Education in Radical Uncertainty

New Directions in Comparative and International Education

Edited by Stephen Carney, Irving Epstein and Daniel Friedrich

This series aims to extend the traditional discourse within the field of Comparative and International Education by providing a forum for creative experimentation and exploration of alternative perspectives. As such, the series welcomes scholarly work focusing on themes that have been under-researched and under-theorized in the field but whose importance is easily discernible. It supports works where theoretical grounding is centred in knowledge traditions that come from the Global South, encouraging those who work from intellectual horizons alternative to the dominant discourse.

The series takes an innovative approach to challenging the dominant traditions and orientations of the field, encouraging interdisciplinarity, methodological experimentation, and engagement with relevant leading theorists.

Also available in the series

Affect Theory and Comparative Education Discourse: Essays on Fear and Loathing in Response to Global Educational Policy and Practice, Irving Epstein

Global-National Networks in Education Policy: Primary Education, Social Enterprises, and 'Teach for Bangladesh', Rino Wiseman Adhikary, Bob Lingard and Ian Hardy

Internationalization of Higher Education for Development: Blackness and Postcolonial Solidarity in Africa-Brazil Relations, Susanne Ress

Resonances of El Chavo del Ocho in Latin American Childhood, Schooling, and Societies, edited by Daniel Friedrich and Erica Colmenares

Understanding PISA's Attractiveness: Critical Analyses in Comparative Policy Studies, edited by Florian Waldow and Gita Steiner-Khamsi

Education in Radical Uncertainty

Transgression in Theory and Method

Stephen Carney and Ulla Ambrosius Madsen

BLOOMSBURY ACADEMIC
LONDON • NEW YORK • OXFORD • NEW DELHI • SYDNEY

BLOOMSBURY ACADEMIC
Bloomsbury Publishing Plc
50 Bedford Square, London, WC1B 3DP, UK
1385 Broadway, New York, NY 10018, USA
29 Earlsfort Terrace, Dublin 2, Ireland

BLOOMSBURY, BLOOMSBURY ACADEMIC and the Diana logo
are trademarks of Bloomsbury Publishing Plc

First published in Great Britain 2021
This paperback edition published in 2023

Copyright © Stephen Carney and Ulla Ambrosius Madsen, 2021

Stephen Carney and Ulla Ambrosius Madsen have asserted their right under the Copyright, Designs and Patents Act, 1988, to be identified as Author of this work.

For legal purposes the Acknowledgements on p. viii constitute an extension of this copyright page.

All rights reserved. No part of this publication may be reproduced or transmitted in any form or by any means, electronic or mechanical, including photocopying, recording, or any information storage or retrieval system, without prior permission in writing from the publishers.

Bloomsbury Publishing Plc does not have any control over, or responsibility for, any third-party websites referred to or in this book. All internet addresses given in this book were correct at the time of going to press. The author and publisher regret any inconvenience caused if addresses have changed or sites have ceased to exist, but can accept no responsibility for any such changes.

A catalogue record for this book is available from the British Library.

Library of Congress Cataloging-in-Publication Data

Names: Carney, Stephen, author. | Madsen, Ulla Ambrosius, author.
Title: Education in radical uncertainty: Baudrillard as transgression in theory and method / Stephen Carney and Ulla Ambrosius Madsen.
Description: First Edition. | New York; London: Bloomsbury Academic, [2021] | Series: New directions in comparative and international education | Includes bibliographical references and index. |
Identifiers: LCCN 2021004553 (print) | LCCN 2021004554 (ebook) | ISBN 9781474298834 (Hardback) | ISBN 9781474298841 (ePub) | ISBN 9781474298858 (eBook)
Subjects: LCSH: Comparative education. | Education–Denmark. | Education–Korea (South) | Education–Zambia. | Education and globalization.
Classification: LCC LB43.L3649 2021 (print) | LCC LB43 (ebook) | DDC 370.9–dc23
LC record available at https://lccn.loc.gov/2021004553
LC ebook record available at https://lccn.loc.gov/2021004554

ISBN: HB: 978-1-4742-9883-4
PB: 978-1-3502-1677-8
ePDF: 978-1-4742-9885-8
eBook: 978-1-4742-9884-1

Series: New Directions in Comparative and International Education

Typeset by Deanta Global Publishing Services, Chennai, India

To find out more about our authors and books visit www.bloomsbury.com and sign up for our newsletters.

Contents

List of Illustrations	vi
Acknowledgements	viii
Series Editors' Foreword	ix
Introduction: By Way of Explanation	1
1 A Thousand and One Disturbing Little Stories	5
2 Education in/and the Global	25
3 Into the Darkness	67
4 Writing as Method	105
In Extremis	135
5 A World in/of Fragments	139
6 Comparative Education and Radical Uncertainty	217
Notes	235
References	267
Index	283

Illustrations

1.1	Mask of Dionysus, Louvre. Sketch by authors	13
1.2	Ethnographer in the field After the posed photo of Bronislaw Malinowski in the field from Malinowski, B. (1929), *The Sexual Life of Savages in North-western Melanesia*, London: George Routledge, p. 257. Sketch by authors	18
1.3	Utopia? 'A framework for comparative education analyses'. Figure 1. In Bray, M. and R. M. Thomas, (1995), Levels of Comparison in Educational Studies: Different Insights from Different Literatures and the Value of Multilevel Analyses, *Harvard Educational Review*, 65 (3): 472–91. (p. 475)	21
1.4	Fragment of a queen After the sculpture: Fragmentary Head of a Queen, reign of Akhenaten, Egyptian, 18th Dynasty. Metropolitan Museum of Art, New York. Sketch by authors	22
2.1	Thief entering house. Sketch by authors	30
2.2	Policy borrowing in education 'Policy borrowing in education: composite processes'. Figure 1. In: David Phillips and Kimberly Ochs (2003) Processes of Policy Borrowing in Education: Some Explanatory and Analytical Ddevices, *Comparative Education*, 39 (4): 451–461. (p. 452)	58
2.3	Complete reference network by policy domain 'Complete reference network by policy domain'. Figure 2. In Baek, C., Hörmann, B. Karseth, B. Pizmony-Levy, O. Sivesind, K. and G. Steiner-Khamsi (2018), Policy Learning in Norwegian School Reform: A Social Network Analysis of the 2020 Incremental Reform, *Nordic Journal of Studies in Educational Policy*, 4 (1): 24–37. (p. 30)	59
2.4	Advocacy networks, choice and schooling of the poor in India Ball, S. (2012), *Global Education Inc.: New policy networks and the neo-liberal imaginary*. London: Routledge, figure 3.1, p. 43	61
2.5	Bowl. Sketch by authors	64
3.1	Cathedral, Art Young	75

3.2	Ulysses and the Sirens	
	Illustration from Greek Vase Paintings by J. E. Harrison and D. S. MacColl (Look and Learn)	88
4.1	Minotaur slain by Theseus, the friend of Hercules	
	From illustrations from the Ancients by George Cumberland (Look and Learn)	107
4.2	Excerpt from Portrait of Georg Wilhelm Friedrich Hegel (1770–1831)	
	Jakob Schlesinger (1825), Nationalgalerie, Berlin, Sketch by authors	110
4.3	Grin. Sketch by authors	134
5.1	Mirror in school corridor. Sketch by authors	146
5.2	Poster entitled 'Foreigners, please don't leave us alone with the Danes'	
	Original artwork by Superflex. Sketch by authors	156
5.3	Students enjoying the sunshine. Sketch by authors	160
5.4	Bumper sticker 'Support our soldiers'. Sketch by authors	161
5.5	High school graduation cap and champagne. Sketch by authors	165
5.6	High school party bus. Sketch by authors	165
5.7	School entrance, early morning, Seoul. Sketch by authors	168
5.8	Students sleeping in class. Sketch by authors	174
5.9	Free time. Sketch by authors	178
5.10	Together. Sketch by authors	184
5.11	Witch doctor. Sketch by authors	193
5.12	Waiting game. Sketch by authors	203
5.13	Senior English classroom. Sketch by authors	204
5.14	Destination? Sketch by authors	209
5.15	Game over? Sketch by authors	216
6.1	When a Country Falls in Love with Itself	
	When a Country Falls in Love with Itself (2008). Elmgreen and Dragset, Photograph by Anders Sune Berg. Collage by authors	220
6.2	Sunbird. Sketch by authors	234

Acknowledgements

The authors and publisher gratefully acknowledge the permission granted to reproduce the copyright material in this book. Every effort has been made to trace copyright holders and to obtain their permission for the use of copyright material. The publisher apologizes for any errors or omissions in the above list and would be grateful if notified of any corrections that should be incorporated in future reprints or editions of this book. The third party copyrighted material displayed in the pages of this book are done so on the basis of 'fair dealing for the purposes of criticism and review' or 'fair use for the purposes of teaching, criticism, scholarship or research' only in accordance with international copyright laws, and is not intended to infringe upon the ownership rights of the original owners.

Series Editors' Foreword

The field of comparative and international education requires its researchers, teachers and students to examine educational issues, policies and practices in ways that extend beyond the immediate contexts with which they are most accustomed. To do so means that one must constantly embrace engagement with the unfamiliar, a task that can be daunting because authority within academic disciplines and fields of study is often constructed according to convention at the expense of creativity and imagination. Comparative and international education as an academic field is rich and eclectic, with a long tradition of theoretical and methodological diversity as well as an openness to innovation and experimentation. However, as it is not immune to the conformist – especially disciplinary – pressures that give academic scholarship much of its legitimacy, we believe it important to highlight the importance of research and writing that is creative, thought-provoking and, where necessary, transgressive. This series offers comparative and international educators and scholars the space to extend the boundaries of the field, encouraging them to investigate the ways in which under-appreciated social thought and theorists may be applied to comparative work and educational concerns in new and exciting ways. It especially welcomes scholarly work that focuses upon themes that have been under-researched and under-theorized but whose importance is easily discernible. It further supports work whose theoretical grounding is centred in knowledge traditions that come from the Global South and welcomes those perspectives that are associated with post-foundational theorizing, non-Western epistemologies and performative approaches to working with educational problems and challenges. In these ways, the series provides a space for alternative thinking about the role of comparative research in reimagining the social.

Education in Radical Uncertainty is the fifth volume in the *New Directions in Comparative and International Education* series and its presence strongly affirms its purpose and spirit. In a work that is noteworthy for its eclecticism, breadth and depth, Stephen Carney and Ulla Ambrosius Madsen not only offer a biting critique of the comparative education field, but critically analyse contradictions inherent in globalization theory, the social sciences more generally, Enlightenment thought and the conduct of educational research. Living in a post-Brexit, post-

Trump, Covid-19 era, none of us are strangers to the notion of radical uncertainty. But Carney and Madsen provide us with a robust intellectual frame through which we can appreciate why conventional assumptions regarding the efficacy of comparative educational research and practice are so unproductive. They are able to do so by referencing those dominant ambiguities and tensions within the humanistic and social science paradigms that have shaped modernist thought but have failed to be reconciled, resulting in a failure to address contemporary truths in their complexity and fragmentary nature. Educational prescriptions thus become unsatisfying because of their inherent inauthenticity, perpetuated by a willingness to avoid confronting the consequences of global precarity. The authors illustrate the notion of fragmentation both conceptually and stylistically, at times abandoning the presentation of text in linear form. As a result, reading *Education in Radical Uncertainty* may at times be challenging. However, doing so can also be immensely fulfilling, as the authors' embrace of alternatives to modernist prescriptions is borne out of their commitment to intellectual and ethical engagement, a commitment they eloquently invite readers to share.

Irving Epstein and Daniel Friedrich

Introduction
By Way of Explanation

This is a book about young people, schooling and the world, and the possibilities and limits of educational research. It is an unusual set of pages, especially if one thinks of other texts that have approached these matters in a comparative perspective. It attempts many things – possibly too many – as it overloads theory, method and the already performative task of writing with the fragmentary, poetic and magical. This strategy is deliberate, aimed at manifesting in/as text something of the condition of contemporary life. A renowned figure once remarked that football is a simple game but to play simple football is the hardest thing there is.[1] Our aim is to write ~~about~~ a world that is literally disappearing. Others have written *about* these processes; few have tried to manifest them *as* writing.[2] Writing ~~about~~ nothingness is much harder than you might think.

The immediate response of many will be to question our scholarly competence, even our grasp on 'reality'. To do so will be to misrecognize the text by judging it solely by the academic norms that have dictated most of what counts as legitimate in this particular knowledge community. We suggest that these norms limit our capacity to say much of interest about our current situation. Are there other possibilities? In what follows, we attempt to find spaces where certainty meets doubt, where reason is disrupted and where the total text is lightly torn to pieces. Here, scientific method meets the *Other* of science, provoking the reader to consider what is left out, unseen or deliberately silenced so that the world can be presented with the certainty and comfort of a 'pre-packaged form'.[3] By resisting this urge – one that is central to the project of education and task of educational research – we offer new ways to present educational phenomena and thus alternative directions for thought from those prescribed by academic convention and habit. You may find these pages inspiring, provoking or simply unbearable. Our only request is that you meet them on their own terms.

We open with a deliberately partial sweep of the endeavour that we know as comparative education. It is necessarily partial because we remain unpersuaded that any one definition or understanding can do justice to such a broad, serious but occasionally frivolous endeavour. Robert Cowen is surely right to call this calling 'undisciplined'.[4] We are aware of its histories but more interested in going places that these stories of origin do not. For that reason, we occasionally delve into educational policy studies, a field that is becoming more central, and we acknowledge innovations and radical thought in the broader area of qualitative methodology in education. We provide a similarly broad sweep of various understandings of the global in order to argue that globalization as intellectual concept – far from being exhausted as many are beginning to suggest – best maintains its usefulness when understood through the lens of post-foundational thought. Our take on the 'global' aims to challenge methodological nationalisms of all kinds and lead us away from the study of education as the expression of bounded cultural phenomenon. We challenge the very possibility of pursuing the country-based case study that has been the lifeblood and default setting of comparative education and, for many, its zealously guarded barrier to entry. While a growing number of scholars explore the changing nature of space and place and its role in education, we have not followed the dominant policy analysis approach that, for better and worse, carries the mark of modern science and thus complicates matters further.

We also offer a broad and partial survey of relevant themes in Western philosophy, especially those that construct or fabricate certain narratives about the rational, moral individual and the 'real' that they are expected to master. Such narratives have led many scholars to *believe* in education and its potential to resolve the tensions, dilemmas and ambivalences of modern subjectivity. By contrast, we argue that these tensions, dilemmas and ambivalences are actually central to the constitution of the self and must be understood and embraced if we are to find ways to live on in an age of upheaval. At present we are wont to speak of environmental and biological crisis as an 'invisible threat, what we know but fail to see'.[5] That is certainly right and applies in equal measure to the fate of our own subjectivities which are being slowly unmade by the slow drip of visual media, consumer modernism, technology and, as we shall see, education. This may seem radical (perhaps unconscionable) to many newer readers but it will become clear that we are contributing to a move first made explicit with Michel Foucault's famous 'face in the sand' imagery of more than half a century ago and taken to its extreme by the polemic, troubling, writings of Jean Baudrillard. These theory moves enable us to argue for an approach to the subject that is *object*-centred, and an approach to educational comparison that avoids the conceptual quicksand of unit ideas such as nation, culture and educational system.

Our sections on methodology attempt to mirror the radical uncertainty of the present. We blend the rational, political and aesthetic in an attempt to explore the potential of writing as a research strategy that might transcend the certainties of science. We find it peculiar that while much of the field of educational studies ('paedadogik' in our Danish context) is historically grounded in perspectives from the humanities, that fragile trace is being marginalized by the growing dominance of the social sciences with their lust for fact, measurement, causality and (final) solution. Even those researching and writing *against* quantification, domination and control in education embrace the demands for theoretical comprehensiveness, analytical clarity and methodological rigour. It seems that most are in search for the truth, nothing but the truth.

*

To write in fragments is to honour the world as we find it, not as we want it.

*

As truth disappears behind appearances, we are reminded of the primacy of the fragmentary. Usually, the diligent scholar will bring together distinct 'fact', event and insight to create an image of the world as complete, believable even. We resist this *will to meaning*. Instead, and as an experiment in method, we present ethnographic 'reality' as it has always confronted the analyst: partial, provisional, the pure event. The role of offering 'modest witness'[6] is much more than an exercise in wilful or careless omission. It is the task of the reader to reconstruct the world in their image, not ours. This is the best we can do: science after what Patti Lather called our disappointments with science. Where does all this leave the reader? To wallow in what may well come across as an authorial indifference to the state of the world? That would be the shallowest of readings. The 'data' *created* here attempt to do some justice to the experiences of young people who must come to terms with the impossibility of bridging a growing chasm between imagination and possibility. We write of such things without hope but, equally, without cynicism.

*

The dissident Chinese author Yan Lianke says that the most difficult thing about writing is to stay confused.	↔	Andy Warhol famously suggested that the aim of his art was to always leave them wanting less.

Both aims are in play here.

*

Acknowledgements usually come at the end of the beginning and we honour this convention! The work presented here had its origins in a project entitled 'Redefining Comparative Education in an Age of Globalization: Schooling, Identity and Eduscape across Denmark, China and Zambia', funded by the Danish Research Council for Culture and Communication (Forskningsrådet for Kultur og Kommunikation). One early product was an unpublished Danish-language manuscript entitled 'Education's Other' (Pædagogikkens Andet). Another, also in Danish, was a small introduction to the thought of Jean Baudrillard.[7] Both were authored by Ulla Ambrosius Madsen and the empirical work we present here draws on her extended field work in all three countries. We thank Hans Reitzel Publishers for permission to draw upon some of the data fragments from that volume although note that these have been fundamentally reworked and extended by both of us for this text. We thank Mark Richardson at Bloomsbury who displayed great patience during our writing process. Moving deadlines were necessary in the context of an under-funded public university with limited provision for sabbatical. For us, the contemporary interest in the 'slow professor' movement[8] was no choice. Still, we are genuinely grateful for our institution and the freedom it provided us to research and write on whatever took our fancy.

1

A Thousand and One Disturbing Little Stories[1]

1

Democracy strikes back: Helene saw the red sweater in an exclusive second-hand store in down town Copenhagen. It was expensive, a little worn but imploring her to fall in love: 'I am retro, cool and irresistible. Be mine and we shall be noticed'. She bought the sweater, knowing she couldn't afford it and aware that she would probably never wear it. But it felt good to capture its affection. Getting home, she immediately went to her bedroom, put it on, did her makeup and hair and photographed the trophy. Minutes later, this unbeatable team would be on social media. 'Look at me! Look at us!' It was a painful evening. Three 'likes' from her class of 30 'friends' and a Facebook family of nearly 600. Sobbing, she explained: 'I know it doesn't matter that people ignore me. I don't care that they are not real friends. But it hurts. I didn't even want that stupid, stupid sweater. Why is it so hard to say no?'

*

Nothing happens unless first a dream: Sung's journey to school is quite short. A walk to the train, then fifteen minutes packed tight before the bus that brings her to the front gates of one of Seoul's most sought-after addresses. That's just the beginning. The scary Mr Pak waits at the sentry's box. He uses his eyes to measure the length of my skirt. Then, if these cannot decide for him, out comes the measuring stick. The flat side reads out the centimetres while we hold our breath; the sharp side is for striking the head while we stand stiffly to meet the sting. That's our first exam of the day. At least he never cuts our hair. The boys are not so lucky. Today, I went straight to the assembly hall. A new school year, and the headmaster, teachers and parents are there to celebrate one more step on the way to realizing our dream. 'Recall your duty, study with diligence, bring honour to your family.' I think these are the words from the podium. Pisa, examination, number one, rankings. These are the things that our teachers dream of once the door to the classroom closes. That was a long time ago. Now I'm on the Eiffel Tower! In Paris! City of love and dreams. I made it! Up here everything is simple, quiet, solitary. Life is a long way from me. Korea, a cloud on the horizon. Now, at last, I'm an individual. Free. It's 1.00 am and my sister wakes me. I must have fallen asleep at my desk, again.

*

Truth comes in small drops: Trees are knowledge. Old, tall, strong. Our trees carry memory. They talk if you listen and never judge. They are home to truth. Joseph often sits under the big tree behind the place where he lives. It's cool and seems a long way from the noise and uncertainty of home, the street and school. Here, he can think, putting aside the thoughts that pile up each day and which refuse to sleep at night. Like messy papers, too many to set aside for later. The shadows are safe, but not when the monkeys come. He has thought a lot about monkeys since Mr Kabuta showed a picture of three wise ones during English class. One wouldn't see, another wouldn't hear and the third one held his tongue. Mr Kabuta said that it meant we should not judge each other. Our monkeys have not had this lesson. They know more than we think. You know, our president gave a big speech about how life in Zambia was getting better and that jobs and happiness would soon return. A monkey walked down the branch under the big tree in the palace gardens where the boss was speaking and did his toilet. Our human leader said, 'Hey monkey, you have urinated on my jacket' but the monkey just walked away like it was his right – or maybe duty – to soil us when we start making things up. Maybe he went away to steal something while everyone was busy laughing.

*

When all's been said and done: Educational studies, education policy, comparative education and educational research are established fields carrying the ballast of 'science' but, also, varying degrees of its opposite. Some of these areas have sheltered and nurtured radical thought, others have struggled with, even actively resisted, forms of opening up, provocation, transgression and estrangement. In acknowledging the debt we have to recalcitrant thought in education, we ask ourselves: Where do we start when theory and method have already mapped our world to its vanishing point? What is left to say? What is *allowed* to be said? How can that be written? Do spaces remain between the authoritative academic text and the most radical of performative alternatives? What would be the point? What repetitions are at play when we claim to think anew? What is overlooked? Suppressed? Denied?

*

How can 'research' with a comparative ambition approach a world of entanglements that seems to have pushed far ahead of our capacity to map, understand and tame it?

*

Beware the scholar: The academic text claims to be original, indeed, must be original to be taken seriously. It must also acknowledge the history, contexts and ideas of others who have laid the *well-worn* paths we claim to be brave enough to travel. Ironic that we pretend originality by following routes signposted by the proper line of argument, the thorough literature review, the rigorously argued case and the defensible analysis:

> Academia is as preoccupied with its fetish for originality as it is suspicious of its appearance. Academics need to be assimilated. So this pursuit of originality – by which each writer attempts a position against the heavy bibliography he or she must employ – leads to a profound and tightly felt academic bondage. Which gives another slant on the joke: I've seen the best research ideas of my generation destroyed by a brief literature search.[2]

*

An anti-manifesto: If we avoid the impulse to do 'science' that serves the reality principle on which it is based, what new ways of seeing become possible? If we reject the imperative to capture 'culture', how can we reimagine place, context and lived experience? If we defer judgements of good and bad, right and wrong, with what commitments can we meet vastly uneven educational worlds? Is our task to reveal, re-inscribe, guide, open, close, fool, subvert, mystify or enchant? What are the limits of *experimentation* in education research? Who says? Why?

*

A path less travelled: The short vignettes that open this chapter were *crafted* from a study of youth and schooling in three countries: Denmark, South

Korea and Zambia. The study, funded by a major research agency, took place over a period of five years. It involved all the usual elements of policy literature and analysis, extended field work in and across places as well as our participation in a number of extended 'cultural' visits by Danish schools to their contemporaries in Africa and Asia. The connection to current research themes and the grounded, gritty, ethnographic flavour of the project promised relevance to a number of educational areas, not least comparative education and global education policy studies. Notwithstanding a familiar veneer, our project attempted to unfold additional perspectives on globalization, education and youth in order to push scholarly assumptions and limits in the search for new thought. Hopefully, our early vignettes will have aroused your suspicions that something different is afoot here. Our starting point was to question the coherence of contemporary meaning systems in education. We wanted to explore the ways in which they were now overloading and collapsing under the weight of unruly global flows for which they were never calibrated. We felt that while processes of seduction and simulation were challenging, even displacing, the 'real' in social life, education research (and especially work with a comparative ambition) continued to delay the inevitable break down of the system; finding meaning where ever it could be grasped, converting that into fuel for a system of reason, purpose and action that appeared to be dying. In the pages that follow, we let the objects of our study express themselves with complexity, contradiction and banality. Often, they are given a helping hand as we blur the sacred boundaries between truth and fiction, using the latter to shed a different light on that which we habitually take for granted. These pages contain the impassioned, profane, reasonable, magical, distressing and perfunctory. There is science (always ready to fill a crack!), politics (but whose?) and an aesthetic form of expression that belongs to no one and everyone, nothing and everything. By refusing to close down or reduce phenomena to neat, familiar or acceptable closures, we attempt to accelerate the tensions between messy worlds in semiotic crisis and those idealized ones that continue to hypnotize educational planners and their bedfellows in the academy. Let's call it a *fatal* approach to research work.

A fatal research strategy aims at undermining the system of meaning, pushing it to breaking point. Wreakers or redeemers? Along the way, it gives up the pretence that theory can tame the world or that data is somehow (still) out there to be captured and made reason-able. Scratching, cynically, at the absurd in education, its venture is to *write* a disappearing world, perhaps until it finds new ways to express itself.

2

The best of times, the worst of times: The broad idea alluded to here was conceived as an experiment in method at a time when interest in the 'global' was at its high-water mark. That trope was by no means easy to unravel, not least because of its collision (collusion?) with the similarly narrative category of modernity.[3] When viewed as the spatialization of modernity,[4] globalization became a comfortable and compelling way to talk about the world of places, people and forces in one breath. Globalization was a harbinger of deeper inter-cultural integration and economic prosperity as well as a force for political renewal. Others were less certain, sensing a new if not dangerous phase of societal unravelling. A world of winner-take-all cosmopolitans but also one of wasted lives played out on shadowy peripheries.

The notion of modernity set free (or at least unravelling) from the confines of place, history and culture has important implications for the project of schooling. Does 'globality' entail a deep and permanent form of connectivity within the world? Is that connection a promise or contract of political, material and personal betterment? What forms of exclusion emerge or are built into the project of global schooling? How do people read and enact messages of hope and abjection?

In posing such questions, we were interested to understand more about the 'chimerical, aesthetic, even fantastic' worlds of those imagining 'metropolitan life' from the side-lines, as well as the 'deeply disjunctive relationships'[5] emerging from global flows. That interest resonated with our own experiences of engaging with young people, their teachers and families in the so-called Global South, as well as in 'high-performance' education systems in Europe and East Asia. In many cases, it seemed that notions such as 'citizen' or 'schooled subject' just didn't capture the aspirations of the young but, equally, cosmopolitan identities linked to these global flows were harder to name and still harder to embody. A focus on irresolution offered a more challenging way to understand schooling in the emerging global *cultural* economy. This orientation – more a vague awareness at the beginning of our journey – offered a difficult but promising line for research. If many cultural flows are disjunctive, *what*, exactly, do we study and how? If globality involves processes of displacement and decentring, *where* precisely do we study the 'global'? Where do the subjects of education fit into these emerging spaces? What does 'culture' mean to subjectivities on the move? How does all this change what we understand as the *subject* of education?

An interest in complexity, hybridity and contradiction was central to the cultural anthropological approach of writers like Arjun Appadurai and gained considerable purchase as stocks in the theorizing of globalization rose during the late 1990s and early 2000s. Initially celebrated as a way to understand the contours of a post-Westphalian world, the focus on scapes and flows enabled us to study modernity *as* globalization and provided new optics for exploring the state, politics and power. Ultimately, though, the mission of social science was still to counter *indeterminacy*. These academic concerns were interrupted by a unique and spectacular jihad in the very heart of twentieth-century modernity. Scholars, not least within educational studies, were quick to recommit to a normative science aimed at exposing injustice, advocating humanism and outlining new forms of social engagement. Surprisingly to us, Appadurai himself offered an 'atonement' for anthropology's foundational interest in culture as a 'cabinet of curiosities',[6] advocating that it play a leading role to 'improve(ing) the planetary quality of life'.[7] The game had narrowed to making a *difference*. To taking sides.

That terrible event in New York insisted that academic work clarify and focus its political aims precisely at a moment when it was becoming harder to ignore the possibility that the world itself had simply moved on to another order of 'reality', one that we argue is increasingly incommensurate with the ambitions of modern 'science' and research work. While it would have been possible to dismiss terms such as 'post-historical', 'post-political' and 'post-factual' in the 1990s when the globalization heuristic was riding high, they are used increasingly as markers of our contemporary condition. While not necessarily capturing the global zeitgeist, if that were possible, they may well be proxies for it. Rather than simply being the latest instalment of a centuries-old lineage of cultural pessimism[8] we are now facing a vague unease that, this time, things are different, less repairable and, even, less comprehensible.

3

Going nowhere too fast:[9] With globalization theory as a frame and Appadurai's (initially expansive) notions of scapes and flows identified as one way to imagine globality and/ in education, we set out to study people and places, things and ideas, connections and abjections. All at once. A type of multi-sited ethnography of schooled life between hope, disappointment and deferral. This was almost bound to come up short. It seemed to us that schooling in particular presented a fascinating porous container from which to explore the disjunctive effects of new visions and narratives about how to live in a fast moving world. Schooling is grounded and situated but, equally, ephemeral and imagined. A great canvas on which youth are promised the opportunity to be something unique. Often, that promise appeared disproportionate to the actual situation in which schools found themselves, with those anchored in the most challenging of contexts offering young people the wildest of dreams. Acknowledging the sticky materialities that shape the project of schooling, we wanted to understand how the global comes into being in education through registers of anticipation, hope, fear and humiliation.[10] There were undoubtedly other ways to conceptualize the seductive pull of schooled identity, but our earlier work, especially in Nepal, attuned us to the notion that schooling in our current age generates meaning by its relation to what it is not, but *might* become.[11] One version of this spectre emerges from the contemporary lust for international assessment and comparison. For example, the 'global' might be thought of as beginning to take root in Danish educational thinking during the 1990s after a series of sobering results in early reading and mathematics tests: the so-called Togo-shock[12] when children, suddenly thrust forward as proxies for the nation, were ranked alongside their historically invisible African cousins. A system bathed in the light of European exceptionalism, now cloaked in shame. Our sputnik. An earlier, *distant* ground zero.

Rather than identify a single political, economic or cultural logic to educational places, we understood globalizing education as constituted by the circulation of ideas and practices that 'scientific' comparative scholarship with its stubborn methodological nationalism had struggled to acknowledge. Writing from Denmark, our project was about understanding global flows, schooling and Danish youth at a time when educational policies and identity politics had shifted into overdrive and seemed only partially the product of local thought. As we viewed the Danish context relationally, we selected cases (a dubious term at best) that were at the forefront of the imaginative scape as that was unfolding at home. That included the threat and opportunity of a resurgent Asia and a continued if not intensified sense of obligation-cum-entitlement that shaped Danish engagements with the Global South. Are the two related? For all its problems, our study became one where Danish schooled identity was framed by myths of what we are, unease about what we were in danger of becoming and a vague sense of foreboding that our fate lay in the hands of others. The responses to that – at the level of policy, political rhetoric and schooling practice – say something about the collective consciousness in this small and shrinking corner of Europe. We hope that our configurations of literature, image, data and fiction – fragments that will induce much 'painful halting'[13] along the road to meaning making – will also say something about a range of other things.

We grounded our empirical work in three contexts. It could have been otherwise but as our cases are mobilized for the purposes of experimentation rather than systematic knowledge production, it hardly matters. And, as systematic knowledge production in an orgy of dreams, imaginings and 'truth' is conceit, it's hardly possible.

4

Dreams and drunkenness:[14] The text that emerges from this general interest owes a debt to Nietzsche's first radical book, *The Birth of Tragedy*, his broadside against Greek metaphysics. Prior to Socrates, the Greeks had the 'horrific realization that the world not only lacks meaning but it is profoundly indifferent to human suffering'. By overcoming that lack of meaning, Socrates gives us hope and purpose. This 'decadence', nurtured later by Christianity and, finally, by humanistic philosophy, employs dialectical reasoning to expose, clarify and make good the world by employing the intellect to imagine a 'phantasmagoria' of another, better, life. To make a 'tyrant of reason'.[15] Our point here is that this tyranny lives on in the modern era in the 'distraction' and 'cheerful optimism'[16] of education.

Nietzsche presents the pre-Socratic world of Greek theatre as the highest attempt to deal with the pain of life. Here, we find two forces in play: Apollo and Dionysus. Light, reason, calculus and precision confronting the shadows, chaos, instinct, emotion and passion. The Apollonian dwells in architecture and the plastic arts of sculpture and painting. Solid, smooth, certain, permanent. It is also present in the world of dreams that promise a higher truth: revelation and clarity. By contrast, the unruly, 'grotesquely uncouth'[17] Dionysian lives in music with a 'drunken reality' that 'seeks to destroy the individual and redeem him by a mystic feeling of Oneness'.[18] Drowned in consciousness, wisdom and beauty, the 'sculptor-god' is 'principium individuationis'[19] split from nature and thus himself. Enter Dionysus and the promise of union:

> Now the slave is free; now all the stubborn hostile barriers, which necessity, caprice or 'shameless fashion' have erected between man and man, are broken down. Now, with the gospel of universal harmony, each one feels himself not only united, reconciled, blended with his neighbour, but as one with him; he feels as if the veil of Mâyâ has been torn aside and were now merely fluttering in tatters before the mysterious Primordial Unity.[20]

It is in music and tragic performance that the two art-deities come together, 'erasing the individual spirit and awakening impulses which in their

Figure 1.1 Mask of Dionysus.

heightened forms cause the subjective to dwindle into complete self-oblivion, while the spirit is mystically transported to a transcendent state of bliss or horror'.[21] By overcoming our impulse to rationalize, map, understand and control, we come to terms with the hard truth of the world and are set free to dwell in its beauty and promise. Man is 'no longer an artist, he has become a work of art'.[22] For Nietzsche, the encounter with Dionysus induces a 'terrible awe' where we are 'suddenly unable to account for the cognitive forms of a phenomenon, when the principle of reason, in some of its manifestations, seems to admit of an exception'.[23]

*

Education: A cynical trade?

> A distraction from the brutality of existence, education introduces brutalities of its own. The indifference of the world is replaced by the moral imperium of education, far from indifferent when it comes to human lives. Despite its consolations, despite pasting meaning and order into existence, education attaches to that existence its impossible excess: the unearthly goal of wisdom.[24]

What starts out as the promise of self-actualization dies with a whimper as training for the marketplace. How high our cynicism soars when our lofty ideals meet worlds in which meaning and purpose are dissolving.

*

The absurd: Is the world absurd? Hardly, the absurd emerges before our eyes, 'through us'. We produce the absurd by how we 'position ourselves in relation to the universe'. The absurd is a 'disease of the intellect bred to revere higher things'. Our tragedy is that the mind demands the universe to 'mirror its ideas of justice and reason'.[25]

*

Tragedy is here to stay: To embrace tragedy is to embrace something more fundamental about the world: 'there is no sun without shadow, and it is essential to know the night'. Albert Camus asks us to *imagine* Sisyphus, toiling endlessly with his boulder: 'If the descent is thus sometimes performed in sorrow, it can also take place in joy'.[26] Education, building on the Socratic promise, chooses to identify and strangle the tragic in the hope that it might wither on the vine. That belief in purpose and action is the metaphysical contract of faith underpinning the educational transaction: we *shall* make a difference. An empire of the good[27] in every classroom, flowing from every textbook and lesson plan, the sublime; that place *beyond* Sisyphus' small mountain summit. As educationalists, we avoid thought that might lead us to the absurd essence of our endeavours. Not only do we battle with tragedy, we turn it into a particularly modern form of decadence where 'misfortunes are greedily embraced as opportunities to display refined, compassionate sensibilities'.[28]

*

What cynicisms are required in order to maintain the illusions on which education, grotesquely disfigured, lumbers on?

*

Nihilists! Putting aside the 'real' for just one moment, how might we deal with indifference, absurdity and our contemporary educational cynicism? Should we dwell in incommensurability as a 'more self-conscious mode of interruption that resists recuperation?'[29] We might grasp this modern cynicism by the tail, following it to its deepest recesses. We could turn it on its head as comedy or farce. If we reject unities, holisms, coherences and avoid the 'successful' text, we might write in fragments that reflect the world *as it is*, resisting the urge to bind together half-glimpsed experiences, fumbling action, partial truths and total deceptions into one glorious remedy for an impossible condition. By putting hope to one side, we might find a way to explore the world and education with joy. It might be cathartic to let go, affirm life, even if only temporarily.

*

On Nihilism: A term defiled by superficiality. Nihilism can go either way: 'a sign of weakness or a mark of strength. Unable to accept loss and anxious about death, the partial nihilism of the modern humanistic atheist is a sign of weakness. For the writer who suffers the crucifixion of selfhood, nihilism is the mark of the cross. On Golgotha, not only God dies; the self also disappears'.[30]

*

The end: Embracing our fallibility makes it possible to offer a text that is radical and dangerous but, in its own ways, familiar and comforting. Our aim is to explore – indeed look for – the breakdown in meaning within and around the project of global schooling and to understand something of the processes of seduction, disappearance and return that might help us overcome our absurd condition. It is a text that attempts to explore 'the end' (of the social, the self, research as 'science') but where that end is placed permanently on hold. This text inhabits a space somewhere between the radical certainty inherent in the Eastern philosophies of nothingness and the radical scepticism of post-classical theory that marks the current limits of Western thought.

5

The real: When the last man, basking in his 'wretched contentment' asks 'What is a star?' and proceeds to blink, Nietzsche is left to despair.[31] What if, as we now know, these fantastic markers of energy, depth and life actually burnt out long ago? What does it mean to know that stars offer us nothing more than the *illusion* of presence? The 'real' is the great foundation on which many of our most cherished ideals rest. For some, it takes form as indisputable 'facts'. For others (utopians knowingly or otherwise), it's a desperate struggle to articulate political commitments. For most, it's a forgetting that our representations are just that. But, somewhere, some time ago, something changed. Jean Baudrillard – a key inspiration throughout these pages – attempted to embrace the insight that our current age is overrun with 'the truth, nothing but the truth'.[32] The suggestion here is that we have moved through certain stages of reality where notions of originality were undermined by industrial-scale processes of reproduction and, in our time, dissolved entirely by the numbing spectacle of media society. What remains is a world given way to simulation and appearances. On the cusp of the pure simulacrum, the distinctions between the real and imaginary begin to blur. Hope and disenchantment – those hallmarks of the modern – give way to indifference. Some have called this a 'post-society' configuration that defies sociological 'classification and explanation' and which can be best understood as an 'endless cycle of the reduplication and overproduction of signs, images and simulations that leads to an implosion of meaning'.[33]

*

Hyperreality: Faced by a surfeit of images and ideal worlds where the boundaries between empirical fact, information and entertainment blur, the hyperreal replaces the blandness of everyday life. In the hyperreal, subjectivities are 'fragmented and lost' in a 'media-saturated consciousness (which) is in such a state of fascination with image and spectacle that the concept of meaning itself (which depends on stable boundaries, fixed structures, shared consensus) dissolves'. Are our old theories up to the task of charting this 'carnival of mirrors' in which everything is present and undifferentiated and where 'depth, essence, and reality all disappear'?[34] What status do we give empirical research when faced with the *illusion* of the real?

*

'Reality is a bitch': The main problem with reality is its 'propensity to submit unconditionally to every hypothesis you can make about it'. In Baudrillard's graphic language, it is the 'product of stupidity's fornication with the spirit of calculation – the dregs of the sacred illusion offered up to the jackals of science'.[35]

However, don't think that 'the real' (the unknowable that lies *behind* appearances) has been erased or eliminated by the uncontrolled proliferation of meaning made possible by our faith in reason and the sciences of measurement. Entertain the thought: the more we attempt to capture the essence of things (i.e. their 'real' form), the further we erase that possibility and accelerate their transformation into the hyperreal:

> Any good physicist can repeat the brilliant theory fiction (for Baudrillard all theory is fiction), in which the table is understood as a mass of swirling atomic structures and substances. Indeed the physicist may also point out that the spaces in between the atomic substructures occupies more of what we conceive of as the table than to the atomic substructures themselves. Whatever the 'real' table is remains hidden in these swirling atomic masses under the realm of the appearances (which we perceive as flatness, coolness, motionlessness, stability etc.). The *illusion* of the world . . . .[36]

*

What if we embrace the idea that there is an unknowable and enigmatic basis to the world that remains beyond our reach? How might we bring something of that mystery into play when we write about education, schools, textbooks, teachers and dreams?

6

Taking centre stage: Ethnography has a long history of putting enigma in its place. The impulse to explanation through a deductive form of reasoning where the 'real' is progressively unfolded has been, in succession, celebrated, problematized and, lately, rehabilitated. In much of educational 'science', we find a blissful (or wilful?) ignorance of the epistemological wars of the past thirty years and in the best of the rest we find a self-reflexive minority struggling with issues of representation, authenticity, voice and purpose. 'Colonialisms' persist as the ethnographer takes centre stage in the narrative, keeping alterity alive in spite of everything. We may have become self-conscious and thus less prone to dominating our own stories, but we retain our privileges as 'authentic knower': the one who was there, the one who must pass on the world to our reader. We have barely understood the provincialism at the core of our craft:

Figure 1.2 Ethnographer in the field.

> It may be that when the ethnographer enters the culture of the group that is the subject of her study she may be in the position of the stranger (and therefore other to the other) but when the process of narrativizing (writing) is engaged, she, as the writing/speaking human subject in the text, is fixed at the centre.[37]

*

When things overflow: What sort of ethnography might mirror a world of fragments surrounding an unknowable core that obscures the absurdity of our existence? Why are we so determined to separate the real from the fantastic?

7

The Magical and the real: A magical orientation to the world suggests 'a form of writing that employs paradoxes in relation to time, reality, and space' where 'past, present, and future run alongside each other'. It is writing where 'space is a montage in which the centre and periphery are overlaid or overlapping; reality and truth are separated and their inherent relationship called into question by the revelation of fantasy and desire residing between the two'. A magical realist approach views irony and tragedy as 'the face behind the mask of the comedy that underscores tragic futility'. Here, the real is 'the colonialist overlay that imperils life and culture, while the fantastic is that which operates in direct antithesis to the European super-civilization in an attempt to negotiate the persistence of colonial memory'. The aim is nothing less than to bring to life a future that 'neither represses the past nor is permanently mutilated by it'. Freedom, then, comes about by 'simultaneously holding in one hand dystopia (ill-place) and utopia (non-place) to establish a hybrid, dis-place (other place) or heterotopia'.[38]

Rejecting false distinctions between inner and outer worlds, between time past, present and future and our pathological urge to sort out victors from vanquished, a magical approach to writing might possibly do justice to our cause. Here, we might use irony to establish distance to the world and its inevitable hardships. We might play with tense and tenses as well as take liberties with place and space. Who can say what happened, when and where? And isn't that one way to approach the 'delirium of excess'[39] that marks our age? And might it not put the authors in their place? Like Taussig's magical evocation of the State,[40] we might find a transgressive way to present the world and its actors that is allowed to run free, proliferating, outrunning the proselytizers and cynics who wait at the gates of academic integrity ever ready to sort fact from fiction, reality from fantasy, expert from fool.

*

Fabulous lists: In this study of global schooling we introduce the usual characters of the educational drama: determined and despairing teachers, anxious and attentive parents, children shaped by fear, passion and promise as well as those who live their days without anticipation. There are 'high-performing' schools, 'world-famous' pedagogies and 'schools in crisis'. A world of difference packed into vague homogenous spaces that rank and level while they promise and deny. There are also peculiar sights: buses without wheels, libraries without books, classrooms without learning. Floating in and out of view are flying pianos, melting glaciers, floating words, dream worlds and schools overflowing with popcorn but dry of sustenance. Pythons, birds and monkeys share the stage with their human counterparts.

Foucault was thoroughly taken aback when he read Borges' famed essay that included mention of a certain 'Celestial Emporium of Benevolent Knowledge'. Here, it 'written that the animals are divided into:

a. belonging to the Emperor
b. embalmed

c. trained
d. piglets
e. sirens
f. fabulous
g. stray dogs
h. included in this classification
i. trembling like crazy
j. innumerables
k. drawn with a very fine camelhair brush
l. et cetera
m. just broke the vase
n. from a distance look like flies'[41]

For Foucault, it is not the strange animals that are peculiar, but 'the narrowness of the distance separating them'. What 'transgresses the boundaries of all imagination' is the act of listing such creatures alphabetically, of placing them in relation to one another when common sense would dictate that they be kept well apart. In the 'act of enumeration' we find the 'power of enchantment'.[42] Using this inspiration, his archaeological writings show how the configuration of knowledge changed completely in what we call the modern era. His evocation of Borges' Chinese encyclopaedia where the fabulous, banal, indeterminate and paradoxical are brought together within one 'system of thought' was aimed at illustrating the 'stark impossibility' of such heterotopic thinking in our own time. In modern systems of reason, 'juxtaposition', 'monstrosity', 'absurdity' and 'enchantment' are tamed by the episteme of science, designation, measurement and modern purpose. The resulting utopias allow fabulous reasoning because they let language run free across places that are never quite real. A world redrawn by desire. A sense of how things *could* be:

> Utopias afford consolation: although they have no real locality there is nevertheless a fantastic, untroubled region in which they are able to unfold; they open up cities with vast avenues, superbly planted gardens, countries where life is easy, even though the road to them is chimerical.[43]

The interest in what Borges called the 'arbitrary and conjectural'[44] nature of systems of classification would stay with Foucault and inform his greatest writings. He was especially taken by the potential of heterotopias as they 'desiccate speech, stop words in their tracks, contest the very possibility of grammar at its source; they dissolve our myths and sterilize the lyricism of our sentences'.[45]

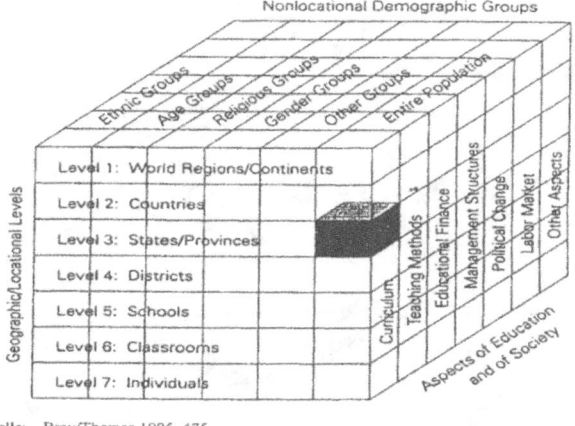

Figure 1.3 Utopia?

Of course, heterotopias not only abound but may well be the original state, kept perpetually out of sight behind the blinkered machinery, faith and systemic violence of the moderns and their madness for method.[46] What if, deploying another type of arbitrariness, we celebrate the unruly and, instead, look upon the modern system of utopian reason and classification as grotesque? Is it possible to write a fragmented, heterotopic text, based on a fragmented and heterotopic engagement with the world and have that acknowledged as *comparative education*? Put another way, in a world where our *kosmos* is fundamentally different from the one that earlier comparativists tried to mirror, who is ready to accept the challenge and *write* into being that which exists *beyond* 'The Order of Things'?

*

Fragment of a queen: The origins of this sculpture from ancient Egypt, now held in a New York museum, remain a mystery. It is often spoken about as being more alive as fragment than fully documented archaeological artefact. Free and defiant, it suggests that 'the fragmentary does not precede the whole, but says itself outside the whole, and after it'.[47]

*

Fragmentation is the 'first movement' and 'spells out that philosophy speaks a *different language*. It no longer speaks of imagined universals, of an expected

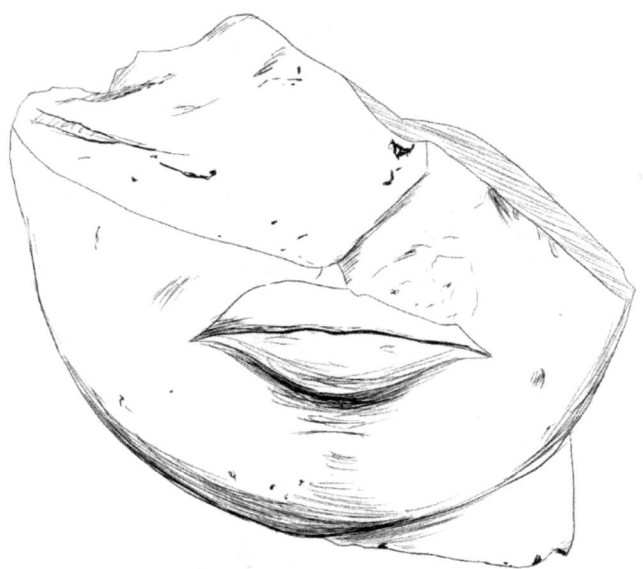

Figure 1.4 Fragment of a queen.

whole, but of disconnection, plurality, of fragment'. Fragmentation is, as Blanchot suggests, a 'passion for the unfinished'. And it must remain that way. 'That is its beauty, its meaning, its *raison d'être*'.[48]

*

Radical? Maxims, aphorisms, fragments. Guicciardini (1520s/30s), La Rochefoucauld (1660s), Nietzsche (1880s), Adorno (1940s), Debord (1960s), Baudrillard (1990s). The baroque, romantic, performative, consensual, political, aesthetic, erotic. The fragment as poem, as manifesto, as hope, as ghost. The fragment as possibility. If, as Debussy claims, it is in the silences that music is made, what might emerge from the fragmented, incomplete text; one that offers insight through what it leaves out or fails to notice?

*

Don't think that fragmentary writing is new. But wonder at its absence within educational studies and ponder why it is simply beyond the horizon of comparative education.

8

Writing, aimlessly: With a focus on global interconnection, we posited that comparative scholarship must become something other than itself. History and context matter but must be thought of as expressing themselves through new arrangements of ideas and things that are no longer bound by place, peoples, habit or custom. Studying education on the 'operating table'[49] of nation in order to evoke the grids of culture and particularity will not do. Youth, seemingly connected by the universal goal of self-fulfilment, are paradoxically made acutely aware of the unequal chances for attaining it. Rather than bridge these and other chasms, we challenge the educational optimism that insists on marking out space, closing gaps and pushing onwards. Recognizing the absurd in the educational endeavour, we seek out day *and* night, joy *and* disappointment, resisting the habit, so well-honed by educationalists, to read the world through the lens of sorrow. While the absurd meant something quite particular to Camus in the wake of world war and threat of nuclear obliteration, we nonetheless see the absurd in a world of unattainable ideals put out of reach by a surfeit of 'reality'. Subjects racing towards a vanishing prize, overwhelmed with information (we might add 'data'?) that can hardly 'survive the moment in which it was new' in contrast to the power of narrative which 'preserves and concentrates its strength'.[50]

*

Might narrative fill the void of hyperreality? Writing the world in fragments, filling our pages with the fantastic, the paradoxical, the sublime and pedestrian may take us further from the facts but enable us to access a *different* awareness, one that can be 'perceived, lived, and relived over and over again, in all its freshness, each time as if it were occurring for the first time'.[51] Perhaps we can *write* another reality into the picture.

*

An empty bag: I like school. It will take care of me. And besides, it's a better way to kill time than wandering around the fields back home. I told 'Big Expert' that schooling was my future, the only future. There are expenses and now that the sickness took my parents someone must help. Things will look good tomorrow.

Money changed hands, of course. Expensive textbooks would save one life, right? With the plane awaiting, Big Expert visited the school once more to give thanks and lay down a final memory to be later conjured to life in this text. A living place soon to morph into ethnographic stone. Joseph was early that day. Gone were the shabby shorts and T-shirt, replaced instead by the costume of the global schooled elite: crisp white shirt, trousers, shoes gleaming like deep mirrors. And an empty school bag.

> Big Expert: What's this? Where are your textbooks? How will you study? What's the point of selling the books you wanted to buy a uniform and an empty bag?
>
> Joseph: Relax Big Expert. I look like a proper student now. I'm ready for the world, right? And this bag. It's not empty. Take a closer look.

Big Expert's gaze moved from the spectacle of this boy reinvented, onto the crimson red backpack. With pride, the bag was opened to the bright morning light and held up so that Big Expert might enter its depths. Beyond the cold dark opening, over the cusp, was a silence to match the emptiness. Big Expert couldn't see a bloody thing but Joseph still beamed rays of truth. The boy said that something began to move within. See, it's full of stuff! There are books. And certificates. There are more schools, friends and far off places. Even a plane is in there, waiting for my orders. There's an office block, high in the sky. He said it was bigger than his favourite tree but easy enough to climb. And the light. Sensing that Big Expert was confused, he asked 'just *imagine* what I can see'. Hmmm. 'Ok', he said: 'it's out of reach for now, but definitely in there'.

*

Joseph as object, recalcitrant subject or trickster? Maybe all of them swirling on a scene that flickers between truth and fantasy. How can we write of such things? Can we glimpse a greater truth behind appearances? Perhaps it is silence and our capacity as writers to invoke it that can lead us to the 'fundamental question'.[52] If it is right that language will always fail us, 'never reaching far enough into the abyss in order to extract its most radioactive gradient',[53] we have little choice and no greater purpose than to express the stillness within, around and beyond things. It is here that we might glimpse our absurd condition, pause for breath and begin to consider our next steps.

2

Education in/and the Global

1

Our moment: studying education across peoples, institutions and borders invites an encounter with the dominant trope of our time, globalization. When defined as a 'multifaceted phenomenon with economic, social, political, cultural, religious and legal dimensions, all interlinked in a complex fashion',[1] globalization seems to capture something distinctive about our age but, by virtue of its vagueness and conceptual looseness, is often dismissed as simplistic, unworkable or, even, banal.[2] While some have already performed the post-mortem[3] on this broadest of signifiers, debates about the usefulness of giving our times a distinctive label continue. Scholarship framed by claims of 'planetary complexity'[4] and shared consciousness has certainly burgeoned during the past twenty-five years. Much of this has been led by discipline-based efforts to comprehend our current situation although, often, that scholarship was 'limiting' and 'skewed' by those same disciplinary interests.[5] Across traditions, much work has privileged the economic sphere, encouraging a sense of capitalism-meltdown. Irrespective of its focus, globalization is understood as the natural successor to nation-based industrial society and to the projects of modernization (and its twin colonialism) and 'development'.[6] It is positioned by specialist scholars as distinctive and demanding of attention, a phase of history that breaks with the past.

While globalization offers a new language with which to grasp our present, it nevertheless resonates with things we have lived with for centuries. Biological transformation, cross-border trade, migration, colonialism, missionary work and other forms of human conquest are not new. One can thus speak of continuities *and* ruptures. Notwithstanding such entanglement, the keen observer will note that a certain language produces a certain way of seeing:

> the rationale of much previous thinking about humanity in the social sciences has been to assume a linear process of social integration, as more and more

people are drawn into a widening circle of interdependencies in the movement to larger units: from families to bands, to tribes to regions, to nations, to states, to blocs of states and eventually to the world-state or global level of social organization. In this sense the global is conceived as a limit, a final stage in the integration of humanity.[7]

Commentators doubtful of such claims are nonetheless aware that using the term tends to bring it into being. In this sense, the global is first 'imagined' and 'subsequently *made*'.[8] They are also attuned to ways in which its reification consolidates a Eurocentric attraction to cosmopolitan concerns and ideals as well as to assumed processes of cultural homogenization and reproduction, more often than not on those same, parochial, cosmopolitan terms. Notwithstanding such critique, early globalization scholarship did at least attempt to address the rampant methodological nationalism that shaped much of social science, demanding that analyses of the social adjust their gaze and ambition to address forces that were clearly of a new scale and intensity. From this vantage point, the container of state or nation is an inadequate basis on which to understand peoples and places. Relatedly, it challenged the idea of 'culture' as separate and historically contingent. Rather, culture, if that is the right term any more, is something to be understood as taking form in 'specific'[9] practices of identity construction that are increasingly global in scope and grounded in the 'non-rational constitution of desire'.[10]

2

Unpacking a word: if it is useful to speak of a global era and a global consciousness, how might we do that in ways that enable us to tease out the complexity of the multiple forces at play? One starting point is to establish distinctions between *globalization* as process, *globalism* as ideology and *globality* as the experience and practice of being in and making the world.[11]

Viewing *globalization* as process centres issues of space and time and attunes us to the deep structural changes and realignments that have shaped recent history. This includes notions of flows, scapes and scales and what these mean for changing relations and dynamics between states, institutions and peoples. It includes new understandings of reflexivity and subjectivity and refashions much older vocabularies concerned with autonomy, emancipation, alienation and exclusion. In a tone reminiscent of Kant's great Enlightenment call to individual awakening, Ulrik Beck was one of the loudest voices to announce a new world:

> A new kind of capitalism, a new kind of economy, a new kind of global order, a new kind of society and a new kind of personal life are coming into being, all of which differ from earlier phases of social development. Thus, sociologically and politically, we need a paradigm-shift, a new frame of reference.[12]

How this alleged paradigm-shift, what Jonathan Friedman calls 'the final confrontation with everything bounded',[13] is defined and unfolded is conditioned by one's philosophical commitments and experiences of the world: one's notion of *globalism*. One form of globalism – often referred to as hyper-globalism – celebrates a new era of movement, integration, isomorphism, networks, one-ness. For those enamoured by liberal political ideology, such phenomena herald a new 'flat earth' overflowing with economic and cultural riches. People, ideas, technologies, goods and the good life framed by the language of 'play' and its associations with rules, order and opportunity. The fantasy of a single space; of oneness, destiny:

> While We Were Sleeping
> While many of us had some knowledge that outsourcing, trade agreements and technology were levelling the playing field, few of us were really aware of the truth. The playing field isn't being levelled, it's being flattened. Today, more people than ever are able to collaborate and compete for increasingly different kinds of work from diverse corners of the world. The flattening of the world means we are now connecting all the knowledge centres on the planet together into a single global network which has the possibility of ushering in an amazing era of prosperity and innovation.[14]

Some critical commentators, while sceptical of the transformative power of markets, nevertheless found potential arising from the decentring of power relations and intense interconnections arising from global capital flows and an emerging shared consciousness. Drawing both on Marxism and the thought of Foucault and Deleuze and Guattari in particular, Hardt and Negri envisage radical social transformation in a world marked by the rising importance of 'immaterial labour', further decentrings within disciplinary societies of control and (post-human) bodies that are 'completely incapable of submitting to command'.[15] From this vantage point, a different type of 'Empire' is on the way: one of interconnection, resistance and social activism that threatens to shatter the privileged position of the imperial centres of power. In its wake will come a new 'multitude' willing to re-appropriate space and constitute itself as a different *type* of subject:

> The passage to Empire emerges from the twilight of modern sovereignty. In contrast to imperialism, Empire establishes no territorial centre of power and does not rely on fixed boundaries or barriers. It is a decentred and deterritorializing apparatus of rule that progressively incorporates the entire global realm within its open, expanding frontiers.[16]

Another globalism is more measured, if not hostile towards a world of markets and marketization, de-regulation, cheap goods and credit, new places and lifestyles. Sceptical globalist accounts introduce us to faceless corporations moving mountains of cash, things and people at an instant. Bigger than presidents, bolder than states, free of history, driven only by returns and the eternal search for more. Here, there is transformation, Western telos, hubris and dissent. The Washington 'consensus' is just that: a consensus on the terms set by Washington and its satellites. Globalization is uneven, unfair and unprincipled. It thus becomes a site of contestation: 'what is generally called globalization is a "vast social field" in which hegemonic or dominant social groups, states, interests and ideologies collide with counter-hegemonic or subordinate social groups, states, interests and ideologies on a world scale.'[17] While the classical anthropologist might speak of *roots*, and the researcher of mobilities in terms of *routes*, it is also necessary to acknowledge the *rout* or displacement of peoples and their ways of being.[18] Humanity in the grip of the base impulses of penetration and extraction that, while framed as something new, manages to keep peoples everywhere 'mysteriously handcuffed to history'.[19] Framed by indignation and the imperative of justice, sceptical globalization research questions the optimism if not self-delusion of hyper or pro-globalization scholarship. Instead, research reads political, economic and social transformation through a dialectic of light and dark[20] with resolution possible only through awareness, engagement, politics and struggle.

These two waves of globalization scholarship – both hopeful in their different ways – continue, albeit with the supplement of a new 'common sense'[21] tradition of enquiry that focuses on the materiality of our current condition, in order to 'reach past illusion to truth'.[22] Withholding judgement on whether our world is characterized by movement, fixity, compliance or resistance, *globality* can also be understood in terms of experiences; how contemporary forces are understood and lived and where our starting point is to accept 'no givens, no structural necessities, no historical inevitabilities and no unfolding teleology of human progress or decay'.[23]

Globality, then, can be grasped as the 'totality of global flows, networks, interactions and connections' that 'triggers a shift in the organization of human affairs and in ways of thinking about social relations and enacting them'. It is a different type of science, playing 'fast and loose with disciplinary canons and notions such as discrete levels of analysis'.[24] While it can never capture this 'totality', or uncover the extent of transnational connection or consciousness, its aim is to keep in play the 'forces, connections, and imaginations'[25] that give our notion of 'the global' intellectual purchase. It will be cautious of 'false universals', 'unreflexive aggregation', the privileging of economic phenomena and 'elite perspectives' and be sensitive to an always creeping Euro-centrism.[26] It will attempt to give depth to various 'shades of the global' where 'global facts take local form'[27] and place becomes an event.[28]

*

Global flows challenge our capacity as researchers: Rather than outline 'any one program of global-future commitments', we might instead commit ourselves to exploring an 'uneven and contested global terrain', one made through connections – real and imagined – but without the expectation of predictable effects.[29] 'Complexity rather than direction'.[30] Diversity and difference rather than cultural uniformity:[31]

> Imagine the landscape nourished by the creek. Yet even beyond the creek's 'flows', there are no stable landscape elements: Trees sprout up, transforming meadows into forests; cattle browse on saplings, spreading meadows past forest edges. Nor are forests and meadows the only way to divide up the landscape. Consider the perspective of the earthworm, looking for rich soils, or the weed, able to flourish in both meadow and forest, though only when each meets certain conditions. To tell the story of this landscape requires an appreciation not only of changing landscape elements but also of the partial, tentative, and shifting ability of the storyteller to identity elements at all.[32]

Constructivist and interpretative approaches often come to the fore here, finding a space between the settled and hardened positions of 'naïve phenomenology' at one end and 'brute structuralism' at the other.[33] This might be a refreshing break from the dominance and dogma of high theory but one that must remain cautious of presenting global dynamics through a 'simple empiricism' where social 'reality' is located in the eye of the beholder. As difficult as it may be for commentators to accept, the 'intellectual fragmentation of the world has undermined any attempt at a single interpretation of the current situation.'[34] Where, then, are we to start?

3

When water runs: if the imaginary of penetration captures something brutal about a world at the mercy of dominant forces, the imaginary of circulation – also appealing to social scientists – brings forth bodies and things on the move: interaction, sharing, co-existence, hybridity and uncertainty but where things are rarely neutral or benign. Some have asked that we imagine water flowing down a hillside. Water has no inclination for equity, social justice or reparation. Water 'rushes down, it carves rock and moves gravel; it deposits silt on slow turns; it makes and remakes its channels'.[35] It takes the easy way, avoids obstructions and moves without conscience. Global flows might establish new interconnections but they also deepen and consolidate existing channels, forge new islands and further isolate old ones.

Transformed economies create new constellations. Migrants, mobile middle-classes, cities within cities and cities beyond states. Cultural flows bring diversity and awareness as well as the 'fear of small numbers' where *nation* gives vent to its *nationalist* Other.[36] Vernacular practices, new localisms, lost

Figure 2.1 Thief entering house.

Did you know?
In 2017, at the height of the European refugee crisis, the Danish People's Party ran advertisements with the stock image of a thief and the message that the open border policy of the European Union had led to more break-ins and street crime in Denmark. The advertisement claimed that since the removal of national police from border posts in 2003, there was now 'free entry for European gangs' who could travel to Denmark, 'fill their trucks with stolen goods and return without risk'.[37]

bearings, anger and anxiety. In the age of economic globalization, markets may be king but they also give the political elite new purpose in attempting to manage complexity. Unwieldly flows of ideas, new technologies and a state desperate for relevance.

*

The master event of globality may well be the terrorist attacks of 9/11 where the fruits of Western modernity (air travel, information technology, and 24-hour media saturation) were returned to their source. Was this the last *real* event; one that defied interpretation through any earlier experience and which captured widespread animosity towards the universalizing tendencies of globalization or, at the very least, elicited a solemn acknowledgement that something in the world order was desperately broken?

*

What does it mean to know that those twin towers – lighthouses of modern achievement and hubris – had a structural weakness at their centre?

*

Globality, then, sees localities and peoples brought into play with specific supra-national ideas and techniques as well as with abstract visions and ideals, allowing us to rethink the social and local on a more complex terrain. Depending on how we configure our 'field', our gaze may make visible vast, invasive systems of economic and political entrapment that consign the marginal further into the shadows. It might show us how those with advantage receive even more. It might also bring into view benign and banal encounters where people across space and place are connected in fleeting moments of colour, sound and movement, seemingly without lasting significance or deep attachments. Schooling occurs in there somewhere. Depending on our gaze, tools and political commitments, it might be a central mechanism of global(izing) capitalism, an arrow head for national policies of in/ex-clusion, a site of resistance or a peripheral social space struggling to keep pace in a world that simulates a taken-for-granted 'real'. Our current situation, while requiring an awareness of the materiality of global dynamics, also requires that we give attention to the role of the imagination in creating, living and enduring the global. How do people *think* the global?

4

The work of the imagination:[38] The spatial turn in the social sciences made possible new ways to view phenomena in motion, acknowledging their historicity and situatedness but recognizing a seemingly new de-territorialized dimension to life. One important move was to theorize the emerging global economy in *cultural* terms. For Arjun Appadurai, global dynamics must be seen as a 'complex, overlapping, disjunctive order that cannot any longer be understood in terms of existing centre-periphery models (even those that might account for multiple centres and peripheries)'.[39] This new order – if we assume for a moment that we are witnessing something new – is framed by the forces of disorganization, disjunction and rupture. The imagination (rather than the purely material) becomes 'a constitutive feature of modern subjectivity'.[40] Here, we must move beyond the 'purely emancipatory' or 'entirely disciplined' to view the imagination as a 'space of contestation in which individuals and groups seek to annex the global into their own practices of the modern'.[41]

The imaginary of global scapes and flows places into profoundly unsettled relation the global configurations of finance, technology and media as well as those of mobile populations/peoples and ideas. The last of these is especially important for our purposes. 'Ideoscapes' in a globalizing world are of course many and not necessarily coherent. At this time and in this increasingly shared space, a 'chain of ideas, terms, and images, including freedom, welfare, rights, sovereignty, representation and the master term democracy'[42] suggest the emergence of a new type of person. This 'global subject' is shaped by the language and imagery of movement (and its *other*, fixity), experience of new forms of interconnection (and its *other*, exclusion), and the need to transform (and its *other*, the shame of stasis).

*

In 2016, China's foreign ministry had to deny reports that Chinese food companies were engaged in 'canning human flesh and selling it in Africa as corned beef'. The country's state-run Xinhua news agency said that 'one tabloid newspaper in Zambia was falsely quoting an unnamed woman living in China. She said Chinese firms were collecting dead human bodies, marinating them and packing them in tins. Chinese spokesman Hong Lei said the reports were "irresponsible".[43]

*

In the 'struggle for authenticity' – and here one should most certainly include young people confronted with the promises of formal education – these imaginaries become powerful 'means of identification'.[44] Should it surprise us that the 'lines between the realistic and the fictional' become 'blurred' such that 'the farther away these audiences are from the direct experiences of metropolitan life, the more likely they are to construct imagined worlds that are chimerical, aesthetic, even fantastic'?[45] Perhaps, like Nietzsche's 'star', the realities behind such imaginaries are extinguished by the time they reach distant eyes.

*

The transnational vulgate: Approaches that prioritize or even fetishize movement, displacement, hybridity and cosmopolitanism are seen by some as promoting a new moral principle for anthropological work rather than examining empirical 'fact'.[46] One line of critique is to question the current obsession with transnationalism by considering the place of locality *within* global structures. Evoking Bhabba, Jonathon Friedman notes that difference and heterogeneity were central to all societies, only to be erased, silenced and subsumed into the nation-building projects that characterized colonialist versions of Western modernity. With the fading of those projects, it is no surprise that heterogeneity *seems* to re-emerge, this time not in antagonism to modernity as colonialism but, rather, to certain ideals of Western cosmopolitanism:

> It is said that globalization has changed the world profoundly. It is dismantling our old categories of place, locality, culture, even society. The contemporary world is one of hybridity, translocality, movement and rhizomes. Is this an intellectual development or discovery that the world has really changed, i.e. before we were local but now we are global, or is it the expression of the experience of those who themselves move from conference to conference at increasing velocities and are otherwise totally taken with the facility of internet communication across the world to their colleagues? . . . It is the discourse of global elites whose relation to the earth is one of consumerist distance and objectification.[47]

Looking down upon the 'multiethnic bazaar'[48] and viewing that as representative of a new and improved epoch made possible by displacement, difference and cultural accommodation says as much about the researcher of global flows as it does about the state of the world.[49] Not surprisingly, therefore, some viewed Appadurai's thesis – tentative as it was – as part of the initial 'enthusiastic embrace of the disembedding tendencies of globalization'.[50] Others worried that he presented a view of geography as comprising neither 'places or placeless flows' and a view of history that was simply 'distorted'.[51] The prominence thus given to the imagination was questioned. Can it be so 'independent of national, transnational and political-economic structures' that facilitate, even dictate, flows of people, things, and ideas'?[52]

Anticipating such critique, Appadurai, like others, actually noted that global dynamics are always 'radically context-dependent'.[53] However, while particular trajectories might be shaped by earlier histories of colonialism, very little could now be taken for granted. In this sense, cosmopolitanism may be about warm associations with faraway places as well as a refusal of the 'demands of localism'.[54] It might be 'transnationally organized resistance against the unequal exchanges produced or intensified by globalized localisms and localized globalisms', what de Sousa Santos calls 'insurgent cosmopolitanism'.[55] It can also be solitary acts of restlessness, suspicion, defiance and irony, 'sometimes camouflaged as passivity'.[56] The subject of global flows finding ways to 'live on'.[57]

*

The problematic, and a problematization: 'The world we live in now seems rhizomic, even schizophrenic, calling for theories of rootlessness, alienation, and psychological distance between individuals and groups on the one hand and fantasies (or nightmares) of electronic propinquity on the other. Here, we are close to the central problematic of cultural processes in today's world.'[58] Does the metaphor of the rhizome catch our zeitgeist? Endless becomings laced with potential maintains our faith in the world and the possibility of human futures, but does it capture a contemporary uncertainty framed by an indifferent system?

*

To be meaningful, the trope of globalization must capture something distinct: A renewed focus on capital accumulation and exploitation, greater bureaucratization, control and surveillance, new ambivalences and deeper alienation and further individualization are actual concerns, for sure, but rehashed motifs chained to the great concerns of modernity: reason, progress and emancipation. Do we need globalization theory to confront such concerns? Might an intellectually interesting and original globalization theorizing be found by going outside the gaze of foundational social thought where issues of truth, 'reality', representation, place, history, narrative and voice are destabilized and thought afresh? What might a *fatal* approach to the global look like, one that pushed the concept to its breaking point? And why haven't we seen that yet?

*

Where context matters: globalization research is not simply the result of the meeting of 'reasonable' concepts with empirical 'fact'. It also reflects the positionality of certain 'knowledge-geographical traditions'.[59] For example, we have come to understand much post-war French theory as questioning the grand Enlightenment metanarratives of universality, classical forms of representation and the authority of the author. Some have called this a 'superficial play with images (and) sensations'.[60] To apply such thought is to transform research into a space for experimentation. Of course, not all have accepted this challenge. If one can generalize about a German philosophical tradition, the word-games of French 'post' thought become an actual moment of philosophical apathy and invitation to renewed fascism. Here, the death of the social is little more than ahistorical speculation and a 'frame of mind or subjective stance' that obscures the possibility of political action to shape social life.[61] This brand of German thought is never far from the philosophy of Hegel where modernity is an idea buttressed by a theory of the state brought to life by concerted political effort. Progress through the nation and a *will* to modernity. This perspective can be further contrasted by the British tendency to gradualism where notions of reflexivity, choice, risk and uncertainty are prioritized.[62] Here, the focus is on processes of economic intensification that lead to inevitable socio-structural change.[63] This is modernity as empirical fact, not ideology, with moral action following careful social diagnosis.

The reception of globalization theorizing in the United States draws upon these traditions and responds to earlier lines of struggle around the meanings of post-foundationalism. When, for example, Jameson, writing in his groundbreaking *Postmodernism; or the Cultural Logic of Late Capitalism*[64] groups together French thinkers as diverse as Barthes, Derrida, Foucault, Lyotard and Baudrillard, he positions them as the main 'rival hermeneutic' to the Marxist tradition and thus a fundamental threat to the mode of analysis dominant in the US academy but, also, to a host of sparkling careers.[65] Post-foundationalism appears to have been received in the United States primarily as a political rather than onto-epistemological category and is deployed in ongoing ideological battles over 'which "ideology of the text" would shape North American intellectual life at a time of theoretical flux'.[66] What appears to start as an aesthetic movement morphs into debates about the 'trajectory of capitalism',[67] where postmodern art and architecture are presented as offering a parallel meaning form to the economy. However, by always seeking out the 'safe house of neo-Marxism',[68] such engagements prioritize representational projects that are indebted to idealized political visions and the creation of alternatives to the only world we have. For some, this leaves us with analyses that are 'solemn in their politics, almost humourless (and) still addressing the virtuality of political emancipation from the position of class guilt and/or sadness'.[69]

In essence, what started as a set of fundamental critiques of the 'grand cultural projects of western modernity' solidifies in the dominant Anglo-American scholarly literature as a limited number of spatial and temporal theories that are 'tamed and safely integrated into the current social order'.[70] This will be a recurrent theme in our analyses. This limiting of the broad project of challenging modern modes of thought and analysis might be the result of the ascendency of English-language academic knowledge-production processes where a modest, practical and cautious academic/political agenda finds voice through hegemonic networks for the distribution of scholarly output. Not surprisingly, then, much alternative social thought is viewed as having limited 'practical and theoretical' relevance.[71] In relation to globalization research, we see a particular rendering of radical thought that enables us to re-read capitalism in order to 'grasp the whole' and 'act to change the world'.[72] Perhaps our problems are rooted here.

5

The world, Northern style: It goes (almost) without saying that globalization theorizing – post-foundational or otherwise – is more than Anglo-American reduction to empiricism or practical responses to actual or perceived societal developments. Rather than recording the victory of one set of priorities over others, globalization theorizing bears the more general stain of hegemonic Northern thought that assigns to obscurity and silence most forms of knowing. For all its attempts to write about and reflect the complexity of the world, it does so principally through the medium and interests of Northern intellectual, political and moral concerns. An obscenity gone largely unnoticed by the rulers of this tiny minority. Seduced by a Kantian notion of *universal* cosmopolitan man and a hard-to-kill Hegelian idealism in the form of the powerful narrative that the development of freedom is part of our collective destiny (*Geist*), the refined and polite globalization text represents a 'performative unity of writer and reader'[73] and, thus, the exclusion of other viewpoints. Connell's commanding review of the literature makes for grim reading:

> Here, for instance, are the authors whom Hardt and Negri consider helpful for thinking about transition from the possible to the real: Lukács, Benjamin, Adorno, Wittgenstein, Foucault, Deleuze. Not Gandhi, not Fanon, in fact no one with a black face, no women, and no one from outside Europe.
>
> Neither Bauman nor Beck, nor Robinson nor Kellner nor Sassen, refers to nonmetropolitan social thought when presenting theories of globalization. Nor does Robertson, despite his career in development studies. Evans's (1997) review of the state under globalization uses metropolitan sources with hardly an exception; so does Guillén's survey of the sociology of globalization. In Martinelli's (2003) introduction to the International Sociological Association presidential session papers on globalization, every citation is Northern. At the end of *Runaway World* Giddens helps the reader with an annotated reading. All 51 books mentioned are published in the metropole, and only one of them centrally concerns a nonmetropolitan point of view. Giddens's account simply does not address nonmetropolitan thought about globalization. It is a striking fact that this body of writing, while insisting on the global scope of social processes and the irreversible interplay of cultures, *almost never* cites nonmetropolitan thinkers and *almost never* builds on social theory formulated outside the metropole.[74]

Producing silence of such kinds is only half the trick, with much writing about globalization unable or unwilling to name the metropole itself, the traditional site of 'cultural domination' and 'accumulation'. Having an 'embarrassed relationship' with Marxist-oriented systems thought and engaged in theorizing power as dispersed *across* and *through* cities, such writing succeeds in 'conceal(ing) the conditions of its own existence'.[75]

*

Is our project in these pages one of concealment? Northern taste masquerading as something else?

*

The Northern foundation of so much of what passes for grand social theory has not gone unnoticed. Far from it. For some, modernity itself is a European phenomenon 'constituted in a dialectical relation with a non-European alterity that is its ultimate content'. Here, we find the 'rational "concept" of emancipation' furthered by its twin, 'genocidal violence'.⁷⁶ 'Western thinking' can be conceived of as 'abyssal', existing within a space beyond which lies 'only non-existence, invisibility, nondialectical absence'.⁷⁷ We are thus confronted not only with the erasure of 'nonmetropolitan experience' but, at the same time, its absolutely central role in producing what *can* be said:

> Modern knowledge and modern law represent the most accomplished manifestations of abyssal thinking. They account for the two major global lines of modern times, which, though being different and operating differently, are mutually interdependent. Each creates a subsystem of visible and invisible distinctions in such a way that the invisible ones become the foundation of the visible ones. In the field of knowledge, abyssal thinking consists in granting to modern science the monopoly of the universal distinction between true and false, to the detriment of two alternative bodies of knowledge: philosophy and theology ... that cannot be fitted into any of these ways of knowing. On the other side of the line, there is no real knowledge; there are beliefs, opinions, intuitions, and subjective understandings, which, at the most, may become objects or raw materials for scientific inquiry.⁷⁸

In the empty spaces created by abyssal thinking we find the most astounding of creatures. Who, in our time, would not be appalled by Thomas Babington Macaulay's 1835 Minute on Indian Education and the infamous sleight that 'a single shelf of a good European library was worth the whole native literature of India and Arabia'?⁷⁹ How many of us can trace its children in the latest 'development' report, especially the faith in 'official languages' and 'core skills' that, while well-meaning, may be little more than smoke and mirrors aimed at keeping subalterns in their place?

A 'southern knowledge' perspective can unsettle the geography of reason⁸⁰ that has produced a univocal, partial and provincial world view where concerns for wholeness, completeness, order and control have suppressed another truth we are not quite ready to accept: that 'the understanding of the world by far exceeds the West's understanding of the world'.⁸¹ Instead of a dominant knowledge that is realist, critical, universal, binary (true/false), scientific, clarifying, solving and reducing, we might instead explore ecologies of knowledge that encompass (broader) scientific and analytical approaches *as well as* myth, superstition, the performative, literary, magical and non-human forms of understanding. The main aim here is to resist the urge to cut through, clarify and resolve and, therefore, to maim and silence the 'pluriversality' of ways of making sense of the world around us.⁸² A southern knowledge perspective might invite such plurality, at least if it remains alert to the impulse of Western philosophy to think in universals. 'Incorporative solidarity' (Dussel) and 'insurgent subaltern cosmopolitanism' (de Sousa Santos) provide new ways to think about cognitive *justice*, political *struggle* and human *freedom* but are, always, one textual leap from the pull of Marxist idealism and its Eurocentric ontology. 'Hegemonic domination', 'human suffering', 'powerlessness' and 'rebellion'[83] are never more than *particular* and *partial* ways to read the world.

How, then, do we take seriously the challenge posed by southern perspectives but where we resist the divisions and certainties of Cartesian thought that naturalize binaries such as northern/southern; European/other; perpetrator/victim; inclusion/abjection and justice/prejudice? What about one that avoids the teleological impulse to think of time as unfolding, moving forward as change, growth, development and, even, *self-actualization*? Is there a southern orientation that can work for humankind by displacing the subject from the centre of attention? Can we avoid our colonial (Western scholarly) guilt, the assumed innocence/romance of the subaltern and an understanding of alterity as a form of otherness constrained, limited and trapped *within* the sacred boundaries of the subject? Attention to absences might unearth buried riches and new beginnings – and much more – but must that necessarily be directed towards the old/new universals of justice and freedom and the silenced peoples that they purport to serve? Can it also be a more general strategy of scholarly disruption; one that views the world as ephemeral and fragmented and which resists the conceit of converting that unknowability to urgent causes, coherent categories and large-scale plans of action? How are we to understand what de Sousa Santos calls the 'marginal or subordinate versions of modern Western thinking'[84] that are also silenced by much of the academy?

*

Aware of the diversity of knowledges and positions in the world, making no claims to universality or epistemic superiority, we must surely be allowed to dwell within the realm of marginalized Western thought.

*

6

'Never less, always more':[85] In this sense, a southern perspective, rather than being limited to the voices of forgotten subalterns and their made-to-be-invisible life-worlds, can be more generally concerned with going beyond our 'existing referents'. It can be an imagining of 'what we cannot imagine as a result of the limits of our realms of intelligibility and experience, and the constitutive foreclosures happening as a result of what has been normalized as real, ideal, knowable, and desirable'.[86] For our purposes, that includes a scepticism towards all claims of a singular and penetrable 'reality', modes of analysis and strategies of representation that get to the heart of things in order to rejoice in or redeem them. It includes a wariness towards subject-focused theorizing, myths of origins and the power of text to lay bare and simplify. In short, a leaving behind of most of what the Northern researcher – wherever geographically located – has been seduced and empowered to be.

*

'If we cannot lay our own lives on the line, this is because we are already dead':[87] One starting point for thinking differently would be to distort the world in order to gain new purchase on the entangled relation of imagination, desire and what Friedman calls 'the more spectacular aspects of capitalist consumption'[88] that characterize our age. Once again, Baudrillard chances his arm with radical imaginaries charged with ambivalence about our fate. Drawing upon Marx's provocation that history moves from authenticity to farce, the spread of Western modernity is viewed as a process of 'carnivalization' where hegemonic models ('technical and military' as well as 'cultural and ideological') result in an 'extraordinary process of reversion' where power is 'slowly undermined, devoured or "cannibalized" by the very people it "carnivalizes"':

> It is this dual – carnivalesque and cannibalistic – form we see reflected in every corner of the world, with the exportation of our moral values (human rights, democracy), our principles of economic rationality, growth, performance and spectacle. They are taken up everywhere, with greater or lesser degrees of enthusiasm, but in a totally ambiguous way, by all those 'underdeveloped' peoples who have not so far heard the good word of the universal and, hence, provide fertile ground for missionary work and forced conversion to modernity, but who, more even than being exploited or oppressed, are simply made a laughing stock and transfigured into caricatures.[89]

This, however, is not the end but a beginning. If globalization includes the rampant and violent spread of the singularity of Western culture (a universalism of sorts), and we acknowledge that this is taken up unevenly and ambiguously by the rest of the world (cannibalized), all singularities (cultural differences and locally relevant meaning systems) are undermined. The result is a form of distorted homogenization but, also, a mystification of the original that is eventually lost in simulation. Carried by globalized flows and devoured in our hunger for the exotic, these shallow duplicates return to their source, devaluing the uniqueness of the Western original itself. Modernity accelerated but towards its own decomposition. In this version of the 'abyssal' line, the psychology of colonialism with its themes of dehumanization and dependence meets a form of mimicry that devours Northern taste and fancy with gusto. However, rather than a triumph for the liberated subaltern, such mimicry is a dangerous invitation to match the unprecedented death drive built into the theatre that is Western globalization:

> And it is this indifference and abjection that we throw out to the others as a challenge: the challenge to debase themselves in their turn, to deny their own values, to lay themselves bare, to make their confessions, to own up – in short, to respond with a nihilism equal to our own.[90]

For Baudrillard, and in light of the perspectives on culture outlined earlier, we can use this line of thought to estrange our understanding of the 'global' encounter. If we view others as discarding their cultural singularity by 'sacrifice(ing) themselves on the alter of obscenity, transparency, pornography and global simulation',[91] it is we in the West who are now dying from the loss of *all* singularities, caught up in the whirlpool of world-wide connection, assumed cultural correspondence, intense banality and the poisoned gift returned tenfold.

*

A gift poisoned and returned: Joseph and his magical bag, rather than a tenuous example of academic overreach, might actually hint at our condition and allow us new purchase on the study of 'global' education. Consider:

> In the so-called Global South, we see a fixation with schooled identity inscribed largely in Western/modern terms but presented as universal. Here, we will find an inability for many to convert that gift of salvation on the terms offered although a powerful enthusiasm to devour its symbols, promise and magic. Ultimately, the new universal (education for all, education for life, education *as* life) is reduced, in this case, to a school bag; quite literally an empty container for something unreachable. Misrecognition? Recalcitrance? Indifference?
>
> If the West (in this case the Organisation for Economic Co-operation and Development) wants to spread its obsession with testing, claiming this to be

a universal necessity and desire, don't be surprised to encounter subaltern enthusiasm (to excel, to obey, to escape) that will embrace this obsession, allow it to devour its own youth but then return it with interest. With impossible levels of achievement that disgrace and discourage the global masters and their *own* children, the gift repaid might be a form of obedience to mantras of global interconnection but, also, a call to competition that causes us, collectively, to defile the very essence of what it means to be educated.

When Scandinavian policy makers insist on using multilateral development and humanitarian agencies to spread their culture of individualized rights and ideology of self-responsibility and improvement, don't be surprised when that returns as an intensified pressure for self-promotion, success and life-long happiness. Individualization exported is not only Northern self-aggrandizement and contentment but, also, intensified angst, self-doubt and self-harm: a hollowing out of the Enlightenment principles on which modern identity is based.

*

All is not lost: As singularities morph through the spread of superficial Western 'culture', so too does the original universal (Western culture itself). In its place remains a 'perfectly in-different (un)culture' and a mass of emaciated singularities which threaten to unleash 'wild' forces that are 'heterogeneous', 'antagonistic' and 'irreducible'. Contrary to those globalist sages who see either hope or despair, man may well be entering a 'void'[92] where nothing is certain beyond an absence at the core. Hope, if that is the right word any more, may lie in that space where, paradoxically, the levelling of difference invites new thought and expression.

7

A generous space: educational research has its own purchase on such musings, offering an array of concepts and strategies with which to challenge the modern 'project'.[93] If, for a moment, one groups together the related terms 'post-structuralism', 'post-modernism' and 'post-foundationalism', one can summon up a rich literature within the areas of teaching and curriculum, schooled identities, leadership and organization, research methodology and globalization and education. In many cases, feminist scholarship, especially its 'hard-won epistemological and political achievement' in identifying the situated nature of knowledge and the importance of 'positionality, reflexivity, voice, and power',[94] has been the driving force behind a suspicion towards all 'seductive claim(s) of truth-making'.[95] Lagging behind innovations in the social sciences, post-foundationalism in educational research eventually made its mark and has taken root as a legitimate alternative to a mainstream that continues to view otherness as a 'miasma of the indeterminate and unpredictable' and thus 'the source and archetype of all fear'.[96] Notwithstanding its successes, alternative thought in education remains limited to certain intellectual communities and knowledge production processes beyond which older battle lines constantly appear.

Much post-foundational writing in education attempts to distance itself from a dominant Marxist tradition of enquiry, challenging representational projects and problematizing the taken-for-granted place of structures, resources and material interests in defining the social. One inspiration for new thinking is found in Derrida's challenge to 'first principles' within thought systems as well as his life-long struggle to give metaphysics 'the slip'.[97] Many early encounters with French post-foundational thought in education were heavily influenced by Foucault's analysis of power and his genealogies of the self. These proved especially amenable as resources with which to relate to but transition from structural-functionalist analyses of schooling, class, gender and politics. Ironically, much of this writing reflects the challenge Foucault himself faced in shedding a Marxist logic of production and invites totalizing portraits of *the* self-managing school,[98] *the* performative teacher,[99] *the* cosmopolitan citizen[100] and, even, *the* child.[101] For a time, Foucault became a new orthodoxy in educational studies but, of course, the caravan moves on.

More recently, post-foundational theorizing in education has been shaped by notions of difference, multiplicities and intensities. Revisiting Spinoza's doctrine of one-substance, Deleuze and Guattari argue that the natural world comprises elements that are real but which lack form and function. Here, we find movement and rest, as well as slowness and speed:

> They are not atoms, in other words, finite elements still endowed with form. Nor are they indefinitely divisible. They are infinitely small, ultimate parts of an actual infinity, laid out on the same plane of consistency or composition. They are not defined by their number as they always come in infinities. However, depending upon their degree of speed or the relation of movement and rest into which they enter, they belong to a given Individual, which may itself be part of another. Individual governed by another, more complex, relation, and so on

to infinity. . . . Thus each individual is an infinite multiplicity, and the whole of Nature is a multiplicity of perfectly individualized multiplicities.[102]

This perspective, derived from the most radical thinker of the Enlightenment,[103] has fostered a new ontological perspective on the social. Notions of de and re-territorialization and the rhizome open up new pathways for the study of educational flows, assemblages and networks and appear most fruitful when avoiding the old default setting where human consciousness and object representation dominate the analysis of 'intensities of encounter'.[104] Life as transcendence, immanence and becoming makes possible a different vocabulary for understanding educational subjectivities, taking us well beyond the binary oppositions and Cartesian dualisms of classical Western thought while holding on to the transformative, even revolutionary, potential of agency within the enlarged 'cybernetic triangle' of human, animal and machine.[105] Here we glimpse a becoming orthodoxy, one that positions human consciousness as a 'minor sideshow' in the history of humankind. The current interest in 'embodiment, materiality, and affect' displaces the traditional subject of educational research, reconfiguring humans among 'birds and beasts'[106] and acknowledging, as Haraway had done decades earlier, the difficulty of assigning humans a particular autonomy over their consciousness or a separateness from other species or actants.

The affective turn is of particular relevance, especially if we consider global flows to constitute a 'cluster of promises'[107] of the good life that become partially realizable through strategies of immediate material betterment and which are always expressions of optimism that life can be made 'bearable' even as it 'presents itself ambivalently, unevenly, incoherently'.[108] This affective dimension to the study of the global is an emerging focus in cultural theory in particular but provides no single or clear way to make sense of the subaltern. Affect deals with 'complex, self-referential states of being, rather than to their cultural interpretation as emotions or to their identification as instinctual drives'.[109] Affect, then, is neither biological impulse nor socially mediated response. The focus on affect recognizes that the self is a fragile achievement in Western thought; one complicated by recent challenges to the culture concept, as well as to the notions of space as bounded and time as linear. For some, affect is unfolded as emotions, especially those of loss, repression and political pessimism.[110] Others take a more affirmative route to explore the 'pleasure that is bound up in the activity of world-making'.[111] Here, the interest is in 'thinking about the ordinary as an impasse shaped by crisis in which people find themselves developing skills for adjusting to newly proliferating pressures to scramble for modes of living on'.¹¹²

While such range gives us the possibility of returning to the question and problem of the subject without assigning to it the properties of rational, deliberative or autonomous thought, it can also be understood as 'way out' of a 'perceived impasse' in cultural studies. From this position, a focus on becoming 'someone other than who we currently are' reclaims voice and purpose in social life, enabling us to overcome the 'pessimism of social determinist perspectives' by inserting a new 'hope of freedom' into post-deconstruction enquiry. However, rather than prioritize the 'good affect' and the 'more productive frame of mind' it invites, a focus on the affective helps us to conceive of the individual in a 'circuit of feeling and response'.¹¹³ The concern here lies less in how each everyday life is 'organized' by capitalism but, rather, with how the ordinary is disorganized and made sense of by intensified global flows of signs, movements of bodies, forms of consumption and fantasies of the future.¹¹⁴ Whether theory aims at hope and purpose – in effect to rescue the *idea* of the subject – or to take us a step closer to its annihilation, is very much a matter of intellectual taste.

The subject of the Subject does not end there. Virtual reality, artificial intelligence, cybernetics, 'post-truth' and our impending environmental apocalypse are all so well established in whatever we take to be consciousness that it can only be a most radical form of denial that keeps us in debt to 'human exceptionalism and bounded individualism'.¹¹⁵ Challenging the purported truth of Man's uniqueness and supremacy over Nature, it fell to 'fabulists, including non-Western and non-civilizational storytellers, to remind us of the lively activities of all beings, human and not human'. That task, we are told, must now be shared:

> The time has come for new ways of telling true stories beyond civilizational first principles. Without Man and Nature, all creatures can come back to life, and men and women can express themselves without the structures of a parochially imagined rationality. No longer relegated to whispers in the night, such stories might be simultaneously true and fabulous. How else can we account for the fact that anything is alive in the mess we have made.¹¹⁶

By resisting familiar narratives of progress that serve to obscure the richness of the world and our precarious place in it, Tsing reflects well an emerging focus for empirical scholarship, in this case, travelling with the humble mushroom, adopting a 'third nature' perspective to re-read a world in the twilight of capitalism. Like mushroom picking, this is about looking for 'eruptions of unexpected liveliness' and developing 'ongoing practices of living in the ruins'.[117] Whether we name our age the Anthropocene, Capitalocene or Chthulucene, we are introduced to a place of human and non-human, 'multispecies assemblages' and processes of 'sym-poiesis, or making with' instead of the 'auto-poiesis or self-making' that has characterized a millennium.[118] This radical reconfiguration of the world and its contents is viewed as necessary if we are to counter the 'Big Thing called Globalization'.[119] How does it change our understanding of education and its role in the present?

*

'Becoming-human':[120] Post-human perspectives aim to be experimental, affirmative, inclusive, non-representational, partial and interested in 'animating lifeworlds'. Post-humanism is about diffraction,[121] dispersed methodologies and a heightened awareness of everything around us:

> I imagine that post-inquiries are like crystal wind chimes – they dance in the breeze as small, vibrant rainbows and glimmers of light flash and disappear against the backdrop of delicate, spontaneous melodies. Sometimes the wind chimes produce momentary refrains that open other languages for research. Yet, attempts to isolate individual notes overlook what the larger entanglement of wind and crystals and light and sounds produce: varied and constantly changing movements. That is the beauty.[122]

The empirical reach of such work is, unsurprisingly, enormous. Objects such as stones, water, sun and wind are no longer necessarily separate or secondary to Man who must find a new place in a Great Chain of Being that is compressed, blurred, reshuffled, if not discarded. If, as Yeats warned, the centre cannot hold, then nor can the edges. Things, technologies, animals, senses, intuitions, fears, joys – even empty school bags – all have their moment in the 'biochoreographies, zooethnographies, and multispecies ethnographies' of the future. With Spinoza's monism, and Deleuze's call to experimentation dwelling throughout, we have the prospect of a genuinely alternative (southern?) perspective: one that might decentre the assumed primacy of European ways of seeing in order to 'make kin in lines of inventive connection as a practice of learning to live and die well with each other in a thick present'.[123]

*

'Telling true stories':[124] One exemplary field in which we see a renewed focus on ontology is in early years research where the 'intransigent nature/culture

binaries'[125] that frame Western thought are sidestepped by children who encounter beings and things in ways that challenge our assumptions about how the world 'is asking to be named'.[126] Following the nomadic philosophy of Deleuze and Guattari as well as Karen Barad's notion of entanglement as the 'lack (of) an independent self-contained existence'[127] we enter a world where sand, sticks, mud and lizards blend into one field of energy, coming alive *as* children-water-sticks-lizards:

> Neither stick nor child is separate. They can no longer be considered isolated beings or objects. Their intra-action has connected them and changed them both, creating a new assemblage of bodies and sense.[128]

From a new materialist perspective, thinking about the subject moves from an 'epistemology of human consciousness to a relational ontology' with a focus on the 'not containable, in excess of meaning, rather than rationality or disciplining or socializing or interpellating'.[129] 'Animal becomings' are unique, almost ephemeral, and demanding of a new, intense commitment to empiricism where matter matters and things are taken at face value:

> It is also clear from the sticks/water/bodies video that sticks are not homogenous or generalizable, each stick is different, they present vastly different possibilities to the children. The huge stick/tree branch, for example, presents all sorts of challenges for moving it, the stick with the E shaped prongs offers possibilities for lifting out weed, some sticks simply invite flapping and splashing, and other sticks also become objects of desire. Sticks invite parts of bodies and combinations of bodies, they splash and wet bodies and sometimes even endanger bodies. They engender language that is specific to each stick and stick moment. They transform and enable other things to transform as sticks become fishing rods and weed becomes fish. It is never just sticks in general but one specific material stick, one moment, the 'agential cut' of intra-action when each material body, stick and child, comes into temporary being.[130]

Such thinking continues the efforts of the 'posts' who tried to 'work in the ruins' of modernist science but who nevertheless found that work impossible because it remained 'so deeply mired in humanism'. The solution, of sorts, is to reimagine empiricism and the material with a new ethical commitment to 'acknowledge the destruction of the world humanism and its science projects encourage with their man/nature, human/nonhuman binaries' and to look instead for a 'justice-to-come' grounded in 'irreducible relations of responsibility'.[131] Celebrating (clinging onto?) philosophies of becoming with their 'belief in the world',[132] provides a promise of/for the future. 'Man' (as child) reimagined *through* nature gives us another chance of living into the coming post-Anthropocene. A kindly stay of execution that casts deftly to one side centuries of Western intellectual struggle to imagine man in and of the world and which now begins to appropriate indigenous ontologies in the service of our (never in doubt) third coming.

8

Mapping, madness and the will to know: While such post-foundational thought flourishes within the generous expanse of educational studies, it lives precariously within the burgeoning field of globalization and its relation to education. Here, we can discern two areas of scholarship worthy of attention – comparative education and global education policy studies– both of which engage with alternative thought but seem determined not to abandon the safe harbours of modernity.

*

Fear of the dark: Comparative education is perhaps the earliest iteration of a global approach to education and one growing in import through the policy fetish for international assessment studies and big data that can illuminate 'what works'. There are thankfully many comparative educations, not all of which are reducible to studying (and learning from) the educational progress of nations. Binding them together as is expected in the scholarly survey is far from straightforward, or wise. Where to start? The new entrant to the 'field' may note a fixation on origins and a pathology of self-doubt. One can find a multitude of surveys and summaries of the 'forms' of comparative education,[133] explanatory models[134] mappings of knowledge positions,[135] attempts to understand the socially constituted nature of these positions[136] and regular efforts to persuade a broad church to remain faithful to an enterprise that often seems desperately 'nebulous'.[137]

*

A full and balanced understanding: Myths of origin usually start with the father figure Marc-Antoine Jullien de Paris who offered a *Plan for Comparative Education* in 1817. Here, we find the first hint of a relation between education and national development that continues to 'legitimate(s) our nineteenth century positivist classification and methodological patterns including juxtaposition and notions of the gradualist improvement of societies through the power of social science'.[138] Jullien's Plan is often considered to have birthed the dominant modernist comparative education taken further by historical functionalist and positivist approaches.[139] As a product of its time, such comparative education dovetailed nicely with Durkheim's 'science of education':

> By comparing, identifying the similarities and eliminating the differences, we can constitute the generic types of education that correspond to the different species of society. . . . Once these types are established, it is necessary to explain them . . . thus obtaining the laws that dominate the evolution of education systems.[140]

The conjuring of such laws brings education into view as a catalogue of nations and regions, demographic groups and knowable phenomena such as 'curriculum, teaching methods, finance, management structures, political change and labour markets'.[141] The ultimate form of the 'illusion' of knowing[142] becomes Noah and Eckstein's attempt to ward off indeterminacy with a 'science of comparative education' where, with 'one foot firmly planted in pedagogy and the other in the wider area of the social sciences' the 'problems of bias, utility of results, and eclecticism in both methodology and data' can be overcome.[143]

A modernist comparative education views the world through an 'allegedly onto-epistemic grammar' but manages to treat as innocent its 'Cartesian, logocentric, teleological, anthropocentric, universalist, or utility-maximizing reasoning'.[144] Increasingly, it is paid for by development agencies frantic to recognize difference in order to kill it. Increasingly, it paves the way for an age 'marked by numbers' and little else.[145] Increasingly, it erases the necessary frictions between academic scholarship, 'science' and policy. One of the many consequences of this lust for controlled knowing is the silencing of histories, peoples and places that fail to meet the standards, dispositions and, even, whims of 'planet North'.[146] Modernist comparative education struggles to acknowledge its 'entanglement(s) with colonialism'.[147] One strand of that entanglement saw education as 'the means by which peoples of *retarded* culture may be brought rapidly to the *common* level (emphasis added)'.[148] While blatant racism is rejected in our post-colonial present, comparative educationalists remain at the forefront of a 'scientific approach' that aims to help liberated peoples reach the benchmarks set by a distant and privileged few.[149] Unsurprisingly, it is not difficult to find an unproblematized 'moral purpose' at the root of much of the field.[150] Astute commentators note that much of this genre fails to grasp that what was 'once deliberately shaped to be an architectural masterpiece' is anything other than 'rubble'.[151]

*

Through the ages, a common theme: Comparative education has never truly left its modernist harbour:

> that mode of thought called 'science', the strengths of its explanatory power, the necessary primacy of hypothesis-formulation and control in research.[152]
>
> much, and perhaps most, research requires multilevel comparative analysis in order to achieve a full and balanced understanding of its subjects.[153]

This is not to suggest that comparative education is doomed to irrelevance. One alternative is an 'academic' approach that finds itself concerned with issues of 'epistemology and modes of academic understanding'[154] and which acknowledges that 'comparative wisdom' remains 'elusive'.[155] With no agreed form but many strands, academic comparative education attempts to reimagine the context or subject of our enquiry, the contours of place and space and, ultimately, revisit questions of purpose as we make sense of education in a global(izing) cultural economy. Some suggest our starting point must be a commitment to estrangement rather than the '"naturalization" of solutions that come from a unifying vision of education'.[156] This is what Barthes calls a 'science of difference'.[157] There have been nascent attempts at such radical thought that have offered a post-modern reading of the world,[158] others that view the violence of modernity as resolvable through dialogues with alternative world views[159] and a host of more moderate perspectives that interrogate our notions of time, space and meaning making. Riches among ruins.

One recent move, echoing the ambitious cartographic project of Roland Paulston,[160] attempts to position comparative education in relation to other equally legitimate time/space universes. One rich seam is unfolding in relation to Japanese educational traditions, especially the philosophies of nothingness and negativity of the Kyoto School.[161] Alongside this work is a new performative, increasingly experimental, contribution that invokes inspirations as diverse as Lewis Carroll's white rabbit, to the witches and pagan rituals of Baltic folklore. Here we find provocations and estrangements made possible by going beyond the conventional boundaries of a scholarly discipline.[162] Such authors write freely of their 'interwoven positionalities' and occasional complicity in stifling or taming the otherness and entanglement that is always and necessarily present in modernist comparative education.[163]

We could have joined these moves, unsettling comparative education with inspiration from beyond its horizon. Instead, and in the original spirit of Paulston's project, we elect to dwell *within* the Western canon, illustrating its long history of openings, closures, forgetfulness and an always present violence aimed at closing down wayward thought. Our aim is to show that significant possibilities for new thinking exist *within* the Western canon itself. While alterity, estrangement, difference and otherness lie on the fringes of the Western philosophical project, they are actually central to it! However, unlike Paulston, we do not dwell in the attempts of comparative education to position itself, viewing this theory work as largely derivative. Rather, our interest is to trace otherness, excess, excrement, bodily pain, ecstasy, incommensurability, the mundane and sublime as these exist *within* the foundational ideas on which comparative education stands.

9

Reframing context: The question of how we read context is central to the comparative project. In some of the most substantial of mainstream attempts, we learn about 'Preschool in three cultures'[164] or 'Culture and Pedagogy' in five primary school systems.[165] Such case-based scholarship digs deep to uncover the rich historically contingent origins of social practices, conflating culture, nation and state in a comfortable alliance that both depicts and creates the object of interest. In the case of Alexander's tour de force, these national studies are bound together by the author's own distaste for the British defiling of education through neo-liberal ideology. In effect, the world is read *through* the agonies of Thatcherism. In the study of pre-schooling by Joseph Tobin and colleagues, one might wonder why certain 'cultural' practices were first noticed and later exemplified as worthy of detailed examination. Who decides on what counts? What goes unseen? Such work is in debt to the logic and limits set by methodological nationalism as well as the passions and positionality of the researcher.

The spatial turn in comparative education attempts to counter the urge to simplify our units of analysis and is indebted to radical thought from anthropology, political science and geography in particular. Common to all three disciplines is the recognition that the 'inherently fragmented space' that made the study of cultural difference possible was little more than intellectual complacence wedded to projects of imperialism. Here, the 'presumption that spaces are autonomous has enabled the power of topography to conceal the topography of power'.[166] Rather than separate spaces brought into dialogue by projects of political and cultural control – and scholarship – the new challenge is to comprehend their connectivity and mutual constitution. When distances are collapsed and communication is instantly possible across peoples, places and levels of society from global policy makers to local activists and when cultural flows make possible new imaginaries for how to live 'here' as they do 'there', the impulse to think in 'levels' becomes not only an 'intensively managed fiction' but an urgent 'ethnographic problem'.[167]

One way to address this problem is to view place as event[168] and localities as 'articulated moment(s) of social space' where 'conflict, discursive manoeuvring, and compromise'[169] produce subjectivities that are both relational *and* scalar. Rather than accept accounts of the apparent 'pulverization of the space of high modernity' by deterritorialized global flows, we might consider how our current condition creates estranged relations between peoples, things and places:

> We need to account sociologically for the fact that the 'distance' between the rich in Bombay and the rich in London may be much shorter than that between different classes in 'the same' city. Physical location and physical territory, for so long the only grid on which cultural difference could be mapped, need to be replaced by multiple grids that enable us to see that connection and contiguity – more generally the representation of territory – vary considerably by factors such as class, gender, race, and sexuality, and are differentially available to those in different locations in the field of power.[170]

*

Academic comparative education rejects 'neatly packaged matter-of-fact cubes'. Context is no longer viewed as 'a unity that is always already-there' but as 'the *practice* of identifying categories and analytic topics (spatial, temporal, institutional, discursive, theoretical) that intersect, overlap, and change over time'.[171] Context is now about 'processes rather than essences'.[172] Space, then, becomes something quite other than the 'neutral grid on which cultural difference, historical memory, and societal organization are inscribed'.[173] It is contested, pregnant with interests, passions and emotions. It is unstable, becoming, entangled and, even, intractable. A moveable feast? Comparative education becomes the subtle art of making sense of objects, events, ideas and people all of which move at great speed without the rule-governed predictability of earlier eras. This is the comparativist's worse nightmare but greatest opportunity.

*

Entangled times: Where, then, do we focus our attention in order to understand both the specificity of things *and* their connectedness? One approach focuses on policy itself, viewing this as a 'social and political space articulated through relations of power and systems of governance'.[174] The anthropology of policy follows ideas as they transform into (legitimate) public utterance and then to text and law. Policy becomes an optic with which to connect ideas across time and space, to trace relations of power and the dramas of decision-making across different types of actors and contexts and to begin to understand the forces of conformity, coercion and contest that mark its journey to the 'policy moment' of fruition. This suggests that we follow processes of formation, solidification, contestation and reformation across time and place. Here, the focus is on the policy object as it moves through the space of institutions, bending to the will of key actors and the vagaries of meaning-making efforts.

This ambition to understand global education as *process* is elaborated further in vertical case study research. This approach attends to the micro-, meso-, and macro-levels of educational reform, placing them in horizontal comparative relations to 'distinct locations' before, finally, undertaking a transversal dimension of enquiry in order to capture how globalizing processes 'intersect and interconnect people and policies that come into focus at different scales'.[175] Like the anthropology of policy, this approach is indebted to the multi-site ethnography of George Marcus,[176] especially the ambition to capture 'people, connections, associations, and relationships across space' and where the global, now tamed, is 'collapsed into and made an integral part of parallel, related local situations, rather than something monolithic or external to them'. This is the new ethnographer: master of the 'spatially dispersed field'.[177]

Vertical ethnography links the transnational, nation and local by identifying 'flows of influence, ideas, and actions through these levels' as they reconstitute this space.[178] This approach aims to ensure that 'local' practices are understood as being in a mutually constitutive relation to transnational rhetoric, policy and action. Not only does the vertical case attempt to give form to the idea of global connection, it provides a way to refashion comparative work beyond the multi-country study. Like all ethnographic work, this approach promises rich understandings of context and considerable potential to give voice to subaltern actors in whose name so much education policy research is conducted. Unlike many studies that *do* focus on subaltern perspectives, it locates these voices as part of an extended national, regional and transnational *chain* of relations. This requires 'broader conceptualizations' of education and necessitates an approach to 'local-level research whose boundaries encompass fieldwork sites hundreds or thousands of miles away as well a careful consideration of history and political economy'.[179]

Multi-sited ethnography, with its recognition that we can no longer study social phenomena in the ways that the greats of anthropology once viewed the isolated village, provides an ethnographic method to deal with 'container' thinking in the study of education policy. However, critics find much of its programme problematic. One strand – favourable to the Malinowskian emphasis on deep, context-rich insight – suggests that this diffuse approach to engaging with field(s) may rob ethnography of its greatest strength.[180] An opposing strand worries that a discredited heritage of unity and holism is being rehabilitated through work that takes for given the primacy and pre-existing matter-of-factness of certain places or processes. This goes against the 'basic principle that space is socially produced'.[181] Others go further, charging multi-site ethnographers with failing to recognize the arbitrary nature of site-selection and the pragmatics of access that have always shaped anthropological enquiry.[182] Even though adherents to this approach claim a '(geographical) spatial de-centredness' and thus a research object greater than a collection of locations or places, the task of following specific phenomena across time and space suggests that multi-sitedness is 'not synonymous with perspectivism'.[183] Others are less generous, dismissing multi-sited ethnography as a 'buzzword', the significance of which has been lost through 'mechanical(ly)' use.[184] For some, the 'first generation' of multi-sited ethnographers were seduced by the 'worldliness' of a programme of thought which promised an elegant solution to a debilitating critique and thus starved its adherents of the capacity for 'self-critical reflection'.[185] A more measured view is that while advocates of multi-sited research are at pains to make clear its distinctiveness from multi-*country* research, it essentially *restores* a 'spatialized (cultural) difference' into the equation:

> it is not important how many and how distant sites are, what matters is that they are *different*. This must be a requisite, because without it there would be absolutely no point in moving around. But it also seems to bring us dangerously close to the supposedly-conventional model of bounded culture.[186]

Yet another related body of work approaches the spatialization of education through the 'anti-structural structural concept' of assemblage. The aim here is to elevate issues of 'emergence, heterogeneity, the decentred and ephemeral' but to do so within an overall framework that seeks out an assumed deeper order and coordination of 'social life and social interactions'.[187] Assemblage thinking enables the analyst to 'spend less time trying to crisply demarcate the boundaries between an object of interest and its "context", and instead to direct our energies towards understanding social embeddedness'.[188] Global assemblages have been identified in many areas of life. One area of relevance for education considers how 'global forms of techno-science, economic rationalism, and other expert systems gain significance' as 'tool(s) for the production of global knowledge'.[189] Unlike other approaches to networks where social relations take a determining position, analyses of financial markets have viewed global knowledge production through the lens of what some term the *scopic system* where participants respond not to 'embodied, pre-reflexive occurrences' but, rather, to the features of the 'reflected, represented reality'.[190] This 'way of seeing' tends towards a 'single collective' and produces a level of 'global inter-subjectivity' that 'derives from the character of these markets as reflexively observed by participants on their computer screens in temporal continuity, synchronicity, and immediacy'.[191] Rather than spatially configured and dispersed, such markets become 'communities of time' integrated into one 'temporal stream of sequentially connected prices and transactions'.[192] Here, we become attuned to a new mode of capitalist representation and its distribution across time and space. Education policy scholars can quickly grasp that *scopic systems* such as the OECD's PISA programme or various systems for the global ranking of universities crystalize pasts, present and futures on one 'surface' and have the power to reimagine what education is and should be for.

In attempting to bridge the spatial logics of flows and place, the notion of assemblage offers the persuasive imaginary of the global as singular and comprehensible albeit messy and provisional. While diversity and complexity are lost in the presentation of the world as fractal, assemblage-thinking risks a return to the seductive world of 'classic social theory' and 'structural' thinking where the new assembled 'object' is given 'materiality and stability'.[193] However, by tracing the notion of assemblage as it is frequently used in contemporary social science, we arrive at the 'radical or deviant' philosophy of Deleuze and Guattari where key concepts have less definitive meanings than those often attributed to them.[194] Some have noted that early English translations of Deleuze and Guattari's concept of *agencement* settled upon the more familiar term 'assemblage' which has its French equivalent but which in English is used in a more limited way to characterize the coming together or 'collage' of 'diverse' objects.[195] *Agencement*, for Deleuze and Guattari, 'implies specific connections with other concepts' and is actually concerned with 'the *arrangement* of these *connections*'.[196] Rather than denoting some settlement or final and stable new state of being, *agencement*, for Deleuze and Guattari, draws upon Spinoza's idea of the 'common notion' to suggest that:

> All bodies have in common the states of extension, motion and rest; but when two or more bodies come into contact or otherwise enter into a relationship they

form a composition. A *common notion* is the representation of this composition as an independent unity.[197]

This 'independent unity' is viewed as an 'event' and remains, necessarily, in a 'state of becoming' where we can (only ever) develop 'adequate ideas' about it and where the 'knower' 'participates in a further stage of becoming not reducible to his knowledge'.[198] The assemblage is thus 'inherently unstable and infused with movement and change':

> the intent in its aesthetic uses is precisely to undermine such ideas of structure. It generates enduring *puzzles* about 'process' and 'relationship' rather than leading to systematic understandings of these tropes of and the common discourse that it has shaped.[199]

Persuasive heuristics such as the scopic system can thus be a productive imaginary while ever it retains a playful and respectful distance to the mechanisms it attempts (fleetingly) to bring together. Describing such systems as 'being based on a comprehensive summary view of things'[200] where 'one global educational reality'[201] is on show may capture the sense that (some) participants have of such events but may say more about the desires of researchers to reduce the world to meaningful and total representation than it does of globalized phenomena per se.

*

Borges reminds us: 'A man sets out to draw the world. As the years go by, he peoples a space with images of provinces, kingdoms, mountains, bays, ships, islands, fishes, rooms, instruments, stars, horses and individuals. A short time before he dies, he discovers that that patient labyrinth of lines traces the lineaments of his own face'.[202]

*

Eduscape: In recognition of the traps awaiting the scientist of assemblage, and following Appadurai's lead to explore globalization as a disjunctive, contradictory and entangled cultural phenomena, the notion of policyscape has been used to attempt theoretical and methodological innovation without the urge to nail down the specific dynamics, flows and nodal points of reform.[203] By bringing together disparate educational contexts and placing them in juxtaposition, this approach to comparison provided a means to reconsider the role of the state under conditions of globalization, acknowledging its centrality to reform efforts without being beholden to it. It has also framed culture and agency in terms of the production of locality, thus avoiding the debilitating global/local binary or methodological nationalism that holds sway in mainstream comparative analyses. By focusing on the precarious project of managing one's own schooled subjectivity – as administrator, teacher, student or parent – the reader comes to view the saturated space[204] of global reform as beyond the control of social science enquiry strategies. Policies, passions, materialities, emotions and happenstance. In effect, a research approach that attempts to reflect the world as it is.

Positioned as a radical contribution, the study of educational 'policyscapes' is, in other respects, fundamentally tied to the modernist logic it attempts to challenge. Here, one might observe a continued commitment to the 'real' (albeit via a new spatial configuration) and to classical notions of truth and representation. More troublingly, one could question the 'policyscape' concept for inadvertently revitalizing a Marxist logic of production where humans 'act(ing) upon and transform(ing) the material world into commodities with surplus value'.[205] This was the predictable consequence of attempting to take seriously Hardt and Negri's claim that an emerging global 'Empire' of universal norms, interconnectivity and social activism would undermine the hegemonic position of the metropolitan centres and their institutions, heralding a new era where the coordinated voices of what they called the 'multitude' would challenge and ultimately dismantle the old order. Such claims were, in many ways, wildly overheated.

10

The profitable business of map-making: This impulse towards capturing the essence of an unwieldly world lies at the heart of the growing field of global education policy studies. Interest here has focused on the new role of the national state in policy formulation, the rise of non-state actors such as private providers, entrepreneurs, supra-national policy and development agencies and transnational advocacy networks. It has explored teachers, curriculum and youth, issues related to professionalization, minorities, gender and post–Second World War regimes of rights and entitlements.[206] While much of this work focused upon particular places, peoples and policies, there is also an increasing interest in large cross-country/context investigations that have at their core a desire to chart new constellations of power and interests; what some frame as 'joined up' policy.[207] The gaze here includes the global governance of teachers and higher education, student mobility, new educational markets and the emergence of new school forms.

Much of this genre is awash with overarching frameworks, typologies and maps aimed at exposing and thus demystifying transnational reform processes. In its most simplistic form, it views policy as an instrumental movement of stages of 'borrowing', relying solely on rational and strategic actor-centric understandings of change. Such work aims at identifying the 'smoking-gun' of reform.

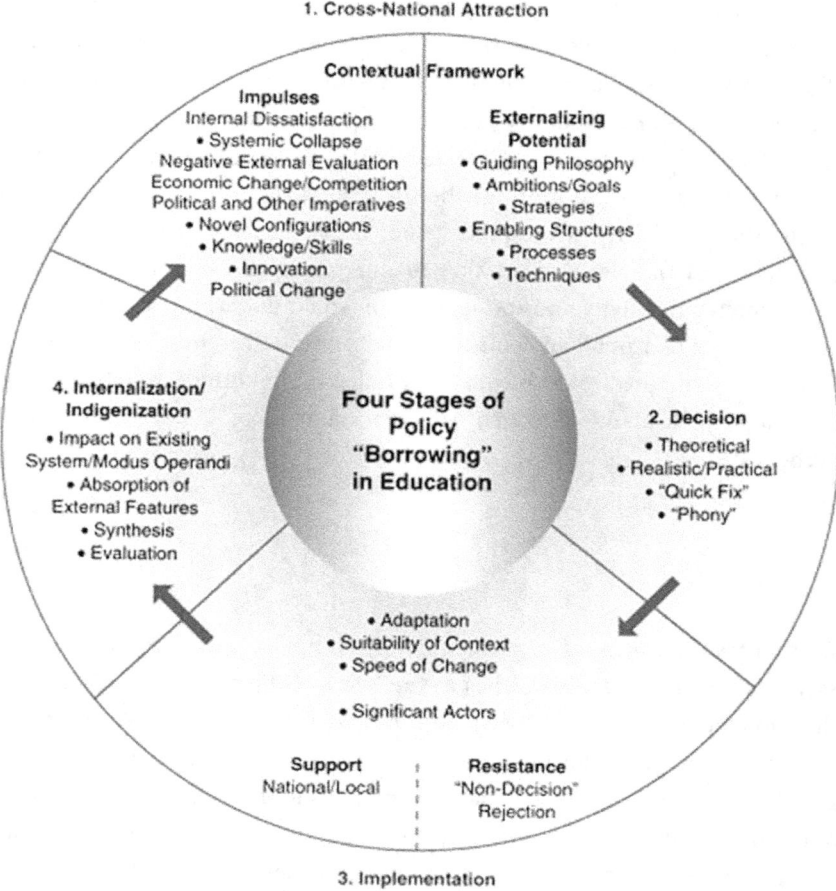

Figure 2.2 Policy Borrowing in Education.

Other approaches consider reform as a deep process of cross-national historical development conditioned by norms that trend towards global convergence. One approach in this genre offers the spectacular prospect of nailing down *the* culture of the world.[208] Another prioritizes the unique logics of different meaning systems within globalizing spaces,[209] an orientation that resonates with classical anthropological perspectives that insist upon the continued primacy of localized culture itself.[210] Culturalist perspectives buttress one another: they consolidate a modernist research ambition to identify and explain reform processes and interests in order to re-establish some semblance of order and control in the face of growing complexity. Such work thrives on an explicit reality principle, never saying more than can be gleaned from 'evidence' and 'experience'. The truth, nothing but the truth.

Various forms of network analysis take the reality principle to its zenith as they seek the 'coherent research framework that examines the effects of the complex mix of data infrastructures, data flows and new policy actors in constituting networked educational governance'.[211] Such work traces emergent – often *sub*merged – interconnections between global, local, state and non-state actors in ways that attempt to expose new mobilities of governing and new scalar relations between actors, places and ideas. From this perspective, the global education policy field itself becomes the culture or system to be studied, with place becoming very much secondary and occasionally irrelevant.

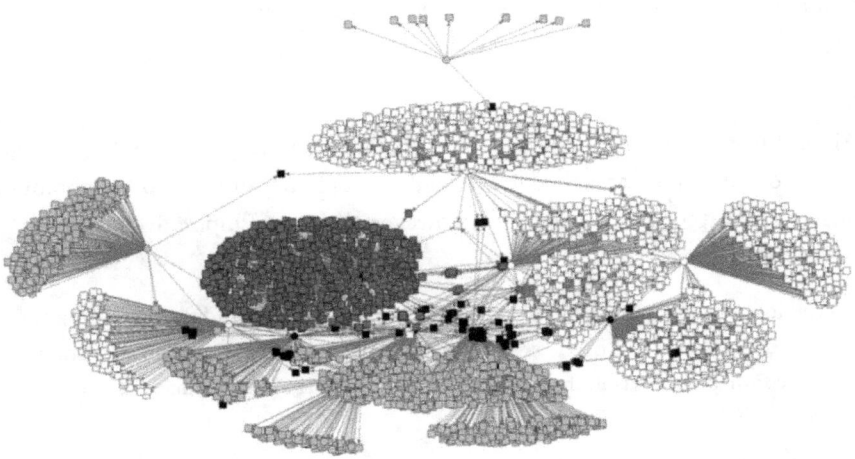

Figure 2.3 Complete reference network by policy domain.

Network analysis requires a different 'geographical imagination',[212] especially an awareness that policy does not simply link and integrate places but, rather, change our perception of place itself 'as geographies are stretched, contracted and folded'.[213]

A socially oriented approach to network analysis is a seductive way to explore neoliberalism as *process*, especially when this is understood as the 'disarticulation and re-articulation of governance'.[214] Such research has explored the processes by which policy texts are developed and embedded globally and has gazed into these networks with a form of ethnography freed from its traditional commitment to ethnos.[215] In its place is the internet and powerful network browsing programs that bring rich and diverse nodal points of data into one frame of reference. Indeed, network ethnography appears limited only by the extent of the ambition and computer software available to the analyst. One nodal point leads to another and then to a dozen more as the research object proliferates. Here, the researcher *creates* the scopic system assumed to be at the black heart of the neo-liberal project. Often, there is little awareness that network analyses tend to take the same visual form, suggesting something more profound about the limits of social science method.[216]

*

By limiting itself to an unproblematized notion of the real, such forms of analysis appear to mirror the contemporary policy fixation with fact and measurement that it otherwise questions.[217] Our madness with method.[218]

*

All of this was described long ago by Borges who tells of an ancient land where the art of cartography reached great heights. Here, maps mirrored the contours of space 'point for point'. Inevitably, however, the great Empire declined and its maps rotted away:

> The following Generations, who were not so fond of the Study of Cartography as their forebears had been, saw that the vast Map was Useless, and not without some Pitilessness was it, that they delivered it up to the Inclemencies of Sun and Winters.[219]

Borges' fable is a call to humility for those engaged in the profitable business of map-making, and one that Baudrillard pushes to the limit:

Today abstraction is no longer that of the map, the double, the mirror, or the concept. Simulation is no longer that of a territory, a referential being, or a substance. It is the generation by models of a real without origin or reality: a hyperreal. The territory no longer precedes the map, nor does it survive it. It is nevertheless the map that precedes the territory – precession of simulacra – that engenders the territory, and if one must return to the fable, today it is the territory whose shreds slowly rot across the extent of the map. It is the real, and not the map, whose vestiges persist here and there in the deserts that are no longer those of the Empire, but ours. The desert of the real itself.[220]

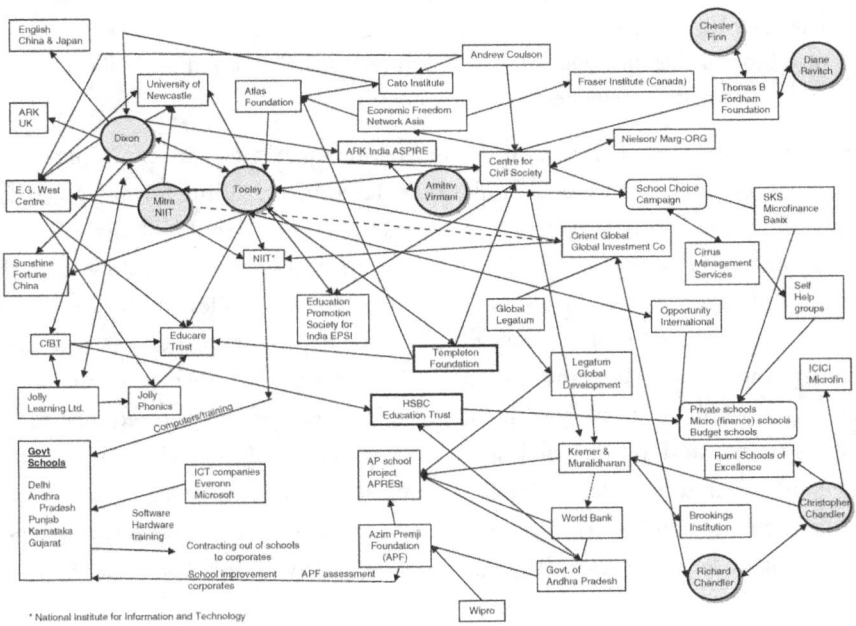

Figure 2.4 Advocacy networks, choice and schooling of the poor in India.

11

Looking in the wrong places: Across the social sciences we find an increasing sense that the motif of globalization has outlived its purpose. What became ascendant in the 1990s as a loose descriptor to catch the profound impact of aggressive Western liberal economic and political thought in the wake of the Soviet 'collapse' has struggled to explain the persistence of key, if not determining, structural categories that give contemporary global political dynamics a familiar, tragic, character.[221] States have been transformed, but certainly not dislodged. The subject has weathered profound cultural and economic flows to remain standing. Conflict, violence, negotiation and cultural hybridity continue, possibly intensified but nonetheless recognizable as part of the ongoing project of modernity rather than as a break from it:

> It should now be commonly accepted that much of globalization theory is zeitgeist sham. It seems equally clear that the 1990s represents a conjunctural rather than an epochal shift, and that globalization theorists misread the relationship between space and time under conditions of modernity. Too much talk of globalization is woolly, imprecise and faddish. At times, the concept takes on a borg-like texture, appearing as structure, institution, assemblage, ideology and, on occasion, as smokescreen and mirage.[222]

Notwithstanding such rejection, there is still much merit in exploring how various elements of the global landscape interconnect, calling for an approach to enquiry that might overcome the 'brutal confinement'[223] of disciplinary forms and can embrace methodological diversity and ontological difference.[224] Such challenges are yet to be met. Within education policy studies, we find a tendency towards more technically sophisticated research perspectives that banish the overheated language of early globalization theory, challenging narratives of indeterminacy with a faith in the power of numbers, connections, nodal points and refashioned social cartographies of precision. Maps laid elegantly over terrain tamed after the political and intellectual chaos of the immediate post-1989 period. More research, more science, more certainty and yet a glaring lack of acknowledgement of the 'reality' of the world that flickers before our eyes.

One challenge must be to counter a double gesture where research reflects Northern intellectual concerns (for improvement, social justice, reality, validity and generalizability in methods of enquiry) which are promoted by Northern authors who struggle to comprehend their own well-meaning provincialism. Education policy studies has moved into new areas, abandoning the structural comforts first of Marxism and, later, Foucault, for the seductive becomings and potentials of Deleuze. The notion of deterritorialization is one way to work with educational phenomena free from many of the disciplinary conventions that framed earlier perspectives but remains compromised by the normative and moral DNA of education which strives to 'preserve consciousness from doubt'.[225]

One example – central to our efforts here – is the so-called 'post-human' turn in the social sciences which is now a mainstream orientation within educational studies and an emergent concern within comparative education. Current efforts to de-centre the enlightenment subject (for example by giving nature an equal billing or by expanding our definitions of the human) build on a long tradition of radical thought but avoid the 'very real spectre'[226] that humanity is in danger of disappearing into hyper-simulation where events become mere signs and objects revenge themselves by their capacity to seduce us. Trapped in discourses of 'truth', fixated by the need to end the illusion (and mystery) of the world, mankind embraces media, digitalized technology and a confident new empiricism and binds these forces together as a cocktail of alleged facts, experientially driven common sense and emotion. Behind this illusion of knowledge and order is a world where 'absence is sovereign' and meaning seeps away. How we respond to this becomes the major intellectual concern of our time. Should we fight uncertainty with the belief that indeterminacy can be overcome or do we embrace its promise to help us re-enchant a world *overflowing* with meaning?

> there is one thing worse than living in uncertainty: living in a world where there is none – where everything is mapped, modelled, predictable and planned – a world without computer viruses, disease, terrorism: without evil. All these things are protecting us from something worse – total consensus – unless that is what we are secretly dreaming of?[227]

Globalization theorizing – borne out of Northern, modern, interests – will always struggle to capture the complexity of the world while ever it is tied to the logic of a social science that prioritizes defensible, universal and superior 'knowledge' over provisional, disruptive and partial awareness. Embracing this alternative awareness becomes an invitation to a different type of research engagement, one that is open-ended, world-making and which reserves judgment.[228] It is one where theory can only exist as challenge because 'anything else is quickly consumed with banality'. With the death of the real and the collapse of traditional political categories, theory thus becomes fiction and 'a space that stands in for liberty and authenticity in an epoch that recognizes neither'.[229] This is a call to education – not least comparative education – to renew itself on different terms.

*

Beyond our compulsion for certainty: If for a moment we reduce the modern to the metaphor of the cube, and our discussion of comparison in education has already drawn upon that privileged geometry, we find the solid, closed receptacle offering the straight lines of containment, order, certainty and control. The cube 'solicits the reduction of sensory information' and is 'intolerant of ambiguity and contradiction'. The cube enables us to tame the world, and our collective anxiety borne from its complexity. By contrast, we might ponder the shape of the bowl: open to interpretation and rich with potential for contamination. The bowl avoids the strictures of Euclidean geometry and Cartesian epistemology that subordinate thought and life to the preordained. Instead, it invites interpretation without insisting upon one gaze or course of action. 'Soft, vague shapes and edges' in contrast to the 'sharp, precise, definitive' boundaries of the cube.[230] Overflowing and thus *part of rather than separate from* the world. It is within such spaces that thinking freed of constraint and obligation might be possible.

Connecting to Eastern thought, we might embrace the bowl – and a flawed one at that – as a metaphor for our research orientation. Imperfect. If we are able to celebrate imperfection, the way opens for a form of awareness that reflects the unspoken but knowing human experience:

> nothing is perfect, everything is in a constant state of change, and everything evolves from nothing, only to devolve back to nothing . . . . The challenge is to view things with *muga* (no mind), thus seeing them as they truly are and involve oneself in understanding the metaphorical representations of universal forces of impermanence, imperfection, and the cycle of creation and decay.

Figure 2.5 Bowl.

The challenge is to unlearn reason and simply see clearly, without pretence and without intellect.[231]

*

Beauty in the flawed or imperfect: The Japanese practice of Kintsugi

Kintsugi has been heavily influenced by prevalent philosophical ideas. Namely, the practice is related to the Japanese philosophy of *wabi-sabi*, which calls for seeing beauty in the flawed or imperfect. The repair method was also born from the Japanese feeling of *mottainai*, which expresses regret when something is wasted, as well as *mushin*, the acceptance of change.[232]

*

Such a perspective sets comparative education with an enormous challenge:

Mind can only create the qualities of good and bad by comparing. Remove the comparison, and there go the qualities. What remains is the pure unknown: ungraspable object, ungraspable subject, and the clear light of awareness streaming through.[233]

3

Into the Darkness

1

Sapere Aude? While we have illuminated the subject of/in education through the optique of globalization, we might also consider philosophies of modernity as a way to understand subjectivity, the 'real' and 'truth'. Here, we find openings, and closures, cautions and invitations. As well as possibility. In comparative education, we find a dominant commitment to a certain expression of the modern that obscures or denies a long tradition for thought that makes space for doubt, darkness, estrangement, nihilism and nothingness. Time to step back into the shadows.

*

Our ambition is to recall those things that have been suppressed and forgotten during the search for light. Perhaps it is here that this book finally begins!

*

What is enlightenment? Writing in Berlinische Monatschrift in 1784, Kant gave the following response to an official from the Prussian government who had addressed this question earlier:

> Enlightenment is man's emergence from his self-imposed nonage. Nonage is the inability to use one's own understanding without another's guidance. This nonage is self-imposed if its cause lies not in lack of understanding but in indecision and lack of courage to use one's own mind without another's guidance. Dare to know! (Sapere aude.) 'Have the courage to use your own understanding', is therefore the motto of the enlightenment.[1]

As human beings, we have the capacity to emerge from immaturity through self-reflection and will. For Kant, the problem is that 'laziness and cowardice' fasten us to ignorance, inviting others to direct our lives. Immaturity comes naturally: 'if I have a book to serve as my understanding, a pastor to serve as my conscience, a physician to determine my diet for me, and so on, I need not exert myself at all'. Immaturity thus becomes part of human 'nature', creating further barriers to personal autonomy. Here we must recall Kant's distinction between the public and the private uses of reason. While the latter refers to the use of reason in civic positions, the public use of reason is what we offer 'before the entire literate world'. Enlightenment requires the loyalty of men who serve the monarch but, and because of this restriction, an inclination to free thinking: to using one's own understanding. The basic principle of the age is, thus, the compromised call to 'Argue as much as you want and about what you want, but obey'. To act freely, using one's reason, is to act morally and that, again, is a sign of maturity. The moral subject will work towards freedom from immaturity. This leaves us with the tension between 'imperative morality' and 'will' and the challenge of how to define our morality in relation to will.

*

In education, we heed the call to act with maturity, autonomy and morality. If only it was that simple.

*

In his *Critique of Pure Reason* Kant outlines four cases of antinomy that continue to guide much of Western thought. One of the most controversial is that space and time are functions of the mind. The ideas that preceded Kant were those of a pre-existing divine foundation, a world made by God. Writing at a time of political upheaval in Europe and influenced by Newton's law-governed universe with its promise that reason would provide the means to control nature and develop social forms free of superstition, Kant wanted to establish categories and rules for how the subject could gain knowledge about the world in order to become self-determining. In his first Critique, he challenges dogmatic belief systems that object to Descartes' proof of the existence of God, accepts (some of) Hume's ideas that our knowledge is determined by our senses and that what we sense is historical and contingent, and dismisses Locke's notion that our mind is a 'blank sheet'[2] on which the world comes to us. This is a move from a stable, ready-made existence to a dynamic and becoming world. The consequence was a radical reassessment of what we can know and how we can be understood as human beings. Bridging the 'gulf between dogmatism and scepticism', this position becomes a 'critical path' that can 'bring human reason to full satisfaction'.[3]

Kant refers to his fruits as a philosophical Copernican Turn[4] where the thinking subject becomes the focal point for making the world and universe intelligible. Of course, Copernicus opposed the *belief* that the earth (and a human perspective) was the centre of the universe, thus making possible a form of scientific enquiry that sought the truth. By contrast, Kant centres the human subject but, significantly, establishes certain conditions for how we might interpret the world around us. Subjects can only perceive objects through frameworks and never in their own right. We conceive things through space and time which are *a priori* categories that steer our perception. What we perceive, then, is not *things in themselves* but things as they *appear* to us. The distinction between things in themselves and appearances is the condition for how we can understand knowledge:

> all our intuition is nothing but the representation of appearance; that the things that we intuit are not in themselves what we intuit them to be, nor are their relations so constituted in themselves as they appear to us; and that if we remove our own subject or even only the subjective constitution of the senses in general, then all the constitution, all relations of objects in space and time, indeed space and time themselves would disappear, and as appearances they cannot exist in themselves, but only in us. What may be the case with objects in themselves and abstracted from all this receptivity of our sensibility remains entirely unknown to us. We are acquainted with nothing except our way of perceiving them, which is peculiar to us, and which therefore does not necessarily pertain to every being, though to be sure it pertains to every human being.[5]

As such, the 'highest degree of distinctness'[6] of intuition will still fail to understand objects as they are constituted in themselves. We are left, therefore, to inhabit the space between a world of appearances – what Kant calls 'the real world' – and an unknowable 'world in itself'. This leads to what appear to be incompatible positions: one where knowledge is derived from empirical data, the other where knowledge is produced through *a priori* categories. It also suggests that God and being are independent of empirical evidence. What we can understand and grasp is already *always* in relation to what we cannot. Our intuition – our contact with things through the senses – is nothing but a representation of appearances not an insight into the 'true' nature of things. If we remove the subject, then the nature of objects in space and time, and their relations, disappear. Indeed, so too does space and time themselves.

*

Many comparative educationalists note that space and place are changing and that the researcher must adapt.[7] Following Kant, we ought to understand that space and time for that matter are not 'encroachments upon experience', but the very 'boundaries within and according to which experience is made possible in the first place'.[8]

*

While intuition offers a source of knowledge about the world of appearances grounded in immediate, passive, perceptions, Kant reminds us that human cognition arises from 'two fundamental sources': a faculty for receiving impressions in the mind and our subsequent capacity for 'cognizing an object by means of these representations'.[9] Strangely enough, spontaneity and cognition are connected to certain rules and functions. Central to this is a grey zone of sense-making between a deterministic nature and human spontaneity. Building on Leibniz, Kant's subject is considered to be 'aperceptive', charged with the ability to reflect and be aware of what one perceives in the world. Intuition is defined as that which is 'given to us' through reception, spontaneity is connected to apperception and judgement, linking moments of experience through *a priori* rules for organizing such experiences. This is what Kant calls categories or pure forms of understanding. As we have seen, we are restricted in our understanding in that we cannot access and know about the world in itself: only its appearance. To come further, Kant develops a comprehensive theory of what we can know based on *a priori* categories and concepts for space and time. In that sense, the human mind is able to *produce* the world. It is thus reason that creates the idea of spontaneity and, like other ideas, this starts to 'act from itself, without needing to be preceded by any other cause that in turn determines it to action'.[10] Ideas that originate from reason can operate freely, since they are without 'the determinations applying to natural phenomena since they deal in appearances, which are nevertheless "nothing more than mere representations" which means that "they must have a ground which is not phenomenal"'.

Many have found this argument to 'complicate the relationship between the realm of reason and the realm of nature, since one is informing the other, and vice versa':[11] a trap from which we have never fully emerged. Kant – like a good number of us – places his faith in the autonomous subject, one capable of acting critically and who is able to develop spontaneous originations beyond causal determinations. Such action is ethical. Indeed, morality is 'ultimate rationality'.[12] Enlightenment man is able to *believe* in the capacity to exercise 'unconditioned, free thought'.[13] It is this (blind) faith in reason – a reason laced with morality – that lingers with us into the present.

*

In comparative education, the sheer volume of those *a priori* categories leaves little to the imagination! Has there ever been sufficient place for doubt?

*

It is often forgotten that Kant, the philosopher of epistemology and guardian of rationality, was also concerned to map the contours of knowledge and the place of human beings in a world bereft of theological bedrock. Finding places for thought *beyond* the scope of reason becomes his pressing concern, with his *Critiques* an attempt to reconcile science and religion, making space for both. Kant *needs* a God as a basis for universal moral laws and moral faith but he must also acknowledge the existence of things beyond our comprehension. His account of the tripartition of science, morality and aesthetics aims to put unintelligibility in its place as part of a comprehensive account of reason and knowledge. This will of course become influential and serve to inform the analytical approach of Habermas, one that remains central to educational studies. For over three hundred years, Kant has helped to keep the darkness at bay.

2

A blinding light: If Kant is an important reference point for Western thought, Hegel is the profound junction through which much twentieth-century philosophy struggled to pass.[14] Inspired by Kant but also the Greeks, Hegel offers something akin to a systematic philosophy of everything. Building on the great concerns of German Enlightenment, he blends rationality and pious Christianity but adds to the mix a radical understanding of history that sets him apart within the Idealist tradition. His aim is nothing less than to elaborate 'a grand vision of reality' where *the* abstract 'Idea', embodied in 'Nature', is swept along by 'Spirit' or Geist understood as a growing consciousness that moves towards its own self-realization. 'Heavy-duty metaphysics'[15] meant to stop in its tracks the timid limits to the problem of knowledge established by Kant.

In the Idealist tradition, Hegel views 'structures of thought' as being 'identical with those of the world'[16] and thus takes issue with Kantian attempts to distinguish forms of thoughts from what they are forms of. The separation of mind and matter, so central to the early Enlightenment thinkers, creates an 'impassable gulf' that is 'most naturally closed either by making the mind material, or by making the material mental'.[17] For Hegel, Kant accentuates the very problem of unknowability that was the object of his original enterprise. His inability to 'unite subject and object leads to a subjectivism that makes knowledge, *sensu eminentiori*, impossible'.[18] By contrast, Hegel views forms of thought as arising historically through interactions between subject and world from the most simple and primitive reactions to stimulus to the advanced conceptualizations that we find in science and philosophy. Rationality is not only in the mind, but in the world itself and this changes not only for different people but in relation to a notion of History that is imbued with purpose. It is a 'fractal' system where his philosophies of logic, nature and spirit are present at all levels. In the system, we find an outer world (or 'externality') that is 'only the mirror of ourselves' and a 'free reflection of spirit'.[19] Hegel, like a number of idealist philosophers wanting to 'go beyond the limits of experience', takes metaphysics to new heights, seeking nothing less than the 'underlying ground of the cosmic order' in the form of 'God, pure freedom, or final Self-Consciousness'. 'Absolute idealism' thus adopts an 'elevated moral tone' as well as a 'religious' belief in the idea of progress and the embodiment of spirit in nature.[20] Man and his world basking in the pure light of the sun.[21]

*

When our leaders claim that 'the arc of the moral universe is long, but it bends toward justice' or that one is in danger of being 'on the wrong side of history', we see a naïve Hegelianism in action.[22] When educational researchers talk of a 'world culture' of schooling or maintain faith in some abstract, general notion of progress or justice we see something similar.[23]

*

While profoundly interested in the relation of finite man to an infinite world shaped by historical forces, this is no simple empiricism. Unlike Locke and Hume who, in their different ways, view data as coming to the senses and thus mediating what we know, Hegel views sense-data as contingent, waiting to be filled with meaning through concepts which are negative until applied. All claims depend on other claims. Truth statements and conceptions remain open to revision through an ongoing process of negation. This dialectical process views understanding as emerging through continuous negations that provide the possibility for openings to more advanced conceptions and understandings but which are always developed in relation to what they are not. A thing/conception only becomes 'positive', because it always relies on 'what it is not to be itself'.[24] This is vitally important as self-consciousness is thus understood as arising out of the encounter with the other where we become aware of ourselves through a recognition of our difference from, but dependence upon, something which is necessarily out of our control.[25] The logic of the world hangs on identity-in-difference. Hegel's 'final solution' is a 'speculative philosophy'[26] that embraces difference in order to overcome it: a 'systematic attempt to secure the *identity* of identity and nonidentity and the *union* of union and nonunion'.[27]

It is well known that many contemporaries questioned the emphasis in Hegel's system (the mysticism/materialism divide being one) as well as its potential to capture all otherness *within* the system. What is important for us is that Hegel lingers in our time as a mode of thought aimed at accounting for difference, excess and absence through the victory – however unlikely – of complete subjectivity. Heidegger saw it as the endpoint of metaphysics, a 'transcendental reduction' that 'gives and secures the possibility of grounding the objectivity of all objects (the Being of this being) in its valid structure and consistency, that is, in its constitution, in and through subjectivity'.[28] This ambition to assimilate and overcome difference within the system can be thought of as announcing nothing less than the 'completion' of modern philosophy.[29] In popular interpretations, the realization of the Absolute through the vehicle of human consciousness has been described as marking the 'end of history'.[30] However, Hegel's project was far more complex, viewing life in its immediacy as shaped by tension and oppositions. It is here that meaning and value reside. Remove the struggle and life falls into a fatal sameness.

*

Is difference always and only to be found in relation to a centre? *Within* a system? Can it be outside or beyond our frame of thought? In the margins or shadows? Forgotten? An unaccounted for and unaccountable leftover? If so, what can we do with it? Should we pretend it isn't there?

*

Hegel was not alone in considering the relation of self to other and there are many variations of German idealism of importance here. For Fichte, it was foolhardy to distinguish neatly, as Kant had attempted, between things in themselves, or noumena, and the apparent world of phenomena. Such indeterminacy was an invitation to scepticism. Similarly dissatisfied by Hegel's sublimation of man to the force of the Absolute, Fichte focuses instead on a subjective subject-object relation where an 'absolute I' establishes a whole within which the relation between subject and object can be perceived. Collapsing the distinction between different avenues for knowing, he argues for an understanding of consciousness that emerges from *within* itself. This move attempts to reposition the subject at the centre of knowledge creation. Through the 'absolute I', the objective world becomes relative to the subject. Freedom for Fichte thus lies in our ability to transcend the finite world in order to shape phenomena to our will rather than submit ourselves to causality or live with an acceptance of things as they are. By contrast, Schelling argues for an objective subject-object position where Nature has an all-encompassing constitutive whole. His dialogue with Fichte captures a major tenet of nineteenth-century thought that resonates into our own time. Here, he takes issue with the notion that 'nature has no speculative significance, only a teleological one' and challenges Fichte by asking 'are you really of the opinion, for example, that light is only there so that rational beings can also see each other when they talk to each other and that air is there so that when they hear each other they can talk to each other?'[31]

Like Fichte, Schelling is critical of the Kantian dualisms of subject/object, appearance/world in itself, nature/God. However, he dismisses the idea of a merely objective nature, attacking Fichte for assuming that this could ever be a passive resource in our service. Instead, nature must be understood as having a subjective dimension that *produces* subjectivity: 'thinking is not my thinking, and being is not my being, for everything is only of God or the totality'.[32] For Schelling, nature then becomes the absolute producing subject. Criticizing Fichte's absolute – itself a response to Kant's spontaneous subjectivity – and as a way to overcome dualistic thought, Schelling challenges the understanding of the subject as an initiating and absolute principle. With gestures to Spinoza, Schelling suggests that in order for something to be an 'I', it must be conscious of its relation to something which it is not: to an 'other'. Deploying Hegel's terminology but with an important twist, we get the formulation: 'Nature is visible Spirit; Spirit is invisible Nature'.[33]

*

Figure 3.1 Cathedral.

If nature is *productive*, perhaps the 'field' shapes the educational researcher at least as much as *we* shape *it*?

*

Idealism invites a romanticism that seeks an 'all-inclusive conception of reason'[34] although no absolute truth. Unlike Hegel, the journey is one of *discovery* not a *return* to the self. Romantic philosophy – at least its early forms – emerges alongside idealism and in addition to the principle concerns of that tradition (what can we know, what is beyond our reach, how can the subject be realized? etc.) it is concerned with the rise of scientific and technological thought and its encroachment into questions that were hitherto the domain of speculative philosophy. If any thought captures this latter aspect, especially the widespread anxiety about the fragmentation of life under early industrial capitalism, it is Schiller's *On the Aesthetic Education of Man*.³⁵ Being 'chained to a single little fragment of the whole, man himself develops into nothing but a fragment'.³⁶

*

This fracturing of modern life, later so well described by Marx, was central to romantic thought, especially its literary manifestations. Rousseau's novel *Julie* – the first blockbuster of Western literature – captured this sense of incompleteness:

> I'm beginning to feel the drunkenness that this agitated, tumultuous life plunges you into. With such a multitude of objects passing before my eyes, I'm getting dizzy. Of all the things that strike me, there is none that holds my heart, yet all of them together disturb my feelings, so that I forget what I am and who I belong too.³⁷

How can this calamity of disintegration with its attendant nihilism be reversed? In Schiller's 'aesthetic utopia', art is given a 'virtually social-revolutionary role'.³⁸ Art serves as a 'catalyst, as a form of communication, as a medium within which separated moments are re-joined into an uncoerced totality'.³⁹ Unlike Hegel's system where negativity would eventually be overcome and replaced by absolute identity, early romantic thought dismisses the hunger for truth, looking upon such cravings with a certain dread. Who, indeed, would wish to live in a world without doubt? While Kant is often the subject of scorn in romantic philosophy, his *Third Critique of Reason* invites art and the artist to move beyond the boundaries of rule-based thought. Rather than art adhering to a particular form, it emerges from the 'talent' of 'genius' and since such talent is an 'innate productive ability of the artist' it 'belongs itself to nature'. In essence: '*Genius* is the innate mental predisposition *(ingenium) through which* nature gives the rule to art'.⁴⁰

Versed in Kant but cautious of his certainties, the early romantics – certainly Novalis, Schlegel, Hölderlein and Schleiermacher – distanced themselves from systematic explanation that would spin from itself. Being and the world cannot be subject to rational scrutiny. At the time that Hegel argued for a philosophy grounded in reason – something beyond 'animal muck' as he called it – others were considering how to integrate aesthetic values and morality. Schiller's controversial poem *The Gods of Greece* ('Die Götter Griechenlandes') from 1788 evoked a mythical classical past where humanity found fulfilment through values higher than those of Christianity and where a union with the natural world could overcome the disenchantment of industrial society and the rationalizing state:

> Oh beautiful world, where art thou flown?
> Oh face of nature's purest bloom, return!
> Now only in the fairy land of song
> Still lives the image for which we yearn.
> And barren mourn once blooming fields
> No Godhead lights up nature's visage
> How from the world's every living image
> Naught but a shadow yields![41]

Schlegel and Schelling in particular envisaged a union of philosophy and poetry that might 'heal the wound which had been festering since Plato's *Republic* between the claims of philosophy and literature'.[42] For Schlegel, the modern age had no mythology but might rediscover one through the poetic. Art thus became a turning point in discussions of how to overcome the fracturing of modern man. In Habermas' terms, such thinkers hoped that art might 'guard(ed) the flame of that absolute identity that had once been enkindled in the festival cults of religious communities of faith'[43] and it could be called upon once more to save reason from itself. Art would 'reacquire its public character' as a 'new mythology', thus enabling philosophy to 'flow back into the ocean of poetry from which it had once come'.[44] This ambition seemed thoroughly achievable for Schlegel who viewed the beautiful as separate from morality and truth. Its roots are therefore Dionysian:

> for that is the beginning of all poetry, namely to overcome the operation and laws of rationally thinking reason and transpose us again into the lovely confusion of fantasy, into the primordial chaos of human nature, for which I know of no more beautiful symbol that the abundant throng of the classical gods.[45]

While Schelling agreed that a new mythology was needed, he was less convinced that art and reason could be easily separated, relying instead upon an 'intimate relationship of the true and the good in the beautiful'.[46] As he matured, Schelling's philosophy turned towards more radical perspectives on knowing. Rejecting Hegel's 'positive' philosophy of revelation[47] where the negation of negation presupposes intuition and immediacy, he turned towards spontaneity, defining being as will and willing as 'the last and highest instance'[48] of being. Ultimately, this is the basis of reality and, in contrast to Kant, he does not link will to rationality or self-determination. Instead, it becomes 'a capacity for good and evil':[49]

> Nobody . . . has chosen their character; and yet this does not stop anybody attributing the action which follows from his character to themself as a free action. . . . Common ethical judgement therefore recognizes in every person – and to that extent in everything – a region in which there is no ground/reason [*Grund*] at all, but rather absolute freedom. . . . The unground Un*grund*] of eternity lies this close in every person, and they are horrified by it if it is brought to their consciousness.[50]

For the later Schelling, it is our 'groundlessness' that frees us from determinisms and necessities and which connects us to being in a world which itself appears groundless. Here we see the beginnings of a new mysticism quite different from that of Hegel's faith in Spirit as well as a scepticism that would pave the way for Schopenhauer's focus on will and desire and, later still, philosophies of self-transcendence, leaving and letting go.

*

Perhaps it is Romanticism – against all odds – that maintains 'a trace of the past that continues to haunt our living present'. Perhaps this is the modernity that we are 'unable to believe, but which we are unable to leave',[51] where the metaphysical urge to see beyond things as they present themselves, to collect disparate thoughts together, and to sleep at peace from the chaos of unwieldly dreams, takes over.

3

Hegel travels, new horizons open: If our aim was to be comprehensive, we might revisit Marx and the Young Hegelians who questioned idealist philosophy on materialist grounds but that tradition is well known and very much alive in educational studies. Less familiar will be the different receptions of Hegel in the mid-twentieth century, and what have these meant for thinking about the subject, world, meaning making and writing ↔ science in our time. Hegel's philosophy spawned an entire intergenerational program of thought in Germany but was interpreted in France, and later beyond, through the radically different influence of two men who shaped the formative years of many post-war intellectuals of that country. One of these, Alexandre Kojève applied Hegel's dialectic to desire, 'the most primitive form of self-consciousness'.[52] This was grounded in Hegel's understanding that humans seek recognition but can only achieve it via 'another object through whose negation it can assert itself'. Ultimately, this requires that the subject 'negates its own self-sufficiency and demonstrates its dependence on the object of its desire'. The resulting 'struggle between desiring subjects'[53] leads to *self*-negation. To achieve full self-awareness, therefore, one must face death:

> for Hegel, the truth *is* the way, and the way is the *Phenomenology of Spirit*. Hegel and his fellow wayfarers pass through the dread and despair of the Stations of the Cross on their way to the satisfaction and fulfilment enjoyed in the kingdom of absolute knowledge. This arduous journey to selfhood begins with desire and reaches its turning point in the confrontation with death (crucifixion) in the struggle for recognition.[54]

Kojève was writing and teaching in the shadow of a catastrophic half-century where Hegel's 'secularized theology of history'[55] provides a way to redeem humanity through bonds of interdependence. Religion is not eliminated but, rather, refashioned as a *faith* in the responsible and accountable state. It is through the modern state – for Kojève the Soviet manifestation – that history would become complete. Following this thesis, violent conflict, oppression and exploitation cease, as does philosophy itself 'for since Man himself no longer changes essentially, there is no longer any reason to change the (true) principles which are at the basis of his understanding of the world and of himself'.[56] While some in our own time view the end of history as emerging through the victory of liberal democracy, an earlier generation viewed the very same end as possible only through the achievement of socialist utopia. Irrespective of the ideological vehicle, such interpretations of a challenging and complex oeuvre of nineteenth-century thought end, fantastically, with the promise of perpetual happiness.

Equally significant was Jean Hyppolite who took issue with Kojève's attempt to erase life's tragic element, suggesting instead that its 'irresolvability'[57] was central to Hegel's project. Hyppolite was especially draw to Hegel's notion of unhappy consciousness and the power of death as an opening into self-awareness. While death 'is the most terrible thing', it is central to the 'life of the Spirit' which 'assumes death and lives with it':

> Spirit attains its truth only by finding itself in absolute dismemberment. It is not that (prodigious) power by being the Positive that turns away from the Negative, as when we say of something: this is nothing or (this is) false and, having (thus) disposed of it, pass from there to something else; no, Spirit is that power only to the degree in which it contemplates the Negative face to face (and) dwells with it. This prolonged sojourn is the magical force which transposes the negative into given-Being.[58]

According to Bataille, one of many French post-war scholars versed in Kojève and influenced by Hyppolite and who sought productive openings from within the systemic totality of dialectical reasoning, Hegel offers a 'violence of understanding' where the Positive must be confronted with the Negative in the search for resolution. By facing the Negative, and dwelling within it, difference is negated but, in the process, life is lost. What, then, of 'pure beauty' which lacks consciousness and thus 'cannot act', remaining forever 'impotent'?[59]

> Through action it would no longer exist, since action would first destroy what beauty is: beauty, which seeks nothing, which is, which refuses to move itself but which is disturbed by the force of the understanding. Moreover, beauty does not have the power to respond to the request of the understanding, which asks it to uphold and preserve the work of *human* death.

To be 'awakened in dismemberment' with the 'lucid gaze, absorbed in the negative' is man's 'violent and laborious struggle . . . against nature and is its end'. The fate awaiting dialectical reason. It is here that 'man constitutes himself as "subject" or as "abstract I" of the "understanding", as a separated and named being'.[60] In this way, both Hegelian idealism and those later romantic attempts at synthesis and holism become destructive strategies that devalue life and condemn man in negativity.

*

Like Hegel, is modern education research – for all its false humility – 'the apotheosized and sovereign Sage, (its) pride swollen with human vanity'?[61]

*

Hyppolite also drew upon Heidegger's radical perspective on language, insisting that Hegel's logic – like all systems of thought – is constrained by what can be thought and said with words. Our dependence on language ensures that meaning remains provisional and that otherness dwells forever beyond full negation. The subject thus remains the precarious achievement, if not fiction, of modern philosophy. This approach sets the tone for the so-called post-structuralism of Deleuze, Foucault and Derrida:

> In a manner similar to Marx's revision of Hegel, Hyppolite stands Kojève's account of Hegel on its head. While Kojève reduces logic to man in the form of the negativity of desire driving history, Hyppolite reduces man to logic in the

form of language or discourse speaking through man. This results in the radical decentring of the subject, which leads to thoroughgoing antisubjectivism.[62]

The impact of this re-reading of Hegel was profound. Understanding its entirety as an effort to 'reunite the opposites sundering self and society', Hyppolite is able to link Hegel's thought to phenomenology as well as structuralism: Hegel emerges as a 'structuralist *avant la lettre* and structuralism little more than latter day idealism'.[63] However, rather than reject Hegel, others emerging from Hyppolite's sphere pushed his idealism to breaking point in order to open up new planes for understanding. Merleau-Ponty, for example, develops a 'dialectics without synthesis'[64] that highlights the play of perception, language and art in processes of sense, not truth, making. Bataille explores the things that *cannot* be negated and which thus remain as an accompaniment to death. Lacan applies Hegel's notion of desire to psychoanalysis to suggest that 'since there is always an Other "within", the subject can never coincide with itself and thus is forever split', ensuring that the 'wound of subjectivity' remains forever open. Here, and to spite Hegel, otherness is present but never named. Blanchot offers 'baffling fragments' that invite 'non-philosophical dialogue'.[65] Derrida's use of Hegel is perhaps the most profound, opening the path to deconstruction, the very *opposite* of absolute knowing and consciousness. Rather than outright condemnation, he sees in Hegel's system the invitation to write on:

> The horizon of absolute knowledge is the effacement of writing in the logos, the retrieval of the trace in prousia, the reappropriation of difference, the accomplishment of what I have elsewhere called the *metaphysics of the proper*.
>
> Yet all Hegel thought within this horizon, all, that is, except eschatology, may be reread as a meditation on writing. Hegel is *also* the thinker of irreducible difference. He rehabilitated thought as the *memory productive* of signs. And he reintroduced . . . the essential necessity of the written trace [*trace écrite*] in a philosophical – that is to say Socratic – discourse that had always believed it possible to do without it: the last philosopher of the book and the first thinker of writing.[66]

The aim here is not to advocate for one or another reading of key sources in the Western canon. Rather, it is to note that Kant's unknown, Hegel's irresolvable otherness and the romantic notion of poetic realization – to take but three themes introduced here like 'a landscape glimpsed from a speeding train'[67] – have been largely ignored or rejected for their assumed inferiority to the analytical, practical and normative perspectives that have lodged themselves firmly in the bosom of education. It is a feature of our time, and a backdrop to these mediations, that the scholarship of our age is so quick to turn away from the darkness!

4

Destroyer par excellence:[68] The societal diagnosis laid bare by Schiller at the end of the eighteenth century was part of the larger concern to re-establish meaning in the wake of the loss of religious authority. How were people to find purpose in an 'uncertain universe in which neither the *ideal* or the *divine* existed'?[69] Some found it in reason, others in the state and still others through nature. Nietzsche would have none of it, rejecting the task of developing a further philosophy of reason and '*bid(ding) farewell* to the dialectic of enlightenment.'[70] The loss of absolute values *defines* modern society. Science fills the void by annihilating myth but replaces it with another less sacred one. Emerging commitments to equality and rights attempt to make up the shortfall. Religion persists with its faith and promise as well as its deference to authority and easy distinctions between evil and virtue. Metaphysical thought remains a deadly trap. The apparent and the 'real' world, this world and the next, man and God. All in place to keep us from embracing life as it is.

For Nietzsche, life was denied while ever it was lived by false ideals in a spirit of blind faith, ignorance or nay-saying. Why does society retain its zealous belief in values and morality when no higher power exists to adjudicate them? Christian morality is decadence, all religions 'affairs of the rabble'.[71] Priests are a 'malicious species of dwarfs'[72] who steal our souls and mortgage them to a fantasy. Kant, that 'cunning Christian',[73] slipped a dangerous moral philosophy into his earnest attempt to codify what we could know. The state – at least as it was emerging in Germany – was corrupted by petty interests that strove for something purer than itself but which invariably landed in the quagmire of vulgar mediocrity, chauvinism and nationalism. Idealism was no answer: denying reality, always striving for something more. The German *problem*. Theoretical culture is just another metaphysical sleight of hand. Modernity is decadence: nothing less than a process of the devaluation and disappointment. Myth, the essential other of reason, is destroyed by modernity and no higher values are developed to replace it.

> How shall we comfort ourselves, murderers of all murderers? What was holiest and mightiest of all that the world has yet owned has bled to death under our knives: who will wipe this blood off us? What water is there for us to clean

ourselves? What festivals of atonement, what sacred games shall we have to invent? Is not the greatness of this deed too great for us? Must we ourselves not become Gods simply to appear worthy of it? There has never been a greater deed; and whoever is born after us – for the sake of this deed he will belong to a higher history than all history hitherto.[74]

*

Overcoming: As we have seen, pre-Socratic philosophy viewed life as a balance between the forces of reason and instinct. Since Plato, we have been lumbered with the task of resolving the tension between them, overcoming uncertainty with a shaky reason that only perpetuates uncertainty. For Nietzsche, we must accept that these forces co-exit. It is through embracing their incommensurability that the richness of life will present itself. Our task is to find joy in experiences that, while conceptualized as incomplete and lacking, are not only all we have but an invitation to self-awareness. Good needs evil as night needs day. While Socrates insists that 'pleasure in understanding can heal the eternal wound of existence',[75] Nietzsche's response is to let Apollonian science and certainty dance alongside Dionysian ecstasy and sensuality.

*

An aristocratic radical: Georg Brandes was one of the first European intellectuals to take deep note of Nietzsche's writings, lecturing on Nietzschean themes in Copenhagen in 1888. He found much to admire. For Nietzsche, man is endowed with an aristocratic core that has nothing to do with one's inherited status, wealth or power. Rather, we are distinct because of our originality and capacity to rise above the herd mentality that levels society to the basest of values and estranges us from our judgment or capacity. The will to power is thus a call to become what you are! This requires diligence and alertness but most of all 'amor fati'.[76] Hermann Hesse, deeply influenced by Nietzschean thought captures this call in *Demian*, his post–First World War novel of spiritual awakening:

> There was only one true vocation for everybody – to find the way to himself. He might end as a poet, lunatic, prophet or criminal – that was not his affair; ultimately it was of no account. His affair was to discover his own destiny, not something of his own choosing, and live it out wholly and resolutely within himself. Anything else was merely a half-life, an attempt at evasion, an escape into the ideals of the masses. Complacency and fear of his inner soul.[77]

*

When a post-foundational thinker is labelled a 'Nietzschean aristocrat'[78] we understand the violence of the insult. However, we could easily return the sleight by referring to the accuser as decadent modernist or, worse, democratic parasite who seeks to level all others, disabling their potential in the fulfilment of a personal will to power.

*

Is education research constrained by decadence, idealism and denial?

The Nietzschean: Find your own values: they are within you.
The Modern: Reach for an ideal: it is more than you are.

*

Philosophy with a hammer: While attempting to break away from a current of thought that had set the tone of philosophy in Germany, Nietzsche nonetheless drew heavily on what had come before him. His mode of thought is dismissive of the mysticism of idealism and unconvinced by the easy to find naturalism of the romantics. Nevertheless, like the romantics, he saw great potential in the arts to provide 'an overwhelming feeling of unity leading back to the very heart of nature'.[79] Art offers illusion which, itself, is a 'promise of freedom from illusion'.[80] Dionysian lust, when displayed musically and in the sphere of poetry:

> does not lie beyond this world, like some chimera of the poetic imagination; it seeks to be the very opposite, the unvarnished expression of the truth, and for this very reason it must reject the false finery of that supposed reality of the cultured man. The contrast between this intrinsic truth of nature and the falsehood of culture, which poses as the only reality, is similar to that existing between the eternal heart of things, the thing in itself, and the collective world of phenomena. And just as tragedy, with its metaphysical comfort, points to the eternal life of this kernel of existence, and to the perpetual dissolution of phenomena, so the symbolism of the satyr chorus already expresses figuratively this primal relation between the thing in itself and the phenomena. That idyllic shepherd of the modern man is but a copy of the sum of the culture – illusions which he calls nature; the Dionysian Greek desires truth and nature in their most potent form – and so he sees himself metamorphosed into the satyr.[81]

It is through art that the painful revelation of the meaninglessness of life is possible and it is through art that we can come to admire, celebrate and reclaim meaning. Drawing on Richard Wagner from who the early Nietzsche found deep affinity, art was posited as saving religion once religion reduced itself to art 'in that it grasps the mythic symbols (which religion wants to believe are true in a real sense) in terms of their symbolic values, so that the profound truth hidden in them can be recognized through their ideal representation'.[82] Like Schelling who viewed the new mythology of art as the 'invention . . . of a new race',[83] Nietzsche saw art as a path to collective redemption:

> Only through the spirit of music can we understand the ecstasy involved in self-annihilation. One thinks of today's rock festival-goers, or of Nietzsche describing his response to *Tristan* as having laid his ear against the heart of the universal will and felt the tumultuous lust for life as a thundering torrent . . . the Bacchic choruses of the Greeks. Intoxication, music, singing and dancing were the activities in which the *principium individuationis* was lost. Here was the Dionysian response to the pain of life.[84]

Archaic culture had found a way to overcome tragedy by embracing it aesthetically. While the Nietzschean vision of the tragic owes something to the naturalism of early romantic thought, his relation to 'theoretical and practical reason'[85] is far less accommodating. Can reason ever bring man to 'maturity'? For Nietzsche, a truly mature gaze that applies reason to its limits will accept our insignificance and the meaningless of our purpose:

> Once upon a time, in some out of the way corner of the universe which is dispersed into numberless twinkling solar systems, there was a star upon which clever beasts invented knowing. That was the most arrogant and mendacious minute of 'world history', but nevertheless, it was only a minute. After nature had drawn a few breaths, the star cooled and congealed, and the clever beasts had to die . . . when it is all over with the human intellect, nothing will have happened. For this intellect has no additional mission which would lead it beyond human life.[86]

Loosing oneself in Dionysian ecstasy also implies a 'merging with amorphous nature within and without' and a 'kind of redemption that eliminates all meditations'. The consequence of this is a turning away from the 'emancipatory content' of enlightenment. Instead, we have the prospect of a 'decentred subjectivity, liberated from all constraints of cognition and purposive activity, all imperatives of utility and morality'. For Habermas, therefore, Nietzsche's dismantling of the 'principle of individuation' becomes an 'escape route from modernity'. From the perspective of twentieth-century social critique, that leads Habermas to the conclusion that Nietzsche has entered 'the realm of metaphysically transfigured irrationality'.[87] This of course is the 'will to power' exercised to break free of the past (not reclaim it) and look forward to a world yet to be made. For Habermas, it is equally a 'will to illusion' and 'simplification' made possible by restricting oneself to an aesthetic perspective.[88] It is this great objection that has stayed with Nietzsche since his death: one that keeps post-foundational *perspectivism* in educational studies on notice.

*

Is there more than the aesthetic sphere? What do we make of a political sphere that appears broken? What of a scientific one that has overflown into all others? How do we make sense of our faith in modernity when it appears to be running on fumes?

*

Modernity constitutes a 'last epoch in the far reaching history of a rationalization initiated by the dissolution of archaic life and the collapse of myth'.[89] Nietzsche's perspectivism invites us to shed the illusion of a singular approach to enquiry, of the pretence of a world that is independent of interpretations and of the danger of ever lurking morality. And it takes up Schopenhauer's invitation to look beyond Western thought, to embrace the abyss.

5

Reclaiming damaged life: Nietzsche's critique of scientism – the ideology of 'technical modernity' that threatens to 'straightjacket our perception of the world' – set the terms for a certain type of philosophical countermovement in the early twentieth century.[90] For our purpose, an important starting point is found in early critical theory which considered how we should read a world poisoned by uncaring capitalism, rampant nationalism and expansionism, personal alienation and, most catastrophically, industrial-scale human destruction. What prospect for the subject? For progressive politics? What of the Marxist prophecy that capitalism would collapse under the weight of its own internal contradictions. Wishful thinking? Enlightenment fantasy? More radically, does 'damaged life' emerge from Enlightenment itself? How do we respond when, as Theodor Adorno writes, 'Our perspective of life has passed into an ideology which conceals the fact that there is life no longer'?[91]

Adorno's polemic text *Minima Moralia* was started during a second catastrophic global war, this time with antisemitism at its core. He described a bleak outlook where life had been reduced to 'appearance' and 'consumption', 'dragged along as an appendage of the process of material production, without autonomy or substance of its own'.[92] Critical consciousness was now so endangered, and circumscribed by a form of technical rationality, that the subject, while 'still for-itself', is 'no longer in-itself'. How could it be otherwise after the 'nullity' of the concentration camp?[93] Such writing – in the hands of Adorno and, separately, with his long-term collaborator Max Horkheimer in their 'incendiary'[94] *Dialectic of Enlightenment* – mirrors as method the uncertainties, incoherence and despair of the times. Blending analysis, polemic and fragment and by juxtaposing wildly disparate cases and examples, such writing ignores the traditional reliance on philosophical depth and coherence, rejecting the 'impoverished and debased language' that passes for proper academic thinking.[95] With its radical critique of bourgeois capitalist culture, the call is for a very different philosophical project, one that might 'displace and estrange the world, reveal it to be, with its rifts and crevices, as indigent and distorted as it will appear one day in the messianic light'.[96]

Founded upon the conviction that the development of civilization had come at the cost of human suffering and the exploitation of nature, the *Dialectic of Enlightenment* is a grim account of the development and state of modern society. By connecting myth and metaphysics, fascism and capitalist consumption as well as art, music and aesthetics, they offer the radical assessment that the Enlightenment search for truth contains its own dark motor of domination, suppression and exploitation. Reason and power, forever entangled, provide no possibility for completely free thought or, therefore, full human freedom. What starts as myth – stories aimed at giving the world meaning and coherence – becomes a frame to condition thought, shaping reason so that it might conquer nature and, ultimately, man himself.

*

'*Myth is already enlightenment and enlightenment reverts to mythology*'.[97] Horkheimer and Adorno's most known phrase leaves us with the stark possibility that modern reason, contrary to a great heritage of thought from Kant to Hegel and onwards, is in actuality the *enemy* of man, condemning him to banality, alienation and disenchantment.

*

Figure 3.2 Ulysses and the Sirens.

Tied to the mast: Like Nietzsche, Horkheimer and Adorno turn to Greek mythology – notably Homer's *Odyssey* – to excavate the origins of the modern subjectivity, *homo oeconomicus*. Wary of the allure of the Sirens and determined to avoid the destiny of earlier sailors, Ulysses is tied to the mast and his crew deafened to the sweet tunes from the shore. In this way, he avoids the trap and a calling that draws him towards seductive beauty, false promise and the decadence of man.

> *Ulysses and the Sirens:* 'And if I beg you and order you to release me, then you are to tighten yet further ropes on me'.[98]

No one who hears the song of the Sirens can escape their call. Ulysses, the prototype modern subject, sacrifices himself with a defiance that is both rational and shrewd. By defying the natural call, man places himself above nature, disenchanting it and 'mortifying what is natural within him'.[99] This is bourgeois enlightenment. Prehistory, Ulysses teaches us, is that which has already been 'neutralized as the yearning of those who pass it by'.[100] The bondage to which Ulysses submits becomes a symbol of the dangers of reason in an era to come. Self-preservation requires mastery and in the process of exercising such mastery, human beings subject nature and its vagaries to human control, objectifying humanity, sacrificing themselves. Perhaps, to navigate a life worth living, one must choose between 'cheating and going under'.[101]

Horkheimer and Adorno argue that the reduction of rational thought into narrow forms of calculation have resulted in the standardization of social life and a form of intellectual enquiry that becomes an 'instrument of unreflective power'. Modernity's dialectical underside emerges as reason loses its 'critical edge'.[102] Empiricism and positivism overwhelm historical analyses of the interaction of the social and the subject. Rationality excludes from thought a critical analytical reflectiveness of how we are and have come to be part of our surroundings: our non-human otherness. While marginal to modern science, such thoughts are essential to the philosophy of classical antiquity, numerous world religions and to the broad program of the Enlightenment but are placed under severe pressure by a scientific mode of thinking which determines what counts as valid knowledge. For modernity, nothing can remain unknown, to lie unformed in the darkness, 'since the mere idea of the "outside" is the real source of fear'.[103]

*

And what of the Sirens themselves? Banished and defeated? Hardly. They live on, 'neutralized' as the 'wistful longing of the passer-by' who confronts fate, uncertainty and nature and defeats them all. To a point. The silencing of the Sirens heralds a transformation of language as man becomes defiant by using his cunning to remake things as he wants them.

*

Modern existence is complicated further by a 'culture industry' that breeds more sameness by obliterating difference, nuance and the capacity for self-conscious thought. 'Culture' was supposed to promote diversity and innovation but has morphed into its opposite, spreading mass deception as part of an apparatus of conformity. Amusement thus becomes the 'prolongation of work under late capitalism'.[104] In commodified society, where thinking is determined *a priori* and concepts that lack firm 'scientific' meaning (for example freedom, solidarity, equality and justice) are placed beyond the scope of rational scientific operations, our thinking becomes framed by the basest of values and interests. To counter these forces, Horkheimer and Adorno proposed a form of 'subdued, post-Hegelian' dialectics that aims to heal or reconcile the schisms of modern life:

hope could not be pinned on magical formulas or instant solutions. Only through critical reflection – one mindful of its tendential complicity with power – was reason able to break the spell of (ancient or modern) mythology and reification. Only in this manner was reason capable of regaining its liberating élan: an élan whereby enlightenment transcends domineering rationality by regaining access to a nature 'which becomes perceptible in its otherness or alienation'.[105]

The way to approach this goal is to offer 'healing mediations' devoid of the Absolute or 'any kind of comprehensive or totalizing synthesis'.[106] In his *Negative Dialectics,* Adorno takes issue with Hegel's demand that experience should be subject to concepts and examination. While Hegel acknowledges the 'fact' of experiential otherness, diverse phenomena are nonetheless subject to 'holistic synthesis governed by reason'. This impulse reduces actual phenomena to little more than 'exemplars of concepts' where 'the moment of negativity serves almost exclusively for the purposes of annexation and subsumption'.[107] Adorno confronted this hegemonic dialectic thinking with an 'attentiveness to non-thought or reason's turn toward the (conceptually) "non-identical"'.[108] The corrective to Hegel, and indeed to philosophy itself, is an insistence on non-totality, on nonidentity – to things, phenomena and experiences that fall outside of what can or should be conceptualized. Negative dialectics is thus open to 'voices otherwise excluded by modern reason'. It means that we seek out and respect the 'potential slumbering in things' and to atone for the violence of forcing them into our predetermined categorizations.[109]

*

Can aesthetics heal the wound of modernity? The early critical theorists wrote in the wake of Nietzsche's explosion of subject-focused philosophy. They built on the legacy of Hegelianism but rejected its mystic notion of Geist which smacked of an unjustified faith in progress. While Adorno maintained a dialectic between the subjective and objective, he did not seek to negate *all* negation. Freedom lies in the possibility of things remaining *non*-identical – of not hanging together. This is the chance to redeem *all* of modernity. This redemptive task had become urgent because history had unfolded radically differently from the projections inscribed in Hegel's System. Technology and mechanization led to heightened forms of capitalist control and domination. New processes of individualization, and alienation, alongside intense self-consciousness, gave the modern era a uniqueness and terrible potential. Systematic philosophy could not address this threat because it tended towards conclusions that were already built into its initial premises. For Adorno, 'True thoughts are those alone which do not understand themselves.'¹¹⁰ It is here that art becomes important because it eludes total capture by thought, thus enabling subjectivity to comprehend the essential incompleteness of the world and the impossible challenge set the subject in mastering life. Art, then, makes possible a 'continuity from reflection to reflection, of the multiple aspects and movements of subjective possibility. . . . It is precisely the artwork's unfinishedness that holds the greatest promise for the subject.'¹¹¹

*

Adorno penned the famous phase 'True thoughts are those alone which do not understand themselves' as part of his attempt to explore the possibility of art in a world brought down by what he elsewhere called the Culture Industry. It is unclear how he would respond to the current offer on Amazon.com to purchase his famous phrase as a 'high quality' fridge magnet for only $5.49 (free shipping included).¹¹²

*

In much of his writing Adorno was attracted to the plays of Samuel Beckett, especially his capacity to generate a 'positive nothingness' that makes one aware of what is at stake without allowing that to be comfortably resolved.¹¹³ Adorno's aesthetic theory builds on Beckett's 'refusal to interpret his own work'. This is 'the expression of the hermeneutic impropriety of any attempt to extract a philosophical meaning from an artwork'.¹¹⁴ If we avoid interpretation, we invite the absurd so what type of interpretative strategy does justice to the work of art? For Adorno, the paradox of aesthetics is that the truth of art can never be fully unveiled through philosophy but neither can it be uncovered without thought. 'Art needs a philosophy that needs art'.¹¹⁵ The solution here is to embrace the meaninglessness in art, 'making a meaning out of the refusal of meaning that the work performs without that refusal of meaning becoming a meaning'.¹¹⁶ Adorno refers to this as a 'positive nothingness'. In order to maintain a negativity in the system, this nothingness cannot be 'reclaimed as a positive meaning'.¹¹⁷ As Critchley explains: 'this does not mean that we stop speaking, but rather that we are unable to stop – *pour finir encore*.'¹¹⁸

*

Enough of darkness! The standard of critical theory is passed further and a new generation of intellectuals come to the fore. Most significantly, Adorno's student Jürgen Habermas views the *Dialectic of Enlightenment* as an exercise in sombre defeatism that extinguishes hope and the possibility for reason to shape humanity after the darkness of the Holocaust. What else can be expected when thought is framed through the motifs of Marquis de Sade and Nietzsche?

While he agrees with the critique of positivism and its immodest claims to objectivity and value-neutrality, Habermas cannot accept that modern science is necessarily reduced to questions of technical utility and he doubts that religious worldviews and normative standards have collapsed so totally as to erode a legitimate foundation on which to rebuild the world. The liberating potential of Enlightenment remains! For Habermas, the 'real problem is too little rather than too much enlightenment, a deficiency rather than an excess of reason'.[119] Modern science, morals, justice and, indeed, autonomous art provide entries to reason. They are not mutilated by the dialectics of purposive rationality but, instead, enabled by them. The analysis of art and mass-culture in the *Dialectics of Enlightenment* is devastatingly oversimplified, ignoring the rational in cultural modernity. Enough of wilful nihilism! To restore reason to a guiding role in the progress of humanity one must first *believe* that it is possible to tame the violent gene in modernity. One must have *faith* in reason. Critical of German idealism and transcendental philosophy with their subject-object orientation, Habermas turns instead towards pragmatism, considering human beings in terms of a number of fundamental interests. Perhaps of most importance here is the desire to communicate and to do so without distortion. Human beings wish to be understood and make sense of the world through dialogue. Unlike the instrumental endeavour of production through labour (another of his fundamental interests), communication requires judgment and good faith. Instead of the mystified ahistorical subject of idealism, Habermas envisages a horizon for shared understandings that emerge and unfold through dialogue. Language and lifeworld replace the earlier tropes of subjectivity and consciousness. Language is the exercise of reason, a practice through which we come to an understanding of each other and of the world around us. In an ideal speech act, subjects should not regard others as objects for the promotion of one's own interest but, rather, attempt to transcend individual interests. Herein lies the democratic potential of communication and the battle cry for a post-war generation of educationalists!

Habermas sees a desire for dialogue as already dwelling in our wish to be understood and to understand. One condition for *undistorted* communication is the existence of symmetry in communicative acts, requiring an egalitarian and respectful political sphere. Perhaps of most importance to us is the need for dialogue to support our ethical commitments. Non-distorted communication, and all it promises, requires much more than the will of individuals of good faith (Kant's reasoning subject). Progress comes through a cultivation of the social. Once again, Hegel can be heard whispering in the background, encouraging us to engage, negate and actualize. For Habermas, however, there is nothing mystical or pre-given on the hard road to emancipation. Still, a light beckons.

While critical of the 'uninhibited scepticism' of Horkheimer and Adorno, Habermas nevertheless acknowledges that ideology critique had become exhausted as the 'forces of production no longer developed any explosive force' and class conflicts lacked a 'unified consciousness', becoming 'fragmentary' rather than 'revolutionary'.[120] What seems less acceptable is the retreat into an 'attitude' of aesthetic modernity[121] most radically pioneered by Nietzsche. This is the 'force which neutralizes both the morally good and the practically useful, which expresses itself in the dialectic of secret and scandal and in the pleasure derived from the horror of profanation'. By trusting only in art, 'the *lie* is sanctified'. In the 'terror of the beautiful', we avoid being 'imprisoned by the fictive world of science and morality'.[122] Ultimately, and especially in his *Aesthetic Theory*, Adorno 'seals the surrender of cognitive competency to art', viewing avant-garde art as the 'single witness *against* a praxis that in the course of time has buried everything once meant by reason (Vernunft) under its debris'.[123] The realization of the great aims of enlightenment – including a banishing of this darkness – cannot come through the personal, subjective and emotive forces of art alone but, instead, through an understanding of reason as a 'noncoercive intersubjectivity of mutual understanding and reciprocal recognition'.[124] Enlightenment is a practical political project.

The scorn for the early critical theorists is intensified in Habermas' response to Foucault and, by association, the wave of post-war French philosophy that proved so enticing to new readers. He is especially sceptical of Foucault's understanding of power and its intricacies, as well as his use of the genealogical method which denies, avoids or simply misreads the 'essentially ambiguous phenomena of modern culture'.[125] Like many since Hegel, Habermas shares Foucault's rejection of subject-focused philosophy and the 'paradigm of consciousness'.[126] What he struggles with is Foucault's analytical strategy, noting a 'performative contradiction' arising from 'using the tools of reason to criticize reason'. This positions his genealogical approach 'embarrassingly' close to the '"sciences of man" he so tellingly criticized' where 'The ideas of meaning, validity, and value that were to be eliminated by genealogical critique come back to haunt it in the spectral forms of "presentism", "relativism", and "cryptonormativism".[127] How is Foucault's new historian to write when consigned to the 'horizon of reason'?[128] Truth is buried in practices, 'incapable of recognizing the *will to truth* that pervades it'.[129] There are no origins, only 'contingent *beginnings* of discourse formations'. History, then, 'makes use not of *Verstehen* but of the destruction and dismantling of that context of effective history which putatively links the historian with his object and with which he enters into communication only to find himself in it'.[130] For Habermas, this unthinkable abdication leads the archaeologist to turn 'talkative documents into mute *monuments,* objects that have to be freed from their own context in order to become accessible to a structuralist description'.[131] Such critique positions the analyst of discourse as a destroyer of historiography and an enemy (or ambivalent house guest) of enlightenment, one who is able to 'fill the space of history, without gaps and without meaning':[132]

> Under the *stoic* gaze of the archaeologist, history hardens into an iceberg covered with the crystalline forms of arbitrary formations of discourse. But since the autonomy proper to a totality without origin accrues to every single one of these formations, the only job left for the historian is that of the genealogist who explains the accidental provenance of these bizarre shapes from the hollow forms of bordering formations, that is, from the proximate circumstances. Under the *cynical* gaze of the genealogist, the iceberg begins to move: Discourse formations are displaced and re-grouped, they undulate back and forth. The genealogist explains this to-and-fro movement with the help of countless events and a single hypothesis – the only thing that lasts is power, which appears with ever new masks in the change of anonymous processes of overpowering.

From the perspective of a 'critical' approach to philosophy, this is an invitation to further darkness and the eventual erasure of humanity.

6

Into the desert of the real: While the great modern philosophers debated subjectivity, consciousness, redemption and emancipation, the world moved on. Could aesthetics restore meaning and humanity to man? Could it do so only by integrating it within a progressive political vision? Was it more productive to chart shifting discursive formations and, where possible, identify cracks in the artifices of power from where new, limited, acts of resistance could emerge? What intellectual tools remain with which to pick up the pieces of an epoch in ruins? What was the lesson from the failed protests of May 1968? Did surplus value still lie in the bosom of labour or was that exhausted? What of class struggle once the worker loses his attachment (and chains) to the factory and *becomes* consumer society with its borderless origins, promiscuous friendships and mirage(s) of utopia? What of power, resistance and the 'real'? What if indifference and unease slipped silently into the picture, replacing the great organizing (and mobilizing) motifs of oppression, alienation and social justice?

> Images detached from every aspect of life merge into a common stream, and the former unity of life is lost forever. Apprehended in a *partial* way, reality unfolds in a new generality as a pseudo-world apart, solely as an object of contemplation. The tendency toward the specialization of images-of-the-world finds its highest expression in the world of the autonomous image, where deceit deceives itself. The spectacle in its generality is a concrete inversion of life, and, as such, the autonomous movement of non-life.[133]

In the months before Adorno's death, Guy Debord published his polemic account of society as 'spectacle'. Written as the 1968 revolt was fermenting, it presents a further 'critical' analysis of capitalism and its tendency to stifle collective life. 'Modernization', 'unification' and 'simplification' lead to an 'ideology' of democracy that is little more than 'the dictatorial freedom of the Market, as tempered by the recognition of the rights of Homo Spectator'.[134] With a direct lineage to Marx and thus Hegel, Debord views religious faith as undermined by modernity and re-energized through consumerism, a life form that deceives human beings into mistaking the sign for the real. This analysis proclaims late modernity to be the grotesque extension of history, one where capital is accumulated to such an extent that it transforms into pure image. In a world of images, the firm boundaries between real and mirage, true and false, right and wrong dissolve. In a house of mirrors, it is hardly worthy to even debate the possibility of identifying Kant's 'thing-in-itself'.

Like other 'situationalist' readings of consumer-modernity, Debord sees the internal contradictions of the spectacle as inviting revolt. By holding on to the 'materiality of the real'[135] he maintains the hope that we might unearth referents to navigate by, to claw a way back to authentic life. Too little, too late?

Much has happened in the half-century since the publication of *The Society of the Spectacle*. And much *hasn't* happened. Certainly, any fundamental revolt is still to come. Perhaps a threshold has been crossed into an order where meaning has become *relational* rather than *referential*.[136] The rise (or, finally, identification) of fake truth, virtual reality, digital identity, clones and codes suggest we take the courageous step into another mode of analysis, another way of seeing what's left of a world that earlier thinkers viewed as manageable by reason and/or faith but which now seems to allude 'analysis'. From metaphysical depths to slippery surfaces.

*

Post-truth, *adjective*

Relating to or denoting circumstances in which objective facts are less influential in shaping public opinion than appeals to emotion and personal belief.[137]

*

The *desert of the real*:[138] Baudrillard, possibly the most radical thinker of late modernity, emerged from structural Marxism and situationalist politics himself but took this perspective to the *other* obvious conclusion: that history and dialectical reasoning were now outdated and that class analysis and political mobilization were in vain. Analyses of economic exchange, the commodification of everyday existence and the role of media culture in distorting the 'real' change everything. Explored by others – notably by Marshall McLuhan who examined the changing role of print and visual media and Frederick Jameson who attempted to outline the 'cultural logic' of late capitalism, Baudrillard went much further. Now, workers *were* consumers. Abjection had been a great fear in industrial capitalism. To stand visibly excluded from the system was a form of death: physical, moral, spiritual. Now, as consumers, man would be 'courted by the system which extracted surplus value from (the) consumption'. While 'vague malaise, emptiness, individual isolation' would remain, these would be experienced as 'internal exclusions'.[139]

What has been variously described through history as the populace, the people, the citizenry and most recently the multitude, is reduced under conditions of consumer modernity to a mass that lies beyond representation or mobilization.[140] Language and signs – the blind spots in Marxist-inspired materialist analyses and something that even Habermas had underestimated – had turned the people into an unmanageable and unresponsive mass. Not nihilistic, for that would be a presumption as well as suggestive that a position or stance, once *held*, could be re-established and directed with intent into the political sphere. More drastically, it seemed that the system was now in the grip of indifference, the worst of all malaises. Here, 'everyone was simultaneously made personalized and anonymous, free and controlled. Consumer and consumed'. The new order was one of indeterminacy.[141]

> Interviewer: Are you wholly intent on demoralizing the West?
>
> Baudrillard: The demoralization of the West is constitutive of its history. I didn't invent it. 'The new sentimental order', the order of disaffection, repentance and the 'victim society', is the extension of a crisis of meaning which began in the nineteenth century with the fallout from the Industrial Revolution and colonialization, and has continued throughout our long twentieth century.[142]

How had this state of things come to pass? Baudrillard, in his way with an obvious debt to Foucault's *The Order of Things*, suggested that we had moved through certain stages of reality from the real to hyperreality and, finally, an impending 'fractal stage' characterized by the impossibility of meaningful exchange. This final destination, a utopia of sorts, was most evident for Baudrillard in his reflections on the banality of life in contemporary America. The original desert of the real.

If you hunger for the authentic Venetian experience you might want to try Las Vegas, Nevada, not the Veneto region of Italy.[143]

There's a scaled-down replica of the ancient city inside the glitzy Venetian resort casino, complete with canals, gondolas and even a pocket version of the Piazza San Marco. It's fake, of course – but then so is the real Venice.

Professor Potter says the increasingly consumerist, individualistic and technology-dominated nature of daily existence is pushing people to seek surety in nostalgia. 'We look for the authentic in things that are antitechnological, anti-individualistic, more communitarian and anti-consumerist', he says. Hence the rise of the 'hipster' trend, craft-brewing and the resurgence of vinyl, Professor Potter says.

'It's almost like a lot of us are playing at being old-fashioned or old-timey', he says. 'It reaches back to the set of social and economic and cultural circumstances that we tend to dimly think were if not better, at least a more innocent time. We react against the cynicism and the manufactured aspect of our existence and we move back to the authentic.' But that can be counterproductive, not just problematic, he warns, as attempting to create authenticity only results in increased artifice.

In an increasingly digital world, are we losing our grip on reality? – ABC News (Australian Broadcasting Corporation), By Antony Funnell.

---

*

For many of those working on the edges of modern social theory, this analysis came to frame how we might imagine the future where the 'ultimate terminus' of the 'commodity production system is the triumph of signifying culture and the death of the social'. This is a 'post-society configuration that escapes sociological classification and explanation, an endless cycle of the reduplication and overproduction of signs, images and simulations that leads to an implosion of meaning'.[144] Baudrillard explained this as 'crossing into a space':

> inaugurated by a liquidation of all referentials – worse: with their artificial resurrection in the systems of signs, a material more malleable than meaning, in that it lends itself to all systems of equivalences, to all binary oppositions, to all combinatory algebra. It is no longer a question of imitation, nor duplication, nor even parody. It is a question of substituting the signs of the real for the real, that is to say of an operation of deterring every real process via its operational double, a programmatic, metastable, perfectly descriptive machine that offers all the signs of the real and short-circuits all its vicissitudes. Never again will the real have a chance to produce itself – such is the vital function of the model in a system of death, or rather of anticipated resurrection, that no longer even gives the event of death a chance. A hyperreal henceforth sheltered from the imaginary, and from any distinction between the real and the imaginary, leaving room only for the orbital recurrence of models and for the simulated generation of differences.[145]

The last great dinosaur: Such pronouncements were met as 'weak thought' by those who were invested with the hope that use value could find ways to counter indeterminacy.[146] Devoid of a better idea, most hitched their wagons to capitalism itself, 'eager to extract its subversive energy'. For Baudrillard, such attempts came too little too late. How could we introduce a truncated revolutionary form of human presence and consciousness into a system that had jumped tracks and become 'irreversible' and 'inhuman'?[147] Marxism was thus no answer. Indeed, it was a large part of the problem: simply a 'mirror of bourgeois society, placing production at the centre of life, thus naturalizing the capitalist organization of society'.[148]

This perspective is presented most forcefully in Baudrillard's startling attack on Michel Foucault in a pamphlet provocatively titled 'Forget Foucault'. Submitted to the journal *Critique* (where Foucault himself was a board member) the essay was both an acknowledgement of a debt to a heavyweight of the French intelligentsia and a rhetorical challenge that he move beyond a mode of analysis that was boxed in by its own timid limits.[149] Baudrillard challenged Foucault's fascination with power which, like the Marxists he was distancing himself from, remained focused on the order of *production*, and its effects. Because power (whether despotic or disciplinary) still belonged to the objective order of the real, Baudrillard saw Foucault's entire project as 'still turned towards a reality principle and a very strong truth principle', an orientation that suggested a continued belief in 'a possible coherence of politics and discourse'. With remarkable parallels to Habermas' critique of Foucauldian method, Baudrillard identifies a similar flaw in this 'perfect' writing,

> in that the very movement of the text gives and admirable account of what it proposes: on one hand, a powerful generating spiral that is no longer a despotic architecture but a filiation *en abyme,* coil and strophe without origin (without catastrophe, either), unfolding ever more widely and rigorously; but on the other hand an interstitial flowing of power that seeps through the whole porous network of the social, the mental, and of bodies, infinitesimally modulating the technologies of power (where the relations of power and seduction and inextricably entangled). All this reads *directly* in Foucault's work which is also a discourse of power. It flows, it invests and saturates the entire space it opens. The smallest qualifiers find their way into the slightest interstices of meaning; the clauses and chapters wind into spirals; a magistral art of decentring allows the opening of new spaces (spaces of power and discourse) which are immediately covered up by the meticulous outpouring of Foucault's writing. There's no vacuum here, no phantasm, no backfiring, but a fluid objectivity, a nonlinear orbital, and flowless writing. The meaning never exceeds what one says of it; do dizziness, yet it never floats in a text too big for it: no rhetoric either.[150]

For Baudrillard, Foucault's fixation with power traps him in a 'transparency principle', 'force(ing) what belongs to another order (that of secrecy and seduction) to materialize'.[151] This impulse to 'let everything be produced, be read, become real, visible, and marked with the sign of effectiveness . . . transcribed into force relations, into conceptual systems or into calculable energy' was part of what Baudrillard saw as the 'natural condition' of Western culture but a fundamentally misguided way to read our contemporary situation.[152] Foucault followed the trail of power as it 'pulverized into micro-devices', never daring to cross the 'threshold of a current revolution' to consider if it might have disappeared altogether.[153] By detaching power from its original symbolic form and converting it with semiotics to the order of production, power becomes not only visible but 'visibility steered toward its most extreme form'[154] which, for Baudrillard is the 'hyperreal', a place where things (objects) are presented as their visible selves but where their essential secrets – and essence – are obscured in the obscene overproduction of image, description and fact. Obscenity, then, is the 'all-too-visible, the more visible than visible',[155] our culture of 'monstration' which is 'ruled by the transparency principle governing all forces in the order of visible and calculable phenomena: objects, machines, sexual acts, or gross national product'.[156] This is Foucault's mistake, and ours, whenever we attempt to override the symbolic order by semiotic production aimed at clarity, completeness, science. It is the death of the 'illusion of the world' replaced by the 'truth'.[157]

Foucault's 'monstration' of power was also applied to its 'twin', desire. Here, Deleuze came into the firing line. Just as power is rethought by Foucault as something 'positive, active, and immanent' rather than as a repressive or judicial tool, so is desire transformed as the 'positive dissemination of flows and intensities'. Like power, desire is 'purged of all negativity, a network, a rhizome, a contiguity diffracted ad infinitum'.[158] Baudrillard was 'struck' by the similarities here:

> Foucault is part of this molecular intertwining which sketches out all of the future's visible hysteria: he has helped establish a systematic notion of power along the same operational lines as desire, just as Deleuze established a notion of desire along the lines of future forms of power. This collusion is too beautiful not to arouse suspicion, but it has in its behalf the quaint innocence of a betrothal. When power blends into desire and desire blends into power, let's forget them both.[159]

Whether a political or libidinal economy, these are 'production channels' that 'render visible' processes of seduction, but always reducing them to their (trivial and obscene) material forms that, for Baudrillard, are the forms of analysis typical of a 'collapsing' 'classical age' of which Foucault is the 'last great dinosaur'.[160] By focusing on forces of consumption rather than production, Baudrillard brings *objects* to the fore. The object is never silent or compliant but, rather, 'fired with passion', with 'autonomy' and endowed with 'a capacity to avenge itself on a subject who is over-sure of controlling it'. In Baudrillard's enigmatic terms: 'it's no longer the subject which desires, it's the object which seduces'.[161] Herman Hesse captured this zeitgeist in its infancy:

> Above all I learned that these little playthings, fashionable accessories and luxuries are not just tawdry kitsch, invented by money-grabbing manufacturers and dealers, but quite legitimate, beautiful and diverse objects. They constitute a small, or rather large, world of things, all of them designed with the sole aim of serving Eros, refining the senses, breathing fresh life into the dead world we inhabit and magically endowing it with new sexual organs, from powder and perfume to dance shoes, from rings to cigarette cases, from belt buckles to

handbags. These handbags were not handbags, the purses not purses, flowers not flowers, fans not fans – no, all of them were visual and tangible material of Eros, of magic, of stimulation. They functioned as messengers, touts, weapons, battle cries.[162]

*

Objects seduce: Ultimately, Baudrillard wasn't *critiquing* Foucault but following his thought to its logical terminal point; daring him to go to what he called 'the mysterious point where he . . . stops and finds nothing more to say'.[163] What comes next? Do things magically cease to transform once they assume microscopic or dispersed form? Baudrillard's move was to switch our attention to the object. This is not the object we understand from Marxist thought. Devoid of referents and beyond fetish, this object has no origins. All meanings attached to Baudrillard's object are contingent, shifting, fleeting. For Marxism, the object is caught in a metaphysics of production that *creates* rather than *satisfies* needs. Even the dialectic of subjective/objective is cast aside in Baudrillard's effort to find a new foundation for thought. While Adorno uses subjective irony to re-establish and reinforce the relation between the two, the society of simulation implies a world in which objects have broken free of fixed reference and are thus meaningless. Also implied here is the disappearance of the analyst and his replacement by the writer.

*

The end? Echoing our earlier reflections on metaphysics since Kant, Baudrillard distinguishes between the *illusion* and *simulation* of the world. Here, illusion is the way that the world presents itself to us, always protecting its hidden essence or true state. Simulation, by contrast, refers to our attempts through media, mapping and the research efforts of knowledge industries to manufacture truth, fact and certainty. To establish origins in order to master them. It is our saving grace that the order of seduction is an original state of being and *beyond* the logic of production. The world remains, as always, hidden behind appearances. Like the molecular nothingness at the core of the physical.

The more that we attempt to identify the origins or essence of objects (i.e. their 'real' form), whether that be through the uncontrolled proliferation of meaning systems (PISA?) or the deliberate application of reason through analysis and investigation (education research), simulation intensifies, taking us further from the real and into the hyperreal. As soon as we reach out for the object (which we can only do through language) it obscures itself in 'reality' only to become more enigmatic. Here, the illusion of the world is 'guaranteed by the fact that the real always hides behind appearances and that we "know" it through discourse'.[164] This is the inconvenient truth of science, one the congregation seem determined to ignore. In seeking more 'reality' we aim to cheat death. If we accept the claim that the system of equivalence is now in a spiral of decay – where more knowledge gives less meaning, more fact less certainty, deeper commitments to education greater cynicism and where hyperreality renders the real obsolete, forever buried behind the superficial, deceptive and deceitful simulation – we are invited to consider the parallels to human life which is also governed by the inevitability of death and disappearance. How should we respond? Unlike Ulysses, we might take our medicine, accept our fate, succumb to the pull of the shore. Rather than resist death and deny the absolute rule of life, we might, through our own symbolic death, open a pathway for renewal. Paradoxically, by accelerating the death drive of the system – by adding further acts of indeterminacy, we return the gift (of clarity, precision, 'reality') with its symbolic opposite. By *writing* the world, we overload a system seeking meaning and create an opening for thought and a 'reserve of possibility'. This is the journey into night 'in which one cannot find a position, where the body refuses to lie still'. The 'spectral night of dreams, of phantoms, of ghosts'. If any desire remains in the system, it could be 'nocturnal': 'an impossible and insatiable desire for that which is by definition denied to the movement of comprehension'.[165] Baudrillard states the aim of writing the world back to existence in equally dramatic terms:

> The absolute rule is to give back more than you were given. Never less, always more. The absolute rule of thought is to give back the world as it was given to us – unintelligible. And, if possible, to render it a little more unintelligible.[166]

*

'It is because the world is not finished that literature is possible':[167] Kantian moral autonomy in an age of veiled truth? Hegelian Absolute and Geist in the society of proliferating signs? The naïveté of Romanticism with its 'complete transformation or aesthetic revolution of life and culture'.[168] And communicative practice? Where to start if we accept that one's choice of language determines one's notion of the 'real'?[169] Dialectical thought and seduction by dualism? That peculiar Western impulse to split, order and resolve? This legacy of thought has brought us valid and reliable social science, ethical commitments and social justice. It has also sired 'effective' schools, 'professional' teachers, large-scale

assessments, 'big-data'-driven policy and the chauvinism of euro-centrism which is morphing in our time into a new Anglo-American manifest destiny.

None of this is to suggest that the rich tradition of thought outlined here should be abandoned outright for there are forgotten traces that we would do well to remember. Kant's unknown and the spontaneous, Hegel's philosophy beyond the subject, romantic poetic realization, Nietzschean perspectivism, Adorno's non-identical and the possibility of art, Baudrillard's impossible exchange and the inevitable reversals that follow. Such strands provide direction for a different type of educational project. Thought fit for our time.

How can we fight the pull of reason and purpose, to remain open to unknowing and meaningful non-meaning? What if we accept the impossibility of singular truth and the new 'reality' that signifier and signified are now 'joined by uncertainty'?[170] How can we work in the margins of modern thought and find something *else* to say? Perhaps all that is left to us is the possibility of a 'poetic resolution'[171] of the world, turning theory, and for that matter, data, into fiction.

4

Writing as Method

1

The 'success' of the book is actually its 'failure'.[1] The Book has a long history and in the Western tradition keeps a sacred fire burning. It connects us to origins and the original event and secures the self in the great chain of being. It keeps us moving forward, hopeful. It is promise. The Book keeps the idea – and the *ideal* – of humankind alive. The fate facing those in search of a (pre)scribed end will be the Book already written. Such books provide outlets for concern, fear, indignation, absolution and redemption.[2] Such writing stays true to its purpose. Seduced by the Siren's songs of reason, moral purpose, justice, equity, validity, generalizability, value and relevance, it sails on, towards the rocks, never offering more than is promised, but with its deficit intact: 'reality' falling short of the unreachable ideal. By elaborating a problem, examining facts and exposing deficiencies, the book already written invites for more research.

Did Ulysses *really* outwit the sirens? Did he succeed in enjoying their music but avoiding their deadly gift? Even though the story says that he avoided a catastrophic ending – for the writer, meaning submission to the pull of dominant values and morals – like all journeys, his continues in the shadow of seduction. The sirens, far from vanquished, remain entombed within the pages of *The Odyssey* and thus within the Western literary tradition,[3] always calling us towards the familiar, the comforting and the pleasurable. The predictable narrative and reason-able conclusion. A space where heroes are elevated, monsters vanquished and loose ends tied off like ropes on a ship.

*

The thread: How have we learnt to master the uncertainty that accompanies a journey into the unknown? The Ancients offer us yet another story to guide us further. Poseidon gifted King Minos of Crete a white bull but the King could not bear to sacrifice the animal as commanded. In punishment, Poseidon mated the animal with the King's wife Pasiphae and the Minotaur was born. To restrain the beast, Daedalus built a labyrinth of such complexity that all who entered its depths would be lost. Still, the Minotaur threatened. So much that the King demanded the City of Athens to supply young flesh to satisfy its hunger. Finding this intolerable, Theseus, son of the King of Athens, vowed to destroy the monster. Disguised as one of the doomed Athenians, he entered the chamber intent on slaying the abomination. His journey into that darkness was possible by the gift of a length of thread from the King's daughter Ariadne. That string tied him to the world outside and thwarted the threat of intractability and horror of the unknowable. Our storyline. The essential ingredient to narrative; one that makes possible meaning, coherence and closure. Something we put in place before a difficult journey. Something that guarantees our return and protects us from deaths of all sorts. Whether tied to the mast or tethered to string, our instinct when writing is to conquer uncertainty, turning it towards its opposite. Voluntarily holding ourselves back, walking the line, sticking to the straight and narrow, we enter our task with the presumption of control, ready to commit the violence of omission in the service of a noble end. It is the hallmark of the scientist to know where to head, controlling for difference and uncertainty as the journey unfolds.

*

In the beginning God created the heavens and the earth: Nietzsche asked in despair: 'How could we drink up the sea?':

> Who gave us the sponge to wipe away the entire horizon? What were we doing when we unchained this earth from its sun? Whither is it moving now? Whither are we moving? Away from all suns? Are we not plunging continually? Backward, sideward, forward, in all directions? Is there still any up or down? Are we not straying, as through an infinite nothing? Do we not feel the breath of empty space? Has it not become colder? Is not night continually closing in on us? Do we not need to light lanterns in the morning? Do we hear nothing as yet of the noise of the gravediggers who are burying God? Do we smell nothing as yet of the divine decomposition? Gods, too, decompose. God is dead. God remains dead. And we have killed him.[4]

In the Western tradition, 'God, self, history and book' are 'bound in an intricate relationship in which each mirrors the other'. This is a relation in which '(n)o single concept can be changed without altering all of the others'. What happens, though, when God dies but we maintain the old chain? Nietzsche's lunatic

Figure 4.1 Minotaur slain by Theseus, the friend of Hercules.

feared that the death of the Creator had left humankind with a dangerous void, one greedily filled by the Self. History, that 'temporal course of events' from a 'definite beginning (creation) through an identifiable middle (incarnation) to an expected end (kingdom or redemption)' continues but in *our* service, not His. In this sense, and having lost a chance to be something different, the Book remains a manifestation of divine truth, now mediated by mortals. History remains authoritative and the Book continues on as its holy fruit. 'Page by page and chapter by chapter, the Book weaves the unified story of the interaction between God and self' where 'the logic of this narrative reflects the Logos of history' and where, consequently, the text 'rewrites the Word of God'.[5] Not surprisingly, we continue to approach the Book and its narrative structure with reverence, looking upon any other form of literary expression as profane, distorted, impure and unworthy.

The death of God will continue to amount to little until its 'reverberations'[6] are felt in our understanding of self, history and book. Much of what counts as education 'science' resists this death or, at best, transfers the powers of God to the modern humanist who, in turn, redoubles the effort to craft meaningful stories of origin from fractured events. Valid, reliable, generalizable. The word of God through the hand of Man. Such writing achieves this conceit through constructions of the authoritative text that maintains an allegiance to a notion of History *as* purpose as well as to a belief in Self *as* God. On the contrary, acknowledging the death of God, we might embrace the disappearance of the Self, the end of History and, ultimately, the closure of the Book. What remains or becomes possible? Writing after Self, after History and after the Book becomes an invitation to resist the 'nihilism of humanistic atheism' that, having renounced God 'never reaches the extreme point of questioning the function of truth and the value of value'. Instead, we might wear the cross, viewing the 'crucifixion of selfhood' as our 'mark of strength'.[7] This is the invitation to write without authority, without predetermined purpose on unchartered terrain. It also means resisting the temptation to say everything rather than a little.

*

To wander in dark passageways without purpose is not nihilism but the opposite. Affirmation of the immediacy, finiteness and unknowability of existence. To what end should we use these wanderings?

*

Truth after Hegel: Such musings will inflame most scholars of education who unwittingly toil within the confines of Hegel's System. Here, life is one of opposites, where tensions and differences must be resolved in order for life to be purposeful. Hegel sought to accommodate such opposites within an overall whole where, ultimately, identity becomes the 'mastery of difference';[8] a death struggle where Self and Other settle their scores. A radical reading views this philosophy of everything as both idealist *and* structuralist,[9] placing self, society, rationality, pious Christianity, human history and development on an encompassing canvas from where the Absolute will eventually present itself in readiness for its ultimate realization. For Hegel, difference and otherness are to be understood as residing *within* the whole. For many of his followers, this makes possible their defeat by reason. The achievement of absolute knowledge through complete self-awareness (of the known *and* metaphysical) realizes the fantasy of Western philosophy to capture 'total presence that is neither disturbed by irreducible difference or interrupted by the return of an absolute other'.[10] What remains, then, is a scholarship that moves forward, confident in its capacity to handle, store and manage that which cannot be known or controlled; neatly stowed beneath decks in ships headed for rocky coasts.

As we have seen earlier, at the limits of modern thought, all is resolved via absolute knowledge and rests on a metaphysical contract that lives on in our educational present. However, by asking about the Being of Being (rather than Being and beings), Heidegger challenges the notion that subjectivity emerges from the negation of otherness. Difference is no longer in tension to Being, something to be resolved on the path to greater consciousness but, rather, a fundamental part of it: something that is always revealing *and* concealing itself. Events of 'unconcealment' and 'clearing' may present themselves but are 'always coupled with untruth, openness with seclusion, clarity with mystery. Being withdraws as it comes to presence; it expropriates as it appropriates; it holds back as it gives'.[11] Otherness is not other to Being, and thus something to be eliminated, it is fundamental to its constitution. Consciousness can never be absolute when placed in the hands of reason.

Once we challenge the fiction of the liberated self (and free human consciousness) as having the divine authority that was previously the preserve of God, we give up our search for truth, purpose, unity and resolution. Open to the world, writing embraces difference and the page becomes one of assertion, doubt, blank space and an opening to silence that gives birth to renewed thought. Writing, once self-conscious of its profound limitations, also engenders mirth! Writing after truth means submitting to the currents of logic *and* passion, myth *and* marvel, purpose and nonsense. To write is to be inadequate to the task of dissolving ambiguity. Perhaps all that is left is to 'laugh(ing) at people on the shore from a disabled ship'.¹²

*

In Umberto Eco's great novel of medieval mystery and metaphysics, the senior brothers of a famous monastery fear the uncovering of Aristotle's alleged second book on poetry with its celebration of a laughter that might undermine the word of God. During the search for the source of a series of murders, it becomes clear to the protagonist, William of Baskerville, that there is no one truth. Assumptions, perspectives and, indeed, the application of logic itself, radically alter our perceptions of reality. He surmises:

> Perhaps the mission of those who love mankind is to make people laugh at the truth, to make truth laugh, because the only truth lies in learning to free ourselves from insane passion for the truth. . . . Where is all my wisdom, then? I behaved stubbornly, pursuing a semblance of order, when I should have known well that there is no order in the universe.¹³

*

Figure 4.2 Excerpt from Portrait of Georg Wilhelm Friedrich Hegel (1770–1831).

As his monumental project was coming to completion, Hegel feared that he was losing his mind. Bataille mused that the 'certainty of having attained absolute knowledge' with the 'completion of history' would lead Hegel to a 'state of empty monotony'. Is it possible that Hegel's 'bouts of sadness' were a sign of the 'profound horror' that arose when he, himself, had become God?[14]

*

The thread undone: Georges Bataille survived Kojève's lectures on Hegel. He had developed much of his thinking before this encounter and was now thoroughly opposed to a life aimed at 'the essentially vain attempt at equilibrium and harmony'.[15] Knowledge intent on discovering all has undoubted *utility* but the destruction of all particularities results in a sacrifice of *meaning*. Rather than a puzzle to be solved, the labyrinth is a powerful metaphor for our condition, what he termed the 'principle of insufficiency':

> In isolation, each man sees the majority of others as incapable or unworthy of 'being'. There is found, in all free and slanderous conversation, as an animating theme, the awareness of the vanity and the emptiness of our fellowmen; an apparently stagnant conversation betrays the blind and impotent flight of all life toward an indefinable summit.[16]

Man, in his insufficiency, lives with incompleteness and doubt. The labyrinth is no maze to be solved but, rather, a space of indeterminacy and disorientation to be embraced. In life, we encounter our own labyrinth and the 'hours when Ariadne's thread is broken'. And when we are 'hungry, cold and thirsty', the 'resort to will would make no sense'.[17] In this space of disorientation we confront hopelessness:

> Trembling. To remain immobile, standing, in a solitary darkness, in an attitude without the gesture of a supplicant: supplication, but without gesture and above all without hope. Lost and pleading, blind, half dead. Like Job on the dung heap, in the darkness of night, but imagining nothing – defenceless, knowing that all is lost.[18]

In the supreme logic of Hegelianism, such loss is recovered and the light restored but at the cost of negating the ecstasy and rapture and an experience 'laid bare, free of ties, even of an origin, of any confession whatever'.[19] For Bataille, however, life is governed by a general economy in which organisms must expend the surplus energy or wealth not needed for essential maintenance. If this energy cannot be absorbed it must 'necessarily be lost without profit; it must be spent, willingly or not, gloriously or catastrophically'.[20] By contrast, restricted economies deny such surplus or excess, incorporating or marginalizing it to 'achieve some semblance of the orderly explanation of phenomena'.[21] Restricted economies get their energy by 'drawing, selectively and discretely upon their "outside" . . . and by simultaneously denying that they border an irreducible "outside"'. Science is part of the restricted economy because it gains legitimacy from its usefulness. Its 'accursed share' is 'that which cannot be reduced to the utilitarian project of scientific thought' and consists in 'paradox, anomaly, and in the failure to erect meaningful rather than simply useful foundations for knowledge'. The accursed share also includes the 'inner experience of the thinker, moments of wonder, inspiration, mystery, despair and ecstasy'. Such experience also includes the opulent, obscene, erotic and perverse. Unsurprisingly, such things are denied or suppressed in most academic projects as trivial and disrupting but they will always be the 'non-foundations of the scientific enterprise'.[22] The reason and calculation that allegedly drives our thought owe much to those dark hours when the thread of meaning falls slack.

It is central to Bataille's approach to consider the boundaries between the general and restricted economies; between our deeper inner experiences and those that are suitable for polite society; between use value and meaningfulness; between confinement and excretion. While Hegelian logic denies or claims to dissolve these boundaries, Bataille views them as impossible and unwise to suppress. To live, we must make a friend of the dark.

2

Avoiding rocks or, tips for good living: How might we avoid the restricted economy of scientific research? The 'crisis' in late-twentieth-century anthropology provides an invitation to a broader approach to scholarship, one where the restricted and general economies begin to intersect. Just as Northern knowledge needs to create an abyssal line to legitimate itself as natural and essential, so too must 'science' which is defined in opposition to its literary, poetic and frivolous 'other'.[23] Here, we find science as the provider of signification and objectivity while literature wallows in rhetoric, fiction and partiality. Science establishes fact, pointing the way to 'reality'. Literature 'plays on the stratification of meaning; it narrates one thing in order to tell something else; it delineates itself in a language from which it continuously draws effects of meaning that cannot be circumscribed or checked'.[24] Literature cheats and lies to gain our favours.

Dominated by participant observation and meticulous on the spot notetaking, anthropology has been seriously disabled by a realist 'ideology claiming transparency of representation and immediacy of experience'. In this tradition, the textual is reduced to a final triumphant phase of 'writing-up'.[25] Interventions from cultural studies, post-structuralism and deconstruction made such pretence untenable. Culture is of course 'composed of seriously contested codes and representations' where the 'poetic and the political are inseparable'.[26] The writer has much more than a ringside seat to the action.

By acknowledging that cultural and historical accounts are partial, we must question the intent of interpretative science. We can accept the critique that anthropology (and thus ethnography) emerged from a poisonous cocktail of imperialism, evolutionary science and, if one is being generous, benign nineteenth-century curiosity, but we should not stop at this tale of origins. Ethnography remains embroiled in distorted relations of power that it attempts to counter by rigor and purpose. While the best of such work will avoid deliberate acts of omission, obstruction or mystification, all qualitative enquiry is mired in the loose soil of perspectivism:

> In this view, more Nietzschean than realist or hermeneutic, all constructed truths are made possible by powerful 'lies' of exclusion and rhetoric. Even the best ethnographic texts – serious, true fictions – are systems, or economies, of truth. Power and history work through them, in ways their authors cannot fully control.[27]

This is by no means a call to abandon enquiry aimed at giving voice to the condition of the World or the ways that this is experienced, not least by those on/in the margins. To go beyond the 'banal claim that all truths are constructed',[28] research – in a literary form – can serve to uncover as well as conceal, derail or obscure meaning; all with a higher aim in mind. Once again, this is not wilful destruction but a commitment to maintaining the wonder and power of things so that, to return to Bataille's language, the *useful* may become *meaningful*. Clifford and Marcus remind us of Richard Price's ethnography of the Maroon peoples of Suriname, *First-Time*,[29] especially its 'complex technique of revelation and secrecy' that is as much about the process of imparting knowledge in traditional society as it is about restrained but insightful ethnography:

> These strategies of ellipsis, concealment, and partial disclosure determine ethnographic relations as much as they do the transmission of stories between generations. Price has to accept the paradoxical fact that 'any Saramaka narrative

(including those told at cock's crow with the ostensible intent of communicating knowledge) will leave out most of what the teller knows about the incident in question. A person's knowledge is supposed to grow only in small increments, and in any aspect of life people are deliberately told only a little bit more than the speaker thinks they already know.'[30]

Ethnography, then, remains an undertaking aimed at exploring the social world and the relations and processes that shape it. An expanded ethnographic project treats that world as large, beyond the scope of absolute knowing and necessarily a form of storytelling. Ethnography is 'always caught up in the invention, not representation, of cultures'.[31] From this perspective, the 'smoothed-over, monological form' is cast aside for a mode of writing that is 'literally pieced-together, full of holes'; aspiring to nothing less than a 'serious partiality'.[32]

Ethnography of this type attempts to do justice to the richness of human existence. It spares us from 'imposing crude portraits on subtle peoples'[33] and, of course, from being hoodwinked by sneaky or recalcitrant subjects. It calls upon the researcher to surrender the master fiction of objective observer. An ethnographic awareness invites further introspection. Should it continue to rely so heavily upon speech acts? If we treat silence not only as refusal but as 'something intractable, unspeakable, unreasonable, unanalyzable' we 'trouble the notion of voice as an indicator of authenticity, immediacy or narrative authority in qualitative inquiry'.[34] Where does that leave us? What counts as ethnographic 'sign' and what do we ignore under the time-honoured heading, 'noise'? What might an 'analytic of noise' look like?[35] How might it smell, feel or taste? To embrace Bataille's notion of excess, how might we avail ourselves of these other powerful senses? How do we get those onto paper 'without simply imitating speech'?[36] Can an *excessive* approach to ethnography do justice to the passion, violence, obscenity and banality of things?

*

Isn't it time we faced up to our deep entanglement in creating smoothed out fantasy worlds of meaning where energies of all types – overflowing in plain view – are neatly contained and forgotten?

*

In contrast to such musings, ethnography in comparative education remains staunchly welded to the norms and techniques of critical realist social science where concerns for rigorous analysis and social policy relevance trump all.[37] While such ethnography is open to mixing methods and to accepting the interpretative basis of qualitative enquiry, the so-called crisis of representation heralded by the *Writing Culture* project remains largely marginal in a field where the scientific article continues to dominate the essay as art.[38] If one takes as an earlier starting point Geertz's seminal text *The Interpretation of Cultures*,[39] we can certainly trace in comparative education a heightened awareness of the positionality of the ethnographer and an acknowledgement of the pervasive reach of research discourses and power dynamics in education, but little else. The textual turn in comparative education – ethnographies included – largely amounts to good writing with the author doggedly holding onto 'some kind of depleted mastery over the world through the dogmatic exercise of methodological good sense'.[40]

Like much of the world of qualitative research, most education research that positions itself as comparative in scope has a particular relation to data that 'invokes a positivist ontology which turns the world into nouns and other things' and 'perpetuates the myth that objective observers can make the world visible through their methodological practices'.[41] Apparently, data is 'passive', 'waiting to be coded or granted shape and significance through the interpretive work of researchers'.[42]

*

Haven't we all experienced and celebrated 'good' data, the 'perfect' interview, the 'great' observation, 'significant' findings? How did we fall for such theory-fiction?

*

The vital illusion: Rather than passive ally, perhaps we should think of data as alive, active, on the move, an illusion with its own life force:

> the more the object is persecuted by experimental procedures, the more it invents strategies of counterfeit, evasion, disguise, disappearance. It is like a virus; it escapes by endlessly inventing counter-strategies. This behaviour of the object is also ironic insofar as it breaks the foolish pretentions of the subject, its desire to impose laws and dispose of the world according to its own will, its own representations.[43]

Method is no antidote to the hyperreal. For Baudrillard, the 'secret of the universe' – if there is one – is that 'at the core of every human being and every thing there is such a fundamentally inaccessible secret': a 'vital illusion'.[44] The more we use science and method to uncover the secret essence of things, the more obscured these become by the very data thrown up to expose the 'truth'. This disturbing reversal positions data not as pathway to the 'real' but, instead, as 'a trickster, foiling all the protocols of the subject's experiment, so that the subject itself loses its position as subject':

> Science has got it wrong. It is true that, thanks to the progress of analysis and technique, we actually discover the world in all its complexity – its atoms, particles, molecules, viruses. But never has science postulated, even as science fiction, that things discover us at the same time that we discover them, according to an inexorable reversibility. We always thought that things were passively waiting to be discovered, in much the same way that America is imagined to have been waiting for Columbus. But it is not so. At the moment when the subject discovers the object – whether it is an 'Indian' or virus – the object makes a reversal, but never innocent, discovery of the subject. More – it is actually a sort of invention of the subject by the invented object.[45]

With reversibility, everything becomes less stable. The subject (researcher) is cut lose from a position of authority and control. The object is acknowledged as active, although not necessarily as agentive in the ways that new-materialists are quick to ascribe. Reality becomes 'an obsequious servant', 'obey(ing) any hypothesis, verifying them all in turn, even when they contradict each other'. Reality 'supports all sorts of interpretations because it no longer makes sense, because it no longer wants to be interpreted'.[46] The endpoint here is ironic: objective, dispassionate indifference.

The search for the real will always be in vain. Most know this but few embrace the consequence. For those prepared to look into the abyss, there awaits an invitation for something new. If data is 'virtual and simultaneous', we have lost everything of importance to the traditional empirical undertaking but, at the same time, gained even more. In a 'state of simultaneity and production', data loses its meaning, becoming 'only illusive' and embodying 'all possible meanings'. Rather than sacred fact or window into reality, 'data, texts, images, objects, sounds, dreams, emotions, processes, enactments, and other things' become 'ghosts and proxies'[47] for the real, enabling us to play the only game remaining: to *create* worlds through the dual fictions of theory and data.

*

While realism remains the goal and the author remains sovereign, the complex challenge of 'working the ruins'[48] of qualitative research will remain unmet.

*

This mode of thought will be familiar to those in educational studies who have lived through the 'methodological upheavals' of recent decades and who continue to work within and in the wake of various 'posts' that have, collectively, destabilized old knowledge projects and problematized humanist thought in qualitative research.[49] Challenges to conventional understandings of data – and research – have not had an easy run. In part, this is due to practices of surveillance and policing, by both disciplinary gatekeepers and practices of self-censorship and forgetting. One important study (a meta-analysis of articles in one leading journal championing empirical post-structuralist policy research in education) identifies a 'prevalence of realist representational practices', and a surprising lack of preparedness on the part of authors to interrogate 'their own discursive practices in establishing scholarly authority' or their own 'world-making practices'.[50] In taking seriously the task of interrogating one's own positionality, Bendix-Petersen inserts a 'juxta text' into the scholarly analysis of publication patterns and preferences. This is a separate performance, part of the scholarly article but estranged from it by its positioning under the official text, literally cut off by a heavy dark line. Consciously avoiding depth and thus any claim to 'real' meaning or authenticity, the juxta text serves to remind us that all writing (and scholarship) is discursive, coming from *somewhere*, imbued with intentions. Juxta is a 'bone in the throat',[51] not only for the reader who might otherwise be enthralled by the analytical rigour of the author but, also, to the author herself who can quickly become carried away by the persuasiveness of her own performance. The juxta text – lurking in full view below the official text – aims to 'disrupt the singular authorial voice and call attention to the ways in which authority is sought (and) achieved'. Here, juxta appears as real and engaged as any flesh and blood author and is quick to claim her independence: 'Hey, stop talking about me in the third person. I am right here. This is my space'.[52] Juxta, as strategy, thus offers an 'opening'. Taken alongside the official text above the line, these two texts:

> attempt to enact a different and viable form of social scientificity – one that simultaneously does and undoes. One that both honours and disrupts traditional academic storytelling practices; one that seeks to encourage more courage to grapple publically and practically with the webs of incommensurable expectations embroiling those who desire post-foundational empirical work.[53]

Others have profited from this move to challenge the coloniality of knowledge production in comparative education. Using juxta as a way to disrupt the racial/cultural 'lines of othering' that enables comparative education to position post-socialist society and education as deficient, parallel texts are inserted into the scholarly article to allow the authors to speak in voices that are otherwise silenced in academic work. These are 'stories and reflections' – inserted as text boxes at strategic points in the text – that aim to 'complicate, interrupt, or make ambivalent (the) knowledge claims produced through colonial relations of power'. They serve to 'give voice to those less privileged accounts' that are often stifled by the grand concerns of academic discourses.[54] Critique with a *human* face.

One persistent reflection emerging from post-foundational scholars who struggle in the ruins of positivist science is the difficulty of completely avoiding the 'old habits of humanism and hubris' that got us into our present mess.[55] In the first example introduced here, juxta performs an alternative to the usual post-foundational text but inadvertently presents its own authoritative voice. Perhaps this juxta takes the form of *Juxta*: an independent alter-ego who offers, ironically, a coherent, almost dialectical, stage on which the reader is presented options for thought rather than the freedom to roam? Juxta puts the author in her place by inserting an unlikely but familiar auto-ethnographic other who inadvertently restores post-theorizing to the safety of dialogue and reason. In the second example, we find a similar process at work: a critique of colonial reasoning that opens the way for *parallel* histories and *alternative* knowledge empires. By reasserting voice, presence and purpose, both textual strategies reinforce a mode of post-qualitative enquiry that re-inscribes personhood, subjectivity and meaning making, trapping the text in the very ruins that they wish to transcend. By flirting with the modernist repertoire of dialectical reasoning, common sense and appeals to justice (in one case as 'my' right to be heard and the other as 'our' rights to be treated equally), Juxta is subsumed back into the 'system', thus playing its small (preordained?) role in moving subjectivity towards the ultimate goal of self-realization.

*

Are all attempts to establish alternative voices in educational research thus compromised? Is it ever possible to avoid the pulls of realism and humanism? Is the only way out to leave research behind, to abandon the debris of qualitative science and start afresh elsewhere?

*

When we speak with a voice that serves as 'an indicator of authenticity, immediacy, or narrative authority' we are exercising presence, what Derrida described as 'direct access to fundamentals, such as truth, thought, meaning, or the unbroken integrity of the intact self'.[56] This is of course an unattainable desire to heal the 'wound between Self and Other, as well as the colonial guilt that it produces'.[57] Rather than exercise voice in this sense, we might try to *destabilize* rather than *attain* meaning, produce moments of deceleration, slowing and meaninglessness. We could also accept what Lyotard calls the 'differend' that exists between parties who have equally compelling cases and where any settling of these by applying a 'single rule of judgment' is viewed as violent.[58] And we might listen. Silence is one way to attempt that, letting data be heard through the absence of speech and text. Laughter is another, the ultimate sign of awareness, breaking with solemnity and making clear just how little is at stake.

3

Presenting the unpresentable: We have argued that the legacy of modern thought – still responding to the Hegelian impulse – bends much comparative education towards an impossible striving for the 'truth' by exhausting, integrating and consuming all possible positions. This vanity, occasionally well meaning, often cynical, lies at its heart. By contrast, our project becomes one aimed at finding strategies to present that which is beyond presentation. The possibility of transcending the empirical via aesthetic experience is alluded to in Kantian explorations of beauty and central to the Romantic understanding of the sublime, but must be rethought in an age of hyperreality where objects roam freely, subjectivity dissolves as it de-centres and data reveals itself as wily foe.

*

If data is alive, how can we let it find its own voice?

*

For early Romantic writers, the Absolute, was that which lay beyond grasp. If the idealism of Hegel and his followers can be understood as a journey back to self where one returns to the essential truth that was hidden in the beginning, the Romantics of Jena viewed this journey as necessarily incomplete and ultimately beyond comprehension. One way to unfold this speculative difference is via irony. For Hegel, irony enables us to question truth until it is itself exhausted by the emergence of a *final* Truth. For the Romantics, irony is part of the ongoing journey of unfolding consciousness and presence, with uncertainty the 'essential fact about our being'.[59] We can never know how our World actually *is* and what, if anything, can achieve our integration with it. The aesthetic experience *points to* the 'hidden ground of subject-object identity'[60] but resists the hubris of realizing that as Absolute.

The sublime – this engagement with the unpresentable – is central to Romantic thought. For key figures like Novalis, this was the way to re-establishing 'original meaning'.[61] The sense of nostalgia and longing running through much Romantic art (poetry and painting) has been identified by Lyotard as the essence of a *modern* understanding of the sublime, one that allows the 'unpresentable to be put forward only as the missing contents'.[62] By 'glossing over' the unpresentable, modernity proffers a 'harmony' between form and content and thus 'violates the true nature of aesthetic experience'[63] where imagination and understanding are in necessary disharmony. By contrast, a *post-modern* aesthetic confronts the unpresentable on its own terms, 'den(ying) itself solace of good forms, the consensus of a taste which would make it possible to share collectively the nostalgia for the unattainable; that which searches for new presentations not in order to enjoy them but in order to permit a stronger sense of the unpresentable'.[64] Here, the pursuit of non-meaning aims to 'restore the true nature of the sublime' which is beyond 'complacent comfort', 'pre-established' rules or apparent truths. From this stance, the sublime will treat the event as 'something which is complete in itself'. This is worlds away from the modern sublime that, in its yearning for recovery and self-realization, attempts to locate the event within a 'totalizing logic' that 'violates (its) momentary and independent character'.[65] The 'meta-narrative' of modernity is thus 'dishonest' because it seeks to unify the disharmonious and silence the unpresentable.[66]

*

Has anyone thought to call education research – especially the 'best' of it – dishonest?

*

The pull of romanticism and to aesthetic modes of presentation remains strong. However, rather than aim for a 'complete transformation or aesthetic revolution of life and culture', it must be enough to present a finite world and embrace its otherness. In order to respond to our current context where sign systems are degrading and speculative philosophy has lost its purchase on an elusive 'truth', our approach here is more interested in striving to 'revolutionize the means of presentation'.[67] If, as we suggest, things hide behind appearances, lost behind the 'reality' of data, research practice must find new forms to present the World in ways that might help us *sense* what lies beyond our grasp. How can we present such absence?

A transgressive study of education under conditions of globalization, defined in terms of processes of hyperreality, aims for new thought, renewal and affirmation. It cannot be redemptive, corrective, reparative or nostalgic. To do that would be to defer to the rules and tools of philosophy that will be better equipped to map, clarify and complete a predetermined picture of reality. Then our reader could say: 'Oh, *that* is what you are trying to say . . . why didn't you just come out and say it in the first place?'[68]

*

For art to be meaningful, it must transcend meaning. If art only inspires, it is an aesthetic way to philosophical truth and therefore subordinate to it.

*

Our performative approach must open up and go beyond the constrained boundaries of imagination and understanding in order to touch upon the sublime. This is the place where pleasure and pain run freely, inviting new associations, dissonance and the strength (and gift) to face things as they are. Such writing should express something of the general economy to which Bataille has alerted us: a world of uncontrolled and incommensurate excess. It should also seek to take on data (the object) at its own game: intensifying and exhausting what can be thought and said. Theory and method gone fatal.

This notion of the fatal has its forerunner in the musings on death that run through the thought of our major protagonists. For Bataille, Blanchot and Baudrillard, one's relation to death becomes fundamental to how we approach life, shaping in turn how we understand the task of the writer. Bataille and Blanchot both developed their thought in the shadow of Hegel's system that viewed death as 'at the origin of humanity's self-consciousness'[69] and thus something to be mastered. In heralding the victory of the subject over indeterminacy, Hegelianism heralds the victory of life over death. Death defeated thus becomes central to the accomplishment of life. However, as we have seen, Bataille was fascinated by the excesses built into the general economy: ecstasy, laughter, sacrifice and death. For Bataille, death expresses a radical negativity that emits excessive energy and disrupts the closure of the system. Bataille explains the difference between Hegel's understanding of death and his own through the concepts of 'sacrifice' and 'discourse'. The man of sacrifice lacks discursive consciousness and, instead, has access to sensual experience grounded in 'unintelligible emotion'. Sacrifice presents a certain excitement and '*sacred* horror: the richest and the most agonizing experience, which does not limit itself to dismemberment but which, on the contrary, opens itself, like a theatre curtain, onto a realm beyond this world, where the rising light of day transfigures all things and destroys their limited meaning.'[70] This notion of sacred horror with its radical negativity lies *beyond* thought. Here, 'In order for Man to reveal himself ultimately to himself, he would have to die, but he would have to do it while living – watching himself ceasing to be.'[71] Sacrifice thus becomes the exercise of sovereignty beyond what is possible through instrumental reasoning, something that meaningful discourse with its rational and cautious rules can never accomplish. Death for Bataille thus constitutes the unavoidable undoing of the subject. It defines us *through* and *as* loss. The impossibility of recuperating from death becomes the ultimate form of expenditure, one that is always beyond negation. We must therefore learn to embrace death because it is so central to our being:

> I can only perceive a succession of cruel splendours whose very movement requires that I die: this death is only the *exploding* consumption of all that was, the joy of existence of all that comes into the world; even my own life demands that everything that exists, everywhere, ceaselessly give itself and be annihilated.[72]

Death in the Western context is at the 'heart' of taboo and a source of 'loathing' and 'prohibition'.[73] Like excretion, waste, drunkenness, luxury and eroticism, death confronts us with our loss of control. It is here that Bataille makes his move into the excessive, confronting our alienation from the primitive and from our basic impulses. Evoking the modern abattoir, he notes that death has lost its sacred connection, turning instead in the twentieth century into a productive force, a secret technical activity that governs the slaughterhouses of human life. In a more notorious move, he seeks out the ecstatic in death by extended contemplation of images of torture.[74] Rather than reject or celebrate such imagery, his challenge is that we must respond to the extreme, embracing death as sublime expression, in order to live fully:

> He alone is happy who, having experienced vertigo to the point of trembling in his bones, and being no longer able to measure the extent of his fall, suddenly

discovers the unexpected ability to transform his agony into a joy capable of freezing and transfiguring those who encounter it.[75]

Writing becomes a central way to 'stimulate the anguish and loss of self'[76] that are essential to honouring the general economy but only if it can remain open to the excessive that confronts and surpasses reason and science.

Bataille's struggles with death were well known to his close friend Blanchot, who shared an interest in understanding death in order to go beyond it to that point where writing begins. Death in Blanchot's hands becomes a 'civilizing power and the condition of possibility for freedom, projection and authentic existence'.[77] While Bataille sought to embrace death, harnessing its energy to realize the ecstatic, Blanchot viewed it as impossible to imagine let alone achieve. Death can be the 'object of meaningful activity, my ultimate possibility' or, alternatively, it is the 'ever-futural gulf in which these notions are definitively lost'.[78] Suicide, for example, can never be the ultimate possibility because the person who wills this is displaying an extraordinary mastery of life and individual sovereignty: 'an ecstatic assertion of the absolute freedom of the Subject in its union with nature or the divine'.[79] Death, then, cannot be willed for 'Whoever wants to die does not die, he loses the will to die'. Instead, death can be embraced as a place where the subject enters the 'nocturnal realm of fascination wherein he dies in a passion bereft of will'.[80] Unable to will ourselves to death, our only possibility is to live on in a state of diminished control. This is also the fate of the writer who, like the suicide, has no goal and no mastery over what unfolds:

> Both strive toward a point which they have to approach by means of skill, savoir faire, effort, the certitudes which the world takes for granted, and yet this point has nothing to do with such means; it is a stranger to the world, it remains foreign to all achievement and constantly ruins all deliberate action. How is it possible to proceed with a firm step toward that which will not allow itself to be charted?[81]

Because dying 'transgresses the boundary of the self's jurisdiction' it remains impossible and thus initiates the 'possibility of an encounter with some aspect of experience or some state of affairs that is not reducible to the self and which does not relate or return to self; that is to say, something other . . . . Dying is the impossibility of possibility and thus undermines the residual heroism, virility and potency of Being-towards-death'.[82] In the work of art – for us the book – we capture the essential ambiguity of existence, the '*no-mans*' land between reality and fantasy, intention and chance, control and loss, life and death. Between a literature that unfolds consciousness and delivers it as truth and a literature that reclaims the 'silence and materiality of things as things before the act of naming where they are murdered by language and translated into literature'.[83]

*

Paradoxically, a literary approach aims to put language in its place by ensuring that things are not reduced to the meaning we give to words.

*

Writing, like death, is framed by its own impossibility. As is his way, Blanchot offers another set of poles with which to comprehend our fate. The night is that place where 'everything has disappeared', a state of 'silence' and 'repose . . . where the sleeper does not know he sleeps, and he who dies goes to meet real dying'. This is the place where 'language completes and fulfils itself in the silent profundity which vouches for it as its meaning'.[84] In this first night, we sleep, rest, recharge, banish uncertainty and achieve death each time the day withdraws. However, it is in this darkness that the *other* night shows itself as 'unapproachable', 'impenetrable' and 'impure',[85] and

> he who senses it becomes the other. He who approaches it departs from himself, is no longer he who approaches but he who turns away, goes hither and yon. He who, having entered the first night, seeks intrepidly to go toward its profoundest intimacy, toward the essential, hears at a certain moment the *other* night – hears himself, hears the eternally reverberating echo of his own step, a step toward silence, toward the void. But the echo of his own step, a step toward silence, toward the void. But the echo sends this step back to him as the whispering immensity, and the void is now a presence coming toward him.[86]

To embrace this void is to be 'riveted to existence without an exit'.[87] It is a space where philosophy ends and writing starts. This means 'ceasing to be fascinated with the circular figure of the Book, the en-*cyclo*-paedia of philosophical science' that lusts for 'unity and totality' and that seeks to capture everything. Writing – the other to philosophy – is the 'experience of language unworking itself in an irreducible ambiguity that points towards an exteriority that would scatter meaning – a dizzying absence, the space of dying itself'.[88]

Baudrillard had read both Bataille and Blanchot when arriving at his own position on the relation of death to writing. In his early thought, we can trace Baudrillard's interest in restoring meaning and authenticity by returning to the symbolic foundations of social life. According to Baudrillard, we have entered a stage where biological death has become the dominant criterion for the end of life. In primitive societies, Baudrillard suggests that death is social, interpreted symbolically as part of a reversible cycle and beyond the scope of reason to penetrate fully. However, in modernity, the dead simply cease to exist, with death 'an unthinkable anomaly'.[89] What becomes of writing in a world surrounded by the death of death?

As we have seen, his analysis of the unfolding collapse of meaning in contemporary society found an early outlet in his critique of Foucault, not least what he viewed as Foucault's inability to take death seriously. By focusing on power and its dispersal to the microscopic extremities of the subject, and as relations between things, he held fast to the dominant Marxist tradition of production, failing to account for what happens *after* the dispersal of power. Foucault simply got death wrong, preferring instead to hold onto depleted life. This fixation with the dynamics of power and production would not do and Baudrillard moved to its opposite, processes of seduction. It is here, in *Symbolic Exchange and Death*, that he takes his notion of stages of simulation to their ultimate terminus, death itself. However, as we shall learn shortly, this was premature, for it became even clearer to Baudrillard that the system had no in-built self-destruction mechanism. The death-drive would lead somewhere else. Instead, the fourth of stage simulation would be death in the form of disappearance. Not the extermination of life, but its removal to a realm beyond grasp or recovery. The question, then, is what remains and how might we engage with that? Writing becomes key, not as science, but as strategies to reflect and challenge the disappearance of the World and the hyperreality that drives it. Writing, then, requires that we embrace death, not run from it. The writer must enter the void, let go, write lightly and decline to hope, for the system has no capacity to exchange desire or purpose into authentic life.

Death (of God and Self) thus becomes a call for a different *type* of book: a book of remains engaged in 'wandering without return'.[90] One that exceeds and overflows. One not afraid of the dark or afraid to fall. It is in that space – within and beyond the page, in the margins and in recalcitrant relation to the binary opposites that (con)strain Western thought – that writing takes place. With it comes difference, excess, possibility and the 'erring nomad who neither looks back to an absolute beginning nor ahead to an ultimate end'.[91] To write with death at our side is to write free of constraint and, strangely enough, for the future.

4

A thousand and one disturbing little stories:[92] If we are to keep multiplicity, incommensurability and the differend at the centre of our empirical work, *and* do justice to the fragmentation of social experience that typifies late modernity, one appropriate mode of presentation would be the fragment itself, a form that expresses the 'self-conscious naïveté'[93] of the romantics and our own project. The content of these fragments will vary, encompassing the 'real', the poetic and the brazenly magical. Interspersed among them will be measures of irony and humour aimed to unsettle, provoke and elicit a wide range of emotional responses. Transgression in theory in method.

Fragments as literary forms come from many times and places. They can be "'Ancient", "Romantic", "Modern", "Postmodern" (period terms), or "Philosophical" or "Literary" (aesthetic or generic terms)'.[94] In Greek literature and scholarship, the distinction between 'intended and unintended' fragments was not hard and fast with the text assessed for its overall 'intentionality, truthfulness, authenticity, and sense'. By the renaissance, the fragment becomes an 'allegorical expression of divine power' where the almighty is alluded to through symbol while the 'devil's existence (is) in the detail'.[95] In romantic literature, as we have seen, the fragment elevates aesthetic forms of expression as a strategy of revelation. With Nietzsche, the fragment reflects the partial and fleeting nature of life and becomes an invitation to self-realization in the present. Throughout these ages, the aphorism has been central to the fragmented text, hinting at truths with light writing, wit and critical distance.

In our own era, Adorno and Horkheimer used a fragmentary literary form to express the ruptured, loss of modernity in the mid-twentieth-century West. In Adorno's later masterpiece, *Minima Moralia* – deliberately evoking the *Magna Moralia* of Aristotle (or a later follower) – the shocking events of the Holocaust provide a backdrop to the unfolding disappointments of industrial capitalism, bureaucratic instrumentalism and declining sense of community. However, this 'damaged life' is not to be consoled but, rather, embraced as an invitation to find the good that remains. 'Schooled' in the method of Hegel, he cites the master to outline the enduring power of negation:

> The life of the mind only attains its truth when discovering itself in absolute desolation. The mind is not this power as a positive which turns away from the negative, as when we say of something that it is null, or false, so much for that and now for something else; it is this power only when looking the negative in the face, swelling upon it.[96]

Adorno notes that dialectical theory rejects 'anything isolated' and 'cannot admit aphorisms as such'[97] but suggests that the time for the dogmatic application of technique is past. As the subject fractures and vanishes in the present historical moment, so too does the demand and desire to express the totality of the World in each sentence or formulation. Nevertheless, this is writing that aims to recover some semblance of the good life or at least give hope that things can be made liveable. Walter Benjamin, with support from Adorno, wrote his unfinished *Arcades Project* in a fragmented style that sought to do justice to the splintered reality of nineteenth-century urban modernity and which could serve as the 'threshold to a primal world of fantasy, illusion and phantasm agorias that expressed the dream world of capitalism'.[98] Rather than begin from a structural analysis of the whole, his approach was to gaze into the 'specific nature of modern life experience' in order to find as George Simmel writes, 'in each of life's details the totality of its meaning'.[99]

This tradition of critical realist enquiry that aims to capture a zeitgeist in order to confront and overcome it continues in Debord's *The Society of the Spectacle* with its 221 theses that have the 'deliberate intention of doing harm'[100] to an age of exploitation, disinterest and disintegration. In a text of linked but independent statements, the author attempts to diagnose capitalist society, mirroring its estranged, fragmented but, paradoxically, unifying character. While not explaining his literary method, it is apparent that these semi-independent musings, once connected as coherent text, tell us something about the subtle but effective reach of the Spectacle and thus provide a *situationalist* stance from which to marshal a response.

The situationalist approach was familiar to Baudrillard who claimed membership of this community in the early phases of his work that focused on the rise of semiotic society. For a time, he would support the attempt to expose the hidden mechanisms of capitalism, and the false consciousness it fabricates, as a step to resistance. The catastrophe of the failed student uprising of 1968 changed everything. With the failure of the left (especially the intelligentsia) to mobilize effectively and muster anything like a personal commitment to genuine redistributive public policy, it was clear that politics had now moved into a phase of stasis with the indifference of the citizenry mirroring that of the system itself. By the time of his own *Cool Memories* series of books, aphoristic writing was not aimed at celebrating or lamenting the condition of the World but, instead, riding the indeterminacy and disappearance of meaning to the end. The *ultimate* fatal strategy. For a time, Baudrillard's intent was to invest writing with a richness that might reclaim the myth and mystification that characterized discourse in symbolic society. In the end, and like the fragmented literary texts of Nietzsche, Bataille and Blanchot, the ambition is to 'let go'.[101]

Fragmentary writing thus has a multitude of aims and styles from which one can only proceed after setting one's ontological and epistemological bearings. The fragment can be coercive, consensual, redundant, resolute, hopeful, unfinished, provoking, comforting and estranging. The fragment can implode science and slap down our confident assertions about truth and falsity, our notions of right and our righteousness. Like objects, they circulate. Jewels of simulation in an age of simulacra. The fragment is therefore performative, introducing 'acts of literature, acts of reading, acts of writing'.[102] This performative function means, ultimately, that the fragment cannot submit to a singular definition or purpose. Being independent of any story of origin or destiny, and in unstable relation to their creators, they remain sovereign, beyond the reach of absolute meaning, comfort and closure.

*

Strategies for fragmentary ethnography: Our fragmented approach is not simply the result of scholarly whim, fancy or a lack of capacity to adhere to the standards expected of 'serious' research. Rather, it is a way to ensure an aesthetic route to understanding and awareness that transcends what is possible via philosophy and most certainly what emerges from a naïve confidence in empiricism. Fragments of the sort unfolded here take us to a state beyond appearances, to the silence that always follows hasty attempts to force meaning. They induce laughter and a relief that comes from the realization that we are finally free from the burden of education.

The incomplete text can provide an insight from the 'field', an attempt to give something of the essence of experience, to do justice to 'reality' and situated action. It can reflect the researcher's attempt at sense-making or be a sly move to invent history. The incomplete text may be a deliberate act of omission: to be mischievous, to disrupt vulgar interpretative overreach, to do justice to the wonder of things. The incomplete text may be aphoristic, suggesting truth or fancy, always blurring the lines between them.

*

The fragment enables the researcher to move between the positions of scientist, activist and poet without settling comfortably in any one of these. Is not that how we all live anyway?

*

The fragmented text can seek to disrupt the total text that underwrites the hegemony of scientific scholarship. As 'minor' research, it places the author beyond the conventional modes of engagement within a field of study while nonetheless remaining in dialogue with them.[103] Poetic writing might simply be good prose aimed at enlivening sullen concepts or, more radically, it might aim to transform empirical experiences so that they become alien to the concepts that tend to foreground and hence bound them:

> Unafraid of sensual immersions, subjectivities, mutual constructions of meaningful relationships, and sometimes deliberately fictionalized realities that 'ring true', poetry is a way of constructing lines and meanings in spoken or written work for aesthetic results and more.[104]

Poetic inquiry can take form as poetry itself, providing an alternative to the conventional research genre: saying more with less. It can also be a creative reworking of prose that highlights, suppresses and repositions existing textual utterances so that new responses become possible. That might mean playing with a text: blocking out part or most of what a respondent tells us to highlight what we *think* is important or, even, what is being lost in the business of reading between the lines. It might also be attempts to reshape and format what is usually presented conventionally so that the text, literally, jumps off the page with new life and purpose. This is our way to challenge the pre-emptive seductiveness of data. In the same way, photographic inquiry can provide an alternative way to reflect everyday experience, especially when the conventional image is reworked creatively to expose or highlight that which is hidden in plain sight.[105]

Perhaps the most profound way to disrupt the 'real' is to subject it to the magical and fabulous. That tradition, well known as a literary strategy, 'employs paradoxes in relation to time, reality, and space' and deploys irony and tragedy as 'the face behind the mask of the comedy that underscores tragic futility'.[106] By blending past, present and future (time), placing the fabulous alongside the everyday (reality), blurring 'inner and outer worlds' (space) and moving between 'centre and periphery' (authorial control), we are able to create heterotopias that respond to critiques of ethnography as simplistically realist and Western-centric. The magical can problematize the subject/object distinction, challenge colonialist renderings of events and undermine the status of the writer:

> In this equation, the real is the colonialist overlay that imperils life and culture, while the fantastic is that which operates in direct antithesis to the European super-civilization in an attempt to negotiate the persistence of colonial memory, in the hope of creating a future that neither represses the past nor is permanently mutilated by it.[107]

Comparative education has had little engagement with this tradition, surprising given the preponderance of research interest in addressing power inequalities in Latin America where an important strand of the genre emerged as a corrective to colonialism. However, anthropology, versed in magic as subject matter, has applied the fabulous to the analysis of social life and the representation of culture. One especially relevant example comes to us as Michael Taussig's *The Magic of the State* that explores the mystical or religious underpinning of the modern state in one unnamed Latin American country. In arguing for the centrality of spirit possession at the heart of the emergence of the modern bureaucratic state, he blends dispassionate description, political assertion, poetics and reflections on theory to illustrate how the sacred invests the political in a complex of mutual relations:

> these stories of the coming into being of the state are not only fantastic history but – and here's the rub – precisely as fantasy are essential to what they purport to explain such that any engagement with the thing called the state will perforce be an engagement with this heart of fiction, the very script of whose real and grave purpose presupposes both theatre and spirit possession.[108]

By refusing to name and locate the country in question, by moving between place and context in ways that confuse the binary of modern/other and by inserting himself into the text both as author and protagonist, the text/novel becomes a fluid encounter with modern science itself where, as with nation building, 'Faith is necessary. Always'.[109] Taussig's role as a participant/character in the text is also important as he loses the 'lofty gaze of an omniscient narrator speaking from the centre of power'.[110] While he directs the action – a necessary condition of academic writing – his approach means that the writer becomes an ironic figure swept up in shifting relations of reality/fiction where, ultimately, events are touched by truth but also the opposite. The result is an ethnographic project that 'flows in all directions'.[111]

*

The radical uncertainty of events in magical realist literature resonates with Baudrillard's suggestion that truth has disappeared behind display. By representing the world through the 'deliberate and rigorous, but also playful, use of imagination' we create a 'fictional reality' that at last positions ethnography itself as part of our 'vanishing real'.[112]

*

Why hasn't the modern school, built on and powered by a fantasy foundation (the doctrine of education for all, the myth of enlightenment, the promise of empowerment) been explored by any means other than reason(able) science?

*

New Rules to Live By[113]

New Rules to Live By (amended)

1. We have an ample supply of methodological rules and interpretive guidelines. 2. They are open to change and to differing interpretation, and this is how it should be. 3. There is no longer a single gold standard for qualitative work. 4. We value open-peer reviews in our journals. 5. Our empirical materials are performative. They are not commodities to be bought, sold and consumed. 6. Our feminist, communitarian ethics are not governed by Internal Review Boards. 7. Our science is open-ended, unruly, disruptive. 8. Inquiry is always political and moral. 9. Objectivity and evidence are political and ethical terms.	1. We have an ample supply of methodological rules and interpretive guidelines. 2. They are open to change and to differing interpretation, and this is how it should be. 3. **There is no longer a single gold standard for qualitative work.** 4. We value open-peer reviews in our journals. 5. **Our empirical materials are performative.** They are not commodities to be bought, sold and consumed. 6. Our feminist, communitarian ethics are not governed by IRBs. 7. **Our science is open-ended, unruly, disruptive.** 8. **Inquiry is always political and moral.** 9. **Objectivity and evidence are political and ethical terms.**

5

Reversibility: What might emerge from fragmentary ethnography? We noted earlier that Horkheimer and Adorno saw in Enlightenment new dangers for control and domination, lamenting that reason could easily lead to its opposite. That general warning is one we can apply broadly to our study here. The teacher who embraces student-centred pedagogy submits the student to individual attention and thus the threat of visibility, control and judgment, all in the name of respect, diversity, rights and efficient learning. The nation that embraces international assessment studies as a policy device to improve education opens itself to examination, critique and the interests and whims of others, creating educational goals that may very well be marginal or, even, contrary to national interests. The researcher who employs methods and procedures in the name of greater or even 'full transparency' (the great call of our age) obscures our capacity to understand the object of interest as it disappears in its copy. Conceptual work (including the work in this book!), data collection and analysis do not necessarily make the world more transparent.

In our age, this reversible dimension to life takes the form of simulation. Baudrillard, as we have seen, initially attempted to counter the system of objects and their indeterminacy by overloading it with meaning. To cipher rather than decipher,[114] to make the seemingly straightforward (what we call the 'real' but which is only ever its illusion) enigmatic. To flip the switch on the escalating banality of economic exchange by seeking out the symbolic, understood as that which is beyond calculative reason and which gave primitive societies their depth, authenticity and meaning. Like other French theorists of his era, the problems of modernity would be confronted by recourse to earlier societal forms. This cultural perspective eventually gave way to the realization that it was simply too late to undo what had been done. The unstoppable movement into the digital, clone and code meant that reality had already shifted into the hyperreal, becoming *more* real than the 'real' itself. All we could do was to hold on for the ride, waiting for the system to derail itself:

> Nothing moves any longer from cause to effect: everything is tranversalized by inversions of meaning, by perverse events, by ironic reversals. Acceleration, streams and turbulences, self-potentialization and chaotic effects. . . . Pushed to extremes of sophistication and performance, to a point of perfection and totalization (as is the virtual system of nets and information), the system reaches its breaking point and implodes all by itself. This does not occur through the actions of any critical subject or any historical forces of subversion: it occurs through ultra-realization and automatic reversal, pure and simple. . . . The more these political, social, economic systems advance toward their own perfection, the more they deconstruct themselves.[115]

This reversal is perhaps most evident in the areas of technology and communications that, for Baudrillard, are characterized by an 'excess of information' and a loss of 'real information and real historical events'. What pornography did to sexuality is now being generated by media as fake news, virtual reality, facial recognition technology and advanced algorithms that distort thought, judgement and taste. Yet the illusion of meaning remains even though objects and events disappear behind it.

*

If meaning has been murdered in the erotic and informational spheres why would that be any different in the sphere of (increasingly) performative academic scholarship?

*

Baudrillard had little to say about universities and their scholarly endeavours, apart from that they had ceased to function as sites for the production of knowledge. Like art, having proliferated beyond the point where it could say something original and after exhausting all aesthetic forms, perhaps we can say of research in comparative education that it 'doesn't know it has disappeared and – this is the worst of it – continues on its trajectory in a vegetative state'.[116] Where does this leave us? A condition of stasis obviously invites a radically different type of research perspective: one grounded in a form of art that, while not necessarily seeking to be original, can play with the forces of illusion and disappearance. A fragmented approach thus offers us two major directions for contemplation and action.

Fragments of the sort that follow enable us to engage with the world as the thousands of disturbing little stories evoked by Lyotard. With no attempt to stitch together our scattered data in order to tell the prescribed story, we aim to let the World come to us as we find it.

By allowing every fragment to stand on its own, we treat each little story as an event in itself: a total manifestation of the World in that moment.

By adopting a fragmentary approach, we might also sense what happens as things disappear, lose meaning but nonetheless manage to carry on. For things never disappear and that is the grim message. As each thing dissolves before our eyes, it's 'ghost' or 'narcissistic double' remains. Like Lewis Carroll's infuriating cat, the grin becomes the reminder of that which was once substantial, with referent and value. Now, hyperreality bequeaths us with the cruel reminder of what was and laughs at our vein attempts to capture and reclaim it.

It is here that our fragments begin to speak, but only from the silence that they evoke. Like Baudrillard, we 'gamble(s) on the world being an illusion' where 'there is perhaps nothing rather than something and which "hunts down the nothing that runs beneath the apparent continuity of meaning".[117] Like the bright light from a dead star that continues to illuminate the night long after its death, these fragments speak of what *was* as well as what *remains*. They mock our nostalgia for the comforting and our desire for restoration. They seek to embrace the grin and return it with laughter. In a World that is indifferent to disappearance and unable to reverse it, laughter becomes the frivolous other of research.

Like the Cheshire Cat, we too might disappear, offering in our places rhetorical questions and a form of data that turns back on the reader, always asking for more than it gives. Perhaps our task as writers of radical uncertainty is nothing less than to write ourselves out of the picture? The fragment as grin ensures that it remains an aesthetic gesture beyond the scorn of science and its scholarly moralizing. This position is not one which 'seeks to be obscure or to create nonsense' but is one which 'respects the illusion of the world'.[118]

*

God vanishes, leaving only His judgment in which we silently drown.
    The cat remains to swallow our indignation and return our doubts compounded.
        The subject lingers on without a self.
            The school remains without education.
                Learning without insight.
                      The future without the . . . future

Figure 4.3 Grin.

In Extremis

All research submits to some form of peer review. The following selective assessments of our earlier work span a fifteen-year period and give an idea of the difficulty of penetrating the outer walls of social 'science' in education.

Failed research applications, in the words of external reviewers:

The research should explore solutions to next generation issues.

The Committee finds that the proposal does not sufficiently elaborate the main concepts and subsequently how this conceptual framework is translated into researchable questions and a set of coherent and comparable case studies.

. . . the phenomenon seems to be understood at an abstract level and only in terms of implied government policy rather than at a practical level where data/evidence can be identified, collected and analyzed. In other words, theoretically this could be a very interesting conceptual paper. Nothing more is articulated in terms of the actual methodologies that will be employed and there is not articulation or explicit explanation of how the PI ('Principal Investigator') or his collaborators will develop their methodologies . . . there is not even a methodology for developing a methodology. So, in spite of the fact that this is an interesting idea, there are significant and fatal flaws in the lack of methods, lack of any articulation of the kind of evidence/data that might be collected or analyzed, lack of any hypothesis or direction for an analysis even if there were data (other than that the PI will 'go fishing' for results).

. . . one can only assume that the articles that would come from this project will be based on experiential and anecdotal evidence rather than a scientific and systematic approach to the study.

*

From a conference participant in England, in response to a presentation on young children's experience of primary schooling in the Global South:

I've worked in this country and seen the damage from limited educational opportunities. Frankly, I'm appalled and you should be ashamed to be making such a critique of what everyone agrees is a human right. How can you dismiss schooling and glorify poverty like that?

*

At a research seminar in Denmark, commenting on a study of Danish university governance:

I'm not convinced. I've experienced over a decade of neoliberal reform of higher education and your perspective is politically naïve.

*

From the editor of a journal that focused on qualitative research, explaining the rejection of an article based on ethnographic study of young peoples' experience of education:

Everyone appreciates the impossibility of undertaking extensive fieldwork in the tradition of Malinowski, at least in terms of years of immersion in the field. However, it is simply insufficient to make numerous short visits in the hope of compensating for an inadequate depth of engagement. In future, I suggest you consider planning to be in country for 6 weeks at least. Then your findings will carry weight.

*

From a research symposium in Germany:

I appreciate your post-modern perspective but there are real children in need. Education research must listen and respond.

*

From a dialogue with a colleague and self-described 'scholar of colour':

... given the growing concerns with whose voices (and bodies) get privileged in comparative education scholarship, I believe a scholar in your stature can make some dent in pushing the citational patterns to move beyond Whiteness. Whiteness, or our racialized/gendered leanings are invisible because it's so unconscious. Perhaps, a white reader, or even many non-white readers may not make a big deal about this, but as a scholar of color who always raises questions of whose knowledge counts or is validated, I raised this issue. Similar questions are being asked throughout conferences about having all white panels, or all male-panels, raising critical questions.

*

From a conference participant in Australia:

What worries me is that your perspective only gives a partial look at the problem. The school effectiveness paradigm aims at catching the whole. It's backed by numbers.

*

From a PhD student during the oral defence of the thesis in which one of the present authors was examiner:

I considered your approach but it is a form of madness.

*

On the limits of policy research as writing:

Your piece is certainly a masterpiece of elegance in circling a topic like a belly dancer circles her spectator. Writing is like belly dancing – beautiful to look at but you can't touch.

*

5

A World in/of Fragments

Network of gems: Glass reflects the world, gives back what it catches. When shattered it can cut, blunt, highlight, hide and deceive. Once broken it remains so. A whole replaced by the possible, the implied, the absent. If the writer wishes to take the reader to a predetermined destination, fragments will be assembled coherently to ensure their power to clarify, explain and lead or, depending on one's whim, to deceive. This will prioritize the reading subject over the field or object of enquiry and returns us to the book already written with its invitation to triumph, despair, resignation and hope. If we are true to the fragmented nature of experience, one where an 'infinitely huge network of gems . . . illuminates and reflects all the others',[1] we must configure our fragments without such thought or care. As long as the strictures/scriptures of comparative method are placed to one side, the aware mind will *find* connections and an essential unity. What we know as context is, for the student of Zen, a 'field saturated with energy'.[2] When subject and object are kept in balance, the reading subject becomes one with the field. With the emphasis 'evenly diffused . . . there is the Subject, there is the Object, and the world is seen as a vast, limitless Unity of a multiplicity of separate things'.[3] We know this in education from Alfred North Whitehead who insisted that 'every entity is only to be understood in terms of the way in which it is interwoven with the rest of the universe'.[4] The artificial separation of life into disciplines and fields of study with their differing emphases and a prioritizing of mechanical relations over the organic is at the root of the problem of the project of modernity and a central hurdle in our encounter with education in the present age. If all matter is interconnected and relational, our methods must remain alert to the impulse to dissect, explain and reassemble along parochial (and fickle) academic lines. When faced with the question of whether to prioritize facts or ideas, the answer, as Whitehead suggests, must be to explore 'Ideas about facts'.[5]

To approach fragments through the 'discriminating act of thinking'[6] is to have them quickly shrivel into the poor or inadequate data that has always been the enemy of the scientist and the quick excuse of the dismissive reader. Perhaps, and for the first time in the arena of comparative education, the suggestion is to take a stance akin to 'no-mind'. Instead of dividing and measuring the contents of an opaque world, we might simply bath in the light it emits.

*

The pure event: Baudrillard considered the attacks in America on 11 September 2001 as a 'strong' or 'pure' event that had the effect of bringing together sentiments, hopes and fears that could never be gathered in reality.[7] How should we understand this almost metaphysical insight? From Deleuze, any philosophical concept, by definition, is an event that cannot be reduced to, or identical with an actual happening or the essence of a thing.[8] The pure event is a 'self-referential movement of pure immanence . . . never exhausted by its various actualizations'. It is both 'now-here and no-where' that, for Deleuze and Guattari, is a 'plane of immanence, infinite movement, and absolute survey'. The pure event brings together the totality of imaginative possibilities and is not constrained by either the reality of the world or our knowledge of it, through actual historical events.[9]

*

The great cubist artist Georges Braque was indebted to Paul Cézanne for 'sweeping painting clear of the idea of mastery'.[10] Should an ethnography in fragments be recognized as operating on similar terms? Perhaps the mastery at play is one that weaves together reality and fabrication, so that one not only struggles to grasp the whole from fleeting appearances, but flounders in a surfeit of fact *and* fiction. Might this not silence the always-discriminating mind and enable phenomena to finally speak for themselves?

*

Is it true that 'some truths speak only from the well of exaggeration'?[11]

*

Wishing to reacquaint the reader with the original experience of fragmentation, we have consciously avoided delivering 'data' in a form that would lead to ready pathways of understanding. Some fragments will confirm prejudices while others may challenge them. Some will confuse. Others will offend. Some may close down thought. Others may open it up or just slip beyond reach. All 'data', in spite of our best intentions, tells its own story no matter how hard we seek to control its form and flow. In what follows, the fragments reflect different aspects of the basic formula of anthropological fieldwork:

> Belongings: where places, sites and our global perspective come to the fore.
> This is the 'somewhere' of fieldwork.
>
> Objects: the things and 'something' of research.
>
> Experiences: where subjects gasp for air in the rarefied world of dreams.
> Education always happens to 'someone'.

How these aspects find form on the page will be less apparent as preconceived categories and empirical differences merge together. Weaved in among these excerpts from life are reflections, statements and provocations from the writers who become unreliable commentators and occasional participants in the drama. Best to be on guard here.

*

In the shadows of methodological nationalism: Can we really write about the world without placing context at the centre of our considerations? Most start there and comparative education is well served by the thorough, grounded case study of nation, school and place.[12] If context is as dispersed and fleeting as global cultural phenomenon themselves, need we provide the usual, perfunctory, overview of system, place, site, nation, culture? Isn't that as much discursive trick as conceptual necessity? If we are arguing for a field of endeavour/drama that is beyond neat dissection into national, cultural or systemic action, what are we to do with those well-argued accounts that highlight the distinctiveness of place? Perhaps what will emerge from the following sections is a reaffirmed stance that context matters, but one that acknowledges the pull of global phenomena as central to the practice and experience of education.

*

But how did you do it? Our three country experiments were founded on ethnographic 'field' work over a five-year period. Based in Denmark, and seeing the world to some extent from a Danish perspective, it may be assumed that this aspect of the study was the most thorough. But what is meant by thorough in a post-foundational perspective? The study in Denmark involved two state-funded secondary schools. One was a public-funded boarding school set in a remote rural location. The other was in a large regional town. There were also two upper secondary (gymnasium) schools, one located in central Copenhagen, the other in the suburbs. The fragments presented here reflect perspectives from these visits and interactions and build on more than thirty years of engagement in researching Danish education, youth and school policy. The studies in South Korea and Zambia were built on earlier work in those countries and were concentrated into two longer stays totalling some nine months. The work here focused on two public high schools in Lusaka and two high schools in Seoul, one public and the other private. A research assistant was involved in the South Korean work, although interestingly, this person was a recent high school graduate and was often completely bewildered by the things he was encouraged to see and hear. Our learning emerged alongside his. In most cases, interviews with Korean teachers took place in Korean although the most engaging discussions were usually 'off the record' reflections in English. The Zambian work was conducted solely in English, making some things possible and others problematic. The Danish study was conducted in Danish. The familiarity of mother tongue here was no guarantee of smooth information transmission, whatever that is. In all cases, the students who are central to these pages were in the final years of their educational cycle and aged between sixteen and eighteen. All names are altered, including those of the dead, the missing and the lost.

'Denmark'

Small land demanding much space and attention. Land of freedom, self-determination, wealth and resourcefulness. If you want to live the American dream, move here. Borders now closed. Sorry: the Danes come first. Muslims welcome? Benign colonial heritage? Greenland as problem. World closing in. Asia looming. Global South in her debt, always. Land of democracy, education for life, free education, enlightenment. Hubris. Peace loving after centuries of territorial loss and a fraught relation to the Germans. Now, willing participant in foreign wars and 'coalitions for peace'. Moral compass lost. Advocate for PISA but perennial under performer. Welfare state, but only for some.

Perpetual education reform. School day extended in early years, exam culture introduced. Great teacher resistance turns to apathy and acceptance. Teaching to the test? Never. Well, maybe. Professional teaching force trained in university along the Singaporean example or continuation of the nineteenth century para-professional model motivated by pastoral care and social goals?

Upper secondary school (gymnasium) turns to professional leadership and faces intense competition for students. Or did they become pupils? Bildung/dannelse slowly replaced by training and preparation for work. Death of the myth of educational equality and education for enlightenment.

Pigs outnumber people but the parallel to Orwell is lost in translation. A national politics in debt to a handful of farmers? Aging population. Impossible demographic. National socialism meets progressive conservativism ending in stasis. None of this can continue. Or does it?

*

It is Written

> Education and the school culture as a whole must prepare students for participation, co-responsibility, rights and duties in a society of freedom and government. Therefore, the teaching and the daily life of the school must be based on freedom of spirit, equality and democracy. Pupils must thereby gain the prerequisites for active participation in a democratic society and an understanding of the possibilities individually and jointly to contribute to development and change as well as an understanding of both the near and the European and global perspective.[13]

In the Kingdom of Denmark

The high school's profile can be briefly formulated as creative professionalism and democratic consciousness. We build on traditions and community with a student body where unity and security are central. In our vision, we emphasize an innovative and open approach to the curriculum. This is deepened by our approach to bodily, musical and dramatic expression. We prioritize the development of students' democratic consciousness. All students receive instruction in rhetoric as a part of their general education. We have democratic days, democracy modules, morning meetings, an active student council and many student-led committees. These give a strong and independent platform that feeds into school decision-making. The school strives to be a democratic laboratory.

Good Habits

Morning assembly. Students are called to the main hall by the chime of a single bell followed by Jimi Hendrix's *Purple Haze*. Sleepy heads barely register this anthem of the 1960s but the deputy principal confides that it creates a bond between teachers and students. He starts the assembly by reviewing the school's rules: respect others, dress properly, speak properly, meet people positively, meet on time, meet well prepared, bring your books, materials. Agree with the teachers regarding toilet breaks and bringing food and drink into the classroom. Come to the homework cafés after school. Homework is mandatory. All adults are role models. Smoking is prohibited at school. This applies to everyone: staff as well as students. Some staff have smoked a lifetime but it applies to them also. You must not smoke at school and we define school as the dining room, the kitchen, the hallways, the common room. If you smoke, you'll be sent home initially for three days. Here you'll have time to consider if smoking means more than your education. If it does, you can stay home.

Karl leans over to Andreas and whispers: Then there'll be a lot of teachers going home.

Choose Me!

In her application to join the school, Linda promised to be everything they were looking for:

> I can offer commitment and motivation. A diligent student who wants to contribute to making the high school a good place for students, teachers and staff. I grew up in a home where current events were the focus for family discussions. I want to make a difference for people in the third world who suffer poor conditions compared to us in the privileged world. When I was travelling, I visited a school that left an impression on me. Unlike our schools, the teachers didn't talk to the students. I am from a family where both my parents are university educated and where we have books everywhere. I like to read. I have been to many countries although I am only 15 years old. New York is my favourite city. I am motivated by high grades. I am good at taking responsibility. I'm left wing. I am social. I am interested. I am clever. I am academic. I am intellectual. I am artistic. I am a girl. I am a boy. I am me.

You Just Can't Talk to Them

The last class was hugely ambitious, says the teacher. So ambitious that it was always about grades. You could just feel – all the time – that it was about getting good grades. And only that. You couldn't even talk to them at all without having the feeling that they were going to show how good they were.

Mirror, Mirror on the Wall

International Politics is held on the top floor of Building 2, an old turn of the century red brick structure with high ceilings and ancient heavy wooden windows over-painted in white gloss. It could have easily been another type of institution once but the giveaway is an old enamel sink set low to the floor above which is fixed an unframed mirror that has begun to lose the silver layer of paint on its rear side that provides the reflection. Surely this was an elementary school in a bygone time when the focus of hygiene was both mental *and* physical?

Six times a day, different bodies of students make their way to the top of the stairs to start another class on Marx's stages of development, the Six-day war, Mao's China, the regulative framework of the EU or the dynamics of contemporary geopolitics. And of course the war in Afghanistan and Denmark's new status as an international player punching well above its weight. Without exception, students will never stop to wash their hands at the low sink. Just to stop would create a pile up in the narrow entrance to the room. Equally, without exception, every student sneaks a glimpse into the mirror with its shallow depth and endless mystery. Some have said that it whispers back. Others have said that you shouldn't stand in front of it and definitely not look deeply into it. You may not like what you see.

There's always one who has to learn the lesson for herself and today that was poor Louise. She had to go to the toilet during class and that required passage past the mirror. The class was watching a film in the darkened room. Ordinarily, they would be easily able to see out into the hallway through the glass door and thus to anyone standing still in front of the mirror. On this occasion, the film explored the history of fashion in London's swinging 1960s and that was entrancing most to keep their gaze forward.

Louise passed the mirror on the way to the toilet and was sure that she heard something. That whisper stayed in her head as she made her way back to the class. Coming into the hallway, the mirror seemed to be real, alive, waiting for her alone. She slowed down, pretending to wash her hands at the low sink. Once in position, and with great trepidation, she slowly looked up until she was staring right into the abyss.

Figure 5.1 Mirror in school corridor.

There was nothing in there, she said blankly. Just a long silence that made me feel even more worthless. All the others seemed beautiful and happy while I looked sad and lonely. How will I ever find peace?

The Principal

I'm the first principal in this type of school to have been recruited through a consultancy firm. Modern management: that's what we need in our schools. I was tested in all possible ways and I was employed because the board was convinced that I could improve this school, give it a profile, attract different students from those we have in the local area. We want urban youth: young people with academic ambitions, young people from the cultural elite of the big cities. We have decided that a focus on globalization and cultural encounter will enable that. That is what my leadership should focus on: recruiting students from social and cultural environments that have historically been beyond our reach.

The Principal II

He could feel modern management becoming part of him. He was the first in this country to take a test like this, to pass it. Modern management. He had *become* modern management. He could already glimpse entirely new students, urban youth, cosmopolitan youth, elites. They would be the ones to fill the rooms, to study at *his* school. He could already feel them in the classrooms, the corridors, the playing fields. Elegantly dressed, clever, something useful to say. Reflecting glory. British boarding school. Good morning, Mr Jensen they'd say as he did the rounds. No more 'Hi John'. Just 'Mr Jensen'. Or 'Sir'. Now that's a school! Modern management.

Folk-enlightenment

Our school is culturally open. We include all students, irrespective of ethnic, social or religious background. The cultural encounter is at the centre of our pedagogy in relation to the national and the local, the European and the global.

This school is based on the principle of folk enlightenment. We want to enlighten all aspects of our existence, all the nuances and challenges in order to support the individual in his or her becoming.

We want to focus on dialog between human beings.

We travel all over the world to spread ideas. We want to make a difference with these cultural encounters. We want to show what humanism is: tolerance, humility, respect, empathy. Democracy.

He checked his notes. He got all the words out. What could they say to this? What could anyone say to this?

The Good Samaritan

Walking as a group, the students and their teachers head towards the local church. The pastor welcomes them all individually, providing each one with a book of hymns as they enter the cool, dark silence. The evening service has been especially organized for the new students. The pastor introduces the parable of the Good Samaritan, suggesting it as inspiration for how they might spend the coming year among new faces. It tells us what it means to care for others by not only focusing on oneself. We must value others more than ourselves. That is what the Bible teaches us. Any questions?

A boy of a different ethnicity rises his hand.

Unseen, the lead teacher seems to approve of the pastor's message and then tells the group that they are done here. Let's go outside, and enjoy the rest of the day.

The boy of a different ethnicity lowers his hand.

Trophies and the Crown Jewel

A group of boys acquired an old piano that they had purchased at the local recycling market. It cost 200 kroner and they carried it all the way from town to the school driveway. They hid it behind some bushes for a few days, not really knowing what they would do with it. They certainly couldn't carry it up the hill to the school in full view and didn't have the strength to get it to their second floor headquarters. They needed Kenneth, the new kid from Africa. The three friends took one end and Kenneth bore the brunt of the weight. Before long it was parked in the hallway. They knew they would soon be told to remove it so hatched a plan.

We didn't know what to do with it. It was so big. Much bigger than all this, says Søren, waving to a shelf in their common area which was full of pieces of splintered wood and metal. These are our trophies. One piece came from a guitar that we threw out the window. These were from two chairs, a stool and then some small things. But this one, Søren announces with pride, this one takes the cake. He picked up the shiny shard and brushed off the dust with the sleeve of his shirt. This is our crown jewel. It's from the piano. One day we had to listen to a teacher tell us how much he had done for us and how grateful we should be for everything: that we were educated and that the school was so famous. Then I suddenly knew what we were going to do with that piano. We threw it out the window. It made a fantastic explosion as the keys and strings hit the road. I thought the principal would kill us after that, that he would go totally crazy. But he didn't actually. He almost praised us. It was probably an elegant joke on his part. Very elegant, I must say. Something like that. But what could he say? After all, we didn't do anything we weren't *allowed* to. It's not written anywhere that you can't throw a piano out the window.

Heaven

It's tight in here. About two by three meters. Full of brushes, buckets, floor cloths, a vacuum cleaner, cleaning products. The boys from hallway 3 have lined the cupboard walls with silver paper and posters and set-up a computer. The rule is that everyone should be able to be here. There is no one who's *not* allowed to come in here. We should all be able to be here and it can be done. We've tried it. We were here almost the whole night.

Their secret spot was discovered by the night watchman the following day. Three of the boys were sent home for violating the rules.

It's actually strange, says Mathias. We're the only ones on our floor who are doing what the school says we should: we are interacting together across ethnic lines.

Sit down or Get Out!

In the assembly hall, students gather to listen to visiting students introducing programs at a nearby senior high school. From the window, a group of Greenlandic students start heading down the driveway towards the local convenience store. A teacher, noticing they are leaving the premises, gets up quickly, knocking her chair over in the rush to catch them.

Now this is enough. Fucking kids, she swears to herself. She strides out of the hall, slamming the door, runs down the corridors to the main door and shouts from the driveway: You four! Where do you think you are going?

The girls turn towards her.

This is an important meeting. Actually, we arrange these things in order to support your education. And then you just take off! This is about your future, you know! And it is mandatory. Now get yourselves back in there.

The girls remain standing, clinging to each other.

The teacher puts her hands on the shoulder of one of the girls as if to push her back towards the school.

They walk back, slowly.

By the time they return, there is nowhere to sit so they remain standing with their coats on.

Hey, move out of the way, yells a girl. We can't see anything! You're taking up too much space. Yes, says another. Sit down or get out!

The girls turn around and walk away once more.
At the end of the driveway, they stop, look around.
Then they head towards the local convenience store.

Invitation to Awareness

The Greenlandic students are Danish citizens with equal rights. The Greenlandic students are bilingual (Greenlandic-Danish). Their language skills might depend on family background and on their local origin. Many of the young people have only visited two or three places in Greenland and some have never been to Denmark before. Greenlanders are in general more modest, cautious and hesitant.[14]

Lunch

Those Greenlanders always cause trouble, you know.
   Yeah, always.
And the problems we face with those kids are different compared to other students.
   Yeah, you are right.
They have no watch in their body. Can't tell time. It starts there.
   No, you're right.
I am sick and tired of it.
My mother-in-law knows someone who once went up there.
   Really?
Yeah, she said there is just nothing up there. Just nothing.
   OK.
Yeah, it is like just one street out that goes out into nothing. No shops, just nothing.
   Yeah, I know. I was also very nervous when they started talking about a study-trip to Greenland. I would have refused to join. I don't know. Something about that place just makes me depressed in advance.
Yes. They're out of time. They don't have a watch in their body.
   Yes, you are right about that.

Downpipes

By 10 pm all the exterior doors are locked and the alarm is activated. No one can enter or leave the school without tripping the alarm.

Muhammad, Kalle and Andreas are regulars at a nightclub in the nearby town. They crawl down the drainage pipes at midnight and pile onto the teacher's bike. The town is about an hour if they can manage to steer the overburdened machine.

They usually get back home between 4 and 5 am, leaving the bike exactly where they found it. They crawl up the downpipes and get quickly into bed.

Charity

The Christian message is worth building on. I can only act on the basis of who I am. The young people get a solid foundation. A solid point from which they can find their own path. If nothing else, it gives them a humility towards their neighbours: sense of respect for other people. It asks that they give something of themselves to others. It is also part of the message of charity. It's also important that they get the opportunity to experience other religions: Judaism, Islam. In this way, it is a gift that there are so many nationalities here at the school. They get the opportunity to meet others. It means a great deal to them.

Exclusive Treatment

We cannot accept this kind of exclusive treatment in a culturally open school. David is disappointed that he is not treated with respect, that he does not feel safe among his classmates. It's because he's homosexual. They are all such tough boys. Then I asked him why he just doesn't pick one of the girls. I told him that I saw him holding hands with one of them and then he immediately became very defensive, trying to explain to me that this was just something they did spontaneously. Then I asked him: well, how can you say that you are so clear about your sexuality, if you make so much fuss about holding a girl's hand?

Educational Principles

Extract from an internal school paper on 'our educational approach':

> Open and willing attitude.
>
> To love, acknowledge and affirm the individual within the community, in teaching situations and alone.
>
> To help the student feel acknowledged and recognized socially, educationally, practically.
>
> To equip the student to engage in larger and larger communities: socially, educationally and practically.
>
> Insist that students grow and develop.
>
> To relate to the demands of the world in human and educational terms, and do so with confidence, empathy and persistence.
>
> To develop the student's ability to solve tasks constructively together.
>
> To help the student see the purpose of community in everyday life and to believe in the opportunities that community can bring.

Bloodhound

Jens knows exactly what it feels like to smoke twenty to thirty cigarettes a day. He had to stop. School-policy. At least they know him as the school bloodhound. He'll always pick up the scent and rarely loses it. He can smell the students who break the rules. Always. So far, twenty-five students have been caught smoking despite the ban. Tonight another four. Not bad. Half a packet confiscated, pressed into the silver cigarette box he inherited from his grandfather.

A High Academic Level

I often think that Jørgen just can't handle it, but then he comes through and shows that he's in control. Especially during the oral exams with the external examiners that come in from other schools to check the quality.[15] He knows very well how to produce a high professional level. He gives it full charm and a deep voice. The other examiners are always impressed. The principal is relieved and happy about the good grade average from the English exams. A high academic level is important.

More Than Friends

Tascha got a C for her oral exam which was based on a course text that was selected randomly on the morning of the exam. She got *The tree of knowledge*. Arhh, say the other girls knowingly. That was a good text to get. Yeah, but I got so nervous. That's because it's so hard to concentrate at this school. It's not a school at all. Henrik is not our teacher. He has become our friend. You can fool yourself with a teacher and pretend to know more than you do, but not with a friend.

Nikolaj

It is evening. Jimmy, the night watchman, has come to start his rounds but first sits down to play guitar. Students start to gather around him, including Nikolaj. Jimmy's play is good. He plays in a band. He offers the boys a few tips. Nikolaj moves on to the living room and joins a group of friends in the old sofa. He settles down and talks to Lars for a bit. Morten asks if he wants to play billiards. Yeah, why not. Trine, his girlfriend emerges from the photography studio. She begins to take pictures of him. Many pictures. When she is done, she kisses him and asks what time his exam is in the morning. Hell, I haven't checked. Nikolaj starts asking the group if they know the exam schedule. They don't. He then walks back to Jimmy who is still entertaining the boys in the main entrance area. He gets Jimmy to let him play for a bit and then stops to ask the boys if they know the schedule for tomorrow. Nobody does. Then, it's off to the sports hall where another group are playing indoor football. A short game and then it's time for bed. On the way out he is stopped by a couple of boys who are struggling with a physics book. They ask Nikolaj for help which he provides easily. Physics is a piece of cake. Do you know when to get up tomorrow? No, they answer, don't you know? I can't find the exam plan he says.

I'm damn disappointed with Nikolaj. That he isn't better prepared. That pisses me off. He doesn't care about everything I do for him. It's so clear when he doesn't even bother to turn up for the exam. He'll never get through senior high school. I just know, even though he doesn't. He'll have the same problem after school. In life. Personally, I don't give a damn about his anarchism. He's only destroying his own chances. He'll be bloody useless. I also tell him that he'll need to save for his own pension, because nothing comes from nothing. Nikolaj hasn't progressed at all in school. In fact, he's gone backwards. If it was up to me, he wouldn't be allowed to attend the next exam the day after tomorrow. This behaviour must have consequences. It's for their own sake. Otherwise, they never learn anything from it.

Willy, who is Nikolaj's physics teacher, worries that the principal views the low grades and non-shows as the teacher's fault. It is my responsibility that the natural sciences do not get better grades.

It's true that the exam results here are well below the national average, the school principal says. We're under pressure from the other schools. There's a lot more competition now. Everyone is feeling it. I feel it from the School Board. Our reputation is at stake. It's all about reputation.

Nicholas had overlooked the schedule. I totally messed that up, he says. I often forget that I go to school. But fuck it, that's not why I'm here, either. I wish they'd all just take it easy. School never used to be about exams and performance but that's all they care about now. If they throw me out, then so be it. I don't care. I'll be OK.

Higher Intelligence

We are at a crossroads. We've put down a line because we want to create another type of school. This semester we have expelled fourteen students. A number of others have chosen to leave the school voluntarily. Now we are rid of the ones we didn't want. What's left are students of higher intelligence and better social habitus. That's what we want. That way, they succeed. We succeed.

But how does that fit with the school's vision of being an inclusive and culturally open school?

Academic competence and cultural openness are linked. We need to find and focus on those students who have the skills and background to cope with such cultural meetings. The students we threw out just don't have it.

Star of Bethlehem

Teaching is very different here. You must be careful not to demonstrate that you have knowledge. Here, it's enough just to talk in groups. Do that, and they think you are active and clever. I have lots of knowledge that I got from home in Palestine. That just doesn't count here.

Echoes of a Dark Past

Danish identity politics has been intense since the late 1990s and especially after the 9/11 terrorist attacks. Immigration has been a particularly contested area, leading to a situation today where the major political parties are in agreement about the need to curtail new arrivals, especially of refugee groups that are viewed as unable and unwilling to adopt what is widely expressed as 'Danish values'. These 'values' gained international attention after the Danish Government, led by the ruling Venstre party, proposed to confiscate the jewellery and valuable belongings of newly arrived asylum seekers in order to defray the cost of accommodation and 'processing'. Critics spoke of a dark past.

World Understanding, According to a Teacher

A cultural meeting is a meeting in which your world understanding is challenged or collides with a view that is different to your own. As soon as two people meet, there is a cultural meeting. These meetings take place not only between Danes and others, for example in Africa or between a Pakistani and a Dane. The cultural meeting takes place when you get to the roundabout, turn right and meet the first person there. Then a cultural meeting takes place. It's everywhere. Here, up in the rooms, all over.

Pride and Pity

> You are a Greenlander when you help develop your country / You are a Greenlander when you speak your language / You are a Greenlander when you respect your parents / You are a Greenlander when you are an alcoholic / You are

a Greenlander when you beat your partner / You are a Greenlander when you abuse children / You are a Greenlander when you have been neglected as a child / You are a Greenlander when you have self-pity.[16]

Under the Milky Way

At home in Greenland we help each other a lot.
Teachers have no heart here.
If we say we're sick, we need to come to class anyway.
When we are sick, the teachers never come and ask how we are.
If we say we feel alone here, they just ask us to have positive thoughts.
But it's not about that. It is not a matter of negative or positive thinking.
Everything we do is wrong. Our language. Our appearance. If we chose to be together.
See this picture. It was taken when we arrived. Look how slim we were. And we were so happy.
I miss Greenland. We are 4,000 kilometres away from home.
    When I was preparing to leave to come to Denmark, I went inland and kissed the ice.
        I hope it doesn't melt.
                Greenland is so beautiful.
                        The Milky Way. See my pictures.
            Qivitoq,[17] she mumbles . . . .

War

Muhammad grew up in Denmark to Kurdish refugee parents. He has always had friends. Lots of friends, not least among the Danes. I always hung out with them, but now I tend to hang with the other students, the ethnic ones. Danes are OK. I'm not excluded that's for sure. But when someone is killed in Iraq, like a Danish soldier, then the Danish students always tell us that it's our fault. You killed our soldiers! But the Danes are OK. I like the Danes. I have no problems with them. They are OK. I haven't experienced racism or anything like that. Not me.

On the Wind

Social sciences classes are an unusual combination of theory, history and contemporary events, laced with opinion and common sense. In these early weeks, Peter is introducing Danish electoral history, part of the master narrative of Danish democracy. This is his first year as a qualified teacher and his enthusiasm is clear for the students who enjoy watching him bathe in this sacred material.

He starts with the defeat of nineteenth-century militarism and continues seamlessly into the early worker movements and the unique system of Danish cooperatives. People's enlightenment, public education and the high school movement follow. Then comes the individual: personal development, self-realization, critical consciousness, competences and of course life-long learning and eternal happiness.

As he transferred celebratory word after word onto the board, the students noticed movement. It seemed as if the board was coming loose from the wall but no, it was the words themselves that were on the move. Slowly but surely, the chalk lost its grip and the letters began to slip softly downward before regrouping mid-air. Too important to remain trapped in this small space, having mobilized in correct formation – one that only this chosen tribe from the cold north could fully appreciate – the words began to float towards the open window, picking up speed as they spread across the city and onward to the darker corners of the globe.

FOREIGNERS, PLEASE DON'T LEAVE US ALONE WITH THE DANES!

Figure 5.2 Poster entitled 'Foreigners, please don't leave us alone with the Danes'.

During 2002 this poster appeared on the streets of Copenhagen as a comment on the increasingly harsh public debate surrounding immigration and Government policies of integration.[18]

Culture Course

Last time we reached the Enlightenment, right? The teacher asks in class. Half of the students have come to class, the rest drift in during the opening minutes. Two girls answer. They are the only ones with their folders, books and pencils ready for teaching.

Well, today it's the French Revolution, he adds.

But we have nothing in the materials about that, say the two girls.

No, says the teacher. So go in groups, get on to the internet and see what you can find out. What was the French Revolution all about. If there are words and concepts you don't understand, look them up. For example, autocracy. Find out who Rousseau and Voltaire were. Make a poster that illustrates what the French Revolution is all about.

Grumbling, the students move on to the computer room, form small groups and start surfing the web: Facebook, social media sites, fashion.

Did you know that Nikolaj and Trine have become boyfriend and girlfriend? God... no, I didn't know. She's pretty crazy about him. I can't understand that. He's not my type. Well, let's get started, OK?

They focus on Wikipedia. Socialism, liberalism. Next come lots of printing, cutting and pasting. Pictures of Voltaire and Rousseau.

Cut them out so it looks like they are the ones talking.

An Examiner Calls

There are final exams in physics. The results are not good. Management is keeping a close eye on how things are going. The physics teacher is under pressure. I'm doing better, says Ole the math teacher. The deputy principal has been satisfied.

Anders leaves the exam room. He got an E. The minimum pass. I'm damn happy. Anders gets a D, Mikael an F. Johannes manages a C. Louise got an A. The deputy principal comes by at the moment she is announcing her grade. He listens with pride but then hears the others celebrating their mediocrity. Well, it's whimsical. The average we're picking up here just doesn't work. We can't live with that. I don't understand it. Why are they so happy? There must be a reason for that. We have to find it. We can't live with this. This is our face to the outside. The external examiner is an older experienced teacher from the nearby town. From a private school. A *real* school.

The grades are something else here, that's for sure, but you have different material to work with, he whispers. Waiving the external examiner away, Ole turns and says:

Arhhh! He has such a damn bad breath.

Integration

All the students talk wildly that they would like more integration. They call for initiatives for integration. But it's hollow. When it comes down to it, they wouldn't support it. That's basically why they're here, there are *no* immigrants. If it was so important to them, they could just pick another high school, says one teacher.

Let's Shake on It

In December 2018, the Danish Parliament passed the government's new Law on Citizenship by Naturalization. It was the 100th piece of legislation related to immigration and integration since the government was formed in 2015. Now, it would be a legal requirement that naturalized Danish citizens *physically* shake the hand of the official charged with issuing the certificate of membership to the world's oldest monarchy. Apparently, skin-to-skin contact is an essential part of what is meant by 'Danishness'. A few years earlier, many local councils insisted that kindergartens serve pork to all children, knowing that many come from Muslim communities.

In March 2020, all Citizenship by Naturalization ceremonies were halted because of the fast-spreading Covid-19. Until further notice, no one would (or *could*) become Danish. The Law, apparently intended to strength integration efforts, now inconvenienced (and embarrassed) the entire Kingdom.

Totally Relaxed

It's a totally wild, relaxed environment here. It's absolutely crazy cool.

With clothing, it's not a matter of branding, not at all. Actually, you have to wear plain clothes. The best are those from the second-hand shops. 1950s and 1960s. Relaxed style but elegant.

You can buy that stuff in the second-hand stores or, if you're lucky, get it from your mother or aunt. Lots of them had this style. My grandmother gave me a mega-nice blouse with dots and ruffles. Just totally relaxed.

She poses in front of a glass door, admiring the reflection. Loosening and tightening here and there. All very relaxed.

Information Letter to Students and Parents

Class study trips are approaching and that means a global outlook for the students. As a farm boy from Funen, I still remember my own study trip as a very, very great experience. Warsaw will always stand as the first metropolis I visited. A visit that gave me insight into completely different ways of living and, in 1986, a trip that gave me insight into what was going on behind the Iron Curtain.

This year, our student trips go to Paris, New York, Dublin, Lisbon, Florence, Iceland, Krakow, Sicily, Sarajevo, Rome, Marrakesh and Malta. Great programs are organized.

Our ambition to provide a global outlook should not be blurred by well-known Danish alcohol habits, so the rule is that students can only enjoy alcohol at the closing dinner. No one will be hurt by being reminded about this and I ask parents to reinforce the message as they say their farewells.

High Expectations

I'm really happy with this. It's really good. You really made something out of it. You are good for long sentences, but you need to be able to control them as well. That is really good. The cut is a C this time. We shouldn't display this work but, on the other hand, it's good to know for the exam. Remember Bloom's taxonomy? If you want to get to the highest level, you must reflect and relate to something. Be critical of the text. You just have to rise above what you are working on if you want to reach the highest levels. But as I said, I am very satisfied. You have done well. It creates high expectations.

They Should Study Political Science at Copenhagen University

They're on the bench in the sun. Massaging each other, messing around in each other's hair, hugging cheek to cheek. School is over. Exams done.

The girls from 3.G. A very hard core of students who worked purposefully to score the absolute highest marks. They explained that an average below B would be a problem. They are ambitious, and need to be, if they are to reach their dream education. I did OK says Ellen. B+ offers Marie, but it doesn't matter. I'm not really going to use it for anything. I want to be a transportation engineer. That's easier to get into. A says another. There's a B+ and another A-.

Marie has competed with Ellen throughout high school. Competitor-friends. How have you been, I ask Ellen? She leans forward a little, opening up for the first time in weeks. I'm starting political science at Copenhagen this autumn.

Figure 5.3 Students enjoying the sunshine.

The girls around her shrink into silence. Nobody knew what she wanted to study and that program is really selective. She kept her dream to herself and no one dared to ask. Well done I say. The others smile quietly.

Janne, Afghanistan and Top Level Social Science

I'll finish tomorrow, says Janne. It's the last subject.

Don't think you have time to sit here, says Ellen.

Janne looks at her. Says nothing.

Well, it doesn't mean as much to me as it does to you, voice cracking a little.

She gasps quietly. I don't have such high ambitions. Not anymore. I did once but dropped it. I just didn't want to spend that much time studying.

Oh yeah, Ellen. It's not just about time.

Well no. But.

Janne says that she wants to do her military service. She casts a quick glance at Ellen to gauge her reaction. I've always been attracted to the military and police. You learn a lot from being in the military. It really develops you.

Ellen looks at her sharply, no need for words.

Who, you? Liva chips in.

Camilla adds that to join the military means saying yes to war.

That's not why I want to join the military, Janne says. It is absolutely awful what is happening in Afghanistan, with all those killed. I think it's unreal when you watch it on TV. Especially when they come home in coffins. But I want to defend democracy. The Danish democracy. My mother and her boyfriend wanted to start fresh so they went to Bolivia and became international development workers, serving democracy and everything like that. So I've been really used to thinking about democracy.

Liva has been staring at Janne obliquely throughout the discussion. The mood is turning sour.

Figure 5.4 Bumper sticker 'Support our soldiers'.

Silence.
Liva pushes: Can we then agree that it's hugely political?
No. It's not so political.
Haven't you just had A-level Social Studies? For three years?
Well, yes.
Isn't your final exam in Social Studies tomorrow? At A level? I'm just asking?
Liva gets up and the other girls follow.
Not Janne. She stays seated.
Support our soldiers.[19]

Our Leaders Speak

We sent more soldiers in proportion to our size than most others – and we did so without the 'caveats' many of our allies insisted upon. We did not say no to certain types of operations, nor did we say no to being in the most dangerous places, as many European allies did. In this way, we were the 'good example' that Americans and Britons – who drew the heavy burden – could put forward to the hesitant: 'When Danes can, you can at least try!'[20]

Our Leaders Speak, Again

'Denmark has to cast off its small state mentality.'[21]

Pity

I feel sorry for them. All of them. The girls have completely turned this game into a ruthless competition that they can't control. And they've become its victims.

We have many with eating disorders, stress, depression. Self-harm, cutting. The surface is impressive but don't scratch it. We shouldn't talk about all this. It doesn't look good. The same applies to the boys although they react differently. They drink their brains out. And not just on weekends. Most will drink and get drunk a few times during the week. Yes, we have a lot of issues with cannabis and alcohol, says another teacher. What would you do in their place?

Dentist

That's at least what I say. Only something I say. I want to be a dentist.
I can hear the sound when the word leaves my mouth.
Dentist.
It sounds quite convincing when I say it.
Hold it a bit with my tongue.
Dentist.
Then I smile to show my teeth.
When family and relatives ask what I want to study, I always say that I want to be a dentist.
Dentist.
But it's not true. I would really just like to be a schoolteacher for small children. Not more. Just to spend time with children all day.
Mother? PhD from Oxford. She's the head of a big research unit in the pharmaceutical industry.
Dad? PhD from Oxford, biochemistry.
No space for dreams where I come from.

Hygge

Hygge – or cosiness – is the most Danish of Danish norms. Deployed with charm, far from harmless:

> hands cupping warm mugs; bicycles leaning against walls; sheepskin rugs thrown over chairs; candles and bonfires; summer picnics; trays of fresh-baked buns. To look at them is to long for that life, that warmth, that peace, that stability – for that idealised, Instagrammable Denmark of the imagination.
>
> To Danes, nothing could be less political than hygge – since talking about controversial subjects is by definition not hygge – and yet it is clear that the concept lends itself to political use. Davidsen-Nielsen and Jensen told me that the prime minister, Lars Løkke Rasmussen, was hyggelig – the kind of guy you

could imagine having a beer with. 'He's folksy and informal. He's one of the guys. And he gets away with murder – almost', said Davidsen-Nielsen. 'Hygge is a useful strategy for disguising power. Politically, you can cloak quite aggressive or radical acts with an impression of hygge. Hygge says, let's forget about everything. Let's block out the world and have some candy'.[22]

PP

Short for princesses of performance.

That's what they call us. In the media, in research-reports, everyone seems completely obsessed by that term. Princesses of performance.

What a thing to say. It's derogatory, right? As if we enjoy being trapped in this stuff? A race towards what? Top five, top three, number one? They force us into hurting ourselves just to meet their demands. It's not just snobbery or elitism.

It's something much worse.

      And it's insulting.

            Princesses of performance?

                  Go f**k yourselves.

Lots of Different People

Why did you choose this school, I ask?

Because it's a place with lots of very different types of students.

Different?

Yes, we are completely different. Many different types. It is awesome. It's amazing.

How different?

With style and stuff.

But you all seem very similar. You all like retro fashion for example.

Yes, but it is also totally casual and relaxed here, not at all like other schools which are full of hype. That's what everyone loves about this place.

OK, but maybe not in terms of different ethnic origins?

Well no. That's also very annoying. The student council and the school had tried to attract people from different ethnic backgrounds other than ethnic Danish. We really want to have some with head scarves. They are hugely welcome.

Democracy and Democracy

This is the profile of the school. Democracy. There is democracy in everyday life, students are involved in planning, in teaching, in activities and in the many clubs we have. The student councils are also heard by the school board and staff council. And there is, as you probably know, enormous competition to get accepted to this school. It's crazy.

With all the competition you could even say that democracy becomes a competition. Haha. Who can be more democratic! Having said all that, we're not allowed to be too critical of the school. I mean what does democracy mean when we can't question the focus on competition and success and we can't get the school to provide more places for non-ethnic Danes? In a school that focuses on global citizenship? So, there's democracy and democracy, I guess.

End of the Line

They spill out of the graduation ceremony and it's all over. Hundreds of new people ready to venture off, open to the world. Some will go far, others barely beyond graduation day, falling at the first hurdle. Fate unkind.

Hope, joy and exhaustion on every face. Funny, one says: we talk about the Danish school system as being about learning for life but most of us think life starts when this ends!

The girls graduate in white dresses. Not one, but a multitude of styles. Yes, some are hand-me-downs from home. Casual, well-chosen, fashion. The boys wear black ties. Maybe the last time they'll *ever* wear a tie. They all wear the distinctive cap of the 'student': one who has completed high school. Before the era of mass education that really stood for something. White cloth with scarlet red band and shiny black peak. In our time, it is possible to have these caps personalized with the student's name embroidered on the rear and a wide choice of cap badges for the front. The classic insignia is the 'Dannebrog' cross but it's now possible to order a cap with the star of David, Muslim half-moon and star, communist hammer and sickle, heart, atom and, even, marijuana leaf. The personalized uniform: quintessentially Danish.

Much kissing and hugging. Young people together, parents and teachers blending joy with relief. Crying and laughing. Some are already miles away. I got accepted to Cambridge says Alex so now I'm just waiting. I still hope for military service says Janne. I'm taking a year to travel to South America says Eric. I'm taking a year off to drink says Emil, with beer in hand.

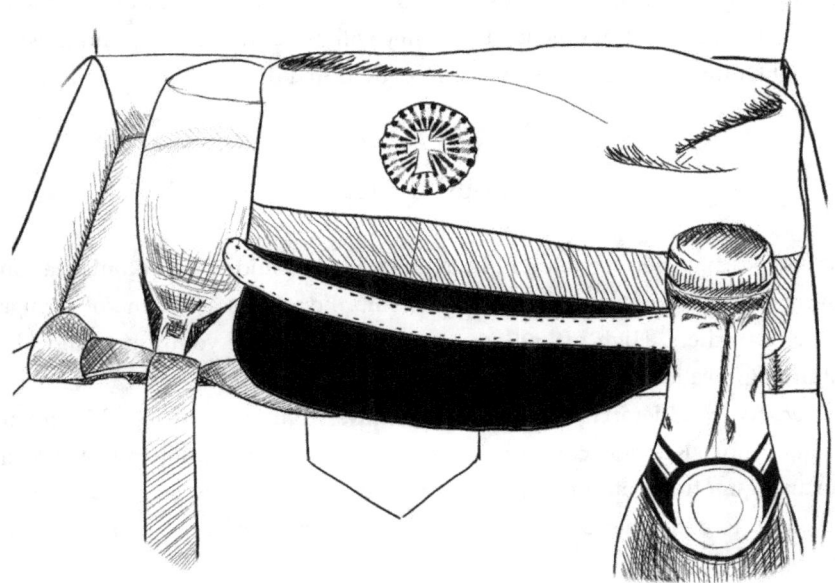

Figure 5.5 High school graduation cap and champagne.

Figure 5.6 High school party bus.

As is tradition, the class climbs aboard a refitted truck hired for the day and tasked to drive them door to door to each other's homes for a quick refreshment. The truck is remade in bright decorations and slogans, music blaring from a portable sound system. As is also tradition, passers-by will shout

out congratulations. Cars will sound their horns, sharing the joy as this rite of passage is passed to a new generation. They will drive all afternoon and most of the night, only pausing to greet the sun on their first day.

'South Korea'

Stereotypes: high performance, PISA, remarkable transition from colonialization, poverty, 'underdevelopment' and dictatorship. Education as engine of change, model for others. High technology, connectivity, mobile youth, pop and film culture. Innovation, entrepreneurship, diversity. Future.

Stereotypes: hierarchy, obedience, family, honour, status, achievement through effort. Religion, conservatism, cram schools, education industry. Hell. Nurturing mothers, absent fathers, stress, anxiety, suicide, waste. Docile youth served up to authoritarian society. Low crime, public order ↔ private despair. Business friendly.

Between heaven and hell: viewed abroad with admiration by policy makers, scepticism by teachers and researchers, hesitation by parents. Is this what we want for our children? Should we listen, respond, catch-up? Where are they going?

*

Welcome, Be Still and Attentive

Mr Yan enters the stage. The teachers and students bow towards their headmaster who returns the gesture. In the back rows, parents raise themselves. Lacking the timing and symmetry of the others, they do their best to indicate deference and gratitude. Most students stand upright. Others are bent and half-hearted.

Welcome, be still and attentive. This year we have received 416 new students. You should try your utmost to be successful, to become future leaders in a global world. You should be proud of your country. Korea is world famous.

We were among the top 10 best schools out of the PISA ranking of 135 schools. We succeeded although some come from poor families.

Our aim is to become a self-governing private high school. That would enable us to send even more students to high-ranking universities.

Index finger pointing up, merging with the bright lights of the auditorium.	Next year, we want to send two more students to our parent university. Someday, this school may be able to send a student, maybe more, to Seoul University: number one in the world.
	I can see that you already improved your uniforms, as I instructed. I am very happy about that. You should be here on time, you should wear your uniform according to the regulations. The length of the girls' skirts must never be above the knees. Boys are not allowed to wear long hair. Remember that! Be good to each other, keep the school clean, listen to your teachers. You are students of one of the best schools in this country. Be proud, have self-confidence. We want to make you leaders of this country. Trust in us.
Spotting two girls as he prepares to leave the stage.	You two! You need to go to the hairdresser immediately. Your hair is too long. Your coats are too short and the colours are too bright. You are not allowed to have long shoelaces. No bright colours.

Something I Heard

I have heard that in the West, university is a place for intellectuals and scientific development.

    I have heard that in the West young people can travel the world, if they want.

        I have heard that in the West, you admire our schools and results.

      I have heard that in the West you have individualism.

        How does that feel?

What Can I Say?

I turn eighteen on Monday, and then I get my identity card. Then I am considered – what can I say . . . a citizen? But it doesn't matter. We belong to the school or our parents as long as we study. No, all of our lives. This is how it is in Korea. It's not good to be here for young people. I'm exhausted. The school is a prison, the country is a prison. I'm angry, I have so much anger in my heart, but I don't know what to do with it. I want to travel to another country. I want to go to Australia. I want to study in Australia and live there and be happy. I want to live in another country and be happy. Many people say that Korea is an amazing country. But I'm exhausted.

Figure 5.7 School entrance, early morning, Seoul.

The only thing it is about is getting to university. The best university. It's like a gun going off in my head all the time. A university, the university, my university.

I have to get away, but I don't know how.

The West, the World and the University

I have heard that in the West young people can **travel**. Travel around the world if they want. That would be amazing. **Talking** to other people and learning. But here in Korea, it's all about the university. It's all about our **lives**. Everyone is talking about university, only university. It makes me **angry**. The university is a place where people need to grow and learn ... not a place for money and careers. Isn't that what you say about studying in the West? Here, universities **steal** our lives. I **hate** my life. Young people in Korea have **no horizons.** The only thing they are allowed to see is the university. There are no horizons here. No one can see anything – beyond the school. **Just darkness.**

> **It's awful.** I have to do something.

Interview with Ann

Ann said her parents did all they could to support their children's education. That's what we do in Korea. The family supports their children and then the children support their families. My parents had the dream to make us fluent in English. That's why we moved to America. We stayed there for ten years and now we're back. Most of us anyway. My sister stayed. Now it's time for me to start university. We planned a career for me as an English interpreter. Then I can easily support my parents when they get old.

So your favourite subject is English?

With a warm, gentle smile she explains: you people, your thing is individuality, needs, rights. So much, that you do not see our culture. Of course, English is not my favourite subject, but that is not important. I need a profession where I can earn enough to support my family. That is more important than any subject.

Five to Six Hours

7 am:	Tutorials in classrooms.
8 am– 4 pm:	Teaching at the school.
4 pm–5 pm:	After-school program and extra teaching.
5.30 pm:	Dinner.
6 pm–10 pm:	Private tuition.
10 pm–10.30 pm:	Pause and TV.
10.30 pm–12 pm:	Private study or extra tuition with private teacher.

Jin says: We get between five and six hours of sleep . . . we get tired. Young people in Korea are very tired.

Comparative Education

There is such a big difference in the classroom in Korea and Australia. In Korea, no one can be free in class. This is because teachers are always right and students are afraid to say anything wrong. It's just best not to say anything. I once asked the teacher in class about something I didn't understand. Afterwards, one of my friends asked me why I had done that. I said it was because there was something I didn't know. But that's not how it works here. The students visit the teachers individually after the class. Don't interrupt the teaching with personal questions. It's different in Australia.

From a Castle in the Air

The teacher reads from an English textbook as she walks around the class, laughing shrilly into a portable microphone.

Knowing what you want and choosing the path that can lead you to the goal will help you make the right choices. Instead of pursuing many goals at once, focus on planning your future. You need to gather the seeds that can create the garden for the dreams you would like to blossom. What does value mean?

The teacher looks around the classroom. No one answers. One student is asleep, leaning slightly to the side, being pushed upright by the student to his left. Another lies with his head in his arms across the table. Sleeping. No one answers.	Imagine that? What does it mean? It's like . . . imagining yourself.
	OK. We move on. One way to connect with what you value in life is to dream for a minute. Imagine yourself in the most perfect role you can imagine. What do you want to be? Photographer? PhD? Want to be the head of a large company?
No one answers. She presents them with a ranking of the 500 most successful companies in the world: Toyota, General Motors, ING Group. Another five pupils have now fallen asleep. They lie with their heads on the table, not even trying to hide their exhaustion.	In the first place is the United States, then Japan, then France, then Germany. England, China . . . and in the seventh place, who do you think we have there?
No one answers.	
	Yes, you are right, Korea! That is exactly right. Korea is in the seventh spot. You must be proud of your country.
She walks over to a couple of the sleeping boys and puts her arm on their shoulder. They straighten up.	You must have unlimited confidence and self-esteem because of your country. OK. We continue. It's important that you build your own air castles, whatever they may be, and work to make them a reality. A Spanish saying goes: If you don't build castles in the air, you can't build castles anywhere.
A boy sleeps. Loudly.	Get up! You have to get up until you are awake.
The boy gets up.	What does it mean – to build castles in the air? What does it mean?
No one answers.	It is not possible to do that, but a Spanish proverb says that we must do it. We must dream, even if it is only dreams in the air, because otherwise we have no dreams at all. Strive. What does it mean?
No one answers.	You must strive to make your dreams come true! You, are you sleeping?

He looks up, shakes his head slightly.

How can we define success? Success depends on yourself, whether you can fulfil it in life the way you want to. So air castles are actually a good thing, but if you want them to last, you have to form a basis for them. Give them a foundation. Otherwise, they disappear.

The lesson ends with a little competition and, as something quite unusual, the teacher has offered a prize to those who can solve the task first. When they have the right answer, they must call her cell phone number. The class is awake now, struggling to solve the task. Some cheat by looking at the textbook under the table. A group calls her to provide the correct answer. Three young men cheer their winnings from an undisclosed castle in the air.

Virtue, Stupid Children and Pop Stars

What is the opposite of a man of virtue? My, how stupid you are! It hurts me every time. I have to explain this over and over again, as if you are hearing it for the first time. It's annoying. Do you realize that? Only wise men know the innermost nature of nature. No one, except wise men can rule a country. Only wise men can, because they have virtue. Only wise men can judge, and only wise men know on what basis to judge people. The perfect virtue is not about ruling and leading people. Confucius said it was about loving the people. It's like with pop stars that everyone loves and screams for. If a man rules a land with virtue and love, the people will automatically follow him, just as girls follow their pop idols.

When the Heart Beats

It's so great to play football, says Kim.
They have played a little on the field in the recess.
Although only ten minutes. It clears the brain.
And if you just feel your heart rate, your heart beating, it helps with stress.
It's so great to do it with my friends.

Exhaustion

Years ago, a boy at the school asked the teacher if he could go home a little early because he was so exhausted after many days of study and too little sleep.

Quite exceptionally and very remarkably, the teacher allowed him. The boy committed suicide and subsequently the teacher was fired. Particularly during the stressful periods around the exams, teachers address the problem of suicide and emphasize that it is wrong to do so, an unacceptable act that merely indicates that students are mentally weak and unable to resist the pressure.

Do you talk to your parents about this?

As we have already told you, we have very little time with our parents. When we get home, we are exhausted after a long day of hard work, so we don't really talk. We don't have time to talk to them. It just goes over our heads. It is important for you to know that we get home well past 10 pm. We are exhausted and so are our parents. Exhausted . . . there is just no energy left.

The Invisible Majority

There are many in the class who keep to themselves. They have no friends. They don't talk to anyone. They eat breakfast alone and sit alone during the breaks. I don't think they have any contact with anyone. I don't think they talk to anyone at all. I just think they fall asleep. They have no one to talk to. They are very introverted. Young people in Korea are very introverted, says Grace.

Mowgli

The teacher is wearing a white shirt with silver embroidered sleeves. And a shiny tie. He is different. Instead of the official bowed greeting, he has introduced clapping and students start as soon as he enters the classroom. He talks about socio-cultural phenomena and how to understand society in a micro and macro perspective. If a boy runs away from home and we look at it in a micro perspective, we may see that there are problems with his family, perhaps that they do not understand him. But if we look at it from a macro perspective, it might be because he has bad grades. Or because of the structure of society.

Is there anyone who can live alone in the community? Can you do that? Do you know any examples?

No one answers.

Mowgli, he says! He is the only one who has been able to live entirely for himself.

The students laugh and the teacher continues: Can any of you tell me how much you love me?

They laugh even louder. One raises a hand.

OK, you there, asks the pop star teacher.

As much as I love my mother, shouts the boy!

No you don't! You can't say that when you're seventeen years old. He imitates the boy: As much as I love my mother!

Wild laughter.

Are there others who want to share their love for me?

A boy gets up and draws a heart in the air with his arms.

Yes, says the pop star, that is much better!

The whole class erupts.

The Pencil Case

Filled to the brim with colours, erasers, clips, rulers, pencils. All sorts of colours. A teddy bear hangs on a ring at one end.

Teacher: On Why They Sleep

Why do you think that they sleep so much during class?
I guess *you* think it's because they're tired?
They sleep because they *are* tired.
Sure, they *have* to sleep.
But it's not just that.
Not just about being tired.
It's more about trying to stay alive.
That's what they think of when they fall asleep in class.
In the end, they simply need to sleep to keep it out. The darkness. The nothing. Those who don't sleep are the ones who'll break down sooner or later. These are the choices.

Escape Route

During a regular consultation meeting with parents in the Spring of the 2008–9 academic year, the school had no choice but to acknowledge a higher degree of absenteeism than was normal or acceptable. At least in the senior classes. This brought to a head a long-running tension between the leadership and the parents association. Apparently, students from the school were seen walking around, dancing even, in the Wangsimni shopping complex each Tuesday and

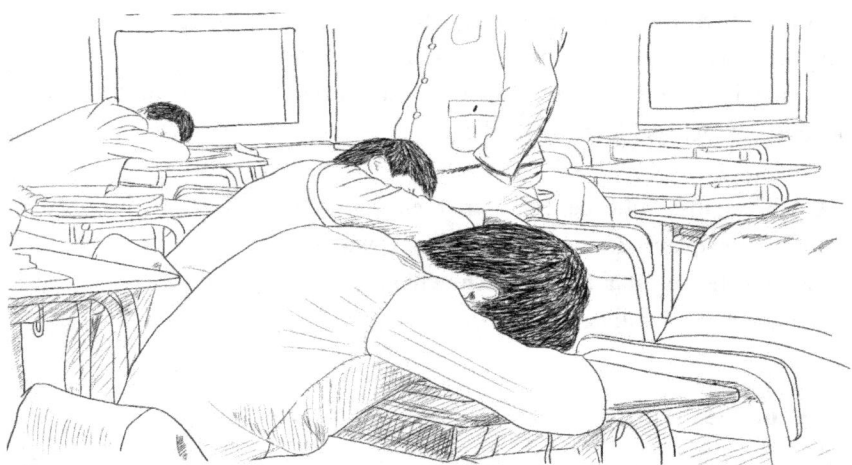

Figure 5.8 Students sleeping in class.

Thursday morning. A number of shop owners had called the school to report the irregularity. Initially, Deputy Principal Kim took note and then went past the senior classrooms to check the roll. Everything seemed to be in order. The same phenomena were reported the following week, this time by the manager of Global Connections Café who rang to say that four students from the school were outside the premises, splashing around in the rock pool. In full uniform! Three boys and a girl. When he confronted the students, they just laughed and disappeared under the artificial waterfall. Mall security was called out, but by then the students were gone. Manager Choi said they were not rude or disrespectful, but 'seemed deaf'. The unauthorized absences continued, usually within the Wangsimni shopping complex and almost always at the same time each week. Principal Yan was at a loss to find the culprits. Things were complicated when teachers began taking the roll at each class but the reports continued. The most recent report was from a metro attendant at Sangwangsimni Station who rang the school to say six students had jumped the entry turnstile and entered the train without a ticket.

The situation – still inexplicable – boiled over when radio station KBS 1FM ran a story about the delinquent students as part of a general report on the declining morality of urban youth. Principal Yan was understandably distraught. Teachers were tense. The parents were now demanding that the school introduce a total lockdown from 7.30 am to 5 pm. No one in, no one out during those hours. School Security Chief Yie had no problem with that and found himself, for once, on the side of the parents. All this, a mere three months before the final exams.

The first genuine crisis of principal Yan's tenure. He'd begun to contemplate retirement knowing that he was unlikely to survive if this didn't stop.

We have Korean History, Citizenship and Democracy on Tuesday mornings and three solid periods of English on Thursdays, says Lucy. I don't know why these periods are best, but they just are. May nodded agreement. Both seemed deadly serious. We often agree where to go, she says. As soon as the class starts we get up and leave. We go separate ways and meet up at the entrance to Wangsimni Subway station. Lots of students do it. On the left behind the bushes is a service door that's never locked. We get in there and then it's easy. You can nearly float the entire way down through the metro and up through the ventilation system into the shopping mall. There's a million service doors down there so we can come into the mall anywhere we like. Yes, adds May, and it's just as easy to slip out again. Usually, we meet in the basement next to the Roman Forum. It's this huge reproduction of ancient Rome where you can eat your food and ice creams. We like the style and feel of that place. It's another world and perfect for dreaming.

You don't get it, do you? Look, as soon, as class starts we lay our heads on the desks, dream of another place, and then go. The teachers never mind. Sure, they try to wake us up a few times but they are used to sleepers. After a while, they give up and it's basically a free morning anywhere in the world. When the bell goes again, it's a bit hard to be sucked back into this world but it's not long before the next class when we can live again.

My mum knows about it, says Mary. She says it's good to dream as it gives ambition and excitement. We just do it to stay alive.

During a Break

The break lasts ten minutes. Students count on the teachers taking a few minutes more to reach the class room. Down the main hallway in an empty room, eight boys have fallen asleep. Heads in arms, tables turn to matrasses. Another group gathers around Kim. He has removed the jacket of his school uniform. Under the pressed white shirt, behind the tie, emerges a black T-shirt emblazoned with the words 'Rock' in silver print. He loosens his pants and undoes the laces from his black shoes. Finally, a shock of thick black hair is roughed into something between fashion and moral danger. Korean pop music blares from a mobile phone. Much talk, laughter, rhythm and movement. Good times. The bell rings. Kim repairs his outfit and gets into character just as the teacher arrives. Silence meets suspicion. Sleeping boys wake without conviction. The student monitor and class leader shouts: Attention, bow! The students get up, pay their deference and sit. Break over.

Woman with Camera

A young woman is sitting in the subway. Rush hour. She's a student for sure. Bags, coat, scarf and a violin. Occasionally, fellow passengers swing over her as the train takes a tight curve through the underground. She doesn't mind. She sits with her camera, finding a small space where she can keep perfectly still in order to photograph herself. Images in different profiles as the shadows change the light. She examines them briefly, discards most. Another one, this time from above while she looks away. That's a keeper!

Adjectives, Ramen and a Life at the Hotel

What kind of life do you want to live? A life of ramen and **poverty** or a hotel life? Let's do our best today and see if we can't prepare for a hotel life. Let's become **heroes in our own lives**. Let's think a little ahead and deal with the difficulties now, so that in two years you will be at university. Look, adjectives are highly developed in Korea. There are for example forty meanings of red but only two meanings in English. That's why Korean writers can't get the **Nobel Prize**. It is because of the adjectives. It is difficult to translate all these feelings. Now don't sleep, you **shame** your country, **Korea**, if you sleep. There are 500,000 lexis for English and only 200,000 – or 250,000 of them are verbs. And only fourteen are interactive. It is very different in Korean. No, now you sleep again. **Wake up**.

What Was the Best Thing about School?

What was the best thing about school?	→	I don't know.
Well – anything you found interesting, good, exciting?	→	I don't know.
Well . . . anything you think of as *good* about school?	→	I don't know how I should answer!
		Am I the one to decide what is right to answer? It's very confusing to me.
Well . . . in this conversation it is up to you to judge, OK?	→	Alright.
What was the worst experience?	→	When they made me cut my hair.

Guests for Dinner

> How do you fancy eating your dinner at home in front of a webcam and letting thousands of people watch? If they like the way you eat, they will pay you money – maybe a few hundred dollars a night . . . a good salary for doing what you would do anyway. This is happening now in South Korea. Is it a kind of voyeurism, food porn, perhaps?[23]

Number 1

Korea is a busy society. We all want to reach the top. Everyone thinks that they are number one, or on their way to becoming number one. Also in my school. In my class. In my family. When I get good grades, I run to my mom to tell her: mom, mom, I've got good grades today! Then she'll say: You can still do much better. And when I get bad grades she'll say: Hmmm. I thought so.

The Best Time of the Day

A group of noisy boys runs between chairs and tables, some preparing for the next class, others at sleep over their desks. A boy puts a video on the screen. Showing a scene with a woman who, after having her breast cut off, eats her nipple, spreading blood all over her face while it drips from her mouth and chest. Cheering, the boys slap those who study and sleep. The glasses belonging to a sleeping boy fall on the floor. He picks them up, setting them safely aside in their container. Lunch break is the best time of the day, he says. Smiling, he puts his head between his arms to catch a few more minutes.

On the Road

From school direct to the private academy. Walking down the dirty lane, they rehearse their homework, play on their Gameboys, buy an ice cream, run after an abandoned ball, tease girls. Arm in arm, through the mall. Stopping to look at a window display. Onward to the evening study school and their parent's dreams. They won't be late.

Pythons and Pizza

We are the lucky ones.
We are from the technical high school.

Figure 5.9 Free time.

Expectations are not that high.

Parents still hope, but deep down they know we will not get to a good university.
    They also don't care. As long as we are happy and earn money.

I have a snake, says Kim. I like to spend time watching it when it eats. It's a python. It lives in a cage in our flat.

I work says Yang. I deliver pizza. I earn so much money that my parents can borrow from me.

Then they can pay the school-fee.

Parasite Director Bong Joon-ho: 'Korea seems glamorous, but the young are in despair'

> 'Korea, on the surface, seems like a very rich and glamorous country now, with K-pop, high-speed internet and IT technology', Bong says, 'but the relative wealth between rich and poor is widening. The younger generation, in particular, feels a lot of despair'. Just as there are people living in tents just around the corner from where we are in central London, so there are homeless people sleeping rough around Seoul's central station, he says. 'People who are in society's blind spots'.[24]

The Art of Flirting

A friend of mine attended an all-boys school, both in middle school and high school. When he came to university, he asked me how to get a girlfriend, how to flirt, how to be sweet and kind when on a date. Everything like that with girls. When he went to middle school and high school, he only studied. He never had the opportunity to meet girls. So when he got to university, he got into trouble with the girls when he finally met them. He didn't know what to do. It's not good. I'm actually glad there weren't boys in my class. That would have disturbed me quite a lot. I think I would have started using makeup and that would have affected my studies. That's also why they split the classes. So that attention is not taken away from the students' studies. At my school, we were only together in the breaks. But at my friend's school, it was a pure boys' school.

High Standards

She hoped he would text her. Their first date went well. He was not particularly good looking, but his hands and nails were clean and well kept. She liked that. At least a sign of standards of some sort. And then he was from Hanyang University. Not that bad, actually. Her mother had been teaching her carefully how to spot standards and would give advice on what men she should date. That was of course all part of the preparations for Seoul University, preparations that had lasted as long as she could remember.

Thinking of that time usually made her cry. It was sad, so very sad how things had turned out. All through her childhood they had been preparing for her to enter Seoul University. She had been studying hard, really hard, to get the marks that were required. Not only her, her mother had been busy organizing her schedule, making sure she had learned the curriculum, connecting her to proper friends. Her father had been working. He was seldom home. She would leave for school at 6 am, and would come home late at night at 11 pm. But she also liked it. That time was full of dreams. Dreams about the social networks she would be part of, what men she should date, what friends she would have, her appearance when she finally could leave the uniform behind her. She imagined herself going out with young people from influential families. Sometimes, when she got older and there was a break between tests at school, she would take the train just to go and look around at the campus of Seoul University. In the beginning, these trips where always together with her mother who would teach her the right attitude when walking around the campus. She had to look self-confident and busy. Not too busy, not scary but as someone who would have important things to do. Later she would travel there alone. As soon as she saw the place, it filled her with joy and excitement. Even now, thinking back on that time, hope and joy rose in her breast. It was everything.

She had done well through high school but her final exam grades fell enough to end her dream of Seoul University. Now she was enrolled at Hanyang, studying of all things, education. The subject was not that important for young women, at least not the women she knew. Had she gone to Seoul University she would have also studied education. The value of female teachers from Seoul is high. Everyone knows that. Seoul University just provides a bright future, high value. A life worth living. Men – young men with career jobs and prestige – would like a wife who earns some money, who can take holidays and who would have time to make sure their children get a good education. She would so much have liked to be such a woman: attractive, with high standards. It could have been me, she thought. It could have been me.

She would soon turn thirty and then things would be really serious. In that sense, she hoped that he would get back to her. But then again, a student from the local university, he would never, just never, be like the prestigious, high-ranking, people she might have known.

Her phone vibrates.

Earth's Weakest Animals

The birth rate in Korea is falling. This is because parents are afraid of how they can manage to pay for education for their children. Because it costs a lot of money. You have to pay a lot of money for your education. Up with your heads! Do you know which animals are the strongest on the planet?

Students answer: Bear! Tiger! Lion! Rhino!

It's the elephant, the teacher says, hardly registering their responses. However, the mammoth was stronger and larger than the elephant. It was just hard for prehistoric man to catch the mammoth. Is man strong or weak? No one answers.

If we now look at a cow or a zebra, their offspring are born with open eyes. After an hour or two, they are able to walk by themselves. They are very strong. Humans take two or three years before they can walk. Man is not very strong. Up with your heads!

If you know the answer to the question I ask, I'll give you an extra point. I did that for the first grade and there were many who got points. They are much wiser than you. So listen now. In the Choson Dynasty, when one's parents died, one had to live close to the grave for three years. Sometimes even more than three years. Do you know why?

One boy: Well, it's a long time. How could they survive there if they had to live in a place where there was no food to be found?

It is Confucianism, the teacher replies. You have to look after your parents because they have taken care of you. It says in the doctrines. Up with your heads!

We are very weak because we have to look after ourselves for the first three years. However, if we look at Korean history, we can see that man evolved to become strong, intelligent and social. Now you get points again if you can answer correctly. Prehistoric man built his own houses. Was it because they were intelligent?

Two boys answer as one: Yes!

The teacher points to one: You get a point.

A boy stands up.

Teacher: what do you want?

The boy: I answered yes, too. And that was right. Why don't I get points?

Because the other boy answered faster than you did. And now you need to sit down!

South Korea's Obsession with Top Marks Is Costing Its Youth

Susan Cheong's days were 'literally jam-packed':

> I woke up at 6:30 every morning to get to school by 8:00am. Quiet reading or self-studying was for an hour, and then classes began at 9:00am. School clocked off at 4:00pm, and I had just enough time to duck home for dinner before I was off again to Hagwon, a private tuition college, commonly known as cram schools. I took Korean, science, maths and art classes three to four days a week. Fortunately, I didn't have to take English classes like the others. The proverbial expression 'practise makes perfect' was ingrained in us, and for each subject, we went through textbook after textbook, going through questions over and over again. We had school homework almost every day and failure to complete meant you were punished in whatever way the subject teacher preferred. Our maths teacher made us come to school an hour early at 7 am to sweep the corridors

and classrooms. Our science teacher made the boys do push-ups on the ground with their feet propped up high against the narrow chalkboard holder, while the girls had to squat 40 times holding their ears. Occasionally the teacher got out the broomstick and whacked us on our bottom.

Corporal punishment has since been banned in South Korea but the gruelling regime of education, pressure to succeed and social conformity continues. Education, youth suicide and low fertility rates shape youth culture in South Korea at least as much as K-pop, high technology and art house film.[25]

Plea from a Principal

> So many diplomas but no true education; this is our reality. As a result, our education is producing only mentally deformed and handicapped members of society who would risk their life to get one more point in a test and smile at the unhappiness of others, annealed only in the competition for competition's sake.[26]

Families That Stick Together

In the short period from 2000 to 2003 more than 1,000 students aged between ten and nineteen committed suicide. This phenomena affects families as well. In 2005, a father was 'so distressed over his son's bad grades that he torched himself, his wife, and their daughter outside his son's school in shame'.[27]

In My Day

Principal Yan always does the rounds just after 9 am. Today he stops outside the Chemistry lab. The windows to the main corridor make it ideal for checking on punctuality, class attitude and teacher enthusiasm. Mrs Lu is scolding two boys in the second row. Her tone is harsh and uncompromising. These two scoundrels are seconds away from extra work, detention and, perhaps, a visit to the deputy's office. The smallest of smiles slips through Principal Yan's defences. He steps back a little, leaving Mrs Lu's courtroom before she passes sentence on the boys. Walking on, Principal Yan drifts back in time some forty years to his own science lab in a far way provincial town. Hmm, he mutters to his past self. It was a different Korea back then. It was the beatings, fear and feelings of inadequacy that he remembered most. Military service afterwards was a piece of cake. He was destined for this job. Not without resentment, he recites the proposition that has carried him through the years: this generation have no idea just how important a good education can be.

A Western Disease?

Does all of this say more about the interests and concerns of two Northern European scholars who have swallowed the 'dominant image of East Asian exam hell' as a place 'devoid of joy and deep learning'? Like other Western visitors, are we stuck in a narrative of 'scandalisation or caricature'?[28] Is 'Education Fever'[29] *our* disease, not theirs?

Obama Says

> Let's also remember that after parents, the biggest impact on a child's success comes from the man or woman at the front of the classroom. In South Korea, teachers are known as 'nation builders'. Here in America, it's time we treated the people who educate our children with the same level of respect. We want to reward good teachers and stop making excuses for bad ones. And over the next ten years, with so many Baby Boomers retiring from our classrooms, we want to prepare 100,000 new teachers in the fields of science, technology, engineering, and math. In fact, to every young person listening tonight who's contemplating their career choice: If you want to make a difference in the life of our nation; if you want to make a difference in the life of a child – become a teacher. Your country needs you.[30]

'Obama Is Absolutely Wrong'

The researcher says:

> 'PISA shows Korea is doing great; thus, Korean education should not change', he said. 'If you reform, it will make you score less . . . . This makes it impossible for you to change'. He thinks the rankings only 'create illusory models of excellence, romanticize misery and glorify educational authoritarianism'. He sees PISA as today's 'most destructive force' that impedes progress of education around the world. And the worst part of PISA rankings is that other countries, obsessed with short-term achievement, blindly imitate countries like Korea. 'Asian countries like China, Singapore and Korea score very high. Everybody thinks we have the best education. So people from other countries copy (them), it destroys their advantages (in their own system)', he said.

Figure 5.10 Together.

For the past half century, Korean education has played a vital role in lifting the country to where it is now today. But for the next 50 years, he believes, Korea will have to revise its authoritarian education system and snap out of its obsession with scores, for further prosperity. He noted the strength of Korean education, which contributed to the country's economic growth in the 1980s and '90s, may not be useful for the creative economy in the 21st century, 'where we have the most educated bartenders in history'. 'Korea passed the stage', he said. 'Old education system was very good for producing workers for assembly lines. But what you need for the next stage, to become an advanced country, you need innovators'. In authoritarian systems, governments, teachers, parents are the authority; students have to comply with them, he said. 'There, they do some things they do not like. They do not even know what they like.'[31]

So Says Teacher Kim

Some say Koreans lack initiative. That they only know how to obey orders. That they need everything to be explained to them. That their schools are hell. Some people say that Koreans don't know whether they are happy or not. That they are busy and exhausted because of the race to the top. You, you come from the happiest country in the world. I guess it means that you take the initiative yourself, that you do not take orders from others, and that nothing needs to be explained to you. Your schools must be paradise!

Is that right?

Kitchen

The wise are also the rich, says a boy who goes to a technical high school. We who go to technical school are not that intelligent. We're not that rich either. And we have more time. More leisure. We can go to the PC café. If we have money. And make money from part-time jobs. Isn't it therefore better to go to the technical high school, I ask? No, because it's stressful. It is stressful because in Korea you are looked down upon if you do not go to university and if you just settle for a regular job. Like what, for example? Like being a cook or chef. I'm studying to be a cook myself but if I become a chef instead of attending university, then my status in society will be low. I'll be looked down upon. It's stressful. Although I am not stressed or depressed myself, the family around me will be disappointed, angry, unhappy. It's hard to be a part of all that.

World in Your Hand

As we talk, a door opens in the adjacent yard, the rear entrance to a café. A young man dressed in the long white apron of a cook appears in the doorway and moves into the warmth of the morning sun. He offers a mound of breadcrumbs up to the wind. His birds sail down to gather up the gift. He seems lost in thought as the small battle cries split the cold silence. Five minutes pass and his break is over. Returning to the world, he extinguishes the cigarette, flicks the butt into a shaded corner of the compound and disappears behind the heavy kitchen door.

Don't Believe All You Read. There Were also Good Times

In high school, everything was different. We couldn't play anymore and we had to be at school all day. It was mandatory. I had no choice. But now, today, when I look back, I can see that it has made me who I am. They punished us physically if we talked to each other or read books that had nothing to do with teaching. The only thing they accepted were the studies. I think that can't work anywhere else except in Korea and Japan. And that's because, we're used to it, it works. But it will not work in other countries. But humans are the only resources we have, and we have to develop what we have. We must accept that. That's what we use education for. We study because we must develop our country and because we must survive. But it was also a good time. We were together twelve hours a day and we got close to each other. We knew each other very well, and we still do. It provides a deep understanding of one's friends when living and learning in such conditions. That was the great thing about it. The bright side. The dark side then was that we focused only on the tests. Nothing practical, nothing like art or an appreciation of music for example. It was only theoretical, abstract. There was no freedom. There were nothing like human rights. But I am also grateful, because it has made me who I am today.

This Is What Happened to My Country: Confessions of a History Teacher

There has just been an investigation. Shockingly, the question was something like: in the event of war, would you fight for your country to protect it? It was just to test patriotism among the young. In all, 50 per cent said they would not. That's shocking! The Korean flag flies in 86 per cent of all Korean homes. But now, for me, I love myself higher than I love my country. So something has changed. A generation or two ago, this was not the case. I think the culture was that you have to love your country just as much as you love yourself. Back then, the country and you were one thing. Now it is shared.

They Won't Break Me

'You look good today! It's a new style', I say to my research assistant as we meet outside the school to start another day of fieldwork. 'Yes, I can afford it', he replies. 'I don't care what the others say. I am not a teacher, nor am I in an internship. I'm just me and I can afford to be casual and relaxed. I will show them before we finish this study that this is how I am'. He has a lot to look forward to: working with a 'big expert' from the West, his own university studies and a girlfriend who expects him to graduate so they can get married. His chances of his courtship to Seeyoung ending well will rise if he passes his final year exams. 'Ironic, isn't it? My final exams to become a teacher are multiple-choice and I need almost 100%'. And he *wants* to be a teacher. Because then he will win Seeyoung who will be content with the match. He'll teach the boys in the upper classes. He likes them. They are so nice, he says, and it breaks his heart to see how stressed they are. 'So was I. I know that feeling. I want to help make it different for them'. When he finishes his education, he will be more relaxed, he says. Not so stressed. And today he has put on his jeans, a coloured T-shirt and is wearing a highly visible gold chain. It's spring and the sun is shining.

Unruly Children: A Teacher Explains

There is so much talk about unruly students in school. But I don't think it's about them being uncooperative as such. It's because they can't cope with the financial problems associated with education. Unlike the rich, poorer students can't afford the best extra tuition. And they then get lower grades. So they become desperate . . . and violent.

Paris

A private company has sponsored the language lab.
New Teaching Technology Applied to Language Learning!
Brian is from America. Peace Corps.
He will teach the class together with Mr Lou. His English is poor, so he is mainly supporting Brian.
He asks Brian if he should roll down the curtains.
Yes, good idea, Brian replies.
He rolls down the curtains.
Large images of famous European architecture.
The Roman Forum.
The Leaning Tower of Pisa.
Big Ben.
The Eiffel Tower.
'This is a cucumber', says the New Teaching Technology Applied to Language Learning.

From the Cover of a Student Exercise Book

Paris is without a doubt one of the most beautiful cities on the planet. Paris stimulates the senses, demanding to be seen, heard, touched, tasted and smelt.

My Mother

My mom says to me all the time: don't have too many kids. You have to have your own life. That's because my mother sacrificed everything for me and my brother. And she doesn't want me to have a life like hers. Actually, I don't think she thinks

I should have children at all. Because it's a tyranny. Education. And if I decide only to have one child, she says, it should be a boy, not a daughter. She'd actually like me to have a girl but our societal status views boys as more important. However, as daughters grow older, it's nicer to have them. More fun. After she got married, she just stayed at home. She thought there should be someone when we got home from school. And someone to make sure we got good grades. Can't you see how the whole thing just keeps going on?

'Why I Never Want Babies'

An increasing number of South Korean women are choosing not to marry, not to have children, and not even to have relationships with men. With the lowest fertility rate in the world, the country's population will start shrinking unless something changes.

I have no plans to have children, ever, says 24-year-old Jang Yun-hwa, as we chat in a fashionable café in the middle of Seoul. I don't want the physical pain of childbirth. And it would be detrimental to my career. Rather than be part of a family, I'd like to be independent and live alone and achieve my dreams, she says.[32]

Queue

We sometimes have to ask if we can go to the toilet during class because the queues are long in the breaks. Teachers are usually very angry about this. We should have managed this in the break. Some teachers hit us. That's not fair. What should we do?

A New Law

A new law was passed to prohibit schooling and teaching after 8 pm. The government wanted to put an end to the private tuition industry, or at least limit it. They'll just find other ways to keep it going say a group of university students. They stand outside the library, taking a short break in the sun with a cup of coffee. Inside, they have their own desk space that they have paid for. I don't think it's possible to stop this at all. It's a disease that's spreading. Everyone gets completely wild and out of control as soon as it is about education. And we do it ourselves. When we finish our own education and have children, it starts all over again. We'll send our own children to school all night.

Test and Child Centred Education

In theory, we should have something about child-centred teaching in schools. All teachers know the principles of it. But the reality is that we have to prepare them for the test. So reality and theory are not related. It is a written test so students do not have to worry about speaking. In a student-centred class, the teacher has the role of facilitator, but in Korea they just keep lecturing. I think the students should be at the centre too, but what do you do when there are forty of them? But there are tensions around teaching. Between the students and the teachers. Also between the old and the younger generations of teachers. After all, the old generations would inject knowledge into the students . . . the younger ones want to interact more.

The Big Difference

We think of education very narrowly. Unlike Europe where there is a broader concept. That's probably the biggest difference between Korea and Europe. Do your young people also suffer?

An Individual Human

What do we want to be when we finish our education? We all have dreams about the world. She points to Sung who wants to go to the Czech Republic, to Prague, for she has heard that it is such a beautiful city. And then she will also donate her organs when she turns twenty. The kidney, we have two of them. And then she will also sponsor a child in Africa and concentrate on becoming a beautiful woman. Something about skin treatments. Kim wants to go to the London Olympics. She wants to go to the UK and see David Beckham. And then she also wants to be a tourist and learn English. In fact, she wants to learn all the languages in the world, in all the countries she travels. Me? I want to read history and travel around the world with my sister. She is only a year younger than me, so we are also kind of girlfriends. I dream of living for myself. Somewhere in Northern Europe. Hamlet's Land? In Australia, I learned how Sweden reacted to Hitler's extermination camps, and I found that 90 per cent of the Jews survived in Denmark for that reason. They could go to Sweden. I thought it had to be a good country. Because Korea is a democratic society, we have no royal family, so I would also go to Europe and see the royal families. I want to go to a completely different environment. A place where I can be an individual human being. I would just like that. I so want to live in another place, a place where I can be an individual.

'Zambia'

Proud land, stripped bare. Colonized, freed, colonized once more as capitalism and its secret twin 'development' carry on where kings and bureaucrats stumbled. One Zambia, Education for All, nation under God. State under market. Becoming modern just when the tap is cut off. Economic collapse, abjection, cast out, cast down. Fend for yourself. Corruption, nepotism, incompetence, callousness, brutality: words the northern masters collect and send to their southern 'partners'.

Efficiency, resource allocation. User pays. Quality education, Focus on Learning, Educating our Future. Youthful people. Sector-wide strategies. Decentralization ↔ good governance. Poverty reduction. Millennium Development Goals → Sustainable Development Goals. Learner-centred pedagogy, early learning, learning achievement, curriculum reform, language diversity. Underpaid teachers ↔ professionalization of teachers. National Development Plans. Natural abundance drowned in discourses of good intentions. Endless conditionality. Hope. Resilience. Blind faith.

Young nation, hunted girls. Sickness, absence, loss and trauma. Orphans. Hope without futures ↔ futures without hope. Desperate scramble for food, medicine, dignity. New start: civic action, pride, community schools, low-fee private schools ↔ quality education (again). Hope (again). Progress (again). Cynicism (again). Fend for yourself (again).

New friends and masters. 'Made in China'.

How will it end? Did it already end? Is this a dream or my life? Why doesn't anybody hear me?

*

'Abstinence Is Nicee'

In the main courtyard, this optimistic slogan takes precedence over the school's name and vision statement. The space is shared by other slogans:

> To offer quality education and encourage students to become worthy adults with a good and rooted sense of self-worth in a contradictory world.
>
> A supportive learning environment that leads to academic excellence.

This vision has changed somewhat since the new principal arrived: 'I wanted it to appeal a little more to the young people, so I thought we should use their language – Nicee! And I also thought that we should emphasize that students should have self-esteem and know that we live in a diverse world'. She liked the terms 'supportive learning environment' and 'academic excellence'.

> Such statements and markings are important for both teachers and students so we can always be sure that we are on the right track. We know that it can actually change the lives of these students. It means a lot to them that by training they can change their lives. That development can take place through education – it is important for them to know.

Dream On

Can you imagine? They chose me to lead the prayer at the career exhibition! I liked it. I really liked it.

> Oh, father in heaven, we are grateful to be together here today. We thank you for this opportunity and we wish and pray you will be with us when we plan our career.

They thanked her and then the Secretary of the Training and Skills Department in the Ministry took over:

> You look beautiful! I hope you will all leave this room with a plan, with something you want in your lives. If you want to become a doctor, be one; if you want to become an accountant, be one; if you want to become a witch-doctor, be one. But promise yourself one thing. Get something out of this rare opportunity. Ladies and gentlemen – today it is not boys and girls – today it is ladies and gentlemen. I would like to address you as ladies and gentlemen but also as lawyers and doctors, professors and teachers.

Clapping and screaming.

> I will talk to you about how to concentrate. How to focus. We are talking about careers that you must pursue to be something in life. But before that, I want to ask the question: Who wants to become teachers.

A few hesitant hands rise.

> Why so few? Teachers have the most important position in the world. Those who made you into the people you are today were the teachers. Those who made me

the person I am today were the teachers. The man who was the first president in this country was a teacher. Like me. I fly in and out of the country all the time. I am asked to go around the country to talk to students. And who asks me to do such things? Teachers. So look at me! Look what I have achieved! It can lead to anything. What I want to tell you this afternoon is that the future you are looking for is nowhere else but inside of where you are. It's not somewhere out there. It's from where you are. It must start with you. You must know what you want while you are still young. Mr. Mandela knew what he wanted. In the middle of the prison, he sat down and wrote a book about it. What I am trying to say is that the future you are looking for is not something you find outside, it is what you are holding in your hands today. You have to look into yourself to see the future. If you cannot see yourself as a professor, you will never become a professor. If you cannot see yourself as a lawyer, you will never become a lawyer. If you cannot see yourself as a minister, you will never become one. If you don't have it in your hands, here, right now, here, you won't succeed. That is the problem. That is why many fail. You never asked yourself this question: Why are you at school? You don't even know the reason why you are at school. So, it starts from where you are. You must have a reason for why you go to school. It starts with you. And I can assure you, you can go anywhere. What did I say? ANYWHERE! As long as you have a plan. You must have a plan. You must think about it every day. Each and every day.

A representative from a private university then talks about courses, structures, modules and the jobs open to qualified graduates. There are lots of opportunities:

> Those who would like to participate in Human Resource projects can come here, you can also start your own NGO, and we have courses in sports management. We have education that addresses the decentralized political level, if you want politics. We have entrepreneurship courses if you want to influence political development. We have courses in agriculture, computers, commerce. So, even if there are problems here in Zambia, you can at least use that education in the world. Europe and South Africa. And that way you can establish your own business when you feel ready for it.
>
> Our accommodation is first rate. We offer single rooms, you do not need to share. And then we offer fantastic meals. After three months, our students start complaining that they are getting too much steak and chicken.

A loud gasp goes through the crowd.

A few more presentations and the day is over. 'We are lucky that we have so many opportunities,' says one girl.

From their final year group of 300, the high school will send about 15 to university, 5 or so will complete their studies.

Economic Fortunes

As in its pursuit of access, the government will continue to call on the contributions of communities, cooperating **partners** and the **private sector** in addressing issues of **quality** and **relevance**. The next decade will still be **challenging** because the country will continue to tackle access due to population growth while trying to improve educational **quality**. The challenges for the educational sector will increase in view of **globalisation** and the importance of **knowledge** for nations to be **competitive**. Investments in **human capital** and the quality of such investments will play a **decisive role** in determining the **productivity** of any country and resulting **economic fortunes**.[33]

Figure 5.11 Witch doctor.

Things Fall Apart I

In the second semester, Mrs Mwale had planned for Grade 11 to work with Achebe's great novel *Things Fall Apart*. She was allocated a class set of the novels so that all students could receive a copy. The books were slow in arriving as the order went astray. In the beginning, she read the sole copy of the text aloud, pausing to discuss and ask questions. Three students had personal copies of the novel and occasionally Mrs Mwale asked them to contribute to the reading. To discuss the development of the characters in the book, Mrs Mwale focuses on the main protagonist, Okonkwo, and his relationship with his father. She finishes the section and, looking up, asks: 'How many would like to be different from your parents?' All hands shoot up. They will not drink or smoke like their parents. They will not be lazy and without work. They will look after their children. 'That's why we go to school. We will be different', they say. The teacher goes on: 'Let me know if you would like to spend more time with your parents?' Again all hands shoot up. 'Yes, I probably thought so', Mrs Mwale continues. She wants to know what they are doing when they are with their parents. Several say they see them rarely because their parents are never home. Some say they can be found outside the home, drinking. A girl adds that they often spend time together on chores.

That's not what I mean, Mrs Mwale interrupts. 'How many of you have quiet time with your parents? My kids want quiet time with me! Time to just sit down, drink tea, talk about how their day has been, how mine has been. Time to calm down and help them with their homework. How many of you do this'?

Silence. After a time a boy raises his hand and whispers: 'My parents are dead and I live with my grandparents and other relatives. They don't have time for me'. A girl chimes in: 'We have to be like parents to the little kids. There is no one else'.

Mrs Mwale looks pensive. Then she lightens up:

> Yes, that's right, you have a lot of problems and it's not easy for you. You should have psychological help, if you could get it. Time with a psychologist or counsellor would help. But whatever is the situation, your parents need to spend time with you to check your homework, your notebooks. Otherwise, we teachers need to do that and this is too much work for us. The teachers can't take care of everything, you know. Maybe some of you already have children? You should not go and hide it, but instead think about your responsibilities and then be proud of what you have helped to create.

Hallelujah

Teaching starts at 7.30 am although at that time few teachers have arrived to their classrooms. Most are busy organizing themselves in the staffroom. There are bags to unpack, books to collect, student notebooks to organize. A ritual familiar to schools the world over. Some change their shoes, others read the newspaper. Much laughter, gentle greetings and the occasional dispute or harsh comment. Some teachers have brought food to sell to their colleagues. In all, 1,000 Kwacha for a homemade bun can become 20,000 in a day. A good extra income says Mrs Mulenga. 'Teaching can be profitable' she proclaims solemnly.

At 7.45 am, the door to the staffroom is blocked by a group of students who have gathered outside. They knock cautiously, even though the door is ajar. One asks to know if their teacher has arrived. One teacher comes to the door and explains that Mrs Mwale has not been seen. Another pushes through the huddle and explodes: 'I cannot see her. Can you? Why do you ask? What do you think? Is that your business?' Eventually, they disperse, just missing Mrs Mwale who finally arrives at 8.00 am. According to the schedule, she should have started a double biology lesson with Grade 12 at 7.30 am. It is a busy time for the seniors as exams are fast approaching. She does not appear to be in a rush and today her husband follows her into the staffroom. He begins to chat with her colleagues who are also a part of their private network of friends.

Outside, the students have returned. Mrs Mwale sees them through the opening but chooses to ignore their calls. She sits down after biding her husband farewell. The group of budding biologists has now risen to twelve students and are looking in directly at her. She presses on in defiance, and begins to correct the essays for the afternoon classes. These are private classes that the teachers take in addition to their regular obligations. The extra payments make all the difference. The staffroom remains tightly packed as the first module ends. The teachers correct essays, continue with their newspapers and chat above the din of a local news program on the dusty TV nestled under an iron-barred window. At the break, the school provides tea and coffee for the teachers. The sale of buns takes off in earnest so Mrs Mulenga must be ready and in position. Defeated, the Grade 12 students go back to their dark, cold classroom.

When Mrs Mwale arrives to the classroom it is with purpose and speed. Actually, she should now be teaching literature to Grade 11 in the other building but wants to tell the biologists about the education she is involved in at the university. She's training to become a school supervisor. She will soon be qualified to support children who have been victims of violence and abuse. She will know how to create dialogues with parents to inform them about the damaging consequences of abuse and will have the power to remove children from their homes. A very interesting course, she says. And the extra income is welcome, she confides to me. She often goes to conferences. It is a good job. One that gets her out of the school. The bell rings for the next module to start.

According to the schedule, Mrs Mwale should now be on her way to Grade 10 for literature. She returns to the staffroom, fixes herself a cup of tea, buys a bun from the ever present Mrs Mulenga and begins to correct a short pile of essays.

A quiet girl approaches the door to the staffroom. She remains outside for some moments as if unsure of her next move. Mrs Mwale spots her and commands her to enter: 'Alright, come here quickly. What do you want?' The girl actually wishes to speak with Mrs Musenge but Mrs Mwale will have to do: 'I have a book . . . I do not need it anymore . . . and I thought . . . maybe Mrs Musenge wants to buy it? I know she does not have the textbook for the topic she teaches.' Her eyes swell with tears. 'Now, let me tell you one thing', says an irate Mrs Mwale, 'this is not a marketplace and by the way, Mrs Musenge is not here. Or maybe you can see something that I cannot? No? Well get out of here'!

A Brisk Trade

'Come, come hurry up. Come and see'. The Physics lab across from the staffroom has erupted. Cheap tomatoes for sale, only 60,000 per box. The teachers barrel out of their hideout and rush to the lab. The rear tables groan under the weight of box after box of tomatoes. Flasks, burners and hoses have been pushed to the end of the bench. A queue of teachers develops. All want to catch a glimpse of the fabulous offer. Next door, Mr Banda is underway with Grade 12 mathematics but must abandon his station to join the mayhem. The teachers are animated, filling and measuring bags. Money from buns straight to tomatoes. Precious cargo taken to the staffroom or direct to cars. Phone calls made. This is fantastic, says Mrs Katongo. My sister told me yesterday that she bought tomatoes for 85,000K so this is very cheap. I am really in need of tomatoes so I've bought a large bag. Fortuitously, a group of students are in their usual position outside the staffroom. 'You girls! We need assistance. Kindly help us carry these trays!' A procession of girls, trays on heads, file off to the car park. When they return Mrs Katongo waves them away: 'You are not supposed to be in here. This is the staffroom'!

A boy approaches the staffroom, knocking cautiously at the door several times before the teachers react. Mrs Mulemba waves at him to enter. He is smiling. He carries a big dish of samosa on his head. 'What have you got there'? asks Mrs Musenge. 'Let me see'. He lifts the dish from his head and offers up the prize to the teachers. 'My mother made samosa today', he says. 'Well, well. That does look nice. Let me get a couple of those'. The other teachers are keen for samosa too and within ten minutes he has collected 18,000 Kwacha. Lunch break. The group of teachers in the corner have not left the sanctuary today although the timetable indicates that Tuesday is busy for them all. 'Thank God the morning-classes are part of our normal salary which they can't change', says Mrs Mulemba. Yes, you are right says the usually reticent Mr Mwale. 'Thank God for that. Halleluja'

The Bible or Biology

While the teachers busy themselves with cheap tomatoes, the students have gradually given up waiting for class to commence and, instead, gather outside in some of the clubs for which the school is known and very popular. There are clubs for anti-corruption, the holy scriptures, football, chess, parliamentarianism, poetry, dance, choral singing, citizenship and one entitled 'Youth, Sex and AIDS'. As a rule, the afternoon students gather in the clubs in the mornings when they do not have tuition, and vice versa. Often, both groups of students meet, especially when the mornings are devoid of teaching.

'If you don't feel like it and the boy insists, that's rape', says Mrs Lundu from Grade 11. 'If the boys get drunk and can't control themselves and go to bed with several different girls, then that's what gets dangerous', says another. A girl adds: 'God says nothing is impossible. This means that abstinence is not impossible either. And only abstinence can eradicate AIDS'. 'Yes', the first boy replies, 'but God also says that everything is possible, and that means it is possible to eradicate AIDS'.

'Yes, when we are dead', concludes another.

Mwezi agrees. 'Someone thinks that because I have it, everyone should have it, and then they just go to bed with anyone without protecting themselves. And then we all die'. One boy asks about masturbation: 'Is it a sin? David committed a sin, so even though we are Christians, we may well just commit a small sin. Or what'?

One boy claims abstinence is the only way to survive. Many agree, but it's hard, they say. 'The boys don't fall in love', says one girl. 'They are only with the girls to satisfy their needs. And they do not pay attention to us, not to our feelings or to our safety'. One boy asks if the others use porn to satisfy themselves. Both boys and girls respond in the affirmative. 'Yes, I use it so I can control myself', says a girl. 'When I've seen it, I don't want to be with a boy'. The prefect, who stands with a book published by a Christian congregation, says: 'Here it says Satan has entered sex via porn. And you can also see it in the Bible. The Bible says your body is a sacred temple. You must keep your body free from the immoral'. A girl complements this by citing from the first letter to the Corinthians. 'One should not fool around with one's body. It is dangerous, it can lead to death, and then it is immoral, and not as God wants it.' Another girl, who has recently joined the school because her previous one was plagued by absentee teachers, sits with a biology book open: 'Here it says masturbation is healthy. That it is healthy for our bodies and also for our psyche. That we should get to know about sex'. 'Yes', interrupts the Prefect, 'but it is a book of biology, the Bible says something else. And this is the Bible we must adhere to'. The girl responds: 'Not everyone believes that one should only stick to the Bible. And why shouldn't we use the biology book instead. Then it will be easier'.

'We can't use the biology book', he insists. 'In Zambia, the Bible applies. And it says we are all sinners'. 'That's why we have to die', says another boy. 'Yes, that is why we should all die soon. Because we are sinners'. 'I'm a Tonga man', says a boy and continues with a self-conscious smile. 'That's why I have to have a lot of women. This is how it is for the Tonga people. And the first one has to be a virgin'.

'A virgin! How would you find one'? whispers Mwezi. 'There are no more virgins left. They are all either dead or raped'.

Apocryphal Story I

A development advisor visits the school and talks to children enjoying a break outside.

What do you want to be when you grow up?

I want to be a teacher.

That's very good! And why do you want to be a teacher?

↓

So I can sit in the sun all day and beat the children.

Abstinence – Once More

What does this mean to you all?

> Why do you ask?
> Don't you know?
> Because you are stupid?
> Because you are white?
> Because you are ignorant?
> Because you think we are fools?
> Because you want to have a sugar boy, a sugar girl?
> In that case, give me your phone number and I will make arrangements for you.

Her bright blue bubble gum almost hits my face before she turns and walks away, laughing uncontrollably towards the main building.

I received a text message that evening from a young male student that I had interviewed recently:

'Take me to your dreams tonight, Ma'm. Now you have my number.'

Haunted and Hunted

There are always men lying in wait for young girls, preferably virgins. Melinda from Grade 11 explains that many men are of the opinion that if they have been infected with HIV/AIDS and want to get rid of the disease they must have intercourse with a virgin. She thinks that this is only part of the danger of being a girl. Girls are vulnerable in the streets, at school, in homes. In schools, some teachers trade sex for high marks or for a preview of an exam paper. Sometimes they will just rape them if no one is there to help. In the home, there are particular problems for orphaned children who are vulnerable to relatives who seek a return for the food, lodging and school fees they provide. 'It is dangerous to be a girl in Zambia and it is very dangerous to be a beautiful woman. Many are provoked by the beauty of women and think we should not be so beautiful when they are so sick. That is why it is dangerous to be beautiful in Zambia. We can get AIDS and become pregnant everywhere, in our school, at the market, in the street and at home'.

Fortunate Girl

Memory was 11 when she accompanied her sister to the hospital to deliver her father's body. He had died of AIDS, like her mother a few years earlier. Her sister was married and lives at the other end of town. After visiting the hospital, they ordered a taxi. The sister got out at her stop and Memory continued alone, eager to return to her four younger brothers. Shortly after, the taxi pulled over and the driver raped her.

A few days later, she told her uncle and aunt when they came to take her father's possessions they claimed had always belonged to them. They listened but did nothing. The youngest brothers were sent to distant relatives in the southern part of the country and Memory returned with them to their home where she would help with cleaning, cooking and childcare. Her uncle assaulted her regularly. Her aunt was aware of this but did nothing. Memory decided to leave the family, ending up in a predictable cycle of small-crime and prostitution.

One day, she was approached by two nuns who found their way to her shantytown by the river. She accepted the offer to join their refuge for street children. Memory tested positive for HIV/AIDS but with the support of doctors and psychologists was able to manage her condition. She returned to school where she did well. Over time, she became involved in a number of awareness-raising campaigns on the rights and conditions of HIV/AIDS-infected young people and gained the attention of international donor organizations. Memory represented HIV/AIDS-infected young people when former US president Bill Clinton visited Zambia in 2007. Later, she was invited to a UN conference where she discussed the challenges facing young Africans infected with the disease.

I visited Memory with Mrs Mwansa, her former teacher. Memory was highly pregnant, living in one of the better neighbourhoods of Lusaka. An international NGO provided the large, newly built house. She now served as a speaker and campaign manager, both nationally and internationally. The international donors think my story is exciting and horrible, that's why they support me. So now my job is to tell my story and help other young people in the same situation.

On the way out the door, Mrs Mwansa noticed several bags of cement that were to be used for additional construction. She asked Memory about the price as she was looking for cement for her own house and had been surprised by just how expensive it had become.

'I don't know', Memory replied, 'it's my NGO that pays'.

'Can you just get what you ask for?'

'Yes, if I explain why we need it, they will give it to me.'

'That's good, very good', murmured Mrs Mwansa. 'She is a rich woman, now Memory.'

Very rich.	Even compared to me.	All that cement, and this great house.
	She's been so lucky.	

Combat

> Through girls' own testimonies, this report shows sexual assault of girls in Zambia in the era of HIV/AIDS to be widespread and complex. It documents several categories of abuse that heighten girls' risk of HIV infection, including (1) sexual assault of girls by family members, particularly the shocking and all too common practice of abuse of orphan girls by men who are their guardians, or by others who are charged to assist or look after them, including teachers, (2) abuse of girls, again often orphans, who are heads of household or otherwise desperately poor and have few options other than trading sex for their and their siblings' survival, and (3) abuse of girls who live on the street, of whom many

are there because they are without parental care. All of these situations of abuse must be addressed as part of combating the HIV/AIDS epidemic in Zambia.[34]

Coffins

What we get for funerals these days is not much.
    No, you're right but compared to other schools, at least they pay for the coffin.
    Yeah. That's important. At least they can support us with a proper coffin and funeral.
    You remember the coffin in which we buried Muschenge? That was a fantastic coffin!
    Yes, that is true. A lovely coffin. A really nice coffin. I could go for that too. Good quality and blankets inside.
    Yeah, and lots of flowers on the top.
    And they even picked up his body so we didn't have to bother about that. They gave him make-up, washed him, fixed everything.
    It was different when Catherine died.
    Catherine?
    Yes. She died just after my daughter. Years ago. Don't really remember any longer.
    Wasn't that Mungu?
    No it wasn't Mungu. She died well before that. I am thinking of Catherine. That coffin was silly. You could even see bits and pieces of her body sticking out. Poor creature.
    Yeah, that's right. That was horrible.
    Yes, it was.
    When I think about Catherine I cry. It still makes me cry. God, how terrible.
    Yes. All those coffins.
    At least when the time comes we'll get a coffin.
    Yes, and a good one.
    Yes, at least a good one.
    Will you be there for Victoria's kitchen-party?
    Yes, definitely!
    That will be good. They serve lots of good food at that place.
    Yes, and wine.
    Arrhhh, I should have had a class now.
    Which one?
    Grade 10.

That can wait.
Yes that can wait.
Should I bring you some tea?
Yes, and a biscuit.

Witness

I got up in the witness box, as a mother, as a sister, as a teacher and as a Principal. It was not easy to make the decision. I know teachers are under heavy pressure because of low salaries, expensive houses and an increase in all kinds of costs, not least for the private schools they use in order to give their children a proper education. I have had several hours with him talking about it, I've prayed with him, forgiven him, given him one more chance, one more and then one more. Still, I watch from the window as he sneaks out of the compound when the elder pretty girls leave the school. It has come to a point now where I have to say that I do not know what happens when elder men, teachers like the ones on my staff, assault young girls. People have told me not to do anything since this will be humiliating for his family. But what about the young school girls? It was not like that before we got the traditional healers. They are the ones who carry a huge responsibility in all this, especially because of the ways they claim to cure AIDS. Children are defenceless without parents, families, sponsors. Our society is imploding. Maybe they get some of this wrong because of the Western movies. Maybe they think this is all normal. We need to clean all that up. We need to protect the students. That's what made me stand in the witness box.

At the School Gate

Some are waiting for the bus.
Some sell sweets.
Some flash their fashion clothes.
Some wait for girls to rent out.
Some wait for customers.
Some greet their teachers.
Some greet their customers.
Some greet their students.
Some greet the headmaster
passing through the gate on her way home,
smiling
awkwardly.

Figure 5.12 Waiting game.

Sugar

'The phenomenon of "sugar daddies," unscrupulous older men who entice girls into sex with offers of gifts or money, has been a particular focus of media and other accounts of the impact of HIV/AIDS on girls in Zambia and elsewhere in Africa.'[35] Have we fallen into the trap of viewing that solely from the perspective of Western indignation?

Arriving in Style

I will be leaving earlier from school today, she said. I have business to do.

OK, I said. See you tomorrow.

Yes, see you tomorrow.

What business I thought to myself?

The next morning she arrived for school in style, stepping elegantly out of a black car with dark-tinted windows. She waved goodbye to the older man in the car, and caught my eye as she walked past.

I turned, ready to say good morning. She stopped. Not looking back, she bent down, took off her shoes and ran up the stairs into the main building.

Popcorn

In the courtyard behind the kitchen you'll find a small kiosk from where you can buy sodas, caramels and all kinds of biscuits and cakes wrapped in coloured paper. 'Made in China'. The place attracts a few local merchants. A young woman, about the same age as the final year students, comes in with her infant child tied to her back, and starts to sell homemade cakes. Another slightly older woman arrives with her three children to sell homemade samosas. The most popular fixture is the popcorn machine. It is owned by Peter, a young man with three children, two of whom are of school age. He is convinced that education will enable the family to survive. Sales are going well, especially of the small bags. There are long queues in front of the machine, and he enjoys talking, chatting and teasing the students, most of whom he knows well. He has a helper, a nephew who dropped out of sixth grade. He stands by, watching, ready to assist.

A second machine popped up about a month ago. The new one is owned by the son of one of the teachers. The teacher explains that he wants to fund his son's university studies: I know that the sale of popcorn goes well here, so I bought one for him. At least it's better than the old machine over there. Peter looked despondent as he shared his trade with an unwelcome competitor. A week later he stopped selling popcorn at the School.

Figure 5.13 Senior English classroom.

> Does anyone know where Peter is?
>> Yes, his assistant says. He is dead.
>>> They found his body down by the riverside.

Erica

In the morning. This is the best time for me. Then I am happy. Very happy. I love the mornings. Very early in the morning, I get up at half past three. Because then there is only me. Only me in the whole world. Me! I'm here. I'm all alone. All alone in the world. And anything can happen. And maybe something good will happen that day. Maybe. It's different with the evenings. Then I think about everything that happened during the day. And maybe that's not good. Then the evenings are sad. But in the morning you are someone. Everything begins again, in the morning. And then I'm so happy.

Africa

> Africa, Africa, Africa.
> I love Africa.
> This means everything to me.
> I was born here.
> I'll die here.
> I have my life here.
> My dreams, my future.
> This is where people manage.
> Where people struggle.
> We are Black, we are poor.
> But we care for each other.
> One Zambia – One Nation.
> Yeah man.

Four Girls

We stick together, they say. Then the competition is not so stressful. We always stick together. We help one another. We sit together, also during the breaks. We tell each other everything. We do not want to be dependent on marriage. There are many parents who say their daughters need to get married, even if they are not quite old enough. Because then they will not have to fend for themselves.

But we won't. We want to be independent. That's why we don't hang out with the boys. Especially after school hours. We stay inside. Going out is dangerous. And then we do our homework. We just do homework all the time. Homework, homework. And I dream of my education. I want a career, I want my own house. I want to support my siblings so that we are not dependent on others. I want to become a doctor. I want to be a lawyer. I want to be an economist. That is why we do not go out. We stick together. If you don't stick together, it won't work. That's why we say: school is our boyfriend.

While the President Is Having His Press-conference[36]

It is 11.30 am and the fifth lesson is supposed to start. The teachers showed no signs of moving off to class. Why would they? The president is about to make a great announcement. The TV is on and the president joins them from behind a white clothed table in the garden of the statehouse. He is sitting in the shade of a cluster of trees. Flowers and microphones flank the father, our smiling leader. He addresses the nation on the matter of charges of corruption that have been made against him and the decision of the Western nations to withhold their aid to Zambia. Doctors, nurses and teachers have been striking, demanding a 25 per cent increase in their salaries. The situation in the hospitals is now chaotic. The president is suspected by many – especially those in the staffroom – of pressuring the Supreme Court to withdraw corruption charges against his minister of education.

Students wander around the schoolyard as the teachers wait for the press conference to begin. The Grade 11 students have split themselves into two groups: some working with their English tasks, others with mathematics. A student writes on the blackboard based on notes given by the teacher. The students copy the script into their notebooks. The other half of the class gets support from one of the bright students.

'This is a beautiful country, and Zambians are beautiful people. We work together in this government with only one goal ahead of us – the development of Zambia. We are Zambians, we stand together. That is the thing I am committed to as a real and true Zambian. But let me say this loud and clear so that everybody can understand: I will not take responsibility for what happened under the previous government.' The teachers howl in disapproval.

In a distant corner of the school compound, under the shade of two big trees and hidden by the high grass, a group of students from the scripture-union begins to pray. They stand in a circle, holding hands, eyes closed, invoking God to free the school and the teachers from the evil demons of Satan that want to take their souls. There have been many cancellations of teaching during the strike but we pray that God will bring salvation to the school. One day our prayers will be heard. Halleluja.

'This money comes from taxpayers in Europe. And therefore you have to help me make people understand that it is difficult for our European friends when they see headings of corruption and bribery in the newspapers. This government has taken every possible step against it. And we have established a new commission which will help the ACC look at particularly complicated cases'. Oh no, exclaims a teacher! Not another commission. A despondent sigh fills the staffroom. Their allowances will be more than three times our yearly salary says Mrs Malenga.

Teacher Smith: I have got the idea and I would like to hear your comment on this—maybe Blacks just are corrupt people. Maybe that is why we have these problems with corruption. This is not what one finds in other parts of the world, I have heard. It is only in Africa and among Blacks. So maybe . . . maybe we are just corrupt by nature? Rubbish, says Miriam. Who plundered us? Who took it all? The gold, the diamonds, the copper, even our people? And as what? Slaves! How did Europe become so rich? How did the Indians become so rich? And now it's the turn of the Chinese! They taught us to be corrupt. We got it from them. Can't you see that?

Grade 12. Mock exams are approaching and with those results the students will make their first applications to the colleges and universities. Grade 12 has not had any teaching today.

Time stands still on the screen, in the staffroom and for our president. For seconds everyone holds their breath. Affected but still composed, he wipes the drips from his jacket with a cloth handed to him by a quick-witted assistant. A monkey has peed on him. Yes, that's what drips on the president. The staffroom erupts in joy. Some stand, hands on their heads in disbelief. Others are dancing. You cannot cheat a monkey, says one teacher, sitting back in total satisfaction.

Three boys from Grade 12 are kneeling down in front of the closed door. They came late to class yesterday and their teacher has ordered them to kneel until he comes out of the staffroom. How long have you been here? Forty-five minutes.

In the bus on the way home, a priest has taken the opportunity to preach, starting with the question: Who still believes that we have come from the monkeys?

Development

Young people can tell you many stories about the abuse of girls, not just at home, on the street or in the compound, but also at school. I asked a Danish development professional stationed in Lusaka as part of the Danish support to the education sector about their institutional response to the crisis: 'It is not part of our terms of reference, no, unfortunately. Our focus is on the training of teachers and teaching materials.'

Dreaming

After all, it's hard to regret, says one teacher. I was dancing in the streets, I shouted slogans for democracy and freedom and economic reform. We were so happy. So excited. Now everything would be different, we thought. After Kaunda. But as a nation, I don't know how much we got out of it, this thing they call development. I do not know. It's hard to talk about. There are so many that are excluded. And it keeps on going. Every day there are many people we say no to at school because they can't pay. Have you seen them sitting out in the hallway. All these people with their children. Grandparents begging and asking us to take their children free of charge because they have nothing. Nothing. Can you understand that? They don't even have food every day. They have to take care of their grandchildren and other orphans because their parents are dead. Some kids come alone. I ask them, Who do you live with? They answer, 'I live with my uncle', 'I live with my aunt', 'I live with my grandparents', 'I have my own responsibility', 'we have no adults at home'. And you know what, I'm glad we still have the extended family. Western individualism is a threat to all this. The day it wins, we are seriously lost. And we already see that with the young generation of teachers. They have a completely different attitude to helping the weak. It's absolutely awful. In practice, this is how development has taken shape. That someone has gotten better while most have been shut out. That's not what we dreamed about, says Mrs Kuenda and she starts crying. She apologizes, gets up and leaves.

Africa, According to Joseph

Africa. Africa, it is the village. The traditional way of life. The big family. The greatness, the beautiful nature and the wild animals. Joseph was born and raised in Lusaka and has never visited the village from which he says his family comes. 'I don't know where it is', he says.

One Zambia – One Nation

This slogan dates back to independence in 1964 and Kaunda's declared policy of uniting the nation. It is written on the Zambian flag. Students use the phrase with great diligence, reciting it in chorus at any given opportunity: Where are you from? One Zambia – One Nation. They explain with enthusiasm that, in Zambia, they love each other. No one is discriminated against. No distinction is made between ethnic groups. That is why we have the slogan. Because in Zambia you stick together. You look after each other. In Zambia, all people are together. That's what they mean, with One Zambia – One Nation. Zambia is a beautiful and rich country.

Things Fall Apart II

The teacher asks her class what determines who one is. 'Is it social background, class, race or something else?' There are several bids: money, race, Africa, Black, white. She interrupts and adds:

> The matter of social class is very complicated and a big problem. There are people in the Ministry of Education, indeed, people all over the world, who agree. That's why they say 'Education for All'. They want education for everyone, that's what it means. We all need to have an education and be equal. This means that you have to take advantage of the opportunities you get through education. You have to take advantage that you can come here and learn something. One should not think of background, social class. Especially not in Africa. Here

Figure 5.14 Destination?

you have to share with each other. Share what you have. This education will determine what you become – whether you get eggs and bacon for breakfast, or whether you have to live by air and water. Don't think about social class, you must think – Education for All. The only weapon we have against poverty is education. You are sure that education makes a difference, right? But you need to be serious, determined and work hard to achieve your goals. If you do, you will probably succeed. If you don't, then you might as well go right back to where you came from, your compound, and stay there for the rest of your days. But those who study hard are serious, they come further. We expect all of us to join in, everyone who wants something: One Zambia – One Nation.

And it is only education that can get us to that goal.

Stating the Obvious or, the Power of Science

According to researchers:

> Given the critical role of teachers and the heavy burdens placed on them in low-income countries, policies promoting teacher motivation and adaptive pedagogic practices in resource-poor classrooms could be beneficial.[37]

Apocryphal Story II

At a meeting of education donor agencies in Nepal where ministry officials were to confirm the draft of a World Bank sector strategy document, a Nepali official noticed that the report continually referred to 'The Government of Zambia'. The draft was based on a template that was being pushed all over the world. Sign or sink.

And What Then? Die!

The school is at the end of a long unpaved road. When the wind gets up it is difficult to move because the dirt strikes the face and finds its way into the eyes. Fine reddish brown dirt is everywhere in the school: on the tables, along the walls, in the windowsills. From the classroom, you can see a woman along the railway line selling vegetables, corn rolls, water and biscuits. The train once connected Dar Es Salaam to Lusaka and went on to South Africa. It's closed now. The field in front of the school has become a huge dumping ground. Here. You'll find, old discarded clothes, bottles, boxes, rusted cans. There are women, children and dogs seeking out its treasures. Occasionally, they burn the waste and, of course, the smoke finds its way into the school, even the sacred staffroom. Beyond the waste dump is a brick wall with a painted advertisement: 'Oxford Tuition and Education Centre'. Mutesa starts to writes on the blackboard. Next to her is a small message in white paint: 'And what then? Die!'

Examination

Exams are being held in English Literature for Grade 11B. The exam guard arrives ten minutes late. He is annoyed and scolds the students for being so messy. He sweeps up what he can, throwing the garbage into the corner of the room before cleaning the chalkboard. The desk at the front of the room is covered in notes from earlier classes: chemistry, geography, mathematics. The exam starts and the question reads: Write about African traditions and what they mean to the novel's protagonists. The walls are covered in graffiti. Testimony to another stream of consciousness running through the school or meaningless doodles?

> Virgin fuckers are cool.
> Hash and coke are cool.
> Fuck virgins.
> Fuck sugar daddies.
> Corruption is cool.
> Sex-HIV-AIDS.
> Sexy Mona-Lisa.

AFRICA, by Mona

Africa, Africa, Africa, Africa . . . I love Africa.
It means everything to me.
That's who I am, this is where I belong.
It is there where you . . . find out . . . manage in spite of everything . . . it is there where you do what you must to survive.
We are almost one big family.
The ethnic groups are different, yet we are the same.
We are Black, we are poor.
It is Africa. It is the Africa I love; but also the Africa I want to get away from.
Africa . . . the Africa that kills.

Too Good to Believe

The new popcorn machine was well received and became an essential part of the life of the school. Peter was soon forgotten, although his two school-aged children remained familiar faces outside the main gates, loitering among the young men.

Queues were long and the new unit had a much greater capacity. It was not difficult to have fifty servings ready for the break and to prepare another thirty while the customers lined up. Popcorn wasn't new to the students but there was something about this bright red machine with its shinning chrome features that emitted a sense of **purpose, power and future**. The students loved it and it was not uncommon to see the teachers waiting patiently. Rather than jumping the queue, they too were in thrall to the modern wonder and respected the rules of polite commerce. Indeed, it didn't take long for the wider community to learn about the machine. At first, a few passers-by came into the compound to see for themselves. Before long, the queue was doubled by eager parents, taxi drivers and local traders. Even the occasional celebrity joined in.

The machine emitted a low and pleasing hum. Half the joy of the popcorn was the warm embrace of its vibration that could be felt throughout the compound and across the playing fields. Mrs Mulenga said she could feel it in the staffroom but others could not. They thought she had a special sense when it comes to business.

The teacher's son was now doing so much business that he began to miss his university classes. The teacher himself began to work the machine. Father and son in shifts. As might have been predicted, he began to miss his own classes repeatedly. This was brought to the principal's attention and after some discussions, it was agreed that he would be excused from class provided that a portion of the profits were paid to the school. After a few months, the venture was so successful that the school and the teacher entered a formal partnership, employing the son on a permanent contract. Now, people could not quite remember if there had been another popcorn seller.

The machine was so popular that the School Board gave the teacher permission to run the business all day rather than only during the breaks. An official from the Department of Finance, Ministry of General Education, came to see the machine for herself, hoping to learn how this example could be 'scaled-up' as a form of public-private partnership. Cost-sharing within the sector is essential if we are to reach our goals of providing world-class education, she explained to reporters at a press conference on the day of her field visit. The principal was very content. Zambia on the move, she said to the gathered crowd.

There were considerable logistics involved in feeding the machine. It appeared to have an insatiable appetite and would break down if raw materials were not shovelled constantly into its belly. The teacher made a roster of students who would feed in the corn, replenish the salt levels and ensure sufficient oil. A bit complicated, but crews were always willing. If anything, the machine appeared to be operating a little faster each day. Mrs Mulenga claimed that the hum had changed frequency but others could not notice this.

Problems started one Monday morning when the first teachers arrived to open up. Most went directly to the staffroom. The gate to the adjacent compound was shut tight, even though there was no key or locking mechanism. The maths teacher Mr Banda got a few of the bigger boys to help him force it open and that's when things really happened. The compound was one big white mass. A stream of popcorn raced through the opening, spilling out onto the main entrance, quickly covering every approach to the main building. They couldn't make their way to the machine because the volume of popcorn spewing from its core pushed them back with a determination they had never encountered. Somehow, the machine was now operating independently, sending its **purpose, power and future** in all directions. Children arriving for the day had to climb over the constant flow. Of course, they accepted the challenge with glee. Some managed to ride the wave, most were lost in the white current. Mr Banda wasn't seen again but some could hear him chewing at the bottom. He seemed content and was certainly not yelling for help. The teachers, now trapped in their sanctuary as the levels rose to window heights, looked on helplessly. Some wanted to get into the compound and be part of the miracle. Others shrugged their shoulders and decided to get an early start marking workbooks. All could hear the hum that was now becoming deafening.

The principal, looking down from her first-floor office, marvelled at the sheer majesty of modern technology, the enthusiasm it brought forth and the bright future that lay ahead.

The Librarian

'I have just been appointed librarian', Chomwo tells me with a huge beam across his face. He is proud of his new position. 'It means that I will have a bright future. It is an important step for me in my career. I will have work and education and it means that I can support my family and myself. I will not need any help from anyone.' Chomwo is a tall gaunt young man of eighteen years. His father is dead and his mother is alone with six children. Chomwo is the eldest. His mother is unemployed but tries to manage by selling homemade cakes on the street. She is confident that Chomwo's education is a good investment. And this hope has already turned out to be true. 'We did the right thing', he says.

> I am on the right track, as you see. I'll have to sign up those who come. Put the chairs back, clean and make sure they are quiet so that everyone can study. I do not need anything more except my school. That's what I have to concentrate on. Then my mum and my siblings can get the money for food and clothes. I do not need anything . . . . I will focus on my education. And now I have even become a librarian.

School Without Books

We are missing books, a boy says, and continues: That's right, this is a school without books. They keep saying that we will get books but they never come. A girl chips in: in two subjects there are books, but we never get to take them home. We have to hand them back. When we do our homework, we must read the notes that the teacher has written on the board. It would be good if the library had some books. There are many who steal the books. My geography book has just been stolen. And I can't say it at home, because they just bought it for me and it was expensive. My dad will get angry when he discovers it. Her friend backs her up: yes, when they have stolen the books and you want it back, you can only get it if you pay for it. And we can't. Another adds: they also steal our note books. When we pay to get them back, they are often ruined. Often the important pages are torn out. The notebooks are our books, we need them when we study.

Wealth in Words

The Big Man arrived late. The Parent Teacher Association Meeting starts in about forty minutes but he usually turns up well before that, chats with teachers and discusses the agenda with the principal. The Big Man has been the community representative forever and many consider the school to be his. A well-known businessman with good connections to political parties and local officials, he came from this suburb and returns occasionally for these meetings or to accompany other Big Men as they collect data for their latest report. So many reports that obscure the truth and conjure other futures into being. He hops out of the taxi, jokes with the driver and then heads through the main gates, carried by words.

Secure learning environment: Yes, children must be safe to learn. So many young men waiting outside the gate. It makes the school look important but can't they satisfy their desires somewhere else? He pushes past a familiar face who turns away into the shadows. Peter's orphaned children watch on.

Right to education: That started everything twenty years ago! *The Ministry of Education upholds the principle that every individual has an equal right to educational opportunities.* He has admired and memorized that phrase but wished the poor wouldn't block the main hallway as they plead for free places for their children. So distressing with this begging and so cramped in here.

Successful futures: Yes, good education is relevant education and now we have the national vocationalization plan and entrepreneurship. Young people can create their own businesses. Have you not heard about the popcorn machine? This is a school on the move. He approaches the staffroom.

Dignity: Mutual respect is the cornerstone. Why do these three boys kneel here? Children, please move. This is the teacher's room, not an area for rest or enjoyment. The teachers must have free passage!

Professional teaching force: The big agencies say that teachers work at home because of the lack of space at schools but our new teacher room is enormous and look, they are all in here, enjoying professional relations. The double-shifts tire them out but they are diligent, even taking on additional marking assignments. We are proud of their commitment!

Appropriate learning environments: We need better facilities such as books, chalk, writing boards and chairs. However, the core of the learning comes in the healthy relation between teacher and pupil. Do you know that Mrs Mwale will soon be qualified to support children who have been victims of violence and abuse? The family we create here is a microcosm of the nation.

Learner-centred pedagogy. Our Minister has told the world that we now have child friendly schools. This is achieved by providing water and sanitation, desks for all students and the school health and nutrition program.[38] Some children receive meals as well. With a resounding slap on his huge mid-drift, he reinforces the message that happy learning requires a full stomach.

Life-long learning: Hmmm. He ponders the master term, unsure that it is a real thing, before muttering to himself that the children of his school will never forget the lessons learnt here.

As he disappears into the principal's office, some of the smaller children pick up the deep echo of his belly slap as it reverberates down the hallway and out onto the dusty playing fields beyond. Here, it teases students of all ages as they peck at their meager lunches, rest and play. Swirling around bushes, benches and football posts, this echo is seductive, seeking out the optimistic and their burning longing for knowledge and opportunity. Keeping hope alive.

Figure 5.15 Game over?

6

Comparative Education and Radical Uncertainty

1

Radical uncertainty: 'where the world is changing more radically than thought itself'[1] and where its 'immanent disorder' becomes impossible to deny.[2] The changes we have described here are hardly unknown to educationalists. The ages of industrial, consumer, financial and information capitalism are well documented. The factory, the department store, the 24-hour online shop. The telegram, radio, television, internet and the Cloud. Insight becomes information, news and, finally, entertainment, distraction and the pretence of authenticity. Marx identified the fluidity of modernity, suggesting that ideals and ways of life were melting away. In his wake, modern science has attempted to understand the dynamics of this melting in order to arrest it. We now face an age of proliferation and remainder where purpose, effort and hope are caught in the shifting sand of public discourse and the inchoate stream of communication that gives it form. The space between the world as it is and the world as it should be continues to guide our conscience and feed our guilt. The worldly ideal, notions of heaven, utopia, the sublime and 'development' are but different languages of Western metaphysics all directed to resolving an aching gap, ridding things of their messiness and indeterminacy.

*

Where do we start, not least when place and context, as we have theorized here, are not as simple as that? Space itself remains fleeting. What became standard with the development of the marine chronometer[3] appears now to be remade by global flows. It seems that time and space are indeed inventions ↔ fictions unique to the moderns. Time, once discrete, linear and historical now seems accelerated, slowed *and* reversible.[4]

*

Our argument hangs therefore not on a radical premise but one we have lived with for a generation but struggled to embrace. Is there something rather than nothing? A greater truth waiting to be found? More than this? Can a science of comparative education redeem a world in semiotic chaos? Where do we turn at this late stage? Heidegger considered art as one particular strategy for connecting to deeper currents of meaning.[5] In his analysis of Van Gogh's famous painting *Old Shoes*, he suggests much more than the limited association to worn footwear. Instead, the image evokes the hardship and struggle of the peasant class and thus brings to consciousness an absent world very much alive in modern society that remains dependent on the labour of the exploited. For Jameson, the painting is 'hermeneutical, in the sense in which the work in its inert, objectal form is taken as a clue or a symptom for some vaster reality which replaces it as its ultimate truth'.[6] This was a painting in the age of the meaningful referent and well-aimed signifier: an age of sociological depth where art served the function of connecting history, personal experience and truth. Jameson compares this iconic work to Andy Warhol's equally iconic *Diamond Dust Shoes*, a flat, two-dimensional collage of women's footwear suspended without context or clear purpose like a 'random collection of dead objects . . . the remainders and tokens of some incomprehensible and tragic fire in a packed dance hall'.[7] Here, the hermeneutic circle cannot be closed. Ruptured by flatness and superficiality, it is the very 'inversion of Van Gogh's Utopian gesture' where 'the external and coloured surface of things – debased and contaminated in advance by their assimilation to glossy advertising images – has been stripped away to reveal the deathly black-and-white substratum of the photographic negative which subtends them'. This is no longer a 'matter of content' but of some 'more fundamental mutation both in the object world itself – now become a set of texts or simulacra – and in the disposition of the subject'.[8]

Warhol's art 'evidently no longer speaks to us with any of the immediacy of Van Gogh's footgear'.[9] For Warhol, 'The more you look at the same exact thing, the more the meaning goes away and the better and emptier you feel.'[10] It wasn't always thus. If we think of Edward Munch's equally iconic work, *The Scream*, we might acknowledge Jameson's observation that it provides a 'programmatic emblem' of an 'age of anxiety' where the themes of 'alienation, anomie, solitude, social fragmentation, and isolation'[11] are on full display. Munch's picture suggests a 'complex' era of individuality and autonomy – call signs of modernity – but, equally, imprisonment in the 'mindless solitude of the monad, buried alive and condemned to a prison cell without egress'. By contrast, in our time, the subject appears to fall apart and away, fracturing into a multitude of textual performances and intensities. This is the 'waning of affect' but also the ending of much more:

> for example, of style, in the sense of the unique and the personal, the end of the distinctive individual brush stroke (as symbolized by the emergent primacy of mechanical reproduction). As for expression and feelings or emotions, the liberation, in contemporary society, from the older *anomie* of the centred subject may also mean not merely a liberation from anxiety but a liberation from every other kind of feeling as well, since there is no longer a self present to do feeling.[12]

Perhaps this waning of affect is the closest we will get to liberation. A ground between purpose and meaningless, presence and absence. Existence, almost. Completion, never. As referentials dissolve, we are left with the play of signs and the coming post human. Is this the *becoming* human that so enamours contemporary education researchers or the *almost* human who must negotiate an era where there are 'no essential differences or absolute demarcations between bodily existence and computer simulation, cybernetic mechanism and biological organism, robot teleology and human goals'?[13] This future, hinted at by McLuhan and others long ago, is an actually existing 'reality' to which we cannot turn our backs. Its affects will be different, but a new general economy requires a new range of ways to read the 'global situation', new ways to engage radically with our present. A cultural perspective has been prioritized in these pages, one that draws heavily on ideas of hyperreality, simulation and indeterminacy put forward by Baudrillard and taken in other directions by theorists such as Žižek, Agamben, Sloterdijk and Virilio.[14] These moves put into question the very viability of representational projects in the human 'sciences', and by association most of the oeuvre of comparative education which moves in the tracks laid down by the speculative philosophy of Kant, Hegel and Habermas. If meaningful pathways exist in Western thought, our time seems much more readable through our deliberations on art and writing, sacrifice and death and, ultimately, our own happy letting go.

*

Figure 6.1 When a Country Falls in Love with Itself.

'In those days the world of mirrors and the world of men were not, as they are now, cut off from each other. They were besides, quite different; neither beings nor colours nor shapes were the same. Both kingdoms, the specular and the human, lived in harmony; you could come and go through mirrors'.[15]

*

For Mi-kyong the dream was finally reality. The class trip to Denmark had been a year in planning and now they were here, in Copenhagen, seeing a world that otherwise only released itself in parts though TV dramas, social media and music clips. The cobblestones, rows of English-like terrace houses and sea of white faces felt strangely familiar. Another home. One lodged in her private thoughts that seemed more than real. The school was definitely different. The teachers don't yell and the students come and go when they please. The most disturbing thing was when a boy laid down on a set of tables at the back of the room, using his cycle helmet as a pillow. This didn't stop him yelling out a question over the teacher's explanation of the apartheid system. And the teacher answered, which really shocked me, even though the boy didn't seem to wait for the answer! How can they learn like this and what do their parents say? I also saw that they didn't have to wear uniforms or even comb their hair! Are these wild adults or free people?

The trip to Denmark was the return of the gift that commenced when class 2G went to Seoul last spring. Eskil thought that Korea was cool. Big buildings, narrow dark lanes, 24-hour neon. It's like Blade Runner or something. Lots of people that might be cyborgs but you never quite know. I like the feeling that it's going somewhere but no one knows where. It's busy, but why? The school was pretty stiff but the students were pretty friendly. They wanted to know a lot more about us then we did about them. Most of us wanted to shop and buy electronics but, you know it's not that cheap. I'm not sure I'd like to live there but it was a great place to experience. Like Denmark might become in the future.

Mrs Lungu's Grade 11 English class was all about urban life somewhere else. In the big cities, they have red mail boxes, see the picture in your textbook. It is here that letters are deposited and spirited off all over the world. You can see the picture of this man, a postman like ours, delivering letters in the snow. Yes, snow is like our sun. They have much of it. He will stop to discuss events of the day with the residents. This is community. COMMUNITY is written on the chalkboard. They need each other and this is called interdependence. INTERDEPENDENCE goes up as well. Joseph raises his hand and suggests innocently: don't they use texting like us?

*

A study in/of fragments is *one* way forward, hinting at the disturbing experience of schooled life in the *almost* human. This is an attempt to write the world as it presents itself prior to its submission to the techniques of 'science', the subjective demands of taste and morality and the politics of utopianism. The argument is that a fragmentary approach does greater justice to the world and to our experiences of it. How we *fill* those fragments becomes the battleground for the soul of our (un)disciplined calling. This is where the stakes are highest.

Is hyperreality and disappearance just another *End of History* thesis? The possibility of further meaningful or significant events seems questionable if they must first slip down the rabbit hole of media spectacle and simulation. For Baudrillard, though, hyperreality is only a staging post for the theatre that follows. Globalization, universalism, the spread and normalization of a certain type of humanitarian impulse coupled with a media, communication and political machine that strives for moral improvement, represent the 'unification of things in a totalized world'.[16] This is a desire for immortality where 'the creative will of the transcendent God becomes the destructive will of man sweeping up everything in the vortex of self-assertion'.[17] It is this spectre, now made planetary, that shapes the educational project of schooling and to which we must become better attuned. It is here, in schools everywhere, that we see visions and practices of globality and world-making taking form as acts of impotent self-assertion in jumbled relation to earlier norms of right and wrong, good and bad, pure and profane, noble and decadent. Ours is an age of the Moebius-strip where clear boundaries dissolve and life becomes a procession of clumsy acts performed on a sticky, shifting surface:

> If we were in a face-to-face, confrontational system, strategies could be clear, based on a linearity of causes and effects. Whether one used good or evil, it would be used as part of a plan, and Machiavellianism would not lie outside rationality. But we are in a completely random universe in which causes and effects are piled one upon the other according to this Moebius-strip model, and no one can know where the effects of the effects will end.[18]

For Baudrillard, there is still much at stake in a random universe because this Empire of Good remains locked in a dualistic relation to negativity and death. As the drive for greater achievement, freedom, purpose and self-determination intensifies, it is slowly undone by acts of disruption, misunderstanding and ambivalence, not least when signs outrun their capacity to enable meaning and where imaginaries outrun the possibilities of their realization.

> Youth strive to achieve fulfilment and self-realization. Perverted, this turns to narcissism, the reversal of Western individualism.
>
> Uncontrolled, grandiose attempts at self-love lead to self-doubt, loathing and aggressive posturing: personally and at the collective level.
>
> The celebration of 'reality' leads to dreams of escape. The over-abundance of schooling, opportunity and futures reverts, literally, to stasis and lethargy. Life is lived simulating the world (through gaming culture, fantasy, idealized pop culture, modern schooling with its rhetoric of freedom and possibility) or by simply dreaming oneself away.
>
> The delusional celebration of opportunity in the context of stasis and control leads to disengagement and desperate strategies for living on.
>
> In some places, we see a mania of participation, consumption, gratification, devotion and sacrifice as responses to the helplessness and loss that comes with global abjection: sitting at the big table, not allowed to eat. Window-shopping for beginners.
>
> Cast out and thrown down, blind faith and extreme and profane behaviour become the only rational responses to the increasingly abstract rhetoric of progress and freedom.

The only certainty in our time is the death of our 'reality principle'[19] and the dread that we are headed into an era of *integral* reality: 'an unlimited operational project' where 'everything becomes visible and transparent, everything is "liberated"' and 'everything comes to fruition'. More real than real, a plane on which 'there is no longer anything on which there is nothing to say'.[20] This would be the final solution: a world that has exterminated its own illusion by applying ultimate truth to all:

> Literally, to *exterminate* means to deprive something of its own end, to deprive it of its term. It is to eliminate duality, the antagonism of life and death, to reduce everything to a kind of single principle – we might say a *pensée unique* – of the world. . . . So, by eliminating every negative principle, we might be said to end up with a world that is unified, homogenized, totally verified. . . . Extermination might be said, from this point on, to be our new mode of disappearance, the one we have substituted for death.[21]

*

In Spring 2020, the world was overcome by a 'viral dispersal' of a biological kind, hardly noticing the 'epidemic of value'[22] that had long preceded it.

*

Integral reality is a fate that has not yet overrun humankind, although the present orgy of 'reality' portends to the world to come. At the core of this is what Baudrillard calls the 'fate of value'. Having moved from use value, though exchange and more recently sign value, modernity is now facing its fractal stage where value 'radiates in all directions, occupying all interstices'. As signs break free from signifiers and meaning becomes estranged from action, we see not the destruction of the system of meaning per se but, rather, 'an endless process of self-reproduction' based on 'total indifference' to that which is being generated. Indeed, once things are freed from 'their ideas, of their own essences' they are 'able to proliferate everywhere, to transport themselves simultaneously to every point of the compass'. The consequences are fatal: 'A thing which has lost its idea is like the man who has lost his shadow, and it must either fall under the sway of madness or perish.'[23] Freed from the demands of meaning, referent and intention, ideas run wild. As the categories of politics, aesthetics, sexuality, communication and, not least, education break free from specific meaning universes, they expand into all directions, infecting any realm that is open to the seduction of words without weight:

> Each category is generalized to the greatest possible extent, so that it eventually loses all specificity and is reabsorbed by all the other categories. When everything

is political, nothing is political any more, the word itself is meaningless. When everything is sexual, nothing is sexual any more, and sex loses its determinants. When everything is aesthetic, nothing is beautiful or ugly any more, and art itself disappears. This is the paradoxical state of affairs, which is simultaneously the complete actualization of an idea, the perfect realization of the whole tendency of modernity, and the negation of that idea and that tendency, their annihilation by virtue of their success, by virtue of their extension beyond their own bounds – this state of affairs is epitomized by a single figure: the transpolitical, the transsexual, the transaethetic.[24]

This vision of the future is one of 'total confusion' and the 'impossibility of apprehending any determining principle'.[25] It is a world that is 'identical with itself, identical to itself, by exclusion of any principle of otherness'.[26] It is this polemic provocation of a world to come that we apply to education. Set free from historical commitments and ideals, offered up as an idea without referent, sent to all places and to everyone, education becomes everything, anything and thus nothing. Of course, it will continue to be celebrated for the narrow certainties of instrumental training and skills formation, but the noble aims of self-awareness and meaningfulness beyond mere value are compromised. This loss is alluded to in magical fragments where schooling disappears under the metaphorical weight of popcorn; as young people are sucked into mirrors of false truth; as fleeting fantasies played out in the non-places of baroque shopping malls. As education proliferates everywhere, it disappears into the void.

*

How strange that we look to education for salvation when we should recognize it as central to our predicament.

*

Where do we go when schooling collapses under its own weight? When the carnival of universalized subjectivity is exposed as fiction? When the will to global interconnection and possibility *for all* becomes impossible to sustain? This is our current situation: a time when promises cannot be redeemed but where we are left in wait. Is the subject forever trapped in an *impossible exchange* with the object? In the twilight of modern hubris, after our confidence in the power of planning, development, creation and control, we are left with a morning ↔ mourning after with its enforced sobriety and reluctant soul-searching. Can we write our way out of this carnival?

2

Writing a world that is more real than real: Integral reality changes our understanding of the research process and affects the possibilities for writing. To write ↔ right in the shadow of integral reality means to communicate in ways that are rich, extreme, sensuous, erotic, profane and ecstatic but where meaning is necessarily sacrificed as the text flows over all. Is ours simply another baroque strategy of representation aimed at overloading the senses so that we might glimpse the impossible depths of the human? Hardly. Our form of excessiveness aims to disrupt the orgy, to bring integral reality to a halt, to work our way into its cracks in order to slip away and disappear. Perhaps we disable the 'science' of comparative education by slowing down and reversing the rush to knowledge and certainty that has been the distinctive contribution of our calling to the carnival of the 'real'. If we are to avoid the will to power that gives 'science' its lustre, and if we accept our complicity in further undermining meaning making by overloading things with more 'reality', we may be ready to replace speculative philosophy with meditative thought aimed at letting go:

> the meditative thinker lingers with the negative but, unlike the speculative philosopher, does not negate negation. . . . To live responsibly in a world without redemption, is to live responsibly by always being grateful to the graciousness of every other who lets beings be. Time – what little time remains – is never our own; to the contrary, it is always given and might be taken at any instant . . . to accept the gift of life is to accept the gift of death . . . the elsewhere that is always near.[27]

*

To dance with death 'releases one for the levity of the bearable lightness of nonbeing'.[28] This letting go, or acceptance of what is, becomes part of a fatal approach tasked with riding things to the end, seeing what might be. Not non-action, but non-*directive* action. It is, in the words etched into the tombstone of surrealist artist Man Ray, to remain 'unconcerned but not indifferent'.

*

Is it the tragic fate of the artist to respond only *during* the requiem when that which is disappearing is all but gone?

*

The attempt to find meaning in nothingness and define purpose through non-action is not new and was challenged most spectacularly by Adorno, first in his *Minima Moralia* where he implores philosophy to strive for the impossible goal of redeeming the world, even though historical circumstances appear to work against that task. For Adorno, we must imagine a better world in readiness for the time when it *might* be realizable. Philosophy *always* has a future. Later, in his provocative *The Jargon of Authenticity*, he takes aim at 'German ideology': that tendency or lust to view the world through the lens of ontology, metaphysics and abstraction instead of lived experience, materiality and practice. To talk of meaninglessness is to present a 'straw man'[29] that can be used to *re-inscribe* meaning. To talk of non-being is to open the way for a *new* understanding of being. Philosophers like Heidegger operated with 'bad conscience' for they questioned the possibility of metaphysics but left it standing as a mode of thought that avoided the actual/material horror and fragmentation of the world. To want to 'overcome' and 'produce new values' is 'symptomatic of a reactionary modernism' whose:

> ontologization of the social and facile positivity lead ineluctably to fascism. In this sense, the vocabulary of nothingness and despair becomes part of a masculinist philosophical jargon of resoluteness, decisiveness and hardness that ends up functioning as an *apologia* for immoral intolerance and political barbarism.[30]

Rather than engage directly with the political field, or insist that one can transcend domination through social critique, Adorno sees the highest form of response coming from those works that maintain 'aesthetic autonomy' and ensure the 'refusal of meaning'.[31] It is here that we glimpse the *possibility* of freedom. The application of Baudrillard's ideas to an ethnographic study of schooling suggests a world beyond redemption where there are no obvious paths for restoring meaning or authenticity. It also suggests a world that has pushed beyond the rules of reason and clear, honest, thought. That is a grim message indeed. However, a thesis of hopelessness runs the risk of restoring its opposite. Conscious of the traps of 'bad conscience', we offer a fragmented approach to our topic, brought to life with fragmented data laced with the indeterminate and magical. Rather than lamentation *or* celebration, our aim is to maintain a state of unfamiliarity, conceptual discomfort and to question experience. It is through meditative writing unburdened by fact, necessity or hope that something else can be sensed, and where the 'real' can finally be put to rest.

*

Kim had been struggling to sleep. At the time, it was easy enough to drop out of high school. He had independence, a little money and was well away from the harsh routine of the school and evening slog to keep ahead of the others. There are hardly any jobs anyway so why bother. He had his pet python, friends at the PC centre and time on his side. In the beginning, it was such a relief. No one to tell him what to do except his boss at the café. But he is easy going says Kim. My parents weren't happy with my decision so I don't see them so much. I lost some friends but found others.

Sleep was a blessing when it came but he was growing restless and his strange dreams intensified. Most nights he met Security Chief Yie at the school. Mr Yie didn't say anything but just followed him around as he walked through the empty school. For some reason, these nightly visits to the school always included a stolen glance into Principal Yan's office. He remembers from his time in school that Principal Yan nurtured many plants. Like the botanical garden, you know. Now, in this dreamscape, those plants were weaving themselves into a thick jungle. Principal Yan was still at his desk, even though the vines were beginning to limit his movement. It's funny: I was always so silent when I snuck up to his office and peeked in but every time he always managed to look up at the exact same moment. His eyes pierce you with his judgment. Occasionally, I'd see an animal in there, moving behind the trees. Once I saw my snake on his shoulders. Usually that's when I'd wake. See you tomorrow night Principal Yan!

Being free of school wasn't so liberating anymore. The expectations seemed to be returning. It felt like they were dripping slowly from the ceiling each time he turned to his gaming console to kill a few hours with friends. He felt more and more penned in. Trapped. The apartment is on a busy road in a noisy quarter but that's not it. The ventilation isn't great and if you open the windows you'll be deafened by the noise and covered in fine dust. But that's not it. Tonight, he sleeps deeply even though he feels burdened with some ill-defined worry, as if he was being squashed or flattened. It was becoming hard to breath. Heat all around.

At about 4 am he woke in a blind panic, eyes bulging, gasping for air, desperate to get up but hopelessly pinned down. He immediately turned to the inner wall of his bedroom and the snake house. Resigned, he realized that the python was no longer in Principal Yan's office.

*

Aesthetic autonomy – perhaps little more than a fragile hope in our age – requires a form of writing that *reframes* (not avoids) the question of politics and purpose.

The radical uncertainty of the world is maintained when objects charged with seductive force become impossible to grasp let alone tame. A 'cynical' educational project only intensifies the fiction and tragedy that the metaphysical gap (between subject and object; ignorance and knowledge; experience and utopia) can be bridged. Educational research – like comparative education – is caught in this absurd condition: more 'science' leads to more 'reality' and less awareness as the real is buried further in its illusionary other. Strategies to achieve autonomy are many. We have touched upon the thought of Camus and the need to embrace the absurd condition of the world as a pathway to finding one's personal place in it. To live on without hope but without despair. For Bataille, as we have seen, it is letting the world present itself *in extremis* as a way to fully embrace its general economy and thus derive energy from one's own vital source. For Baudrillard, it is facing processes of hyperreality head on, meeting them with fatal strategies that keep the undecidable in play.

Ethnography also has a place as a strategy to achieve aesthetic autonomy. By evoking the world rather than seeking to catch or represent it, ethnography 'makes available through absence what can be conceived but not presented'. This puts it 'beyond truth and immune to the judgment of performance'.[32] We can even say that if the aim of ethnography is to *evoke* the world, one that is beyond reach by the application of scientific proof, control and pure communication, it becomes *the* method and research orientation of choice for our contemporary 'fantasy reality'.[33] This approach to ethnography – stubbornly dismissed by the majority of a profession in search of precision – prioritizes the 'mutual, dialogical production of a discourse' instead of the 'monologue' of the social-science report driven by the 'ideology of the transcendental observer'. Ethnography was always with us as the sharing of stories that drew upon the fanciful in order to make sense of the 'real'. Now, it returns with new purpose:

> it defamiliarizes commonsense reality in a bracketed context of performance, evokes a fantasy whole abducted from fragments, and then returns participants to the world of common sense – transformed, renewed, and sacralized. It has the allegorical import, though not the narrative form, of a vision quest or religious parable. The break with everyday reality is a journey apart into strange lands with occult practices – into the heart of darkness – where fragments of the fantastic whirl about in the vortex of the quester's disoriented consciousness at the very moment of the miraculous, restorative vision, and then, unconscious, is cast up onto the familiar, but forever transformed, shores of the commonplace world.[34]

Ethnography, then, becomes the 'meditative vehicle' to transcend time and place where meaning is 'not in it but in an understanding, of which it is only a consumed fragment'.³⁵ To *evoke* means, necessarily, that we are free from the straightjacket and conceit of *explanation*. Once we relinquish the goal of representation, we withdraw from an ideological academic field of power, from the illusion of reality and from the age-old struggle to find meaning where it does not exist. This is not a surrender but, rather, a path to a very different type of awareness. Ethnography, when mindful of the limits of science, 'departs from the commonsense world only in order to reconfirm it and to return us to it renewed and mindful of our renewal'.³⁶ However, part of the contract in this therapeutic renewal is to acknowledge that such ethnography, forever subject to the whims of language and perception, remains incomplete. Thankfully, there can be no utopia at the end of the journey. The world will remain fragmented well after our attempts to evoke it into being, just as it has resisted attempts to holism from a scientific endeavour driven by illusion ↔ delusion.

3

Comparison is the thief of joy.³⁷ As we have seen, comparative education is a broad approach to world-making. The contention now is that it has largely run out of conceptual steam, mired in notions of place and context that speak to an earlier era of nation-based, culturally mediated inter-relations, complicated by an ongoing Cartesian, teleological and universalizing logic. Cube thinking but without the all-important cubist goal of attempting to present phenomena from *multiple* perspectives. Its northern epistemological zero point has been one of our areas of attention. Is the very act of mapping and measuring unavoidably parochial, always coming from *somewhere*? Does everything labelled northern necessarily carry the stain of domination and genocide? Our own approach is undoubtedly partial, resting on a familiar northern canon. However, in the post-foundational currents explored here, we have found our own abyssal thread that works to destabilize an over certain mainstream, one that challenges the sovereignty of any one perspective and the voice of any one author. It is the thought that remains when we realize that it is all just thought.

*

If the world is changing more radically than thought itself, perhaps it is time to lose our minds.

*

We are not alone in seeking other paths, with a new wave of scholarship engaged in working the ruins of comparative education. As we have seen, some have interrogated the notions of place, space and time. Others have explored the unit thinking on which comparative work rests. One prominent strand explores actual epistemological diversity in the world and challenges us to find space for southern voices in what continues to be a thoroughly colonialized endeavour. Such work is concerned with not only issues of restorative justice but our environment and planetary survival. However, what problems follow from a project that uses the language and morality of northern thought to argue for the silenced other? Can there be a genuinely southern theory alternative that draws on northern concerns such as the materiality of education, the primacy of politics and the assumed common goal of freedom and self-determination?[38] We would do well to keep all thought at a playful distance, especially as 'everything has its truth'.[39]

A more adventurous path is being taken by those who explore what we might call the archaic in education. By connecting post-Soviet schooling to myth and magic, Silova shows that the modernist period in comparative education was just that: an era and perspective elevated to the place of worldview. What riches were cast aside in the desperate rush to modernize?

> Equally importantly (although rarely acknowledged), it relegated more-than-human worlds and spiritual domains of learning – and being – to our collective pasts, personal childhood memories or imaginations, and worst yet, attempted to expel them beyond the boundaries of the field altogether. In education research more broadly, spiritual domains have been side-lined and 'put at the margins of the academy', restricting our ability to express and practice spirituality inside its walls.[40]

While early Soviet education attempted to suppress differences in the name of modernization, we might argue that comparative education has attempted to do likewise to deviant thought or practice. Can other worlds and worldviews be suppressed for much longer? What do we lose when 'seeking to paper over, rank, or eradicate' differences in the search for 'ultimate similarity'?[41] How do we deal with the legacy of Hegel's distorted philosophy of history with its notion of an inevitable unfolding of historical consciousness towards the realization of a good life that, unsurprisingly, reflects the world of mid-nineteenth-century bourgeois Germany? However, this is not the only stream of Hegelianism at play in comparative education. Any attempt to synthesize traditions, bridge difference, understand and incorporate the 'other' in order to obtain a fuller, deeper or more balanced picture smacks of dialectical reasoning and its deadening negations, what Critchley calls 'a conceptual sadism which forces recognition on things through domination'.[42]

One inspiring effort to get beyond such modern impulses comes from the hitherto marginalized world of Japanese comparative thought. From Kyoto School philosophy, especially that strand developed by Keiji Nishitani, the challenge is to dwell in negativity and to understand education as 'a negative movement of subtraction' that aims to teach the student how to 'let go of the constructs by which one both comprehends reality and separates oneself from reality'.[43] If one considers some of the dominant voices in Zen thought – Hakuin, Dogen, Nishitani for example – we find a striving for a unity of being and non-being. For Nishitani, the major challenge in Western thought is to respond to the nihilism that emerges with the death of God and the purposelessness of history which becomes 'an errant striving for a viable future' that places 'an unbearable burden upon the individual'.[44] Life is not a process of restoring meaning in the world through superior or more appropriate concepts but, rather, becoming aware of its essential emptiness. The ultimate aim here is to reject the 'nihility of nihilism'.[45] In contrast to the Western philosophical tradition, emptiness lies beyond representation. It is not a 'thing' and not in opposition to 'being'. Rather, emptiness lies at the core of the subject/object relation and is *identical* to being. The aim of meditative practice – and, we might add, education or, even, a text of fragments – is to empty things of their thingness. This is not a strategy intended to cheat death but a means to connect death to life in order to leave behind dualistic thought. In the Zen tradition, it is a path to finding the 'reality' of the self and of objects but requires that we transform our field of consciousness. Ultimately, we enter great doubt where the fiction of the independent self is discarded and thought becomes something akin to 'without-thinking'. Standing at the cliff edge, we ignore the warning sign and step into the void. This is radical *certainty*. It is the understanding that there is something beyond the 'impermanent, fractured, empirical self',[46] what Hakuin calls the unchanging Buddha-nature that 'radiates a great pure luminescence'.[47]

*

Eskil was one of 500 that streamed out of the graduation hall for an afternoon and evening of pure celebration. The parties lasted all night and his group of eighteen or so – survivors of three tough years together – made their way to the lake and its summer waters where they would greet the first soft rays of the morning sun. Running on empty, they eventually disbanded, making their way to the local train station. The plan was to return home before meeting again in the city later that day. Taking the stairs to the platform, Eskil was the first to meet the intense light of the sun, now obscured by a thick wall of fog. Immersed in nature's blanket, disoriented but free, he walked over the edge into an oncoming train. No one saw a thing and it was over before the rest of his friends reached the platform. The next day, numb with grief, they made a small shrine of candles in the under pass to the station. Some passers-by cursed that the gathering was limiting their access but only until they saw the framed picture, flowers and wall of candles. As they huddled together, the students sang Eskil's favourite songs and told his funniest stories. After a time, Frederik broke the silence by asking if they thought he felt it. That's the wrong question, stupid! They all looked around thinking that they knew the voice, but of course there was no one else in the tunnel. As they left, Miranda said that it *sounded* like Eskil but no one replied.

*

As we have seen, post-foundational thought, emerging from the broader vein of Western philosophy, has had its own approach to such questions. Nietzsche's challenge to metaphysical reasoning leads us to two different approaches to nihilism: a passive one reflects the limits of Western humanism and an active one works to transgress them. However, while the practitioner of Zen seeks to move beyond representation, the post-foundational philosopher – and some might include Baudrillard and ourselves here – remains trapped in the labyrinth of perspectivism. Even though new approaches to object, self, text and method are brought forth, concepts – however radical they may be – continue to frame and restrict the field of the possible, with a thinking subject/writer never far from centre stage. While the student of Zen attempts to drop thought altogether, the post-foundational *thinker* continues to work the ruins by swapping out one mode of enquiry for another. This is a radical *scepticism* that looks for alternatives but from within the world of ideas. Going on, and without the promise of Ariadne's thread, the post-foundational thinker finds moments of respite but no escape route.

Perhaps these pages can serve as a bridge between a post-foundationalism that is prepared to go all the way and drop thought and that of Eastern philosophy. From the perspective of the Western thought developed here, fatal writing challenges the illusion of 'reality' and the omnipotence of the reasoning subject. It becomes our version of the Japanese koan. Theory as fiction seeks to take academic work beyond the confines of representation and correspondence, questioning everything except the possibility of writing as a strategy of escape and mode of living on. Recognizing the self and ego as precarious achievements, it attempts to disrupt what cultural modernity started with words and images that elude final interpretation and that defer indefinitely the onward march of subjectivity to its bleak terminus.

This fatal approach to scholarship requires that we accept the limits to freedom that come with modern subjectivity, recognizing that there can never be a total resolution or negation of things. We must accept that there is always some remainder, leftover, excess or trace that keeps us 'here' in the world of forms. This is the radical *uncertainty* of the world, a place where images, sensations and codes remain one visceral step ahead of our swift footwork and conceptual counter punches. Can we ever get the jump on the illusion of 'reality'? Maybe. We must first learn to let go,[48] embrace our vulnerability[49] and seek out 'simple joys'.[50]

*

After school, especially on Thursdays when class ends early and the usual club events are over, Joseph and the boys head down to the river to mess around. This time they have the football with them, sneaked out of the sport's room and secreted through the main gates. It's not a long walk but interesting all the same. The bitumen road ends about 100 meters from the school and the streetlights just after that. That's where the shanty town starts. There's always something going on down there. Someone cooking pancakes. Singing. Dogs in mortal combat. TVs blaring through the cracks of flimsy huts. They kicked at the ground blanketed in rubbish but hiding small treasures. One found a bottle opener that could easily be cleaned up. Another took a plastic bottle that, once rinsed clean of dirt and dust, could be used to hold fuel. Not bad. They started playing football, yelling, grabbing each other in the absence of Mr Chanda the referee. These were good times when most other things just drifted away.

Denis kicked the ball far away and it ran and ran all the way to the edge of the riverbank, only coming to a halt at a half-burnt log strangled by grimy plastic and surrounded by the flotsam of an earlier temporary camp: empty tins, cigarette packets, old newspaper, food scraps. It was here, having given up on the business of selling popcorn at the school, Peter drank the dark liquid that set him free. No more promises of salvation.

Joseph ran towards the ball, not knowing the history of this place. He bent over to pick it up, wrapped his hands around the battered surface and paused for a moment without really knowing why. A small sunbird had landed on the log and without the slightest sign of fear returned his glare as it sized him up. Joseph straightened, certain that his sudden movement would startle the creature into flight. It remained completely still, an extension of the charred log and the ground around them. He looked into its eye, an eye that seemed directed at him alone but which also took in everything around the dusty camp. He was now standing over the bird, falling into the darkness of its gaze, deeply connected but strangely distant. He felt that he'd experienced this moment before but how could that be.

They called out and he returned slowly, looking back occasionally. The wind had picked up just then. He re-joined the group, throwing the ball into the scrum. Funny he said. The others looked but could only see a kaleidoscope of colour as the bird fluttered above the ground at one with the breeze, communicating truth to the observant few.

Their game continued until eventually, with the light fading and chores waiting, they turned to head home. Along the way, Joseph asked the others what had happened to Peter's kids. Didn't they used to hang around outside the school? I don't know, said George throwing the ball in Joseph's direction. Remember to get this back to the sports room or we'll all be in trouble. Joseph didn't answer. He was still thinking about the bird as it danced lightly above the world.

Figure 6.2 Sunbird.

Notes

Introduction

1. The Dutch champion Johan Cruyff.
2. Examples include Brown, R. H. (1977), *A Poetic for Sociology: Toward a Logic of Discovery for the Human Sciences*, Chicago: University of Chicago Press; Gordon, A. (2008), *Ghostly Matters: Haunting and the Sociological Imagination*, Minnesota: University of Minnesota Press; Ruiz, X. M. (2019), *Time for Educational Poetics: Why Does the Future Need Educational Poetics?* Leiden: Brill.
3. Malpas, S. (2002), 'Sublime Ascesis: Lyotard, Art and the Event', *Angelaki, Journal of Theoretical Humanities*, 7 (1): 199–212 (p. 200).
4. Cowen, R. (2021), 'Educated Identity: Concepts, Mobilities, and Imperium', in L. Klerides and S. Carney (eds), *Identities and Education: Comparative Perspectives in an Age of Crisis*, 27–46, London: Bloomsbury Publishers (p. 27).
5. Cortada, X. (2020), *The Future Is Here, Now*, Virtual address to Comparative and International Education Society Annual Conference, Miami, March. (https://www.youtube.com/watch?v=4_b2rvlu2Fo&feature=emb_logo&fbclid=IwAR1clt12fEkET3t9ljz0GCpKIW8ysCkgXE4_nnF81lcfzzSEHKrm5ESMCbU).
6. Haraway, D. J. (1997), *Modest Witness@Second Millennium.Female Man© Meets OncoMouse™. Feminism and Technoscience*, London and New York: Routledge.
7. Madsen, U. M. (2018), *Baudrillard og Pædagogik: Fatal etnografi*, Copenhagen: Hans Reitzels Forlag.
8. Berg, M. and B. Seeber (2016), *The Slow Professor: Challenging the Culture of Speed in the Academy*, Toronto: University of Toronto Press.

Chapter 1

1. Lyotard, J.-L. (1989), 'Lessons in Paganism', in A. Benjamin (ed.), *The Lyotard Reader*, Cambridge: Basil Blackwell, 122–54 (p. 123).
2. Allen, A. (2017), *The Cynical Educator*, Leicester: Mayfly books, 6.
3. Jameson, F. (2002), *A Singular Modernity: Essay on the Ontology of the Present*, London: Verso.
4. Featherstone, M. and Lash, S. (1995), 'Globalization, Modernity and the Spatialization of Social Theory: An Introduction', in M. Featherstone, S. Lash, and R. Robertson (eds), *Global Modernities*, London: Sage, 1–24.

5   Appadurai, A. (1996), *Modernity at Large: Cultural Dimensions of Globalization*, Minneapolis and London: University of Minnesota Press, 35.
6   Appadurai, A. (2013), *The Future as Cultural Fact: Essays on the Global Condition*, London: Verso, 4–5.
7   Appadurai, A. (2013), *The Future as Cultural Fact*, 299–300.
8   Bennett, O. (2001), *Cultural Pessimism: Narratives of Decline in the Postmodern World*, Edinburgh: Edinburgh University Press.
9   Mohaghegh, J. (2013), *Silence in Middle Eastern and Western Thought: The Radical Unspoken*, New York: Routledge, 158.
10 Moisi, D. (2009), *The Geo-Politics of Emotion: How Cultures of Fear, Humiliation and Hope Are Reshaping the World*, London: The Bodley Head.
11 Madsen, U. A. and Carney, S. (2011), 'Education in an Age of Radical Uncertainty: Youth and Schooling in Urban Nepal', *Globalisation, Societies and Education*, 9 (1): 115–33; Carney, S. and Madsen, U. A. (2009), 'A Place of One's Own: Schooling and the Formation of Identities in Modern Nepal', in. J. Zajda, H. Daun, and L. Saha (eds), *Nation-Building, Identity and Citizenship Education: Cross-Cultural Perspectives*, 171–87, Springer Science + Business Media B.V.
12 Winther-Jensen, T. (2001), 'Changing Cultures and Schools in Denmark', in J. Cairns, D. Lawton, and R. Gardner (eds), *World Yearbook of Education: Values, Culture and Education*, London: Kogan Page, 178–89 (p. 187).
13 Mohaghegh, J. (2013), *Silence in Middle Eastern and Western Thought*, 154.
14 Nietzsche, F. (1995), *Birth of Tragedy* (trans. by Clifton P. Fadiman), Minnesota and New York: Dover Publications, 1.
15 Nietzsche, F. (2003), *Twilight of the Idols and the Anti-Christ*, London: Penguin, 43.
16 Allen, A. (2017), *The Cynical Educator*, 173.
17 Nietzsche, F. (1995), *Birth of Tragedy*, 6.
18 Nietzsche, F. (1995), *Birth of Tragedy*, 5.
19 Nietzsche, F. (1995), *Birth of Tragedy*, 3.
20 Nietzsche, F. (1995), *Birth of Tragedy*, 5.
21 Prideaux, S. (2018), *I Am Dynamite: A Life of Nietzsche*, New York: Tim Duggan Books, 89.
22 Nietzsche, F. (1995), *Birth of Tragedy*, 4.
23 Nietzsche, F. (1995), *The Birth of Tragedy*, 3.
24 Allen, A. (2017), *The Cynical Educator*, 173.
25 Allen, A. (2017), *The Cynical Educator*, 180.
26 Camus, A. (2000), *The Myth of Sisyphus*, London: Penguin, 109–10.
27 Baudrillard, J. (2005), *The Intelligence of Evil: Or the Lucidity Pact*, London: Bloomsbury.
28 Allen, A. (2017), *The Cynical Educator*, 172.
29 Allen, A. (2017), *The Cynical Educator*, 179.

30 Taylor, M. C. (1984), *Erring: A Postmodern A/Theology*, Chicago: University of Chicago Press, 33.
31 Nietzsche, F. (2003), *Thus Spoke Zarathustra*, London: Penguin, 46.
32 Baudrillard, J. (2007), *Forget Foucault*, Los Angeles: Semiotext(e), 30.
33 Featherstone, M. (1995), *Undoing Culture: Globalization, Postmodernism and Identity*, London: Sage, 19.
34 Kellner, Douglas, 'Jean Baudrillard', in *The Stanford Encyclopedia of Philosophy* (Winter 2015 Edition), Edward N. Zalta (ed.), https://plato.stanford.edu/archives/win2015/entries/baudrillard/ (p. 12).
35 Baudrillard, J. (2008), *The Perfect Crime*, London: Verso, 3.
36 Coulter, G. (undated). *Simulation Is Not the Opposite of the Real—Jean Baudrillard on Simulation and Illusion*. https://noemalab.eu/org/sections/ideas/ideas_articles/pdf/coulter_simulation_real.pdf (retrieved 18 February 2011).
37 Juschka, D. M. (2003), 'The Writing of Ethnography: Magical Realism and Michael Taussig', *Journal for Cultural and Religious Theory*, 5.1 (December): 84–105 (p. 92).
38 Juschka, D. M. (2003), 'The Writing of Ethnography', 84–105 (pp. 92–3).
39 Mohaghegh, J. (2013), *Silence in Middle Eastern and Western Thought*, 154.
40 Taussig, M. (1997), *The Magic of the State*, New York: Routledge.
41 Borges, J. L. (1937) 'The Analytical Language of John Wilkins', *Other Inquisitions* 1952: 101–5 (accessed 28 June 20 at http://www.crockford.com/wrrrld/wilkins.html), p. 103.
42 Foucault, M. (2002), *The Order of Things*, Abingdon: Routledge, xvii.
43 Foucault, M. (2002), *The Order of Things*, xix.
44 Borges, J. L. (1937), 'The Analytical Language of John Wilkins', 103.
45 Foucault, M. (2002), *The Order of Things*, xix.
46 Stronach, I. (2010), *Globalizing Education, Educating the Local: How Method Made Us Mad*, New York: Routledge.
47 Bazzano, M. (2014), *Buddha Is Dead: Nietzsche and the Dawn of European Zen*, Eastbourne: Sussex Academic Press, 14.
48 Bazzano, M. (2014), *Buddha Is Dead*, 14.
49 Here we refer to Foucault's evocation of the famous surrealist credo taken from Lautréamont's poem 'The Songs of Maldoror: "As beautiful as the random encounter between an umbrella and a sewing machine upon a dissecting table"'. In Foucault's hands, that table becomes the 'tabula' or grid upon which things can be subjected to reason and order. de Lautréamont, C. (1914), 'The Songs of Maldoror', *Egoist*, 1 (22): 423.
50 Arva, E. L. (2008), 'Writing the Vanishing Real: Hyperreality and Magical Realism', *Journal of Narrative Theory*, 38 (1): 60–85, citing Benjamin's Illuminations (p. 65).
51 Arva, E. L. (2008), 'Writing the Vanishing Real', 60–85 (p. 80).

52 Bataille, G. (2001), *The Unfinished System of Non-Knowledge*, Minneapolis: University of Minnesota Press, 113.
53 Mohaghegh, J. (2013), *Silence in Middle Eastern and Western Thought*, 153.

Chapter 2

1 de Sousa Santos, B. (2006), 'Globalizations', *Theory, Culture & Society*, 23 (2–3): 393–9 (p. 393).
2 Axford, B. (2013), *Theories of Globalization*, Cambridge: Polity Press.
3 Rosenberg, J. (2005), 'Globalization Theory: A Post Mortem', *International Politics*, 42: 2–74.
4 Tsing, A. (2000), 'The Global Situation', *Cultural Anthropology*, 15 (3): 327–60 (p. 350).
5 Axford, B. (2013), 'You Had Me on "Global" and "Studies" Too, I Think', *Globalizations*, 10 (6): 779–84 (p. 779).
6 de Sousa Santos, B. (2006), 'Globalizations', 393.
7 de Sousa Santos, B. (2006), 'Globalizations', 393.
8 Nienass, B. (2013), 'Performing the Global', *Globalizations*, 10 (4): 533–8 (p. 536).
9 Friedman, J. (1990), 'Being in the World: Globalization and Localization', *Theory, Culture & Society*, 7: 311–28 (p. 312).
10 Friedman, J. (1990), 'Being in the World', 313.
11 Axford, B. (2013), *Theories of Globalization*.
12 Beck, U. (1992), *Risk Society: Towards a New Modernity*, London: Sage, 2.
13 Friedman, J. (2002), 'From Roots to Routes: Tropes for Trippers', *Anthropological Theory*, 2: 21–36 (p. 21).
14 Friedman, Thomas L. (2005), 'The World Is Flat: A Brief History of the Twenty-First Century', Farrar, Straus and Giroux. http://capitolreader.com/bonus/The%20World%20Is%20Flat.pdf (accessed 6 November 18).
15 Hardt, M., and Negri, A. (2000), *Empire*, Cambridge, MA: Harvard University Press, 216.
16 Hardt, M. and Negri, A. (2000), *Empire*, xiii.
17 de Sousa Santos, B. (2006), 'Globalizations', 393.
18 Friedman, J. (2002), 'From Roots to Routes', 22.
19 Rushdie, S. (1995), *Midnight's Children*, London: Vintage, 9.
20 Tsing, A. (2000), 'The Global Situation', 334.
21 Axford, B. (2013), *Theories of Globalization*, 15.
22 Geertz, C. (1975), 'Common Sense as a Cultural System', *The Antioch Review*, 33 (1): 5–26 (pp. 16–17).
23 Axford, B. (2013), *Theories of Globalization*, 14.

24 Axford, B. (2014), Interview with Professor Barrie Axford on 'Theories of Globalization', Global Studies Association. https://globalstudiesassoc.wordpress.com/2014/02/13/interview-with-professor-barrie-axford-on-theories-of-globalization/ (accessed 2 July 2019).
25 Burawoy, M. (2000), 'Introduction: Reaching for the Global', in M. Burawoy, J. A. Blum, S. George, M. Thayer, Z. Gille, T. Gowan, L. Haney, M. Klawiter, S. H. Lopez and S. Ó Raian (eds), *Global Ethnography: Forces, Connections, and Imaginations in a Postmodern World*, Berkeley, CA: University of California Press, 1–40 (p. 5).
26 Nienass, B. (2013), 'Performing the Global', 534.
27 Appadurai, A. (1996), *Modernity at Large: Cultural Dimensions of Globalization*, Minneapolis: University of Minnesota Press, 18.
28 Massey, D. (2004), *Space, Place and Gender*, Cambridge: Polity.
29 Tsing, A. (2000), 'The Global Situation', 330.
30 Tsing, A. (2000), 'The Global Situation', 332.
31 Featherstone, M. (1995), *Undoing Culture: Globalization, Postmodernism and Identity*, London: Sage, 13–14.
32 Tsing, A. (2000), 'The Global Situation', 327.
33 Axford, B. (2013), *Theories of Globalization*, 16.
34 Friedman, J. (1990), 'Being in the World', 312.
35 Tsing, A. (1990), 'The Global Situation', 327.
36 Appadurai, A. (2006), *Fear of Small Numbers*, Durham: Duke University Press.
37 https://danskfolkeparti.dk/politik/kampagner/.
38 Appadurai, A. (1996), *Modernity at Large*, 5.
39 Appadurai, A. (1996), *Modernity at Large*, 32.
40 Appadurai, A. (1996), *Modernity at Large*, 3.
41 Appadurai, A. (1996), *Modernity at Large*, 4.
42 Appadurai, A. (1996), *Modernity at Large*, 36.
43 Source:http://www.bbc.co.uk/newsbeat/article/36341367/china-denies-selling-human-flesh-as-tinned-corned-beef-in-zambia-in-africa (accessed 1 March 20).
44 Friedman, J. (1990), 'Being in the World', 314.
45 Appadurai, A. (1996), *Modernity at Large*, 35.
46 Friedman, J. (2002), From Roots to Routes, 21.
47 Friedman, J. (2002), From Roots to Routes, 26–7.
48 Friedman, J. (2002), From Roots to Routes, 27.
49 In a similar vein, Vickers explores the simplistic world-making that constitutes current innovations in comparative education, illustrating the manner in which Western modernity, colonialism and imperialism are conflated as forces solely external to a uniformly victimized non-western other. Vickers, E. (2019), 'Critiquing Coloniality, "Epistemic Violence" and Western Hegemony in Comparative Education – The Dangers of Ahistoricism and Positionality', *Comparative Education*, 56 (2): 165–89.

50 Bude, H. and Dürrschmidt, J. (2010), 'What's Wrong with Globalization?: Contra "Flow speak" – Towards an Existential Turn in the Theory of Globalization', *European Journal of Social Theory*, 13 (4): 481–500 (p. 496).
51 Heyman, J. and Campbell, H. (2009), 'The Anthropology of Global Flows: A Critical Reading of Appadurai's "Disjuncture and Difference in the Global Cultural Economy"', *Anthropological Theory*, 9 (2): 131–48 (pp. 136–7).
52 Ong, A. (1999), *Flexible Citizenship: The Cultural Logics of Transnationality*, Durham, NC: Duke University Press, p. 11.
53 Appadurai, A. (1996), *Modernity at Large*, 47.
54 Ferguson, J. (1999), 'Global Disconnect: Abjection and the Aftermath of Modernism', in *Expectations of Modernity: Myths and Meanings of Urban Life on the Zambian Copperbelt*, Berkeley, CA: University of California, 234–54.
55 de Sousa Santos, B. (2006), 'Globalizations', 397.
56 Appadurai, A. (1996), *Modernity at Large*, 29.
57 Berlant, L. (2011), *Cruel Optimism*, Durham: Duke University Press.
58 Appadurai, A. (1996), *Modernity at Large*, 29.
59 Lizardo, O. and Strand, M. (2009), 'Postmodernism and Globalization', *Protosociology*, 26: 38–72. These knowledge-geographical traditions are unfolded further in Carney, S. (2016), 'Global Education Policy and the Post-modern Challenge', in K. Munday, A. Green, R. Lingard and A. Verger (eds), *Handbook of Global Policy and Policy-Making in Education* (Handbook of Global Policy Series), 504–18, Oxford: Wiley-Blackwell.
60 Featherstone, M. (1995), *Undoing Culture: Globalization, Postmodernism and Identity*, London: Sage, 44.
61 Lizardo, O. and M. Strand. (2009), 'Postmodernism and Globalization', 44.
62 Giddens, A. (1990), *The Consequences of Modernity*, Stanford, CA: Stanford University Press.
63 Lizardo, O. and Strand, M. (2009), 'Postmodernism and Globalization', 49.
64 Jameson, F. (1991), *Postmodernism; or the Cultural Logic of Late Capitalism*, London: Verso.
65 Lambert, G. (2006), *Who's Afraid of Deleuze and Guattari?* London: Continuum, 16–17.
66 Lizardo, O. and Strand, M. (2009), 'Postmodernism and Globalization', 17.
67 Lizardo, O. and Strand, M. (2009), 'Postmodernism and Globalization', 58.
68 Lizardo, O. and Strand, M. (2009), 'Postmodernism and Globalization', 58.
69 Lambert, G. (2006), *Who's Afraid of Deleuze and Guattari?*, 5.
70 Lizardo, O. and Strand, M. (2009), 'Postmodernism and Globalization', 39.
71 Lizardo, O. and Strand, M. (2009), 'Postmodernism and Globalization', 65.
72 Featherstone, M. (1995), *Undoing Culture: Globalization, Postmodernism and Identity*, 79.

73 Connell, R. (2007), 'Northern Theory of Globalization', *Sociological Theory*, 25 (4): 368–85 (p. 378).
74 Connell, R. (2007), 'Northern Theory of Globalization', 379.
75 Connell, R. (2007), 'Northern Theory of Globalization', 376.
76 Dussel, E. (1993), 'Eurocentrism and Modernity (Introduction to the Frankfurt Lectures)', *boundary 2*, 20 (3): 65–76 (pp. 65–6).
77 de Sousa Santos, B. (2016), 'Beyond Abyssal Thinking', in *Epistemologies of the South: Justice against Epistemicide*, London: Routledge, 118 (pp. 118–35).
78 de Sousa Santos, B. (2016), 'Beyond Abyssal Thinking', 119.
79 Zastoupil, L. and Moir, M. (1999) (eds), 'Minute Recorded in the General Department by Thomas Babington Macaulay, Law Member of the Governor-General's Council, Dated 2 February 1835', in *The Great Indian Education Debate: Documents Relating to the Orientalist-Anglicist Controversy, 1781–1843*, London: Routledge, 166.
80 Gordon, L. R. (2011), 'Shifting the Geography of Reason in an Age of Disciplinary Decadence', *TRANSMODERNITY: Journal of Peripheral Cultural Production of the Luso-Hispanic World*, 1 (2). Retrieved from https://escholarship.org/uc/item/218618vj.
81 de Sousa Santos, B. (2016), 'Beyond Abyssal Thinking', 164.
82 Mignolo, W. (2018), 'Foreward. On Pluriversality and Multipolarity', in B. Reiter (ed.), *Constructing the Pluriverse: the Geopolitics of Knowledge*, Duke University Press, Durham and London, x.
83 de Sousa Santos, B. (2016), 'Beyond Abyssal Thinking', 224–5.
84 de Sousa Santos, B. (2016), 'Beyond Abyssal Thinking', 118.
85 Baudrillard, J. (1996), *The Perfect Crime*, trans. C. Turner, London: Verso, 106.
86 Shahjahan, R., Ramirez, G. B. and De Oliveira Andreotti, V. (2017), 'Attempting to Imagine the Unimaginable: A Decolonial Reading of Global University Rankings', *Comparative Education Review*, 61 (S1): s51–s73 (p. s60).
87 Baudrillard, J. (2010), *Carnival and Cannibal*, Seagull: London, 23.
88 Friedman, J. (1990), 'Being in the World', 313.
89 Baudrillard, J. (2010), *Carnival and Cannibal*, 4–5.
90 Baudrillard, J. (2010), *Carnival and Cannibal*, 23.
91 Baudrillard, J. (2010), *Carnival and Cannibal*, 24.
92 Baudrillard, J. (2002), 'The Global and the Universal', in *Screened Out*, London: Verso, 158–9.
93 Heidegger first uses this term to signify an era marked by a focus on human freedom and self-determination. It's opposite, and our focus here, is captured by Eagleton's (2004) notion of the postmodern as 'the contemporary movement of thought which rejects totalities, universal values, grand historical narratives, solid foundations to human existence and the possibility of objective knowledge'.

In its place, we consider 'pluralism, discontinuity and heterogeneity' (Eagleton, T. [2003], *After Theory*. New York: Basic Books, 13). Somewhat differently, post-structuralism views 'structures as historically and reciprocally affected by practice within contingent conditions of time, particularly conceptual practices and how they define disciplinary knowledge' (Prado [1995], 154 in Lather, P. [2001], 'Postmodernism, Post-structuralism and Post(Critical) Ethnography: of Ruins, Aporias and Angels', in P. Atkinson, Coffey, A, Delamont, S, Lofland J. and L. Lofland (eds), *Handbook of Ethnography*, Sage: London, 475–92 (p. 479). We might do well to note that both modernity and postmodernity – however defined – reflect a certain will to power. (Taylor, M. [2018], *Abiding Grace: Time, Modernity, Death*, Chicago: University of Chicago Press).

94 Ulmer, J. B. (2017), 'Posthumanism as Research Methodology: Inquiry in the Anthropocene', *International Journal of Qualitative Studies in Education*, 30 (9): 832–48 (p. 5).

95 Paechter, C. and Weiner, G. (1996), 'Editorial, Special Issue: Post-modernism and Post-structuralism in Educational Research', *British Educational Research Journal*, 22 (3): 267–72 (p. 269).

96 Bauman, Z. (1990), 'Modernity and Ambivalence', *Theory, Culture & Society*, 7 (2): 143–69 (p. 165).

97 Eagleton, T. (1990), *Literary Theory: An Introduction*, Basil Blackwell: Oxford, 132.

98 Peters, M., Marshall, J. and Fitzsimons, P. (2000), 'Managerialism and Educational Policy in a Global Context: Foucault, Neoliberalism and the Doctrine of Self-Management', in N. C. Burbules and C. A. Torres (eds), *Globalization and Education: Critical Perspectives*, New York: Routledge (pp. 139–52).

99 Ball, S. J. (2003), 'The Teachers' Soul and the Terrors of Performativity', *Journal of Education Policy*, 18 (2): 215–28.

100 Popkewitz, T. (2008), *Cosmopolitanism and the Age of School Reform: Science, Education, and Making Society by Making the Child*, New York: Routledge.

101 Baker, B. (1998), 'Child-Centered Teaching, Redemption, and Educational Identities: A History of the Present', *Educational Theory*, 48 (2): 155–75.

102 Deleuze, G. and Guattari, F. (1987), *A Thousand Plateaus: Capitalism and Schizophrenia*. Minneapolis: University of Minnesota, 253–4.

103 Israel, J. (2010), *A Revolution of the Mind: Radical Enlightenment and the Intellectual Origins of Modern Democracy*, Princeton: Princeton University Press.

104 Epstein, I. (2019), *Affect Theory and Comparative Education Discourse. Essays on Fear and Loathing in Response to Global Educational Policy and Practice*, London: Bloomsbury Academic, 25.

105 Snaza, N. and Weaver, J. (2015), 'Introduction: Education and the Posthumanist Turn', in *Posthumanism and Educational Research*, New York: Routledge 1–16 (p. 5).

106 Snaza, N. and Weaver, J. (2015), 'Introduction: Education and the Posthumanist Turn', 6.
107 Berlant, L. (2011), *Cruel Optimism*, 16.
108 Berlant, L. (2011), *Cruel Optimism*, 14.
109 Thrift, N. (2008), *Non-Representational Theory: Space, Politics, Affect*, London: Routledge, 221.
110 Ahmed, S. (2004), *The Cultural Politics of Emotion*, Edinburgh: Edinburgh University Press.
111 Berlant, L. (2011), *Cruel Optimism*, 14.
112 Berlant, L. (2011), *Cruel Optimism*, 8.
113 Hemmings, C. (2005), 'Invoking Affect: Cultural Theory and the Ontological Turn', *Cultural Studies* 19 (5) September: 548–67 (pp. 549–52).
114 Berlant, L. (2011), *Cruel Optimism*, 8.
115 Haraway, D. (2016), *Staying with the Trouble*, Durham, NC: Duke University Press, 30.
116 Tsing, A. (2015), *The Mushroom at the End of the World: On the Possibility of Life in Capitalist Ruins*, Princeton: Princeton University Press, vii.
117 Haraway, D. (2016), *Staying with the Trouble*, 37.
118 Silova, I. (2018), 'Searching for the Soul: Athena's Owl in the Comparative Education Cosmos', *European Education* 50: 223–7 (p. 225).
119 Haraway, D. (2016), *Staying with the Trouble*, 45.
120 Gildersleeve, R. E. (2018), 'Becoming-Policy in the Anthropocene', *Education Policy Analysis Archives*, 26 (152): 1–12.
121 Barad, K. (2003), 'Posthumanist Performativity: Toward an Understanding of How Matter Comes to Matter', *Signs: Journal of Women in Culture and Society*, 28: 801–31.
122 Ulmer, J. (2017), 'Posthumanism as Research Methodology: Inquiry in the Anthropocene', 841.
123 Haraway, D. (2016), *Staying with the Trouble*, 1.
124 Tsing, A. (2015), *The Mushroom at the End of the World*, vii.
125 Somerville, M. and Powell, S. (2019), 'Researching with Children of the Anthropocene: A New Paradigm?' in *Educational Research in the Age of Anthropocene*, Hershey, PA: IGI Global, 14–35 (p. 17).
126 Somerville, M. and Powell, S. (2019), 'Researching with Children of the Anthropocene', 25.
127 Barad, K. (2007), *Meeting the Universe Halfway: Quantum Physics and the Entanglement of Matter and Meaning*, Durham, NC: Duke University Press, x.
128 Somerville, M. and Powell, S. (2019), 'Researching with Children of the Anthropocene', 24.
129 Lather, P. (2016), '(Re)Thinking Ontology in (Post)Qualitative Research', *Cultural Studies, Critical Methodologies*, 16 (2): 125–31 (p. 125).

130 Somerville, M. and Powell, S. (2019), 'Researching with Children of the Anthropocene', 29.
131 Adams St. Pierre, E. (2013), 'The Posts Continue: Becoming', *International Journal of Qualitative Studies in Education*, 26 (6): 646–57 (p. 655).
132 Deleuze, G. and Guattari, F. (1994), *What Is Philosophy?*, trans. H. Tomlinson and G. Burchell, New York, NY: Columbia University Press (Original work published 1991), 75.
133 Cowen, R. (2014), 'Comparative Education: Stones, Silences, and Siren Songs', *Comparative Education*, 50 (1): 3–14. Cowen provides a formidable overview of the multiple comparative educations, their stories of origin and current iterations.
134 Phillips, D. and Ochs, K. (2003), 'Processes of Policy Borrowing in Education: Some Explanatory and Analytical Devices', *Comparative Education*, 39 (4): 451–61.
135 Paulston, R. (2000), 'Imagining Comparative Education: Past, Present, Future', *Compare*, 30 (3): 353–67.
136 Nóvoa, A. and Yariv-Mashal, T. (2003), 'Comparative Research in Education: A Mode of Governance or a Historical Journey?' *Comparative Education*, 39 (4): 423–38.
137 Nordtveit, B. (2015), 'Knowledge Production in a Constructed Field: Reflections on Comparative and International Education', *Asia Pacific Education Review*, 16: 1–11 (p. 2).
138 Cowen, R. (2014), 'Comparative Education: Stones, Silences, and Siren Songs', 7. Schriewer, J. (2010), notes that this myth of origin brushes over a richer heritage of French Enlightenment thought where 'serious reflection on comparison' was a hallmark, (p. 29). And of course one could problematize the notion of a singular, coherent, Enlightenment project. Israel (2010), for example makes the useful distinction between a 'radical' tradition of pure reason, democracy and Spinoza's doctrine of one-substance and the more familiar 'moderate' tradition of elite rule through the state and traditional institutions where reason is used to justify both change and stasis and as a force separate from nature. Schriewer, J. (2010), 'An Enlightenment Scholar in English Robes', in M. Larsen (ed.), *New Thinking in Comparative Education: Honouring Robert Cowen*, 29–31, Rotterdam: Sense Publishers. Israel, J. (2010), *A Revolution of the Mind*.
139 Epstein, E. and Carroll, K. (2005), 'Abusing Ancestors: Historical Functionalism and Postmodern Deviation in Comparative Education', *Comparative Education Review*, 49 (1): 62–88.
140 Durkheim (1911), p. 1539, in Nóvoa, A. (2018), 'Comparing Southern Europe: The Difference, the Public, and the Common', *Comparative Education*, 54 (4): 548–61 (p. 550) (Durkheim, É. [1911], 'Pédagogie', in Ferdinand Buisson (ed.), *Nouveau*

dictionnaire de pédagogie et d'instruction primaire, Paris: Librairie Hachette, 1538–43).

141 Bray, M., Adamson, B. and Mason, M. (eds) (2007), *Comparative Education Research: Approaches and Methods. CERC Studies in Comparative Education* (Vol. 32), 8, Dordrecht: Springer.

142 Nóvoa, A. (2018), 'Comparing Southern Europe: The Difference, the Public, and the Common', 550.

143 Noah, H. and Eckstein, M. (1969), *Toward a Science of Comparative Education*, London: Macmillan, 115.

144 Shahjahan et al. (2017), 'Attempting to Imagine the Unimaginable', s59.

145 Nóvoa, A. (2018), 'Comparing Southern Europe', 550.

146 Nóvoa, A. (2018), 'Comparing Southern Europe', 551.

147 Takayama, K. (2018), 'Beyond Comforting Histories', *Comparative Education Review*, 62 (4): 459–81.

148 Monroe, P. (1927), *Essays in Comparative Education: Republished Papers*, New York: Teachers College, Columbia University, in Takayama, K. (2018), 'Beyond Comforting Histories', 467.

149 Nóvoa and Yariv-Mashal (2003), 'Comparative Research in Education: A Mode of Governance or a Historical Journey?', 424. Vickers (2019), 'Critiquing Coloniality, "Epistemic Violence" and Western Hegemony in Comparative Education – The Dangers of Ahistoricism and Positionality', reminds us that much education reform is pushed by local elites not distant masters.

150 Philips, D. and Schweisfurth, M. (2015), *Comparative and International Education: An Introduction to Theory, Method, and Practice,* 186, London: Bloomsbury.

151 Cowen, R. (2014), 'Comparative Education: Stones, Silences, and Siren Songs', 6.

152 Noah, H. and Eckstein, M. (1969), *Toward a Science of Comparative Education,* ix.

153 Bray, M. and Thomas, R. M. (1995), 'Levels of Comparison in Educational Studies: Different Insights from Different Literatures and the Value of Multilevel Analyses', *Harvard Education Review,* 65 (3): 472–90. (p. 488).

154 Cowen, R. (2014), 'Comparative Education: Stones, Silences, and Siren Songs', 3.

155 Palomba, D. (2010), 'Maestro Di Pensiero', in M. Larsen (ed.), *New Thinking in Comparative Education: Honouring Robert Cowen*, 81–2, Rotterdam: Sense Publishers.

156 Nóvoa, A. (2018), 'Comparing Southern Europe', 551.

157 Nóvoa, A. (2018), 'Comparing Southern Europe', 552.

158 Rust, V. (1991), 'Postmodernism and Its Comparative Education Implications', *Comparative Education Review,* 35 (4): 610–26; Ninnes, P. and S. Mehta (eds) (2004), *Re-imagining Comparative Education: Postfoundational Ideas and Applications for Critical Times*, New York: Routledge.

159 One could refer to the CER Special Issue on 'Contesting Coloniality', CER 61, S1 (2017), not least Riyad A. Shahjahan, Gerardo Blanco Ramirez, And Vanessa De Oliveira Andreotti (2017), 'Attempting to Imagine the Unimaginable: A Decolonial Reading of Global University Rankings', s51-s73.
160 Paulston, R. (2000), 'Imagining Comparative Education: Past, Present, Future', 353–67.
161 Takayama, K. (2019), 'An Invitation to "Negative" Comparative Education', *Comparative Education*, 56 (1): 79–95. Rappleye, J. (2019), 'Comparative Education as Cultural Critique', *Comparative Education*, 56 (1): 39–56.
162 Silova, I. (2019), 'Toward a Wonderland of Comparative Education', *Comparative Education*, 55 (4): 444–72.
163 Silova, I. and Auld, E. (2019), 'Acrobats, Phantoms, and Fools: Animating Comparative Education Cartographies', *Comparative Education*, 56 (1): 20–38 (p. 20).
164 Tobin, J., Wu, D., and Davidsen, D. (1989), *Preschool in Three Cultures*, New Haven: Yale University Press.
165 Alexander, R. (2000), *Culture and Pedagogy: International Comparisons in Primary Education*, Oxford: Blackwell Publishers.
166 Gupta, A. and Ferguson, J. (1992), 'Space, Identity, and the Politics of Difference', *Cultural Anthropology*, 7 (1): 6–23 (p. 8).
167 Ferguson, J. (2006), *Global Shadows: Africa in the Neo-Liberal World Order*, Durham, NC: Duke University Press, 10.
168 Massey, D. (2004), *Space, Place and Gender*.
169 Gulson, K. (2007), 'Mobilizing Space Discourse: Politics and Educational Policy Change', in K. Gulson and C. Symes (eds), *Spatial Theories of Education: Policy and Geography Matters*, New York, Routledge, 37–56 (p. 45).
170 Gupta, A. and Ferguson, J. (1997), 'After "People's" and "Cultures"', in A. Gupta and J. Ferguson (eds), *Culture, Power and Place: Explorations in Critical Anthropology*, Durham: Duke University Press, 1–29 (p. 20).
171 Sobe, N. and Kowalczyk, J. (2014), 'Exploding the Cube: Revisioning "Context" in the Field of Comparative Education', *Current Issues in Comparative Education*, 16 (1): 6–12 (p. 10).
172 Clifford, J. (1988), *The Predicament of Culture*. Cambridge, MA: Harvard University Press, 275.
173 Gupta, A. and Ferguson, J. (1992), 'Space, Identity, and the Politics of Difference', 7.
174 Wright, S. (2005), 'Processes of Social Transformation: An Anthropology of English Higher Education Policy', in J. Krejsler, N. Kryger and J. Milner (eds), *Pædagogisk Antropologi – et fag i tilblivelse*, Copenhagen: Danmarks Pædagogiske Universitet, 185–218 (p. 190).
175 Bartlett, L. and Vavrus, F. (2014), 'Transversing the Vertical Case Study: A Methodological Approach to Studies of Educational Policy as Practice', *Anthropology & Education Quarterly*, 45 (2): 131–47 (p. 131).

176 Marcus, G. (1995), 'Ethnography in/of the World System: The Emergence of Multi-Sited Ethnography', *Annual Review of Anthropology*, 24: 95–117; Marcus, G (1998), *Ethnography through Thick and Thin*, Princeton: Princeton University Press; Marcus, G. (2011), 'Multi-Sited Ethnography: Five or Six Things I Know about It Now', in S. Coleman and P. von Hellermann (eds), *Multi-Sited Ethnography: Problems and Possibilities in the Translocation of Research Methods*, 16–34, New York: Routledge.

177 Marcus, G. (1995), cited in Falzon, M.-A. (2009), *Multi-Sited Ethnography: Theory, Praxis and Locality in Contemporary Research*, Fanham: Ashgate, 1–2.

178 Vavrus, F. and Bartlett, L. (2009), 'Introduction', in F. Vavrus and L. Bartlett (eds), *Critical Approaches to Comparative Education: Vertical Case Studies from Africa, Europe, the Middle East, and the Americas*, New York: Palgrave MacMillan, 1–18 (p. 11).

179 Vavrus, F. and Bartlett, L. (2009), 'Introduction', 11.

180 Clifford, J. (1997), *Routes: Travel and Translation in the Late Twentieth Century*, Cambridge: Harvard University Press.

181 Falzon, M. (2009), 'Introduction', In *Multi-Sited Ethnography: Theory, Praxis and Locality in Contemporary Research*, Surrey: Ashgate, 1–24 (p. 10).

182 Candea, M. (2007), 'Arbitrary Locations: In Defence of the Bounded Field-site', *Journal of the Royal Anthropological Institute*, 13 (1): 167–84.

183 Falzon, M. (2009), 'Introduction', 2.

184 Hage, G. (2005), 'A Not so Multi-Sited Ethnography of a Not so Imagined Community', *Anthropological Theory*, 5 (4): 463–75 (p. 464).

185 Falzon, M. (2009), 'Introduction', 2.

186 Falzon, M. (2009), 'Introduction', 13, emphasis added.

187 Sobe, N. and Kowalczyk, J. (2018), 'Context, Entanglement and Assemblage as Matters of Concern in Comparative Education Research', in J. McLeod, N. W. Sobe and T. Seddon (eds), *World Yearbook of Education 2018: Uneven Space- Times of Education: Historical Sociologies of Concepts, Methods and Practices*, London: Routledge, 197–204 (p. 200).

188 Sobe, N. and Kowalczyk, J. (2018), 'Context, Entanglement and Assemblage as Matters of Concern in Comparative Education Research', 201.

189 Collier, S. J. (2006), 'Global Assemblages', *Theory Culture & Society*, 23 (2-3): 399-401 (p. 400).

190 Knorr Cetina, K. (2003), 'From Pipes to Scopes: The Flow Architecture of Financial Markets', *Distinktion: Scandinavian Journal of Social Theory*, 4 (2): 7–23 (p. 8).

191 Sobe, N. and Ortegón, N. (2009), 'Scopic Systems, Pipes, Models and Transfers in the Global Circulation of Educational Knowledge and Practices', in T. Popkewitz and F. Rizvi (eds), *Globalization and the Study of Education*, 49–66, New York, NY: NSSE/Teachers College Press (p. 58).

192 Knorr Cetina, K. (2006), 'The Market', *Theory Culture Society*, 23: 551–6 (p. 555).
193 Marcus, G. and Saka, E. (2006), 'Assemblage', *Theory Culture Society*, 23: 101–6 (p. 102).
194 Marcus, G. and Saka, E. (2006), 'Assemblage', 102.
195 Phillips, J. (2006), 'Agencement/Assemblage', *Theory Culture Society*, 23: 108–9 (p. 109).
196 Phillips, J. (2006), 'Agencement/Assemblage', 108, original emphasis.
197 Phillips, J. (2006), 'Agencement/Assemblage', 109.
198 Phillips, J. (2006), 'Agencement/Assemblage', 109.
199 Marcus, G. and Saka, E. (2006), 'Assemblage', 102, emphasis added.
200 Knorr Cetina, K. (2003), 'From Pipes to Scopes', 8.
201 Sobe, N. and Ortegón, N. (2009), 'Scopic Systems, Pipes, Models and Transfers in the Global Circulation of Educational Knowledge and Practices', 61.
202 Borges, J. L. (1998), 'Afterword', in *The Aleph*, London: Penguin, 183.
203 Carney, S. (2009), 'Negotiating Policy in an Age of Globalization: Exploring Educational "Policyscapes" in Denmark, Nepal and China', *Comparative Education Review*, 53 (1): 63–88.
204 Jameson, F. (1991), *Postmodernism; or the Cultural Logic of Late Capitalism*.
205 Luke, A. and Luke, C. (1990), 'School Knowledge as Simulation: Curriculum in Postmodern Conditions', *Discourse*, 10 (2): 75–91.
206 Handbooks such as Munday, K., Green, A., Lingard, R. and Verger, A. (eds), *Handbook of Global Policy and Policy-Making in Education*, provide a sense of the cohesion being produced within such areas.
207 Ball, S. J., Junemann, C. and Santori, D. (2017), *Edu.Net. Globalisation and Education Policy Mobility*, London: Routledge, 15.
208 Meyer, J. W. and Ramirez, F. (2000), 'The World Institutionalization of Education – Origins and Implications', in J. Schriewer (ed.), *Discourse Formation in Comparative Education*, Frankfurt: Peter Lang, 11–32.
209 Schriewer, J. (2012), 'Editorial: Meaning Constellations in the World Society', *Comparative Education*, 48 (4): 411–22.
210 Anderson-Levitt, K. (2003), 'A World Culture of Schooling?', in K. Anderson-Levitt (ed.), *Local Meanings, Global Schooling: Anthropology and World Culture Theory*, New York: Palgrave Macmillan.
211 Gulson, K., Lewis, S. Lingard, B., Lubienski, C., Takayama, K. and Taylor Webb, P. (2017), 'Policy Mobilities and Methodology: A Proposition for Inventive Methods in Education Policy Studies', *Critical Studies in Education*, 58 (2): 224–41 (p. 229).
212 Ball, S, Junemann, C. and Santori, D. (2017), *Edu.net. Globalization and Education Policy Mobility*, 2.
213 Gulson et al. (2017), 'Policy Mobilities and Methodology', 234.
214 Ball, S. J., Junemann, C. and Santori, D. (2017), *Edu.net. Globalization and Education Policy Mobility*, 1.

215 Gupta, A. and Ferguson, J. (1997), 'After "People's" and "Cultures"'.
216 Galloway, A. (2011), 'Are Some Things Unrepresentable?' *Theory, Culture & Society*, 28 (7–8): 85–102.
217 Ball, S. (2012), *Global Education Inc.: New Policy Networks and the Neo-Liberal Imaginary*, London: Routledge, 6.
218 Stronach, I. (2010), *Globalizing Education, Educating the Local: How Method Made Us Mad*, New York: Routledge.
219 Borges, J. L. (1998), 'On Exactitude in Science', *The Aleph*, London: Penguin, 181.
220 Baudrillard, J. (1994), *Simulacra and Simulation*, Michigan: University of Michigan, 1.
221 Rosenberg, J. (2005), 'Globalization Theory: A Post Mortem', 2–74.
222 Lawson, G. (2005), 'Rosenberg's Ode to Bauer, Kinkel and Willich', *International Politics*, (42): 381–9 (p. 387).
223 Coulter, G. in N. Ruiz III (2005), 'An Interview with Gerry Coulter', *Kritikos: An International and Interdisciplinary Journal of Postmodern Cultural Sound, Text and Image*, Vol. 2 (September). https://intertheory.org/coulter.htm (accessed 30 July 20).
224 Lawson, G. (2005), 'Rosenberg's Ode to Bauer, Kinkel and Willich', 42–3.
225 Lyotard, J.-F. (1984), 'Answering the Question: What Is Postmodernism?' in *The Postmodern Condition: A Report on Knowledge*, trans. G. Bennington and B. Massumi, Manchester: Manchester University Press, 71–82 (p. 74).
226 Coulter, G. in N. Ruiz III (2005), 'An Interview with Gerry Coulter', 6.
227 Coulter, G. in N. Ruiz III (2005), 'An Interview with Gerry Coulter', 13.
228 Nancy, J.-L. (2007), *The Creation of the World or Globalization*, Albany: State University of New York Press.
229 Coulter, G. in N. Ruiz III (2005), 'An Interview with Gerry Coulter', 12.
230 Koren, L. (2008), *Wabi-Sabi for Artists, Designers, Poets and Philosophers*, Point Reyes, CA: Imperfect Publishing, 27–8.
231 Cooper, T. M. (2018), 'The Wabi Sabi Way: Antidote for a Dualistic Culture?' *Journal of Conscious Evolution*, 10 (10): Article 4, Available at: https://digitalcommons.ciis.edu/cejournal/vol10/iss10/4 (p. 6).
232 Richman-Abdou, K. (2019), 'Kintsugi: The Centuries-Old Art of Repairing Broken Pottery with Gold', *My Modern Met*, 5 September 19. https://mymodernmet.com/kintsugi-kintsukuroi/ (accessed 30 July 20).
233 Mitchell, S. (2009), *The Second Book of the Tao*, New York: Penguin Books, 13.

Chapter 3

1 Kant, I. (1784/ 1954), 'What Is Enlightenment?' in R. Morse (ed.) and Peter Gay (trans.), *Introduction to Contemporary Civilization in the West*, New York: Columbia University Press, 1071–6.

2. Allan, A. and Goddard, R. (2017), *Education & Philosophy: An Introduction*, London: Sage, 97.
3. Kant, I. (1998), *Critique of Pure Reason*, trans. and ed. Paul Guyer and Allen W. Wood, Cambridge: Cambridge University Press, 704, original emphasis.
4. Kant, I. (1998), *Critique of Pure Reason*, 113.
5. Kant, I. (1998), *Critique of Pure Reason*, 168.
6. Kant, I. (1998), *Critique of Pure Reason*, 185.
7. Larsen, M. and Beech, J. (2014), 'Spatial Theorizing in Comparative and International Research', *Comparative Education Review*, 58 (2): 191–215.
8. Huhn, T. (2004), 'Introduction: Thoughts Beside Themselves', in T. Huhn (ed.), *The Cambridge Companion to Adorno*, Cambridge: Cambridge University Press, 1–18 (p. 7).
9. Kant, I. (1998), *Critique of Pure Reason*, 193.
10. Kant, I. (1998), *Critique of Pure Reason*, 533.
11. Allan, A. and Goddard, R. (2017), *Education & Philosophy*, 93.
12. Williams, B. (1996), 'Contemporary Philosophy: A Second Look', in N. Bunnin and E. P. Tsui-James (eds), *The Blackwell Companion to Philosophy*, Oxford: Blackwell Publishers, 25–37 (p. 34).
13. Allan, A. and Goddard, R. (2017), *Education & Philosophy*, 93.
14. Merleau-Ponty, M. (1964), *Sense and Nonsense*, trans. L. Herbert and Patricia Allen Dreyfus, Evanston: Northwestern University Press.
15. Craig, E. (2002), *Philosophy: A Very Short Introduction*, Oxford: Oxford University Press, 81.
16. Bowie, A. (2003), *Introduction to German Philosophy: From Kant to Habermas*, Cambridge: Polity Press, 275.
17. Blackburn, S. (1996), 'Metaphysics', in N. Bunnin and E. P. Tsui-James (eds), *The Blackwell Companion to Philosophy*, Oxford: Blackwell Publishers, 64–89 (p. 68).
18. Taylor, M. C. (1980), *Journey's to Selfhood: Hegel & Kierkegaard*, Los Angeles: University of California Press, 44.
19. Taylor, M. C. (2018), *Abiding Grace: Time Modernity, Death*, Chicago: University of Chicago Press, 106–7.
20. Blackburn, S. (1996), 'Metaphysics', 68.
21. Hegel, G. W. F. (1956), *Philosophy of History*, trans. J. Sibree, New York: Dover.
22. The first quote is attributed to Martin Luther King, Jr., the second to Barack Obama who was fond of paraphrasing King's original words.
23. Indeed, we find an emerging field of scholarship devoted to exploring the unproblematic unfolding of Western modernity through education worldwide. See Carney, S., Silova, I. and Rappleye, J. (2012), 'World Culture Theory: Between Faith and Science', *Comparative Education Review*, 56 (3): 366–93, for an elaboration and critique of latent Hegelian thought in comparative education.

24 Bowie, A. (2003), *Introduction to German Philosophy: From Kant to Habermas*, 84.
25 A well-known example in Hegel of the relations between self and other is his analysis of the Lord and the Bondsman where the latter subordinates himself to the former in order to stay alive and, by so doing, provides for his desires and demands that build up still stronger ties of dependency. While this example has been applied as a frame for interpreting and understanding history, others emphasize the analysis of subjectivity inherent in the Lord-Bondsman relation: object-subject positions are never fixed but carry the possibility of turning into the other.
26 Speculative: from speculum, meaning 'mirror'.
27 Taylor, M. C. (1987), *Alterity*, Chicago: University of Chicago Press, xxiii.
28 Heidegger, M. (1972), 'Time and Being', in Taylor, M. C. (1989), *Alterity*, xxvi.
29 Taylor, M. C. (1987), *Alterity*, xxiii.
30 Fukuyama, F. (1989), 'The End of History'? *The National Interest*, Summer: 3–18.
31 Schelling, letter to Fichte, in Bowie (2003), *Introduction to German Philosophy*, 103.
32 Schelling cited in Bowie, A. (2003), *Introduction to German Philosophy*, 77.
33 Schelling, F. W. J. (2004), *First Outline of a System of the Philosophy of Nature*, Albany: State University of New York Press, 132.
34 Bowie, A. (2003), *Introduction to German Philosophy*, 103.
35 Schiller, F. (1795/ 1967), *On the Aesthetic Education of Man in a Series of Letters*, New York: Oxford University Press.
36 Schiller, F. (1795/ 1967), cited in Taylor, M. C. (1980), *Journeys to Selfhood: Hegel & Kierkegaard*, Los Angeles: University of California Press, 25.
37 Rousseau, J.-J. (1761), Julie, or the New Heloise, cited in Berman, M. (2010,) *All That Is Solid Melts into Air*, London: Verso, 18.
38 Habermas, J. (1990), *The Philosophical Discourse of Modernity*, 45.
39 Habermas, J. (1990), *The Philosophical Discourse of Modernity*, 50.
40 Kant, I. (1987), *Critique of Judgment*, Indianapolis and Cambridge: Hackett Publishing Company, 174.
41 Schiller, F. (1788/ 1943), 'The Gods of Greece (stanza 19)', in J. Petersen and H. Schneider (eds), *Schillers Werke*. Nationalausgabe, Vol. 2 (1), Weimar, 366.
42 Critchley, S. (2004), *Very Little, Almost Nothing*, New York: Routledge, 99.
43 Habermas, J. (1990), *The Philosophical Discourse of Modernity*, 89.
44 Habermas, J. (1990), *The Philosophical Discourse of Modernity*, 89.
45 Habermas, J. (1990), *The Philosophical Discourse of Modernity*, 90.
46 Habermas, J. (1990), *The Philosophical Discourse of Modernity*, 90.
47 Taylor, M. C. (2018), *Abiding Grace*, 34.
48 Bowie, A. (2003), *Introduction to German Philosophy*, 104.
49 Bowie, A. (2003), *Introduction to German Philosophy*, 104–5.
50 Schelling, F. (1946), 'Die Weltalter', in M. Schröter (1997) (ed.), *Abyss of Freedom*, Ann Arbor: University of Michigan Press, Cited in Bowie, A. (2003), *Introduction to German Philosophy*, 105–6.

51 Critchley, S. (2004), *Very Little, Almost Nothing*, 114.
52 Taylor, M. C. (2018), *Abiding Grace*, 142.
53 Taylor, M. C. (2018), *Abiding Grace*, 142–3.
54 Taylor, M. C. (2018), *Abiding Grace*, 142.
55 Taylor, M. C. (2018), *Abiding Grace*, 145.
56 Taylor, M. C. (2018), *Abiding Grace*, 147.
57 Taylor, M. C. (2018), *Abiding Grace*, 149.
58 Hegel, from the *Phenomenology of Spirit*, cited by Bataille, G. (1997), 'Hegel, Death and Sacrifice', in F. Botting and S. Wilson (eds), *The Bataille Reader*, Oxford: Blackwells Publishing, 279–95 (pp. 282–3).
59 Bataille, G. (1997), 'Hegel, Death and Sacrifice', 284.
60 Bataille, G. (1997), 'Hegel, Death and Sacrifice', 285.
61 Bataille, G. (1997), 'Hegel, Death and Sacrifice', 282.
62 Taylor, M. C. (2018), *Abiding Grace*, 148.
63 Taylor, M. C. (1987), *Alterity*, xxv.
64 Taylor, M. C. (1987), *Alterity*, xxxi.
65 Taylor, M. C. (1987), *Alterity*, xxxii.
66 Derrida, J. (1976), *Of Grammatology*, trans. G. Spivak, Baltimore: Johns Hopkins University, 26 and 41 (cited in Taylor, M. C.) (1987), *Alterity*, 264.
67 Bataille, G. (1994), *On Nietzsche*, New York: Paragon House, 183.
68 Nietzsche, F. (1992), *Ecce Homo*, London: Penguin, 97.
69 Prideaux, S. (2018), *I Am Dynamite: A Life of Nietzsche*, New York: Tim Duggan Books, 371.
70 Habermas, J. (1990), *The Philosophical Discourse of Modernity*, 86, original emphasis.
71 Nietzsche, F. (1992), *Ecce Homo*, 96.
72 Nietzsche, F. (1992), *Ecce Homo*, 49.
73 Nietzsche, F. (2003), *Twilight of the Idols and the Anti-Christ*, London: Penguin, 49.
74 Nietzsche, F. (1974), *The Gay Science*, New York: Vintage Books.
75 Prideaux, S. (2018), *I Am Dynamite*, 90.
76 Nietzsche, F. (1992), *Ecce Homo*, 37–8: 'that one wants nothing to be other than it is, not in the future, not in the past, not in all eternity. Not merely to endure that which happens of necessity, still less to dissemble it – all idealism is untruthfulness in the face of necessity – but to *love* it.'
77 Hesse, H. (2017), *Demian*, UK: Penguin Random House, 103.
78 Kellner, D. (1989), *Jean Baudrillard. From Marxism to Postmodernism and Beyond*, Cambridge: Polity Press, cited in Gane, M. (1991), *Baudrillard: Critical and Fatal Theory*, London: Routledge, 61.
79 Nietzsche, F. (1995), *Birth of Tragedy*, trans. Clifton P. Fadiman, New York: Dover Publications, 22.

80 Cooper, D. (1996), 'Modern European Philosophy', in N. Bunnin and E. P. Tsui-James (eds), *The Blackwell Companion to Philosophy*, Oxford: Blackwell Publishers, 702–21 (p. 708).
81 Nietzsche, F. (1995), *Birth of Tragedy*, 24–5.
82 Wagner, R. *Religion and Art*, cited in Habermas, H. (1990), *The Philosophical Discourse of Modernity*, Cambridge: Polity Press, 87.
83 Schelling, F., *System of Transcendental Idealism*, cited in Habermas, J. (1990), *The Philosophical Discourse of Modernity*, 88.
84 Prideaux, S. (2018), *I Am Dynamite*, 89.
85 Habermas, J. (1990), *The Philosophical Discourse of Modernity*, 94.
86 Nietzsche, F. On Truth and Lies in a Nonmoral Sense, cited in Allan, A. and Goddard, R., *Education & Philosophy: An introduction*, London: Sage, 108.
87 Habermas, J. (1990), *The Philosophical Discourse of Modernity*, 94.
88 Habermas, J. (1990), *The Philosophical Discourse of Modernity*, 96.
89 Habermas, J. (1990), *The Philosophical Discourse of Modernity*, 87.
90 Cooper, D. (1996), 'Modern European Philosophy', 708.
91 Adorno, T. (1974), *Minima Moralia: Reflections from Damaged Life*, London: Verso, 15.
92 Adorno, T. (1974), *Minima Moralia*, 15.
93 Adorno, T. (1974), *Minima Moralia*, 16.
94 Allan, A. and Goddard, R. (2017), *Education & Philosophy*, 114.
95 Horkheimer, M. and Adorno, T. (2002), *Dialectic of Enlightenment. Philosophical Fragments*, trans. E Jephcott, Stanford, CA: Stanford University Press. Quote from the Introduction to the 1972 edition Trans. John Cumming, New York: Continuum, xiv.
96 Adorno, T. (1974), *Minima Moralia*, 247.
97 Horkheimer, M. and Adorno, T. (2002), *Dialectic of Enlightenment*, xviii.
98 Image: Ulysses and the Sirens. Illustration from Greek Vase Paintings by J E Harrison and D S MacColl (T Fisher Unwin, 1894). Quote: Homer (2014), *The Odyssey*, London: Bloomsbury, 130.
99 Allan, A. and Goddard, R. (2017), *Education & Philosophy*, 116.
100 Horkheimer, M. and Adorno, T. (2002), *Dialectic of Enlightenment*, 46–7.
101 Horkheimer, M. and Adorno, T. (2002), *Dialectic of Enlightenment*, 49.
102 Dallmayr, F. (2005), 'The Underside of Modernity: Adorno, Heidegger, and Dussel', in Santosh Gupta, Prafulla C. Kar and Parul D. Mukherji (eds), *Rethinking Modernity*, Delhi: Pencraft International, 22–41 (p. 23).
103 Horkheimer, M. and Adorno, T. (2002), *Dialectic of Enlightenment*, 11.
104 Horkheimer, M. and Adorno, T. (2002,) *Dialectic of Enlightenment*, 109.
105 Dallmayr, F. (2005), 'The Underside of Modernity', 25.
106 Dallmayr, F. (2005), 'The Underside of Modernity', 26.

107 Gibson, N. (2002), 'Rethinking an Old Saw: Dialectical Negativity, Utopia, and Negative Dialectic in Adorno's Hegelian Marxism', N. Gibson and A. Rubin (eds), *Adorno. A Critical Reader*, Oxford: Blackwell Publishers, 257–91 (p. 258).
108 Dallmayr, F. (2005), 'The Underside of Modernity', 25.
109 Dallmayr, F. (2005), 'The Underside of Modernity', 25.
110 Adorno, T. (1974), *Minima Moralia*, 192.
111 Huhn, T. (2004), 'Introduction: Thoughts Beside Themselves', in T. Huhn (ed.), *The Cambridge Companion to Adorno*, Cambridge: Cambridge University Press, 1–18 (p. 8).
112 Amazon.com: https://www.amazon.com/True-thoughts-those-alone-which/dp/B01M64XCE0 (accessed 1 May 20).
113 Critchley, S. (2004), *Very Little, Almost Nothing*, 178.
114 Critchley, S. (2004), *Very Little, Almost Nothing*, 176.
115 Critchley, S. (2004), *Very Little, Almost Nothing*, 176 (citing Zuidevaart).
116 Critchley, S. (2004), *Very Little, Almost Nothing*, 177.
117 Adorno, T. (1984), *Aesthetic Theory*, London: Routledge & Kegan Paul, 220–1.
118 Critchley, S. (2004), *Very Little, Almost Nothing*, 178.
119 McCarthy, T. (1990), 'Introduction', in J. Habermas, *The Philosophical Discourse of Modernity*, Cambridge: Polity Press, vi–xvii (p. xv).
120 Habermas, J. (1990), *The Philosophical Discourse of Modernity*, 129.
121 Habermas, J. (1990), *The Philosophical Discourse of Modernity*, 122.
122 Habermas, J. (1990), *The Philosophical Discourse of Modernity*, 123.
123 Habermas, J. (1990), *The Philosophical Discourse of Modernity*, 68–9.
124 McCarthy, T. (1990), 'Introduction', in J. Habermas, *The Philosophical Discourse of Modernity*, xvi.
125 McCarthy, T. (1990), 'Introduction', in J. Habermas, *The Philosophical Discourse of Modernity*, xv.
126 McCarthy, T. (1990), 'Introduction', in J. Habermas, *The Philosophical Discourse of Modernity*, xvii.
127 McCarthy, T. (1990), 'Introduction', in J. Habermas, *The Philosophical Discourse of Modernity*, xv.
128 Habermas, J. (1990), *The Philosophical Discourse of Modernity*, 247.
129 Foucault cited in J. Habermas (1990), *The Philosophical Discourse of Modernity*, 248.
130 Habermas, J. (1990), *The Philosophical Discourse of Modernity*, 250.
131 Habermas, J. (1990), *The Philosophical Discourse of Modernity*, 250.
132 Habermas, J. (1990), *The Philosophical Discourse of Modernity*, 265.
133 Debord, G. (1995), *The Society of the Spectacle*, New York: Zone Books, 12.
134 Debord, G. (1995), *The Society of the Spectacle*, 9.
135 Taylor, M. (2018), *Abiding Grace*, 48.

136 Taylor, M. (2018), *Abiding Grace*, 49.
137 Oxford dictionaries (2016), International Word of the Year.
138 Žižek, S. (2012), *Welcome to the Desert of the Real*, London: Verso. Žižek uses this phrase well after Baudrillard's evocation of it but studiously avoids reference to Baudrillard in his own writings on the self, society and late modernity.
139 Lotringer, S. (2007), 'Introduction: Requiem for the Masses', in J. Baudrillard, *In the Shadow of the Silent Majority*, Los Angeles: Semiotext(e), 7–31 (p. 12).
140 Baudrillard, J. (2007), *In the Shadow of the Silent Majority*.
141 Lotringer, S. (2007), 'Introduction: Requiem for the Masses', 12.
142 Baudrillard, J. (1998), *Paroxysm: Jean Baudrillard interviews with Philippe Petit*, London: Verso. 15.
143 http://www.abc.net.au/news/2018-04-19/telling-real-from-fake-era-fake-news-digital-technology/9667264 (accessed 20 April 2018).
144 Featherstone, M. (1995), *Undoing Culture: Globalization, Postmodernism and Identity*, London: Sage, 19.
145 Baudrillard, J. (1994), *Simulacra and Simulation*, Ann Arbor: University of Michigan Press, 2–3.
146 Lotringer, S. (2007), 'Introduction: Requiem for the Masses', 26.
147 Lotringer, S. (2007), 'Exterminating Angel: Introduction to Forget Foucault', in J. Baudrillard, *Forget Foucault*, Los Angeles: Semiotext(e) , 7–25 (p. 11).
148 Kellner, D. (2015), 'Jean Baudrillard', in *The Stanford Encyclopedia of Philosophy*, Edward N. Zalta (ed.). https://plato.stanford.edu/archives/win2015/entries/baudrillard/, 6.
149 It was undoubtedly courageous to send the essay to 'Critique'. While Foucault promised to respond to the text, he never did and Baudrillard ultimately published elsewhere. As Lotringer notes, this led Deleuze – himself in Baudrillard's sights – to call him the 'shame of the profession': a peculiar reflection for an intellectual renown for exploring new directions *through* the bodies of earlier philosophers. What is unclear, though, is the extent to which Foucault was lost for words or had simply moved on to other intellectual problems after his famous acid trip in the *actual* desert of Death Valley in 1975. http://www.openculture.com/2017/09/when-michel-foucault-tripped-on-acid-in-death-valley-and-called-it-the-greatest-experience-of-my-life-1975.html.
150 Baudrillard, J. (2007), *Forget Foucault*, 29.
151 Baudrillard, J. (2007), *Forget Foucault*, 37.
152 Baudrillard, J. (2007), *Forget Foucault*, 37.
153 Baudrillard, J. (2007), *Forget Foucault*, 34.
154 Moazami, M. (2016), 'Forgive Foucault, Forget Baudrillard: On the Other Side of Power – Toward the Ecstasy of Seduction', *International Journal of Baudrillard Studies*, 13 (2): 2. https://baudrillardstudies.ubishops.ca/forgive-foucault-forget

-baudrillard-on-the-other-side-of-power-toward-the-ecstasy-of-seduction/ (accessed 6 October 20).
155. Moazami, M. (2016), 'Forgive Foucault, Forget Baudrillard: On the Other Side of Power – Toward the Ecstasy of Seduction', 2 (citing Baudrillard).
156. Baudrillard, J. (2007), *Forget Foucault*, 37–8.
157. Coulter, G. (2010), 'Jean Baudrillard and Cinema: The Problems of Technology, Realism and History', *Film-Philosophy*, 14 (2): 6–20 (p. 14).
158. Baudrillard, J. (2007), *Forget Foucault*, 35.
159. Baudrillard, J. (2007), *Forget Foucault*, 36.
160. Baudrillard, J. (2007), *Forget Foucault*, 30.
161. Baudrillard, J. (2008), *Fatal Strategies*, Los Angeles: Semiotext(e), 141.
162. Hesse, H. (1995), *Steppenwolf*, London: Penguin Books, 155.
163. Baudrillard, J. (2007), 'Forget Baudrillard: An Interview with Sylvere Lotringer', in J. Baudrillard, *Forget Foucault*, 76.
164. Coulter, G. (undated), *Simulation Is Not the Opposite of the Real—Jean Baudrillard on Simulation and Illusion*. Retrieved 18 February 2011, http://www.noemalab.org/sections/ideas/ideas_articles/pdf/coulter_simulation_real.pdf, 3.
165. Critchley, S. (2004), *Very Little, Almost Nothing*, 37.
166. Baudrillard, J. (1996), *The Perfect Crime*, trans. C. Turner, London: Verso, 105.
167. Barthes, R. (1964/ 1972), *Critical Essays* [Editions de Seuil], trans. R. Howard, Evanston: Northwestern University Press, 137.
168. Critchley, S. (2004), *Very Little, Almost Nothing*, 114.
169. Barthes, R. (1977/ 2005), *The Neutral: Lecture Course at the College de France*, ed. T. Clerc, and E. Marty, trans. R. Krauss and D. Hollier, New York: Columbia University Press.
170. Coulter, G. (2014), 'The Embrace of Radical Philosophical Emptiness as a Liberating Conceptualization of Thought in Roland Barthes and Jean Baudrillard', *Frontiers of Philosophy in China*, 9 (2): 194–212 (p. 207).
171. Baudrillard, J. (2000), *The Vital Illusion (The 1999 Wellek Lectures at the University of California at Irvine)*, ed. Julia Witwer, New York: Columbia University Press, 68.

Chapter 4

1. Taylor, M. C. (1984), *Erring: A Postmodern A/Theology*, Chicago: University of Chicago Press, 92.
2. Taylor, M. C. (1984), *Erring*, 76.

3 Blanchot, M. (2003), 'The Song of the Siren's', in *The Book to Come*, Stanford: Stanford University Press, 3–11 (p. 6).
4 Nietzsche, F. (1974), *The Gay Science*, New York: Vintage Books, 181.
5 Taylor, M. C. (1984), *Erring*, 7.
6 Taylor, M. C. (1984), *Erring*, 7.
7 Taylor, M. C. (1984), *Erring*, 33.
8 Taylor, M. C. (1987), *Altarity*, Chicago: University of Chicago Press, xxiv.
9 Hyppolite, J. (1974), *Gensis and Structure of Hegel's Phenomenology of Spirit*, trans. S. Cherniak and J. Heckman, Evanston: Northwestern University Press.
10 Taylor, M. C. (1987), *Altarity*, xxii.
11 Davies, B. (2010), *Martin Heidegger: Key Concepts*, Durham: Acumen, 9.
12 Lotringer, S. (1992), 'Furiously Nietzschean, an Introduction', in G. Bataille, *On Nietzsche*, Paragon House: New York, vii–xv (p. xv).
13 Eco, U. (1983), *The Name of the Rose*, London: Minerva, 491–2.
14 Bataille, G. (1988), 'Hegel', in *Inner Experience*, trans. L. A. Boldt, State University of New York Press, 108–11 (p. 110).
15 Bataille, G. (1988), 'Hegel', in *Inner Experience*, 110.
16 Bataille, G. (1985), 'The Labyrinth', in *Visions of Excess*, 172.
17 Bataille, G. (1988), 'The Torment', in *Inner Experience*, 33.
18 Bataille, G. *Inner Experience*, 35.
19 Bataille, G. 'Critique of Dogmatic Servitude (and of Mysticism)', in *Inner Experience*, 3–9 (p. 3).
20 Bataille, G. (1988), *The Accursed Share*, Vol. 1, New York: Zone Books, 21 (in Pawlett, W. [2013], *Violence, Society and Radical Theory: Bataille, Baudrillard and Contemporary Society*, New York: Routledge, 19).
21 Pawlett, W. (2013), *Violence, Society and Radical Theory*, 20. Pawlett notes that Bataille and Baudrillard are themselves 'heterological' objects that are either expelled or 'partially assimilated' in the disciplines of sociology, philosophy and cultural studies (p. 20).
22 Pawlett, W. (2013), *Violence, Society and Radical Theory*, 21.
23 Derrida, J. (1980), *The Archaeology of the Frivolous. Reading Condillac*, Pittsburgh, PA: Duquesne University Press.
24 De Certeau, M. (1983), cited in 'Introduction: Partial Truths', in J. Clifford and G. E. Marcus (1986) (eds), *Writing Culture: The Poetics and Politics of Ethnography*, London: University of California, 1–26 (p. 5).
25 Clifford, J. in Clifford, J. and G. E. Marcus, (1986), 'Introduction: Partial Truths', 2.
26 Clifford, J. in Clifford, J. and G. E. Marcus, (1986), 'Introduction: Partial Truths', 2.
27 Clifford, J. in Clifford, J. and G. E. Marcus, (1986), 'Introduction: Partial Truths', 7.
28 Clifford, J. in Clifford, J. and G. E. Marcus, (1986), 'Introduction: Partial Truths', 6.

29 Price, R. (1983), *First-Time: The Historical Vision of an Afro-American People*, Baltimore: Johns Hopkins University Press.
30 Price, R. (1983), *First-Time: The Historical Vision of an Afro-American People*, 10, cited in Clifford, James, and George E. Marcus, eds (1986), 7.
31 Clifford, J. in Clifford, J., and G. E. Marcus, (1986), 'Introduction: Partial Truths', 2.
32 Clifford, J. in Clifford, J., and G. E. Marcus, (1986), 'Introduction: Partial Truths', 7.
33 Clifford, J. in Clifford, J., and G. E. Marcus, (1986), 'Introduction: Partial Truths', 9.
34 MacLure, M., Holmes, R., Jones, L. and MacRae, C. (2010), 'Silence as Resistance to Analysis: Or, on Not Opening One's Mouth Properly', *Qualitative Inquiry*, 16 (6): 492–500 (pp. 492 and 498).
35 Ferguson, J. (1999), 'Global Disconnect: Abjection and the Aftermath of Modernism', in *Expectations of Modernity: Myths and Meanings of Urban Life on the Zambian Copperbelt*, Berkeley: University of California, 234–54 (p. 210).
36 Tyler, S. (1984), 'The Vision Quest in the West or What the Mind's Eye Sees', *Journal of Anthropological Research*, 40 (1): 23–40 (p. 25), cited in J. Clifford and G. E. Marcus (1986) (eds), 12.
37 Fendler, L. (1999), 'Making Trouble: Prediction, Agency, Critical Intellectuals', in T. S. Popkewitz and L. Fendler (eds), *Critical Theories in Education: Changing Terrains of Knowledge and Politics*, London: Routledge, 169–88.
38 Denzin, N. K. and Lincoln, Y. S. (1994), 'Introduction: Entering the Field of Qualitative Research', in N. K. Denzin and Y. S. Lincoln (eds), *Handbook of Qualitative Research*, Thousand Oaks, CA: Sage, 1–34.
39 Geertz, C. (1973), *The Interpretation of Cultures: Selected Essays*, New York: Basic Books.
40 MacLure, M. (2013), 'Researching Without Representation? Language and Materiality in Post-Qualitative Methodology', *International Journal of Qualitative Studies in Education*, 26 (6): 658–67 (p. 666).
41 Denzin, N. K. (2013), 'The Death of Data?' *Cultural Studies ↔ Critical Methodologies*, 13 (4): 353–6 (p. 355).
42 Koro-Ljungberg, M. and MacLure, M. (2013), 'Provocations, Re-Un-Visions, Death, and Other Possibilities of "Data"', *Cultural Studies ↔ Critical Methodologies*, 13 (4): 219–22 (p. 219).
43 Baudrillard, J. (2000), *The Vital Illusion*, New York: Columbia University Press, 79–80.
44 Baudrillard, J. (2000), *The Vital Illusion*, 80.
45 Baudrillard, J. (2000), *The Vital Illusion*, 76.
46 Baudrillard, J. (2000), *The Vital Illusion*, 77.
47 Koro-Ljungberg, M. (2013), '"Data" as Vital Illusion', *Cultural Studies ↔ Critical Methodologies*, 13 (4): 274–8 (p. 275).

48 St. Pierre, E. A. and Pillow, W. (eds) (2000), *Working the Ruins: Feminist Poststructural Theory and Methods in Education*, New York, NY: Routledge.
49 Koro-Ljungberg, M. and MacLure, M. (2013), 'Provocations, Re-Un-Visions, Death, and Other Possibilities of "Data"', 219. Here, the authors mention poststructuralist, postmodernist, deconstructive, Deleuzian, performative, affective and material feminist 'turns'.
50 Bendix Petersen, E. (2015), 'What Crisis of Representation? Challenging the Realism of post-structuralist Policy Research in Education', *Critical Studies in Education*, 56 (1): 147–60 (pp. 151–3).
51 MacLure, M. (2006), 'The Bone in the Throat: Some Uncertain Thoughts on Baroque Method', *International Journal of Qualitative Studies in Education*, 19 (6): 729–45.
52 Bendix Petersen, E. (2015), 'What Crisis of Representation? Challenging the Realism of Post-structuralist Policy Research in Education', 148–9.
53 Bendix Petersen, E. (2015), 'What Crisis of Representation?', 158.
54 Silova, I., Millei, Z. and Piattoeva, N. (2017), 'Interupting the Coloniality of Knowledge Production in Comparative Education: Postsocialist and Postcolonial Dialogues after the Cold War', *Comparative Education Review*, 61 (S1): s74–s102 (pp. s77–s78).
55 MacLure, M. (2013), 'Researching Without Representation? Language and Materiality in Post-qualitative Methodology', 666.
56 Derrida, J. (1976), *Of Grammatology* (preface by G. C. Spivak, Trans.), Baltimore: Johns Hopkins. Cited in MacLure, M. Holmes, R., Jones, L. and MacRae, C. (2010), 'Silence as Resistance to Analysis', 498.
57 MacLure, M. Holmes, R., Jones, L. and MacRae, C. (2010), 'Silence as Resistance to Analysis', 498.
58 Lyotard, J.-F. (1988), *The Differend: Phrases in Dispute*, trans. G. Van Den Abbeele, Minneapolis: University of Minnesota Press, xi.
59 Critchley, S. (2004), *Very Little, Almost Nothing*, New York: Routledge, 99.
60 Norman, J. (2007), 'Hegel and German Romanticism', in Stephen Houlgate (ed.), *Hegel and the Arts*, Evanston, IL: Northwestern University Press, 310–26 (p. 322).
61 Novalis, cited in Norman, J. (2009), 'The Work of Art in German Romanticism', in J. Stolzenberg, K. Ameriks and F. Rush (eds), *Internationales Jahrbuch des Deutschen Idealismus*, vol. 6, 59–79 (p. 66).
62 Lyotard, J.-F (1986), *The Post-Modern Condition: A Report on Knowledge*, Manchester: Manchester University Press, 81.
63 Drolet, M. (1994), 'The Wild and the Sublime: Lyotard's Post-modern Politics', *Political Studies*, XLII: 259–73 (p. 262).
64 Lyotard, J.-F (1986), *The Post-Modern Condition*, 81.

65 Drolet, M. (1994), 'The Wild and the Sublime', 263.
66 Drolet, M. (1994), 'The Wild and the Sublime', 263.
67 Norman, J. (2009), 'The Work of Art in German Romanticism', 73.
68 Norman, J. (2009), 'The Work of Art in German Romanticism', 59.
69 Hegarty, P. (2000), 'Bataille, Conceiving Death', *Paragraph*, 23 (2): 173–90 (p. 176).
70 Bataille, G. (1997), 'Hegel, Death and Sacrifice', in F. Botting and S. Wilson (eds), *Georges Batailles. The Bataille Reader*, London: Blackwell Publishing, 279–95 (p. 288).
71 Bataille, G. (1997), 'Hegel, Death and Sacrifice', 286–7.
72 Bataille, G. (1985), 'The Practice of Joy Before Death', in *Visions of Excess. Selected Writings 1927–1939*, Minneapolis: University of Minnesota Press, 235–9 (p. 239).
73 Hegarty, P. (2000), 'Bataille, Conceiving Death', 177.
74 Bataille in *Tears of Eros*, quoted in Noys, B. (2000), *Georges Bataille. A Critical Introduction*, London: Pluto Press, 25.
75 Bataille, G. (1985), 'The Practice of Joy Before Death', 236.
76 Hegarty, P. (2000), 'Bataille, Conceiving Death', 178.
77 Critchley, S. (2004), *Very Little, Almost Nothing*, 77.
78 Crowley, M. (2000), 'Possible Suicide: Blanchot and the Ownership of Death', *Paragraph*, 23 (2): 191–206 (p. 193).
79 Critchley, S. (2004), *Very Little, Almost Nothing*, 81.
80 Blanchot, M. (1989), 'The Work and Death's Space', in *The Space of Literature*, Lincoln Nebraska: University of Nebraska Press, 105.
81 Blanchot, M. (1989), 'The Work and Death's Space', 105.
82 Critchley, S. (2004), *Very Little, Almost Nothing*, 87–8.
83 Critchley, S. (2004), *Very Little, Almost Nothing*, 64.
84 Blanchot, M. (1989), 'The Outside, the Night', in *The Space of Literature*, Lincoln Nebraska: University of Nebraska Press, 163.
85 Blanchot, M. (1989), 'The Work and Death's Space', 164.
86 Blanchot, M. (1989), 'The Work and Death's Space', 169.
87 Critchley, S. (2004), *Very Little, Almost Nothing*, 36.
88 Critchley, S. (2004), *Very Little, Almost Nothing*, 38.
89 Baudrillard, J. (2007), *Symbolic Exchange and Death*, London: Sage Publications, 126.
90 Taylor, M. C. (1984), *Erring*, 93.
91 Taylor, M. C. (1984), *Erring*, 13.
92 Lyotard, J.-F. (1989), 'Lessons in Paganism', in A. Benjamin (ed.), *The Lyotard Reader*, Cambridge: Basil Blackwell, 122–54 (p. 123).
93 Critchley, S. (2004), *Very Little, Almost Nothing*, 113.
94 Elias, C. (2004), *The Fragment. Towards a History and Poetics of a Performative Genre*, Bern: Peter Lang AG, 4.
95 Elias, C. (2004), *The Fragment*, 7.

96 Adorno, T. (1974), *Minima Moralia: Reflections from Damaged Life*, London: Verso, 16.
97 Adorno, T. (1974), *Minima Moralia*, 16.
98 Frisby, D. (2013), *Fragments of Modernity. Theories of Modernity in the Work of Simmel, Kracauer and Benjamin*, Abingdon: Routledge, 3.
99 Simmel, G. (1978), *The Philosophy of Money*, trans. T. Bottomore and D. Frisby, London and Boston: Routledge, appearing in D. Frisby (2013), *Fragments of Modernity*, 6.
100 Debord, G. (1995), *The Society of the Spectacle*, New York: Zone Books, 10.
101 Bataille, G. (1992), 'Response to Jean-Paul Sartre (Defense of Inner Experience)', in *On Nietzsche*, Paragon House: New York, 179–87 (p. 187).
102 Elias, C. (2004), *The Fragment*, 5.
103 Shidmehr, N. (2009), 'Poetic Inquiry as Minor Research', in M. Prendergast, C. Leggo and P. Samesshima (eds), *Poetic Inquiry: Vibrant Voices in the Social Sciences*, Rotterdam: Sense Publishers, 101—9 (p. 101).
104 Brady, I. (2009), 'Foreword', in M. Prendergast, C. Leggo and P. Samesshima (eds), *Poetic Inquiry: Vibrant Voices in the Social Sciences*, ix.
105 Huang, W. (2019), *Photographic Inquiry as Artistic Educational Research: An Investigation through Experiential Processes of Photobook Creation*, Unpublished doctoral dissertation, Michigan State University.
106 Juschka, D. (2003), 'The Writing of Ethnography: Magical Realism and Michael Taussig', *Journal for Cultural and Religious Theory*, 5.1 (December): 84–104 (p. 92).
107 Juschka, D. (2003), The Writing of Ethnography, 92.
108 Taussig, M. (1997), *The Magic of the State*, New York and London: Routledge, 124–5.
109 Taussig, M. (1997), *The Magic of the State*, 124.
110 Juschka, D. (2003), The Writing of Ethnography, 101.
111 Juschka, D. (2003), The Writing of Ethnography, 102.
112 Arva, E. L. (2008), 'Writing the Vanishing Real: Hyperreality and Magical Realism', *Journal of Narrative Theory*, 38 (1): 60–85 (p. 72).
113 Denzin, N. K. (2013), 'The Death of Data?' 355.
114 Baudrillard, J. (1996), *The Perfect Crime*, London: Verso, 105.
115 Baudrillard, J. (2000), *The Vital Illusion*, 78.
116 Baudrillard, J. (2000), *The Vital Illusion (The 1999 Wellek Lectures at the University of California at Irvine)*, J. Witwer (ed.), New York: Columbia University Press, 22.
117 L'Yvonnet, F. (2011), 'Foreword', in Baudrillard, J. *Why Hasn't Everything Already Disappeared?* London: Seagull, 5.
118 Coulter, G. (undated). *Simulation Is Not the Opposite of the Real—Jean Baudrillard on Simulation and Illusion*. Retrieved 18 February 2011, http://www.noemalab.org/sections/ideas/ideas_articles/pdf/coulter_simulation_real.pdf, 5.

Chapter 5

1. Izutsu, T. (1982), *Toward a Philosophy of Zen Buddhism*, Boulder: Prajna Press, 53.
2. Izutsu, T. (1982), *Toward a Philosophy of Zen Buddhism*, 50.
3. Izutsu, T. (1982), *Toward a Philosophy of Zen Buddhism*, 54.
4. Whitehead, A. N. and Schilpp, P. A. (1951), 'Immortality', in *The Philosophy of Alfred North Whitehead*, New York: Tudor Publishing Company, 666–81 (p. 687).
5. Birch, C. (1988), 'Whitehead and Science Education', *Educational Philosophy and Theory*, 20 (2): 33–41 (p. 40).
6. Izutsu, T. (1982), *Toward a Philosophy of Zen Buddhism*, 56.
7. Baudrillard, J. (2002), *The Spirit of Terrorism: And Requiem for the Twin Towers*, London: Verso.
8. Deleuze, G. and Guattari, F. (1994), *What Is Philosophy?*, trans. H. Tomlinson and G. Burchell, New York: Columbia University Press.
9. Smith, D. W. (2004), 'Knowledge of Pure Events. A Note on Deleuze's Analytic of Concepts', in M. Roelli (ed.), *Ereignis auf Französisch. Von Bergson bis Deleuze*, München: Fink, 363–73 (pp. 363–4).
10. Hughes, R. (1996), *The Shock of the New: The Hundred-Year History of Modern Art*, New York: Knopf, 27.
11. Hughes, R. (1997), *American Visions: The Epic History of Art in America*, London: Harvill Press, 609.
12. An ethnographic perspective and post-foundational one are rarely combined, the search being for fact, causality, truth and meaning.
13. High School Act No. 590, 24 June 2005, Aims and purposes of the Upper High School.
14. Excerpt from an information letter from the House of Greenland to the union of boarding-schools.
15. The system of examining in the Danish educational system is based on a foundation of oral exams with two examiners. One is a recognized expert from another educational institution and ensures that the exam procedure is applied properly. This examiner has ultimate responsibility for awarding the grade. The other examiner is usually the course teacher. This creates an unusual situation where the teacher's role changes from facilitator of learning throughout the course or teaching activity to, finally, examiner.
16. Korneliussen, N., *Homo sapienne* in *Politiken*, 1 December 2014.
17. 'Qivitoq is a term that refers to Greenlanders turning their backs on society after a moment of great humiliation and taking to the mountains'. See Jensen, L. (2015), 'Greenland, Arctic Orientalism and the Search for Definitions of a Contemporary Postcolonial Geography', *KULT. Postkolonial Temaserie*, 12: 139–53 (p. 144).
18. Copyright and permission: Superflex.

19. Based on the US original, this car bumper sticker became highly visible in Denmark during the 'War on Terror'. Copyright and permission: Familienetværket.
20. Uffe Ellemann-Jensen, former Foreign Minister, Berlingske Tidende, 1 August 2013, https://www.berlingske.dk/kommentatorer/derfor-var-vores-indsats-i-afghanistan-en-stor-succes (accessed 15 May 20).
21. Anders Fogh Rasmussen, Prime Minister, 2001–2009, cited in *Mandagmorgen*, 11 September 2006. https://www.mm.dk/pdffiles/09ac3-30200602.pdf (accessed 15 May 20).
22. The Hygge Conspiracy, *The Guardian*, 22 November 16. https://www.theguardian.com/lifeandstyle/2016/nov/22/hygge-conspiracy-denmark-cosiness-trend (accessed 26 February 20).
23. https://www.bbc.com/news/magazine-31130947
24. https://www.theguardian.com/film/2020/jan/31/parasite-director-bong-joon-ho-korea-seems-glamorous-but-the-young-are-in-despair#img-1
25. https://www.abc.net.au/news/2016-12-28/south-koreas-obsession-with-top-marks-is-costing-its-youth/8137020
26. Sinking Liner: Korean Education. *The Korea Times*, 12 March 2009. http://www.koreatimes.co.kr/www/opinion/2018/11/162_41100.html (accessed 15 February 20).
27. Beach, J. M. (2011), *Children Dying Inside: A Critical Analysis of Education in South Korea*, Scotts Valley, CA: CreateSpace Independent Publishing Platform, 20.
28. Komatsu, H. and Rappleye, J. (2018), 'Is Exam Hell the Cause of High Academic Achievement in East Asia? The Case of Japan and the Case for Transcending Stereotypes', *British Educational Research Journal*, 44 (5): 802–26.
29. Seth, Michael, J. (2002), *Education Fever: Society, Politics, and the Pursuit of Schooling in South Korea*, Honolulu: University of Hawai'i Press.
30. Obama, B. (2011), State of the Union Address to Both Houses of Congress. 25 January 2011 https://abcnews.go.com/Politics/State_of_the_Union/state-of-the-union-2011-full-transcript/story?id=12759395 (accessed 22 February 20).
31. Obama is absolutely wrong, *The Korea Times* (2014). http://www.koreatimes.co.kr/www/news/nation/2014/09/181_158025.html (Posted 258.5.2014 (accessed 22 February 20).
32. https://www.bbc.com/news/stories-45201725
33. ZMoESVTEE (2014), *Zambia: Education for All 2015 National Review*, Lusaka: Zambian Ministry of Education, Science, Vocational Training and Early Education, 3.
34. Suffering in Silence: The Links between Human Rights Abuses and HIV Transmission to Girls in Zambia (Human Rights Watch Report 2003). https://www.refworld.org/docid/3f4f59890.html (accessed 20 February 20).
35. Human Rights Watch Report (2003), 'Suffering in Silence: The Links between Human Rights Abuses and HIV Transmission to Girls in Zambia'. https://www.refworld.org/docid/3f4f59890.html (accessed 20 February 20).

36 http://news.bbc.co.uk/2/hi/africa/8117649.stm
37 Lee, J. and Simmons Zuilkowski, S. (2017), 'Conceptualising Education Quality in Zambia: A Comparative Analysis Across the Local, National and Global Discourses', *Comparative Education*, 53 (4): 558–77 (p. 574).
38 Siliya, D. (2010), 'Policy Statement by the Minister of Education', Republic of Zambia Ministry of Education. https://planipolis.iiep.unesco.org/sites/planipolis/files/ressources/zambia_policy_statement.pdf (accessed 18 May 20).

Chapter 6

1 Gane, M. (2000), *Jean Baudrillard: In Radical Uncertainty*, London: Pluto Press, viii.
2 Gane, M. (2000), *Jean Baudrillard: In Radical Uncertainty*, x.
3 Taylor, M. C. (2018), *Abiding Grace: Time Modernity, Death*, Chicago: University of Chicago Press, 42.
4 Time is an interesting unit of analysis in comparative education. Undertheorized until quite recently and now hotly contested, some point to the quickened pace of academic life in higher education (Shahjahan, R. (2018), *Review Essay*, Discourse Studies in the Cultural Politics of Education, 1–12. https://doi.org/10.1080/01596306.2018.1550041), while others suggest an opposite movement (Sobe, N. [2021], 'The Slowing Global Order: Space-Time, Boredom and Criss-Crossing Comparative Education Research', in L. Klerides and S. Carney, *Identities and Education: Comparative Perspectives in an Age of Crisis*, Bloomsbury Publishers, (pp. 163–77). As usual, Baudrillard is somewhere else.
5 Heidegger, M. (1964), 'The Origin of the Work of Art', in A. Hofstadter and R. Kuhns, *Philosophies of Art and Beauty*, New York: Random House, 649–701.
6 Jameson, F. (1991), *Postmodernism; Or the Cultural Logic of Late Capitalism*, London: Verso, 8.
7 Jameson, F. (1991), *Postmodernism; Or the Cultural Logic of Late Capitalism*, 8.
8 Jameson, F. (1991), *Postmodernism; Or the Cultural Logic of Late Capitalism*, 9.
9 Jameson, F. (1991), *Postmodernism; Or the Cultural Logic of Late Capitalism*, 8.
10 Appleyard, B. (2011), 'Warhol Rules: But Why?' *The Economist (Intelligent Life)* November/December: 66–77.
11 Jameson, *Postmodernism; Or the Cultural Logic of Late Capitalism*, 11.
12 Jameson, F. (1991), *Postmodernism; Or the Cultural Logic of Late Capitalism*, 15–16.
13 Haynes, K. (1999), *How We Became Posthuman: Vitual Bodies in Cybernetic, Literature and Informatics*, Chicago: Chicago university press, 2–3 (cited in Taylor (2018), *Abiding Grace*, 56).
14 Turner, C. (2005), 'Introduction', in J. Baudrillard, *The Intelligence of Evil or the Lucidity Pact*, New York: Berg, 11.

15 Borges, J. L. (1974), 'Fauna of Mirrors', in Borges, J. L., with M. Guerrero, *The Book of Imaginary Beings* (edited and trans. N. T. di Giovanni), London: Penguin, 67–8 (p. 67).
16 Baudrillard, J. (2003), *Passwords*, London: Verso, 33.
17 Taylor, M. C. (2018), *Abiding Grace*, 254.
18 Baudrillard, J. (2003), *Passwords*, 34.
19 Baudrillard, J. (2005), *The Intelligence of Evil or the Lucidity Pact*, 17.
20 Baudrillard, J. (2005), *The Intelligence of Evil or the Lucidity Pact*, 17.
21 Baudrillard, J. (2003), *Passwords*, 66–7.
22 Baudrillard, J. (1993), *The Transparency of Evil: Essays on Extreme Phenomena*, New York: Verso, 5.
23 Baudrillard, J. (1993), *The Transparency of Evil: Essays on Extreme Phenomena*, 6.
24 Baudrillard, J. (1993), *The Transparency of Evil: Essays on Extreme Phenomena*, 9–10.
25 Baudrillard, J. (1993), *The Transparency of Evil: Essays on Extreme Phenomena*, 10.
26 Baudrillard, J. (2003), *Passwords*, 67.
27 Taylor, M. C. (2018), *Abiding Grace*, 259.
28 Taylor, M. C. (2018), *Abiding Grace*, 259.
29 Critchley, S. (2004), *Very Little, Almost Nothing*, New York: Routledge, 24.
30 Critchley, S. (2004), *Very Little, Almost Nothing*, 25.
31 Critchley, S. (2004), *Very Little, Almost Nothing*, 26
32 Tyler, S. (1986), 'Post-modern Ethnography: From Document of the Occult to Occult Document', in J. Clifford and G. E. Marcus (eds), *Writing Culture: The Poetics and Politics of Ethnography*, London: University of California, 122–40 (p. 123).
33 Tyler, S. (1986), Post-modern Ethnography, 135.
34 Tyler, S. (1986), Post-modern Ethnography, 126.
35 Tyler, S. (1986) Post-modern Ethnography, 129.
36 Tyler, S. (1986) Post-modern Ethnography, 134.
37 Attributed to US President Theodore Roosevelt.
38 Vickers (2020), surveys the various critiques of epistemic violence in comparative education and offers his own powerful critique of these, suggesting that the critics of northern domination must acknowledge their own ahistorism and essentialism.
39 Camus, A. (2000), *The Myth of Sisyphus*, London: Penguin, 44.
40 Silova, I. (2019), 'Toward a Wonderland of Comparative Education', *Comparative Education*, 55 (4): 444–72 (p. 445).
41 Rappleye, J. (2020), 'Comparative Education as Cultural Critique', *Comparative Education*, 56 (1): 39–56 (p. 53).
42 Critchley, S. (2004), *Very Little, Almost Nothing*, 62.
43 Sevilla (2016), p. 643 cited in Keita Takayama (2020), 'An Invitation to 'Negative' Comparative Education', *Comparative Education*, 56 (1): 79–95.

44 Olson, C. (2000), *Zen and the Art of Postmodern Philosophy: Two Paths of Liberation from the Representational Mode of Thinking*, New York: State University of New York Press, 188.
45 Olson, C. (2000), *Zen and the Art of Postmodern Philosophy*, 189.
46 Olson, C. (2000), *Zen and the Art of Postmodern Philosophy*, 86.
47 Hakuin. (1971), *The Zen Master Hakuin: Selected Writings*, trans. Philip B. Yampolsky, New York and London: Columbia University Press, 47.
48 Orellana, M. E. F. (2020), *Mindful Ethnography: Mind, Heart and Activity for Transformative Social Research*, Abingdon: Routledge.
49 Lysgaard, J. A., Bengtsson, S. and Hauberg-Lund Laugesen, M. (2019), *Dark Pedagogy: Education, Horror and the Anthropocene*, London: Palgrave Macmillan.
50 O'Loughlin, I. (2012), '"Man Down!" Aristotle, Epicurus, and the Dude on Friendship and Solidarity', in P. S. Fosl (ed.), *The Big Lebowski and Philosophy: Keeping Your Mind Limber with Abiding Wisdom*, Hoboken, NJ: John Wiley & Sons, 55–66 (p. 61).

References

Adams St. Pierre, E. (2013), 'The Posts Continue: Becoming', *International Journal of Qualitative Studies in Education*, 26 (6): 646–57.
Adorno, T. (1974), *Minima Moralia: Reflections from Damaged Life*, London: Verso.
Adorno, T. (1984), *Aesthetic Theory*, London: Routledge & Kegan Paul.
Ahmed, S. (2004), *The Cultural Politics of Emotion*, Edinburgh: Edinburgh University Press.
Alexander, R. (2000), *Culture and Pedagogy: International Comparisons in Primary Education*, Oxford: Blackwell Publishers.
Allan, A. and Goddard, R. (2017), *Education & Philosophy: An Introduction*, London: Sage.
Allen, A. (2017), *The Cynical Educator*, Leicester: Mayfly books.
Anderson-Levitt, K. (2003), 'A World Culture of Schooling?', in K. Anderson-Levitt (ed.), *Local Meanings, Global Schooling: Anthropology and World Culture Theory*, pp. 1–26. New York: Palgrave Macmillan.
Appadurai, A. (1996), *Modernity at Large: Cultural Dimensions of Globalization*, Minneapolis and London: University of Minnesota Press.
Appadurai, A. (2006), *Fear of Small Numbers*, Durham: Duke University Press.
Appadurai, A. (2013), *The Future as Cultural Fact: Essays on the Global Condition*, London: Verso.
Appleyard, B. (2011), 'Warhol Rules: But Why?' *The Economist (Intelligent Life)* November/December: 66–77.
Arva, E. L. (2008), 'Writing the Vanishing Real: Hyperreality and Magical Realism', *Journal of Narrative Theory*, 38 (1): 60–85.
Axford, B. (2013), *Theories of Globalization*, Cambridge: Polity Press.
Axford, B. (2013), 'You Had Me on "Global" and "Studies" Too, I Think', *Globalizations*, 10 (6): 779–84.
Axford, B. (2014), Interview with Professor Barrie Axford on 'Theories of Globalization', Global Studies Association. https://globalstudiesassoc.wordpress.com/2014/02/13/interview-with-professor-barrie-axford-on-theories-of-globalization/ (accessed 2 July 2019).
Baek, C., Hörmann, B. Karseth, B. Pizmony-Levy, O. Sivesind, K. and G. Steiner-Khamsi (2018), 'Policy Learning in Norwegian School Reform: A Social Network Analysis of the 2020 Incremental Reform', *Nordic Journal of Studies in Educational Policy*, 4 (1): 24–37.
Baker, B. (1998), 'Child-Centered Teaching, Redemption, and Educational Identities: A History of the Present', *Educational Theory*, 48 (2): 155–75.

Ball, S. (2012), *Global Education Inc.: New Policy Networks and the Neo-Liberal Imaginary*, London: Routledge.

Ball, S. J. (2003), 'The Teachers' Soul and the Terrors of Performativity', *Journal of Education Policy*, 18 (2): 215–28.

Ball, S. J., Junemann, C. and Santori, D. (2017), *Edu.Net. Globalisation and Education Policy Mobility*, London: Routledge.

Barad, K. (2003), 'Posthumanist Performativity: Toward an Understanding of How Matter Comes to Matter', *Signs: Journal of Women in Culture and Society*, 28: 801–31.

Barad, K. (2007), *Meeting the Universe Halfway: Quantum Physics and the Entanglement of Matter and Meaning*, Durham, NC: Duke University Press.

Barthes, R. (1964/ 1972), *Critical Essays* [Editions de Seuil], trans. R. Howard, Evanston: Northwestern University Press.

Barthes, R. (1977/ 2005), *The Neutral: Lecture Course at the College de France*, ed. T. Clerc, and E. Marty, trans. R. Krauss and D. Hollier, New York: Columbia University Press.

Bartlett, L. and Vavrus, F. (2014), 'Transversing the Vertical Case Study: A Methodological Approach to Studies of Educational Policy as Practice', *Anthropology & Education Quarterly*, 45 (2): 131–47.

Bataille, G. (1985), 'The Practice of Joy Before Death', in *Visions of Excess. Selected Writings 1927–1939*, Minneapolis: University of Minnesota Press, 235–9.

Bataille, G. (1988) 'Critique of Dogmatic Servitude (and of Mysticism)', in *Inner Experience*, trans. L. A. Boldt, State University of New York Press, 3–9.

Bataille, G. (1988), 'Hegel', in *Inner Experience*, trans. L. A. Boldt, Albany: State University of New York Press, 108–11.

Bataille, G. (1988), *The Accursed Share*, Vol. 1, New York: Zone Books.

Bataille, G. (1992), 'Response to Jean-Paul Sartre (Defense of Inner Experience)', in *On Nietzsche*, Paragon House: New York, 179–87.

Bataille, G. (1994), *On Nietzsche*, New York: Paragon House.

Bataille, G. (1997), 'Hegel, Death and Sacrifice', in F. Botting and S. Wilson (eds), *Georges Batailles. The Bataille Reader*, London: Blackwell Publishing, 279–95.

Bataille, G. (2001), *The Unfinished System of Non-Knowledge*, Minneapolis: University of Minnesota Press.

Baudrillard, J. (1993), *The Transparency of Evil: Essays on Extreme Phenomena*, New York: Verso.

Baudrillard, J. (1994), *Simulacra and Simulation*, Ann Arbor: University of Michigan Press.

Baudrillard, J. (1996), *The Perfect Crime*, trans. C. Turner, London: Verso.

Baudrillard, J. (1998), *Paroxysm: Jean Baudrillard interviews with Philippe Petit*, London: Verso.

Baudrillard, J. (2000), *The Vital Illusion (The 1999 Wellek Lectures at the University of California at Irvine)*, ed. Julia Witwer, New York: Columbia University Press.

Baudrillard, J. (2002), 'The Global and the Universal', in *Screened Out*, London: Verso, 158–9.
Baudrillard, J. (2002), *The Spirit of Terrorism: And Requiem for the Twin Towers*, London: Verso.
Baudrillard, J. (2003), *Passwords*, London: Verso.
Baudrillard, J. (2005), *The Intelligence of Evil: Or the Lucidity Pact*, London: Bloomsbury.
Baudrillard, J. (2007), *Forget Foucault*, Los Angeles: Semiotext(e).
Baudrillard, J. (2007), *Symbolic Exchange and Death*, London: Sage Publications.
Baudrillard, J. (2008), *Fatal Strategies*, Los Angeles: Semiotext(e).
Baudrillard, J. (2008), *The Perfect Crime*, London: Verso.
Baudrillard, J. (2010), *Carnival and Cannibal*, Seagull: London.
Bauman, Z. (1990), 'Modernity and Ambivalence', *Theory, Culture & Society*, 7 (2): 143–69.
Bazzano, M. (2014), *Buddha Is Dead: Nietzsche and the Dawn of European Zen*, Eastbourne: Sussex Academic Press.
Beach, J. M. (2011), *Children Dying Inside: A Critical Analysis of Education in South Korea*, CreateSpace Independent Publishing Platform.
Beck, U. (1992), *Risk Society: Towards a New Modernity*, London: Sage.
Bendix Petersen, E. (2015), 'What Crisis of Representation? Challenging the Realism of Post-structuralist Policy Research in Education', *Critical Studies in Education*, 56 (1): 147–60.
Bennett, O. (2001), *Cultural Pessimism: Narratives of Decline in the Postmodern World*, Edinburgh: Edinburgh University Press.
Berg, M. and B. Seeber (2016), *The Slow Professor: Challenging the Culture of Speed in the Academy*, Toronto: University of Toronto Press.
Berlant, L. (2011), *Cruel Optimism*, Durham: Duke University Press.
Birch, C. (1988), 'Whitehead and Science Education', *Educational Philosophy and Theory*, 20 (2): 33–41.
Blackburn, S. (1996), 'Metaphysics', in N. Bunnin and E. P. Tsui-James (eds), *The Blackwell Companion to Philosophy*, Oxford: Blackwell Publishers, 64–89).
Blanchot, M. (1989), 'The Outside, the Night', in *The Space of Literature*, Lincoln Nebraska: University of Nebraska Press, pp. 163–70.
Blanchot, M. (1989), 'The Work and Death's Space', in *The Space of Literature*, Lincoln Nebraska: University of Nebraska Press, pp. 85–105.
Blanchot, M. (2003), 'The Song of the Siren's', in *The Book to Come*, Stanford: Stanford University Press, 3–11.
Borges, J. L. (1937) 'The Analytical Language of John Wilkins', *Other Inquisitions* 1952: 101–5. http://www.crockford.com/wrrrld/wilkins.html (accessed 28 June 20).
Borges, J. L. (1974), 'Fauna of Mirrors', in Borges, J. L., with M. Guerrero, *The Book of Imaginary Beings* (edited and trans. N. T. di Giovanni), London: Penguin, 67–8.
Borges, J. L. (1998), 'On Exactitude in Science', in *The Aleph*, London: Penguin, 181.

Bowie, A. (2003), *Introduction to German Philosophy: From Kant to Habermas*, Cambridge: Polity Press.

Bray, M. and R. M. Thomas, (1995), 'Levels of Comparison in Educational Studies: Different Insights from Different Literatures and the Value of Multilevel Analyses', *Harvard Educational Review*, 65 (3): 472–91.

Bray, M., Adamson, B. and Mason, M. (eds) (2007), *Comparative Education Research: Approaches and Methods. CERC Studies in Comparative Education* (Vol. 32), Dordrecht: Springer.

Brown, R. H. (1977), *A Poetic for Sociology: Toward a Logic of Discovery for the Human Sciences*, Chicago: University of Chicago Press.

Bude, H. and Dürrschmidt, J. (2010), 'What's Wrong with Globalization?: Contra "Flow speak" – Towards an Existential Turn in the Theory of Globalization', *European Journal of Social Theory*, 13 (4): 481–500.

Burawoy, M. (2000), 'Introduction: Reaching for the Global', in M. Burawoy, J. A. Blum, S. George, M. Thayer, Z. Gille, T. Gowan, L. Haney, M. Klawiter, S. H. Lopez and S. Ó Raian (eds), *Global Ethnography: Forces, Connections, and Imaginations in a Postmodern World*, Berkeley, CA: University of California Press, 1–40.

Camus, A. (2000), *The Myth of Sisyphus*, London: Penguin.

Candea, M. (2007), 'Arbitrary Locations: In Defence of the Bounded Field-site', *Journal of the Royal Anthropological Institute*, 13 (1): 167–84.

Carney, S. (2009), 'Negotiating Policy in an Age of Globalization: Exploring Educational "Policyscapes" in Denmark, Nepal and China', *Comparative Education Review*, 53 (1): 63–88.

Carney, S. (2016), 'Global Education Policy and the Post-modern Challenge', in K. Munday, A. Green, R. Lingard and A. Verger (eds), *Handbook of Global Policy and Policy-Making in Education* (Handbook of Global Policy Series), 504–18, Oxford: Wiley-Blackwell.

Carney, S. and Madsen, U. A. (2009), 'A Place of One's Own: Schooling and the Formation of Identities in Modern Nepal', in. J. Zajda, H. Daun, and L. Saha (eds), *Nation-Building, Identity and Citizenship Education: Cross-Cultural Perspectives*, 171–87, Springer Science + Business Media B.V.

Carney, S., Silova, I. and Rappleye, J. (2012), 'World Culture Theory: Between Faith and Science', *Comparative Education Review*, 56 (3): 366–93.

Clifford, J. (1988), *The Predicament of Culture*. Cambridge, MA: Harvard University Press.

Clifford, J. (1997), *Routes: Travel and Translation in the Late Twentieth Century*, Cambridge: Harvard University Press.

Collier, S. J. (2006), 'Global Assemblages', *Theory Culture & Society*, 23 (2–3): 399–401.

Connell, R. (2007), 'Northern Theory of Globalization', *Sociological Theory*, 25 (4): 368–85.

Cooper, D. (1996), 'Modern European Philosophy', in N. Bunnin and E. P. Tsui-James (eds), *The Blackwell Companion to Philosophy*, Oxford: Blackwell Publishers, 702–21

Cooper, T. M. (2018), 'The Wabi Sabi Way: Antidote for a Dualistic Culture?' *Journal of Conscious Evolution*, 10 (10): Article 4, Available at: https://digitalcommons.ciis.edu/cejournal/vol10/iss10/4.

Cortada, X. (2020), *The Future Is Here, Now*, Virtual address to Comparative and International Education Society Annual Conference, Miami, March. https://www.youtube.com/watch?v=4_b2rvlu2Fo&feature=emb_logo&fbclid=IwAR1clt12fEkET3t9ljz0GCpKIW8ysCkgXE4_nnF81lcfzzSEHKrm5ESMCbU.

Coulter, G. (2010), 'Jean Baudrillard and Cinema: The Problems of Technology, Realism and History', *Film-Philosophy*, 14 (2): 6–20.

Coulter, G. (2014), 'The Embrace of Radical Philosophical Emptiness as a Liberating Conceptualization of Thought in Roland Barthes and Jean Baudrillard', *Frontiers of Philosophy in China*, 9 (2): 194–212.

Coulter, G. (undated). *Simulation Is Not the Opposite of the Real—Jean Baudrillard on Simulation and Illusion*. https://noemalab.eu/org/sections/ideas/ideas_articles/pdf/coulter_simulation_real.pdf (retrieved February 18, 2011).

Cowen, R. (2014), 'Comparative Education: Stones, Silences, and Siren Songs', *Comparative Education*, 50 (1): 3–14.

Cowen, R. (2021), 'Educated Identity: Concepts, Mobilities, and Imperium', in L. Klerides and S. Carney (eds), *Identities and Education: Comparative Perspectives in an Age of Crisis*, 27–46, London: Bloomsbury Publishers pp. 27–46).

Craig, E. (2002), *Philosophy: A Very Short Introduction*, Oxford: Oxford University Press.

Critchley, S. (2004), *Very Little, Almost Nothing*, New York: Routledge.

Crowley, M. (2000), 'Possible Suicide: Blanchot and the Ownership of Death', *Paragraph*, 23 (2): 191–206.

Dallmayr, F. (2005), 'The Underside of Modernity: Adorno, Heidegger, and Dussel', in Santosh Gupta, Prafulla C. Kar and Parul D. Mukherji (eds), *Rethinking Modernity*, Delhi: Pencraft International, 22–41.

Davies, B. (2010), *Martin Heidegger: Key Concepts*, Durham: Acumen.

de Lautréamont, C. (1914), 'The Songs of Maldoror', *Egoist*, 1 (22): 423.

de Sousa Santos, B. (2006), 'Globalizations', *Theory, Culture & Society*, 23 (2–3): 393–9.

de Sousa Santos, B. (2016), 'Beyond Abyssal Thinking', in *Epistemologies of the South: Justice against Epistemicide*, London: Routledge, pp. 118–135.

Debord, G. (1995), *The Society of the Spectacle*, New York: Zone Books.

Deleuze, G. and Guattari, F. (1987), *A Thousand Plateaus: Capitalism and Schizophrenia*. Minneapolis: University of Minnesota.

Deleuze, G. and Guattari, F. (1994), *What Is Philosophy?*, trans. H. Tomlinson and G. Burchell, New York, NY: Columbia University Press (Original work published 1991).

Denzin, N. K. (2013), 'The Death of Data?' *Cultural Studies ↔ Critical Methodologies*, 13 (4): 353–6.

Denzin, N. K. and Lincoln, Y. S. (1994), 'Introduction: Entering the Field of Qualitative Research', in N. K. Denzin and Y. S. Lincoln (eds), *Handbook of Qualitative Research*, Thousand Oaks, CA: Sage, 1–34.

Derrida, J. (1976), *Of Grammatology*, trans. G. Spivak, Baltimore: Johns Hopkins University.

Derrida, J. (1980), *The Archaeology of the Frivolous*. Reading Condillac, Pittsburgh, PA: Duquesne University Press.

Drolet, M. (1994), 'The Wild and the Sublime: Lyotard's Post-modern Politics', *Political Studies*, XLII: 259–73.

Durkheim, É. [1911], 'Pédagogie', in Ferdinand Buisson (ed.), *Nouveau dictionnaire de pédagogie et d'instruction primaire*, Paris: Librairie Hachette, 1538–43.

Dussel, E. (1993), 'Eurocentrism and Modernity (Introduction to the Frankfurt Lectures)', *boundary 2*, 20 (3): 65–76.

Eagleton, T. (1990), *Literary Theory: An Introduction*, Basil Blackwell: Oxford.

Eagleton, T. (2003), *After Theory*. New York: Basic Books.

Eco, U. (1983), *The Name of the Rose*, London: Minerva.

Elias, C. (2004), *The Fragment. Towards a History and Poetics of a Performative Genre*, Bern: Peter Lang AG.

Epstein, E. and Carroll, K. (2005), 'Abusing Ancestors: Historical Functionalism and Postmodern Deviation in Comparative Education', *Comparative Education Review*, 49 (1): 62–88.

Epstein, I. (2019), *Affect Theory and Comparative Education Discourse. Essays on Fear and Loathing in Response to Global Educational Policy and Practice*, London: Bloomsbury Academic.

Falzon, M. (2009), 'Introduction', *In Multi-Sited Ethnography: Theory, Praxis and Locality in Contemporary Research*, Surrey: Ashgate, 1–24.

Falzon, M.-A. (2009), *Multi-Sited Ethnography: Theory, Praxis and Locality in Contemporary Research*, Fanham: Ashgate.

Featherstone, M. (1995), *Undoing Culture: Globalization, Postmodernism and Identity*, London: Sage, 19.

Featherstone, M. and Lash, S. (1995), 'Globalization, Modernity and the Spatialization of Social Theory: An Introduction', in M. Featherstone, S. Lash, and R. Robertson (eds), *Global Modernities*, London: Sage, 1–24.

Fendler, L. (1999), 'Making Trouble: Prediction, Agency, Critical Intellectuals', in T. S. Popkewitz and L. Fendler (eds), *Critical Theories in Education: Changing Terrains of Knowledge and Politics*, London: Routledge, 169–88.

Ferguson, J. (1999), 'Global Disconnect: Abjection and the Aftermath of Modernism', in *Expectations of Modernity: Myths and Meanings of Urban Life on the Zambian Copperbelt*, Berkeley: University of California, 234–54.

Ferguson, J. (2006), *Global Shadows: Africa in the Neo-Liberal World Order*, Durham, NC: Duke University Press.

Foucault, M. (2002), *The Order of Things*, Abingdon: Routledge.

Friedman, J. (1990), 'Being in the World: Globalization and Localization', *Theory, Culture & Society*, 7: 311–28.

Friedman, J. (2002), 'From Roots to Routes: Tropes for Trippers', *Anthropological Theory*, 2: 21–36.

Friedman, Thomas L. (2005), 'The World Is Flat: A Brief History of the Twenty-First Century', Farrar, Straus and Giroux. http://capitolreader.com/bonus/The%20World%20Is%20Flat.pdf (accessed 6 November 18).

Frisby, D. (2013), *Fragments of Modernity. Theories of Modernity in the Work of Simmel, Kracauer and Benjamin*, Abingdon: Routledge.

Fukuyama, F. (1989), 'The End of History'? *The National Interest*, Summer: 3–18.

Galloway, A. (2011), 'Are Some Things Unrepresentable?' *Theory, Culture & Society*, 28 (7–8): 85–102.

Gane, M. (1991), *Baudrillard: Critical and Fatal Theory*, London: Routledge.

Gane, M. (2000), *Jean Baudrillard: In Radical Uncertainty*, London: Pluto Press.

Geertz, C. (1973), *The Interpretation of Cultures: Selected Essays*, New York: Basic Books.

Geertz, C. (1975), 'Common Sense as a Cultural System', *The Antioch Review*, 33 (1): 5–26.

Gibson, N. (2002), 'Rethinking an Old Saw: Dialectical Negativity, Utopia, and Negative Dialectic in Adorno's Hegelian Marxism', N. Gibson and A. Rubin (eds), *Adorno. A Critical Reader*, Oxford: Blackwell Publishers, 257–91.

Giddens, A. (1990), *The Consequences of Modernity*, Stanford, CA: Stanford University Press.

Gildersleeve, R. E. (2018), 'Becoming-Policy in the Anthropocene', *Education Policy Analysis Archives*, 26 (152): 1–12.

Gordon, A. (2008), *Ghostly Matters: Haunting and the Sociological Imagination*, Minnesota: University of Minnesota Press.

Gordon, L. R. (2011), 'Shifting the Geography of Reason in an Age of Disciplinary Decadence', *TRANSMODERNITY: Journal of Peripheral Cultural Production of the Luso-Hispanic World*, 1 (2). Retrieved from https://escholarship.org/uc/item/218618vj.

Gulson, K. (2007), 'Mobilizing Space Discourse: Politics and Educational Policy Change', in K. Gulson and C. Symes (eds), *Spatial Theories of Education: Policy and Geography Matters*, New York, Routledge, 37–56.

Gulson, K., Lewis, S. Lingard, B., Lubienski, C., Takayama, K. and Taylor Webb, P. (2017), 'Policy Mobilities and Methodology: A Proposition for Inventive Methods in Education Policy Studies', *Critical Studies in Education*, 58 (2): 224–41.

Gupta, A. and Ferguson, J. (1992), 'Space, Identity, and the Politics of Difference', *Cultural Anthropology*, 7 (1): 6–23.

Gupta, A. and Ferguson, J. (1997), 'After "People's" and "Cultures"', in A. Gupta and J. Ferguson (eds), *Culture, Power and Place: Explorations in Critical Anthropology*, Durham: Duke University Press, 1–29.

Habermas, H. (1990), *The Philosophical Discourse of Modernity*, Cambridge: Polity Press.

Hage, G. (2005), 'A Not so Multi-Sited Ethnography of a Not so Imagined Community', *Anthropological Theory*, 5 (4): 463–75.

Hakuin. (1971), *The Zen Master Hakuin: Selected Writings*, trans. Philip B. Yampolsky, New York and London: Columbia University Press.

Haraway, D. J. (1997), *Modest Witness@Second Millennium.Female Man© Meets OncoMouse™. Feminism and Technoscience*, London and New York: Routledge.

Haraway, D. (2016), *Staying with the Trouble*, Durham, NC: Duke University Press.

Hardt, M., and Negri, A. (2000), *Empire*, Cambridge, MA: Harvard University Press.

Haynes, K. (1999), *How We Became Posthuman: Vitual Bodies in Cybernetic, Literature and Informatics*, Chicago: Chicago University press, 2–3.

Hegarty, P. (2000), 'Bataille, Conceiving Death', *Paragraph*, 23 (2): 173–90.

Hegel, G. W. F. (1956), *Philosophy of History*, trans. J. Sibree, New York: Dover.

Heidegger, M. (1964), 'The Origin of the Work of Art', in A. Hofstadter and R. Kuhns, *Philosophies of Art and Beauty*, New York: Random House, 649–701.

Hemmings, C. (2005), 'Invoking Affect: Cultural Theory and the Ontological Turn', *Cultural Studies* 19 (5) September: 548–67.

Hesse, H. (1995), *Steppenwolf*, London: Penguin Books.

Hesse, H. (2017), Demian, UK: Penguin Random House.

Heyman, J. and Campbell, H. (2009), 'The Anthropology of Global Flows: A Critical Reading of Appadurai's "Disjuncture and Difference in the Global Cultural Economy"', *Anthropological Theory*, 9 (2): 131–48.

Homer (2014), *The Odyssey*, London: Bloomsbury.

Horkheimer, M. and Adorno, T. (2002), *Dialectic of Enlightenment. Philosophical Fragments*, trans. E Jephcott, Stanford, CA: Stanford University Press.

Huang, W. (2019), *Photographic Inquiry as Artistic Educational Research: An Investigation through Experiential Processes of Photobook Creation*, Unpublished doctoral dissertation, Michigan State University.

Hughes, R. (1996), *The Shock of the New: The Hundred-Year History of Modern Art*, New York: Knopf.

Hughes, R. (1997), *American Visions: The Epic History of Art in America*, London: Harvill Press.

Huhn, T. (2004), 'Introduction: Thoughts Beside Themselves', in T. Huhn (ed.), *The Cambridge Companion to Adorno*, Cambridge: Cambridge University Press, 1–18.

Human Rights Watch Report (2003), 'Suffering in Silence: The Links between Human Rights Abuses and and HIV Transmission to Girls in Zambia'. https://www.refworld.org/docid/3f4f59890.html (accessed 20 February 20).

Hyppolite, J. (1974), *Gensis and Structure of Hegel's Phenomenology of Spirit*, trans. S. Cherniak and J. Heckman, Evanston: Northwestern University Press.

Israel, J. (2010), *A Revolution of the Mind: Radical Enlightenment and the Intellectual Origins of Modern Democracy*, Princeton: Princeton University Press.

Izutsu, T. (1982), *Toward a Philosophy of Zen Buddhism*, Boulder: Prajna Press.

Jameson, F. (1991), *Postmodernism; or the Cultural Logic of Late Capitalism*, London: Verso.

Jameson, F. (2002), *A Singular Modernity: Essay on the Ontology of the Present*, London: Verso.

Jensen, L. (2015), 'Greenland, Arctic Orientalism and the Search for Definitions of a Contemporary Postcolonial Geography', *KULT. Postkolonial Temaserie*, 12: 139–53.

Juschka, D. (2003), 'The Writing of Ethnography: Magical Realism and Michael Taussig', *Journal for Cultural and Religious Theory*, 5.1 (December): 84–104.

Kant, I. (1784/ 1954), 'What Is Enlightenment?' in R. Morse (ed.) and Peter Gay (trans.), *Introduction to Contemporary Civilization in the West*, New York: Columbia University Press, 1071–6.

Kant, I. (1987), *Critique of Judgment*, Indianapolis and Cambridge: Hackett Publishing Company.

Kant, I. (1998), *Critique of Pure Reason*, trans. and ed. Paul Guyer and Allen W. Wood, Cambridge: Cambridge University Press.

Kellner, D. (1989), *Jean Baudrillard. From Marxism to Postmodernism and Beyond*, Cambridge: Polity Press.

Kellner, D. (2015), 'Jean Baudrillard', in *The Stanford Encyclopedia of Philosophy* (Winter 2015 Edition), Edward N. Zalta (ed.), https://plato.stanford.edu/archives/win2015/entries/baudrillard/.

Knorr Cetina, K. (2003), 'From Pipes to Scopes: The Flow Architecture of Financial Markets', *Distinktion: Scandinavian Journal of Social Theory*, 4 (2): 7–23.

Knorr Cetina, K. (2006), 'The Market', *Theory Culture Society*, 23: 551–6.

Komatsu, H. and Rappleye, J. (2018), 'Is Exam Hell the Cause of High Academic Achievement in East Asia? The Case of Japan and the Case for Transcending Stereotypes', *British Educational Research Journal*, 44 (5): 802–26.

Koren, L. (2008), *Wabi-Sabi for Artists, Designers, Poets and Philosophers*, Point Reyes, CA: Imperfect Publishing.

Koro-Ljungberg, M. (2013), '"Data" as Vital Illusion', *Cultural Studies ↔ Critical Methodologies*, 13 (4): 274–8.

Koro-Ljungberg, M. and MacLure, M. (2013), 'Provocations, Re-Un-Visions, Death, and Other Possibilities of "Data"', *Cultural Studies ↔ Critical Methodologies*, 13 (4): 219–22.

L'Yvonnet, F. (2011), 'Foreword', in Baudrillard, J. *Why Hasn't Everything Already Disappeared?* London: Seagull.

Lambert, G. (2006), *Who's Afraid of Deleuze and Guattari?* London: Continuum.

Larsen, M. and Beech, J. (2014), 'Spatial Theorizing in Comparative and International Research', *Comparative Education Review*, 58 (2): 191–215.

Lather, P. (2001), 'Postmodernism, Post-structuralism and Post(Critical) Ethnography: of Ruins, Aporias and Angels', in P. Atkinson, Coffey, A, Delamont, S, Lofland J. and L. Lofland (eds), *Handbook of Ethnography*, Sage: London, 475–92.

Lather, P. (2016), '(Re)Thinking Ontology in (Post)Qualitative Research', *Cultural Studies, Critical Methodologies*, 16 (2): 125–31.

Lawson, G. (2005), 'Rosenberg's Ode to Bauer, Kinkel and Willich', *International Politics*, (42): 381–9.

Lee, J. and Simmons Zuilkowski, S. (2017), 'Conceptualising Education Quality in Zambia: A Comparative Analysis Across the Local, National and Global Discourses', *Comparative Education*, 53 (4): 558–77.

Lizardo, O. and Strand, M. (2009), 'Postmodernism and Globalization', *Protosociology*, 26: 38–72.

Lotringer, S. (1992), 'Furiously Nietzschean, an Introduction', in G. Bataille, *On Nietzsche*, Paragon House: New York, vii–xv.

Lotringer, S. (2007), 'Exterminating Angel: Introduction to Forget Foucault', in J. Baudrillard, *Forget Foucault*, Los Angeles: Semiotext(e) , 7–25.

Lotringer, S. (2007), 'Introduction: Requiem for the Masses', in J. Baudrillard, *In the Shadow of the Silent Majority*, Los Angeles: Semiotext(e), 7–31.

Luke, A. and Luke, C. (1990), 'School Knowledge as Simulation: Curriculum in Postmodern Conditions', *Discourse*, 10 (2): 75–91.

Lyotard, J.-F. (1984), 'Answering the Question: What Is Postmodernism?' in *The Postmodern Condition: A Report on Knowledge*, trans. G. Bennington and B. Massumi, Manchester: Manchester University Press, 71–82.

Lyotard, J.-F (1986), *The Post-Modern Condition: A Report on Knowledge*, Manchester: Manchester University Press.

Lyotard, J.-F. (1988), *The Differend: Phrases in Dispute*, trans. G. Van Den Abbeele, Minneapolis: University of Minnesota Press.

Lyotard, J.-F. (1989), 'Lessons in Paganism', in A. Benjamin (ed.), *The Lyotard Reader*, Cambridge: Basil Blackwell, 122–54.

Lysgaard, J. A., Bengtsson, S. and Hauberg-Lund Laugesen, M. (2019), *Dark Pedagogy: Education, Horror and the Anthropocene*, London: Palgrave Macmillan.

MacLure, M. (2006), 'The Bone in the Throat: Some Uncertain Thoughts on Baroque Method', *International Journal of Qualitative Studies in Education*, 19 (6): 729–45.

MacLure, M. (2013), 'Researching Without Representation? Language and Materiality in Post-Qualitative Methodology', *International Journal of Qualitative Studies in Education*, 26 (6): 658–67.

MacLure, M., Holmes, R., Jones, L. and MacRae, C. (2010), 'Silence as Resistance to Analysis: Or, on Not Opening One's Mouth Properly', *Qualitative Inquiry*, 16 (6): 492–500.

Madsen, U. A. and Carney, S. (2011), 'Education in an Age of Radical Uncertainty: Youth and Schooling in Urban Nepal', *Globalisation, Societies and Education*, 9 (1): 115–33.

Madsen, U. M. (2018), *Baudrillard og Pædagogik: Fatal etnografi*, Copenhagen: Hans Reitzels Forlag.

Malinowski, B. (1922), *Argonauts of the Western Pacific: An Account of Native Enterprise and Adventure in the Archipelagoes of Melanesian New Guinea*, London: George Routledge & Sons, Ltd., New York: E. P. Dutton & Co.

Malpas, S. (2002), 'Sublime Ascesis: Lyotard, Art and the Event', *Angelaki, Journal of Theoretical Humanities*, 7 (1): 199–212.

Marcus, G. (1995), 'Ethnography in/of the World System: The Emergence of Multi-Sited Ethnography', *Annual Review of Anthropology*, 24: 95–117.

Marcus, G (1998), *Ethnography through Thick and Thin*, Princeton: Princeton University Press.

Marcus, G. (2011), 'Multi-Sited Ethnography: Five or Six Things I Know about It Now', in S. Coleman and P. von Hellermann (eds), *Multi-Sited Ethnography: Problems and Possibilities in the Translocation of Research Methods*, 16–34, New York: Routledge.

Marcus, G. and Saka, E. (2006), 'Assemblage', *Theory Culture Society*, 23: 101–6.

Massey, D. (2004), *Space, Place and Gender*, Cambridge: Polity.

Merleau-Ponty, M. (1964), *Sense and Nonsense*, trans. L. Herbert and Patricia Allen Dreyfus, Evanston: Northwestern University Press.

Meyer, J. W. and Ramirez, F. (2000), 'The World Institutionalization of Education – Origins and Implications', in J. Schriewer (ed.), *Discourse Formation in Comparative Education*, Frankfurt: Peter Lang, 11–32.

Mignolo, W. (2018), 'Foreward. On Pluriversality and Multipolarity', in B. Reiter (ed.), *Constructing the Pluriverse: the Geopolitics of Knowledge*, Durham and London: Duke University Press, pp. xi–xv.

Mitchell, S. (2009), *The Second Book of the Tao*, New York: Penguin Books.

Moazami, M. (2016), 'Forgive Foucault, Forget Baudrillard: On the Other Side of Power – Toward the Ecstasy of Seduction', *International Journal of Baudrillard Studies*, 13 (2): 2. https://baudrillardstudies.ubishops.ca/forgive-foucault-forget-baudrillard-on-the-other-side-of-power-toward-the-ecstasy-of-seduction/ (accessed 6 October 20).

Mohaghegh, J. (2013), *Silence in Middle Eastern and Western Thought: The Radical Unspoken*, New York: Routledge.

Moisi, D. (2009), *The Geo-Politics of Emotion: How Cultures of Fear, Humiliation and Hope Are Reshaping the World*, London: The Bodley Head.

Monroe, P. (1927), *Essays in Comparative Education: Republished Papers*, New York: Teachers College, Columbia University.

Nancy, J.-L. (2007), *The Creation of the World or Globalization*, Albany: State University of New York Press.

Nienass, B. (2013), 'Performing the Global', *Globalizations*, 10 (4): 533–8.

Nietzsche, F. (1974), *The Gay Science*, New York: Vintage Books.

Nietzsche, F. (1992), *Ecce Homo*, London: Penguin.

Nietzsche, F. (1995), *Birth of Tragedy*, trans. Clifton P. Fadiman, New York: Dover Publications.

Nietzsche, F. (2003), *Thus Spoke Zarathustra*, London: Penguin.

Nietzsche, F. (2003), *Twilight of the Idols and the Anti-Christ*, London: Penguin.

Ninnes, P. and S. Mehta (eds.) (2004), *Re-imagining Comparative Education: Postfoundational Ideas and Applications for Critical Times*, New York: Routledge.

Noah, H. and Eckstein, M. (1969), *Toward a Science of Comparative Education*, London: Macmillan.

Nordtveit, B. (2015), 'Knowledge Production in a Constructed Field: Reflections on Comparative and International Education', *Asia Pacific Education Review*, 16: 1–11.

Norman, J. (2007), 'Hegel and German Romanticism', in Stephen Houlgate (ed.), *Hegel and the Arts*, Evanston, IL: Northwestern University Press, 310–26.

Norman, J. (2009), 'The Work of Art in German Romanticism', in J. Stolzenberg, K. Ameriks and F. Rush (eds), *Internationales Jahrbuch des Deutschen Idealismus*, vol. 6, 59–79.

Nóvoa, A. (2018), 'Comparing Southern Europe: The Difference, the Public, and the Common', *Comparative Education*, 54 (4): 548–61.

Nóvoa, A. and Yariv-Mashal, T. (2003), 'Comparative Research in Education: A Mode of Governance or a Historical Journey?' *Comparative Education*, 39 (4): 423–38.

Noys, B. (2000), *Georges Bataille. A Critical Introduction*, London: Pluto Press.

O'Loughlin, I. (2012), '"Man Down!" Aristotle, Epicurus, and the Dude on Friendship and Solidarity', in P. S. Fosl (ed.), *The Big Lebowski and Philosophy: Keeping Your Mind Limber with Abiding Wisdom*, Hoboken, NJ: John Wiley & Sons, 55–66.

Obama, B. (2011), State of the Union Address to Both Houses of Congress. 25 January 2011 https://abcnews.go.com/Politics/State_of_the_Union/state-of-the-union-2011-full-transcript/story?id=12759395 (accessed 22 February 20).

Olson, C. (2000), *Zen and the Art of Postmodern Philosophy: Two Paths of Liberation from the Representational Mode of Thinking*, New York: State University of New York Press.

Ong, A. (1999), *Flexible Citizenship: The Cultural Logics of Transnationality*, Durham, NC: Duke University Press.

Orellana, M. E. F. (2020), *Mindful Ethnography: Mind, Heart and Activity for Transformative Social Research*, Abingdon: Routledge.

Paechter, C. and Weiner, G. (1996), 'Editorial, Special Issue: Post-modernism and Post-structuralism in Educational Research', *British Educational Research Journal*, 22 (3): 267–72.

Palomba, D. (2010), 'Maestro Di Pensiero', in M. Larsen (ed.), *New Thinking in Comparative Education: Honouring Robert Cowen*, 81–2, Rotterdam: Sense Publishers.

Paulston, R. (2000), 'Imagining Comparative Education: Past, Present, Future', *Compare*, 30 (3): 353–67.

Pawlett, W. (2013), *Violence, Society and Radical Theory: Bataille, Baudrillard and Contemporary Society*, New York: Routledge.

Peters, M., Marshall, J. and Fitzsimons, P. (2000), 'Managerialism and Educational Policy in a Global Context: Foucault, Neoliberalism and the Doctrine of Self-Management', in N. C. Burbules and C. A. Torres (eds), *Globalization and Education: Critical Perspectives*, New York: Routledge, 139–2.

Phillips, D. and Ochs, K. (2003), 'Processes of Policy Borrowing in Education: Some Explanatory and Analytical Devices', *Comparative Education*, 39 (4): 451–61.

Philips, D. and Schweisfurth, M. (2015), *Comparative and International Education: An Introduction to Theory, Method, and Practice*, London: Bloomsbury.

Phillips, J. (2006), 'Agencement/Assemblage', *Theory Culture Society*, 23: 108–9.

Popkewitz, T. (2008), *Cosmopolitanism and the Age of School Reform: Science, Education, and Making Society by Making the Child*, New York: Routledge.

Price, R. (1983), *First-Time: The Historical Vision of an Afro-American People*, Baltimore: Johns Hopkins University Press.

Prideaux, S. (2018), *I Am Dynamite: A Life of Nietzsche*, New York: Tim Duggan Books.

Rappleye, J. (2019), 'Comparative Education as Cultural Critique', *Comparative Education*, 56 (1): 39–56.

Rappleye, J. (2020), 'Comparative Education as Cultural Critique', *Comparative Education*, 56 (1): 39–56.

Richman-Abdou, K. (2019), 'Kintsugi: The Centuries-Old Art of Repairing Broken Pottery with Gold', *My Modern Met*, 5 September 19. https://mymodernmet.com/kintsugi-kintsukuroi/ (accessed 30 July 20).

Rosenberg, J. (2005), 'Globalization Theory: A Post Mortem', *International Politics*, 42: 2–74.

Rousseau, J.-J. (1761), Julie, or the New Heloise, cited in Berman, M. (2010,) *All That Is Solid Melts into Air*, London: Verso.

Ruiz III, N. (2005), 'An Interview with Gerry Coulter', *Kritikos: An International and Interdisciplinary Journal of Postmodern Cultural Sound, Text and Image*, Vol. 2 (September). https://intertheory.org/coulter.htm (accessed 30 July 20).

Ruiz, X. M. (2019), *Time for Educational Poetics: Why Does the Future Need Educational Poetics?* Leiden: Brill.

Rust, V. (1991), 'Postmodernism and Its Comparative Education Implications', *Comparative Education Review*, 35 (4): 610–26.

Schelling, F. (1946), 'Die Weltalter', in M. Schröter (1997) (ed.), *Abyss of Freedom*, Ann Arbor: University of Michigan Press.

Schelling, F. W. J. (2004), *First Outline of a System of the Philosophy of Nature*, Albany: State University of New York Press.

Schiller, F. (1788/ 1943), 'The Gods of Greece (stanza 19)', in J. Petersen and H. Schneider (eds), *Schillers Werke*. Nationalausgabe, Vol. 2 (1), Weimar, 366.

Schiller, F. (1795/ 1967), *On the Aesthetic Education of Man in a Series of Letters*, New York: Oxford University Press.

Schriewer, J. (2010), 'An Enlightenment Scholar in English Robes', in M. Larsen (ed.), *New Thinking in Comparative Education: Honouring Robert Cowen*, 29–31, Rotterdam: Sense Publishers.

Schriewer, J. (2012), 'Editorial: Meaning Constellations in the World Society', *Comparative Education*, 48 (4): 411–22.

Seth, Michael, J. (2002), *Education Fever: Society, Politics, and the Pursuit of Schooling in South Korea*, Honolulu: University of Hawai'I Press.

Shahjahan, R. (2018), *Review Essay*, Discourse Studies in the Cultural Politics of Education, 1–12. https://doi.org/10.1080/01596306.2018.1550041.

Shahjahan, R., Ramirez, G. B. and De Oliveira Andreotti, V. (2017), 'Attempting to Imagine the Unimaginable: A Decolonial Reading of Global University Rankings', *Comparative Education Review*, 61 (S1): s51–s73.

Shidmehr, N. (2009), 'Poetic Inquiry as Minor Research', in M. Prendergast, C. Leggo and P. Samesshima (eds), *Poetic Inquiry: Vibrant Voices in the Social Sciences*, Rotterdam: Sense Publishers, 101–9.

Siliya, D. (2010), 'Policy Statement by the Minister of Education', Republic of Zambia Ministry of Education. https://planipolis.iiep.unesco.org/sites/planipolis/files/ressources/zambia_policy_statement.pdf (accessed 18 May 20).

Silova, I. (2018), 'Searching for the Soul: Athena's Owl in the Comparative Education Cosmos', *European Education* 50: 223–7.

Silova, I. (2019), 'Toward a Wonderland of Comparative Education', *Comparative Education*, 55 (4): 444–72.

Silova, I. and Auld, E. (2019), 'Acrobats, Phantoms, and Fools: Animating Comparative Education Cartographies', *Comparative Education*, 56 (1): 20–38.

Silova, I., Millei, Z. and Piattoeva, N. (2017), 'Interupting the Coloniality of Knowledge Production in Comparative Education: Postsocialist and Postcolonial Dialogues after the Cold War', *Comparative Education Review*, 61 (S1): s74–s102.

Simmel, G. (1978), *The Philosophy of Money*, trans. T. Bottomore and D. Frisby, London and Boston: Routledge.

Sinking Liner: Korean Education. The Korea Times, 12 March 2009. http://www.koreatimes.co.kr/www/opinion/2018/11/162_41100.html (accessed 15 February 20).

Smith, D. W. (2004), 'Knowledge of Pure Events. A Note on Deleuze's Analytic of Concepts', in M. Roelli (ed.), *Ereignis auf Französisch. Von Bergson bis Deleuze*, München: Fink, 363–73.

Snaza, N. and Weaver, J. (2015), 'Introduction: Education and the Posthumanist Turn', in *Posthumanism and Educational Research*, New York: Routledge, 1–16.

Sobe, N. (2021), 'The Slowing Global Order: Space-Time, Boredom and Criss-Crossing Comparative Education Research', in L. Klerides and S. Carney, *Identities and Education: Comparative Perspectives in an Age of Crisis*, Bloomsbury Publishers, pp. 163–77

Sobe, N. and Kowalczyk, J. (2014), 'Exploding the Cube: Revisioning "Context" in the Field of Comparative Education', *Current Issues in Comparative Education*, 16 (1): 6–12.

Sobe, N. and Kowalczyk, J. (2018), 'Context, Entanglement and Assemblage as Matters of Concern in Comparative Education Research', in J. McLeod, N. W. Sobe and T. Seddon (eds), *World Yearbook of Education 2018: Uneven Space- Times of Education:*

Historical Sociologies of Concepts, Methods and Practices, London: Routledge, 197–204.

Sobe, N. and Ortegón, N. (2009), 'Scopic Systems, Pipes, Models and Transfers in the Global Circulation of Educational Knowledge and Practices', in T. Popkewitz and F. Rizvi (eds), *Globalization and the Study of Education*, New York, NY: NSSE/Teachers College Press, 49–66.

Somerville, M. and Powell, S. (2019), 'Researching with Children of the Anthropocene: A New Paradigm?' in *Educational Research in the Age of Anthropocene*, Hershey, PA: IGI Global, 14–35.

St. Pierre, E. A. and Pillow, W. (eds) (2000), *Working the Ruins: Feminist Poststructural Theory and Methods in Education*, New York, NY: Routledge.

Stronach, I. (2010), *Globalizing Education, Educating the Local: How Method Made Us Mad*, New York: Routledge.

Takayama, K. (2018), 'Beyond Comforting Histories', *Comparative Education Review*, 62 (4): 459–81.

Takayama, K. (2019), 'An Invitation to "Negative" Comparative Education', *Comparative Education*, 56 (1): 79–95.

Taussig, M. (1997), *The Magic of the State*, New York and London: Routledge.

Taylor, M. C. (1980), *Journey's to Selfhood: Hegel & Kierkegaard*, Los Angeles: University of California Press.

Taylor, M. C. (1984), *Erring: A Postmodern A/Theology*, Chicago: University of Chicago Press.

Taylor, M. C. (1987), *Alterity*, Chicago: University of Chicago Press.

Taylor, M. (2018), *Abiding Grace: Time, Modernity, Death*, Chicago: University of Chicago Press.

The Hygge Conspiracy, *The Guardian*, 22 November 16. https://www.theguardian.com/lifeandstyle/2016/nov/22/hygge-conspiracy-denmark-cosiness-trend (accessed 26 February 20).

Thrift, N. (2008), *Non-Representational Theory: Space, Politics, Affect*, London: Routledge.

Tobin, J., Wu, D., and Davidsen, D. (1989), *Preschool in Three Cultures*, New Haven: Yale University Press.

Tsing, A. (2000), 'The Global Situation', *Cultural Anthropology*, 15 (3): 327–60.

Tsing, A. (2015), *The Mushroom at the End of the World: On the Possibility of Life in Capitalist Ruins*, Princeton: Princeton University Press.

Turner, C. (2005), 'Introduction', in J. Baudrillard, *The Intelligence of Evil or the Lucidity Pact*, New York: Berg, pp. 1–16.

Tyler, S. (1984), 'The Vision Quest in the West or What the Mind's Eye Sees', *Journal of Anthropological Research*, 40 (1): 23–40.

Tyler, S. (1986), 'Post-modern Ethnography: From Document of the Occult to Occult Document', in J. Clifford and G. E. Marcus (eds), *Writing Culture: The Poetics and Politics of Ethnography*, London: University of California, 122–40.

Ulmer, J. B. (2017), 'Posthumanism as Research Methodology: Inquiry in the Anthropocene', *International Journal of Qualitative Studies in Education*, 30 (9): 832–48.

Vavrus, F. and Bartlett, L. (2009), 'Introduction', in F. Vavrus and L. Bartlett (eds), *Critical Approaches to Comparative Education: Vertical Case Studies from Africa, Europe, the Middle East, and the Americas*, New York: Palgrave MacMillan, 1–18.

Vickers, E. (2019), 'Critiquing Coloniality, "Epistemic Violence" and Western Hegemony in Comparative Education – The Dangers of Ahistoricism and Positionality', *Comparative Education*, 56 (2): 165–89.

Whitehead, A. N. and Schilpp, P. A. (1951), 'Immortality', in *The* Philosophy of Alfred North *Whitehead*, New York: Tudor Publishing Company, 666–81.

Williams, B. (1996), 'Contemporary Philosophy: A Second Look', in N. Bunnin and E. P. Tsui-James (eds), *The Blackwell Companion to Philosophy*, Oxford: Blackwell Publishers, 25–37.

Winther-Jensen, T. (2001), 'Changing Cultures and Schools in Denmark', in J. Cairns, D. Lawton, and R. Gardner (eds), *World Yearbook of Education: Values, Culture and Education*, London: Kogan Page, 178–89.

Wright, S. (2005), 'Processes of Social Transformation: An Anthropology of English Higher Education Policy', in J. Krejsler, N. Kryger and J. Milner (eds), *Pædagogisk Antropologi – et fag i tilblivelse*, Copenhagen: Danmarks Pædagogiske Universitet, 185–218.

Zastoupil, L. and Moir, M. (1999) (eds), 'Minute Recorded in the General Department by Thomas Babington Macaulay, Law Member of the Governor-General's Council, Dated 2 February 1835', in *The Great Indian Education Debate: Documents Relating to the Orientalist-Anglicist Controversy*, 1781–1843, London: Routledge, pp. 165–189.

Žižek, S. (2012), *Welcome to the Desert of the Real*, London: Verso.

ZMoESVTEE (2014), *Zambia: Education for All 2015 National Review*, Lusaka: Zambian Ministry of Education, Science, Vocational Training and Early Education.

Index

abjection   9–10, 39, 41, 96, 190, 222
absolute   38, 54, 72–9, 81–2, 90, 102, 109, 111, 114, 119–20, 123, 125–6, 128, 140, 158–60, 183–4, 208, 219
abstinence   190–1, 197–9
absurd
   in Camus   23
   in education   8, 23
absurdity   14, 18, 20
abyssal thought   38, 41, 112, 229
academia   7
academics   7
Adorno, T.   22, 37, 86–93, 95, 101, 103, 126–7, 131, 226
aesthetics   71, 87, 90–1, 94, 223
Agamben, G.   219
agencement   55
Alexander, R.   51
alienation   26, 34, 86–7, 90, 95, 122, 218
Anthropocene   46–7
anthropology   10, 51, 53–4, 112–13, 130
anti-manifest   7
Apollo   12, 83
Appadurai, A.   9–10
appearances   3, 7, 16–17, 24, 69–70, 74, 87, 101–2, 121, 128, 140, 155, 179
Ariadne   106, 111, 232
Aristotle   110, 126
art   3, 12–13, 22, 36, 52, 76–7, 81, 84–5, 87, 91–3, 99, 103, 115, 120–1, 123, 133, 179, 181
artist   13, 76, 140, 144, 225
assemblage   44, 46–7, 54–6, 62
authenticity   17, 33, 40, 63, 97, 114, 117–18, 124, 126, 132, 217, 226
author   3–4, 6, 13, 18–19, 22, 30, 35, 37, 50–1, 62, 64, 82, 108–10, 113–18, 127, 129–30, 134, 137, 146, 156, 160–1, 165–6, 168, 174, 178, 183–4, 193, 203–4, 209, 216, 229, 234
autonomy   26, 44, 68, 87, 94, 100, 102, 219, 226–8

awareness   9, 23, 28, 30–1, 46, 60, 63–5, 79, 83, 109, 111, 114–15, 119, 128, 149, 200, 224, 228–9

Ball, S.   61
Barad, K.   47
baroque   22, 224–5
Barthes, R.   35, 50
Bataille, G.   80–1, 110–14, 121–4, 128, 228
Baudrillard, J.
   critique of Foucault   125
   disappearance   101, 125, 133
   illusion of the real   16
   integral reality   222–3, 225
   reversal   103, 132, 222
   simulation   16, 41, 61, 98, 101–2, 132, 219, 221
Bauman, Z.   37
beauty   12–13, 22, 46, 65, 80, 88, 119, 199
Beck, U.   27, 37, 91, 93
Beckett, S.   91
being   2–3, 10–11, 21, 26–8, 38–9, 44–7, 53–7, 60, 68–9, 71–4, 76–80, 88, 92–3, 95, 97, 101, 105, 109–11, 113–15, 120, 122–3, 128–30, 133, 137, 147, 153, 159–61, 163–4, 170, 173, 185, 187, 190, 199, 210–11, 214, 219, 223, 225–7, 229–31
Bendix-Petersen, E.   117
Benjamin, W.   37, 127
Bhabba, H.   33
Bible   147, 197–8
Big Lebowski   266 n.50
binary   38, 44, 57, 98, 125, 130
Birth of Tragedy   12
Blanchot, M.   22, 81, 121, 123–4, 128
Borges, J. L.
   Celestial Emporium of Benevolent Knowledge   19
   map-making   60–1
Brandes, G.   83
Braque, G.   140
Buddhism   265 nn.1–3

Camus, A. 14, 23, 228
Capitalocene 46
Carney, S. 235 n.4
Carnival 16, 40, 224–5
Carroll, L. 50, 133, 244 n.139
Cartesian thought 39
cartography 60
Cézanne, P. 140
Cheshire Cat 134
Christianity 12, 71, 77, 109
Chthulucene 46
civilization 19, 45, 87, 129
Coffin 160, 201
colonialism 17, 25, 33–4, 41, 49, 130
comedy 15, 18, 129
comparative education 1–2, 4, 6, 8, 21–2, 48–52, 63, 65, 67, 70–1, 114–15, 117, 119, 130, 133, 136, 140–1, 169–71, 218–19, 225, 228–30
Confucius 171
consciousness 11–12, 16, 25–7, 29, 44–5, 47, 62, 71–4, 78–81, 87, 90, 92–4, 98, 109, 120–3, 127, 143, 156, 211, 218, 228, 230–1
consumer 2, 33, 95–7, 217
consumption 40, 45, 87, 96, 100, 122, 222
Copenhagen 5, 83, 142, 157, 159–60, 220
Copernican Turn 69
cosmopolitanism 33–4, 39
Cowen, R. 1
Critchley, S. 91, 231
criticism 74, 93
critique 26, 33–4, 36, 54, 68, 71, 76, 85–7, 92–4, 98–9, 113, 118, 125, 129, 132, 136, 226
Cruyff, J. 235 n.1
cube 52, 64, 229
culture
  culture industry 89, 91
cynicism 3, 14–15, 97, 102, 190

Danish 3–4, 8, 11, 30, 136, 141–2, 149, 154–6, 158–60, 162–4, 208
darkness 67, 71, 82, 89, 92–4, 106, 111, 124, 168, 173, 228, 234
data 3–4, 8, 11, 23, 48–9, 59–60, 69, 72, 103, 115–17, 119, 121, 129, 132–5, 139–40, 214, 226

death 15, 35, 41, 63, 79–82, 86, 95–6, 98, 100, 102, 106, 108–9, 121–5, 134, 143, 197, 218–19, 222–3, 225, 231
Debord, G. 22, 95, 127
Debussy, C. 22
decadence 12, 14, 82, 84, 88
decay 28, 64, 102
deconstruction 45, 81, 113
Deleuze. G. 27, 37, 43, 46–7, 55, 62, 80, 100, 140
delirium 19
democracy 5, 32, 40, 79, 95, 142–3, 147, 155, 160, 164, 175, 208
Denmark
  examination system 7–8
  High School Act 156
  House of Greenland 262 n.14
  Hygge 162
Derrida, J. 35, 43, 80–1, 118
De Sade, M. 92
Descartes, R. 68
desire 18, 20, 26, 40, 42, 47, 56, 58, 78–81, 84, 92, 100, 102, 115, 117, 119, 125, 127, 134, 215, 221
deterritorialization 62
development 25, 27, 33, 36–9, 41–2, 48–9, 57, 59, 87, 109, 143, 145, 156, 160, 166–7, 190–3, 198, 206, 208, 217, 224
dialectic
  of enlightenment 82, 87, 92
  negative dialectic 90
  non-dialectic 38
difference 10, 14, 19, 29, 33, 40, 42–3, 49–52, 54, 62, 73, 80–1, 89, 95, 97–8, 106, 109, 116, 119, 122, 125, 127, 141, 144, 147, 169, 183, 189, 195, 210, 219, 223, 230
differend 119, 126
dinosaur 98, 100
Dionysus 12–13
disappearance 15, 101–2, 108, 115, 125, 127, 133–4, 221, 223
disappointment 3, 10, 23, 82, 126
discourse 33, 56, 63, 81, 94, 99, 102, 115, 118, 122, 128, 190, 217, 228
disenchantment 16, 77, 87
dishonest 120
dogmatism 69

dreams 5–6, 11–12, 17, 19, 63, 78, 102, 116, 127, 141–2, 159–60, 162, 168–70, 175, 177, 179–80, 188–91, 199, 205–6, 208, 220, 222, 227
drunkenness 12, 76, 122
dualism 44, 74, 102
Durkheim, E. 49
Dussel, E. 38
dystopia 19

Eastern philosophies 15, 232
Eco, U. 257 n.13
economy
 general 111, 121–3, 219, 228
 restricted 112
ecstasy 51, 83, 85, 111, 112, 122, 123, 225
education
 cynical trade 13
Eduscape 4, 56
Egyptian Queen 21, 22
emancipation 26, 34, 36, 37, 93, 94
Empire
 In Hardt and Negri 27, 37, 57
 Of Good 222
empiricism 29, 36, 47, 63, 72, 128
enactment 116
enchantment 20
enigma 17, 100, 102, 132
enlightenment
 meta-narratives 35
entanglement 7, 25, 46, 47, 49, 50, 114
epistemology 47, 50, 64, 71
Eros 100–1
erotic 22, 112, 122, 133, 225
estrangement 6, 50, 51, 67
ethics 47, 77–8, 93, 102, 131
ethnographic 3, 8, 24, 52–4, 113, 114, 118, 130, 136, 141, 226
ethnography
 multi-site 10, 54
 network 60
 vertical 53
Euclidean geometry 64
Eurocentrism
 and modernity 241 n.76
 ontology 39
 in social science 26
Europe 9, 11, 37, 68, 189, 190, 192, 207

event
 pure/strong 3, 140
evil 63, 77, 82, 83, 207, 222
excess 13, 19, 47, 51, 73, 92, 110, 112, 114, 121–3, 125, 132, 225, 233
exchange 34, 96, 97, 103, 125, 132, 223, 224
exhaustion 110, 164, 170–2
existence 13, 18, 37, 47, 68, 71, 83, 84, 89, 93, 96–7, 102, 108, 114, 122–4, 126, 147, 219
experience 3, 7, 9, 15, 26–8, 31–3, 38, 40, 59, 64, 70, 72, 83, 90, 96–7, 111–13, 115, 119, 120, 122–4, 126–9, 135, 136, 139–41, 151, 155, 157, 159, 176, 218, 221, 226, 228, 235
experimentation, ix 7, 12, 35, 46

fabulous lists 19
faith 14, 17, 21, 34, 38, 48, 62, 71, 72, 77–9, 82, 86, 90, 92, 93, 95, 96, 130, 190, 222
Fanon, F. 37
fantasy 18, 19, 24, 27, 77, 82, 86, 109, 114, 123, 127, 130, 131, 222, 228
farce 15, 40
fatal
 research strategy 8
fear 11, 19, 30, 43, 46, 48, 83, 89, 96, 105, 106, 110, 111, 140, 182, 234
Fichte, G.H. 74
fiction 8, 11, 17, 19, 33, 52, 63, 80, 103, 109, 112–16, 129, 130, 140, 217, 224, 228, 231, 232
Foucault, M.
 acid trip in the desert 255 n.149
 The Order of Things 97
fragments 1, 3, 4, 11, 15–16, 18, 21–3, 29, 39, 51, 76, 81, 87, 93, 126–9, 131, 133, 134, 139–216, 218, 221, 224, 226, 228, 229, 231
freedom 4, 19, 32, 36, 39, 45, 68, 72, 74, 78, 84, 87, 89, 90, 95, 118, 123, 142, 143, 186, 208, 222, 226, 230, 233
Friedman, J. 27, 33
Friedman, T. L. 40
Fukuyama, F. 251 n.30

Gandhi 37
Geertz, C. 115

Geist   36, 71, 90, 102
genealogy   43, 93–4
generalizability   62, 105
Germany   78, 82, 84, 110, 136, 170, 230
Giddens, A.   37
gift   41, 42, 102, 105, 106, 121, 151, 185, 203, 221, 225
global cultural economy   9
global flows   8, 9, 11, 28–30, 33, 34, 44, 45, 52, 217
globalisation
  in comparative education   4
  hyper-, 27–8
  and post-foundationalism   35
  globalism   26–8, 34
globality   9–10, 26, 28, 31, 222
global scapes   32
God
  Death of   108, 231
Golgotha   15
governance   53, 58–60, 136, 190
great chain of being   46, 105
Greek theatre   12
Greenland   142, 149–50, 154–5
Guattari. F.   27, 43, 47, 55, 140
Guicciardini, F.   22

Habermas, J.
  critique of Adorno's Aesthetic Theory   93
  critique of Foucault's genealogical method   93–4
Haraway, D.   44
Hardt, M.   27, 37, 57
Hegel, G. W. F.
  the absolute   73, 74, 90, 102, 109, 119
  history   71–3, 79, 80, 90, 95, 109, 111, 230
  spirit   71–2, 74, 78–9
  subjectivity   73–4, 81, 109, 119
Heidegger, M.   73, 80, 109, 218, 226
Hendrix, J.   143
hero (in literature), 123
Hesse, H.   83, 100
heterotopia
  heterotopic text   21
  heterotopic thinking   20
history   7, 9, 17, 23, 25, 26, 28, 34, 40, 44, 50, 53, 71–3, 79, 80, 83, 85, 86, 88, 90, 94–7, 105, 106, 108, 109, 111, 113, 128, 130, 145, 155, 175, 181, 184, 186, 189, 218, 221, 230, 231, 233
Hölderlein, F.   76
Homer   88
homogenization   26, 41
hope   3, 9–12, 14–16, 22, 42, 45, 77, 90, 92, 95, 98, 111, 125, 127, 129, 136, 139, 140, 155, 164, 178–80, 190–1, 214, 216–17, 226–8
hopelessness   111, 226
Horkheimer, M.   87–9, 93, 126, 131
humanism   10, 47, 118, 147, 232
humanity   25–6, 28, 63, 76, 79, 89, 92, 94, 121
Hume, D.   68, 72
humiliation   11
hygge   162–3
hyperreality   16, 23, 97, 102, 125, 133, 219, 221, 228
Hyppolite, J.   79–81

idealism   36, 39, 72, 74, 75, 80–2, 84, 92, 119
identity
  cosmopolitan   9
  schooled   11, 41, 42
ideology   26–7, 35, 42, 51, 62, 86, 93, 95, 113, 226, 228
illusion
  of presence   16
  of the real   16
  of the world   17, 100, 102, 134
image   3, 11, 16, 30, 32, 35, 56, 77, 95, 98, 99, 116, 122, 129, 176, 183, 187, 218, 233
imagination, ix   3, 20, 29, 32, 34, 40, 60, 71, 84, 120, 121, 130, 162, 230
immaturity   68
indeterminacy   10, 49, 62, 63, 74, 97, 98, 102, 111, 121, 127, 132, 217, 219
indifference   3, 13, 14, 16, 41, 73, 95, 97, 116, 127, 223
inhuman   98
instrumentalism   126
intuition   38, 46, 69–70, 77
irony   18–19, 101, 119, 120, 126
irrationality   85
irreversibility   37, 98

Jameson, F.   35, 96, 218
Jargon   226
Joon-ho, B.   178
Jullien, M-A   48–9
justice   1, 3, 10, 14, 19, 28, 30, 39, 47, 62, 72, 89, 91, 92, 95, 102, 105, 114, 118, 126–8, 221, 230
juxta   117–18
juxtaposition   20, 48, 56

Kant, I.   26, 67–72, 74, 76–7, 81–2, 87, 93, 95, 101, 103, 219
Kaunda, K.   208–9
Kellner, D.   37
Kintsugi (Japanese practice of imperfection), 65
knowledge geographical traditions   35
Kojève, A.   78–80, 111
Kyoto School philosophy   231

labyrinth   56, 106, 111, 232
Lacan, J.   81
language   4, 16, 20–1, 24–5, 27, 32, 36, 38, 46–7, 62, 80–1, 87, 89, 92, 96, 102, 112–13, 124, 149, 154–5, 187, 189–90
La Rochefoucauld, F.   22
Lather, P.   3
laughter   110, 119, 122, 128, 134, 173, 175, 194
Lianke, Y.   3
liberation   219
libidinal   100
literature   7–8, 11, 21, 36–8, 42, 76–7, 102, 112, 123–4, 126, 128, 130, 195, 211
Locke, J.   68, 72, 150, 175, 181, 195, 222
Lyotard, J-F.   35, 119–20, 133
lyricism   20

Macaulay's minute on Indian Education   38
madness   21, 48, 60, 137, 223
Madsen, U. A.   4
Magical
   Orientation in research Magical realism   18
Magna Moralia   126
Malinowski, B.   18, 54, 136

man   12–13, 36, 42, 45, 47–8, 56, 67, 72, 74, 76–7, 79–9, 93–4, 96, 108, 111, 122, 171, 180–1, 183–4, 192, 198, 203–5, 213–14, 221, 223, 225–6
Marcus, G.   53, 113
Marquis de Sade   92
Marx, K.   40, 76, 78, 80, 95, 145
Marxism   27, 36, 62, 96, 98, 101
materialism   73
maturity   68, 85
McLuhan, M.   96, 219
meaning
   meaningfulness   112, 224
   meaninglessness   84, 91, 119, 224, 226
meditation   81, 85
Merleau-Ponty, M.   81
metaphorical   64, 224
metaphysics   4, 43, 72–3, 81, 87, 101, 110, 217, 226
methodological nationalism   2, 11, 26, 51, 57, 141
metropolitan   9, 22, 33, 37–8, 57
Minima Moralia   86, 126, 226
Minos   105
Minotaur   106–7
mirror   2, 14, 16, 18, 21, 24, 38, 60–1, 72, 87, 95, 98, 106, 127, 145–6, 220, 224
modernity   9–10, 31, 33–7, 40–1, 48, 50, 52, 62, 67, 78, 82, 85–6, 89–90, 92–3, 95–6, 120, 125–7, 132, 139, 217, 219, 223–4, 233
modernization   25, 95, 230
Moebius-strip   222
monstrosity   20
multiethnic bazaar   33
Munch, E.   218
music   12, 22, 84–5, 87, 105, 143, 165, 175, 186, 220
myth   11, 20, 38, 40, 48, 76–7, 82, 85–8, 90, 109, 115, 128, 131, 143, 230

Name of the Rose   257 n.13
narcissism   222
nationalism   2, 11, 26, 33, 51, 57, 82, 86, 141
nature   2, 12, 20, 42, 44–8, 52, 54, 63, 68–72, 74–7, 80, 82, 84–5, 87–90, 97, 120, 123, 126–7, 139, 171, 207–8, 231–2

negation 73, 77, 79–80, 90, 109, 122, 126, 224–5, 231, 233
negative dialectics 90
negativity 50, 76, 80, 90–1, 100, 122, 222, 231
Negri, A. 27, 37, 57
Nepal 11, 210
new-materialism 73
Nietzsche, F.
 Birth of the Tragedy 12
 Christian morality 82
 Madman 83
 Star 33
nihilism 15, 41, 67, 76, 92, 108, 231–2
Nishitani, K. 231
Noah, H. and Eckstein, M. 49
non-human 38, 46, 89
non-identical 90, 103
nothingness 1, 15, 50, 67, 91, 101, 226
Novalis 76, 120

Obama, B. 183
object 2, 8, 24, 38, 44, 47, 51–5, 60, 63, 65, 68–70, 72–4, 76, 79, 86, 88, 90, 92, 94–6, 99–101, 112, 114, 115, 116, 119–21, 123, 128, 129, 131–3, 139, 141, 218, 224, 228, 231, 232
obscenity 36, 41, 99, 114
Odysseus 88, 102, 105
OECD 55
ontology 39, 46, 47, 115, 226
orgy 12, 223, 225
Orwell, G. 143
other 1, 4, 30, 59, 81, 109, 119
otherness 39, 43, 50, 51, 73, 80, 81, 89, 90, 109, 121, 224

paradigm/paradigm-shift 27, 93, 137
parasite 84, 178
Pasiphae 106
Paulston, R. 50, 51
pedagogy 49, 51, 132, 147, 190, 215
performance
 performative 1, 7, 22, 37, 38, 43, 50, 93, 121, 128, 131, 133
 performativity 242 n.99, 243 n.121
periphery
 center-periphery 18, 32, 129
 shadowy peripheries 9
perspectivism 54, 86, 103, 113, 232

pessimism 10, 44, 45
phantasmagoria 12
Phillips, D. and Ochs, K. (Policy Borrowing Model in comparative education), 58, 244 n.134, 248 nn.195–8
PISA 55, 101, 142, 166, 183, 187
Plato 77, 83
poetic inquiry 129, 261 n.103
policy
 borrowing 58, 244 n.134
 in education 2, 6, 8, 58, 59, 62, 117
 joined up 58
 transfer 247 n.191, 248 n.201
policyscape 57, 248 n.203
popcorn 19, 204–5, 212, 213, 215, 224, 233
pop idols 171
pornography 41, 132
positivism 89, 92
post-foundationalism 35, 42, 232
post-humanism 46, 63, 219
post-modernism 42, 50, 120, 136
post-society 16, 98
post-truth 45, 96
power 10, 20, 23, 27, 28, 33, 36, 37, 39–41, 43, 48, 50–3, 55, 58, 62, 79, 80, 82–5, 87, 89–90, 93–5, 98–100, 108, 111, 113–15, 118, 123, 125, 126, 130, 131, 139, 163, 195, 210, 212, 213, 224, 225, 229
Price, R. 113
primitive 72, 78, 122, 125, 132
principal 33, 36, 135, 144, 146, 148, 152, 153, 157, 174, 175, 182, 191, 212–14, 216, 227
promise 8, 9, 11–14, 19, 33, 41, 44, 47, 52–4, 63, 68, 79, 82, 84, 88, 91, 93, 105, 131, 144, 191, 224, 232, 233
Python 19, 177, 178, 227

Qivitoq 155
qualitative research 115–17, 136

radical uncertainty 2, 130, 134, 217–34
rationality 40, 45, 47, 71, 72, 77, 85, 87, 89, 90, 92, 109, 222
Ray, M. 225
reality 1, 3, 7, 10, 12, 16, 18, 19, 23, 29, 35, 40, 45, 55, 56, 59, 61–2, 71, 77,

82, 84, 95–7, 99, 102–3, 105, 110, 112, 116, 119, 121, 123, 127–30, 132, 133, 140, 170, 182, 189, 218–20, 222, 223, 225, 228, 229, 231–3
reality principle   7, 59, 99, 222
reason   1, 2, 8, 12–14, 17, 20–1, 34, 65, 68–71, 75–80, 82–5, 87–90, 92–4, 96, 101, 103, 105, 109, 112, 118, 123, 125, 131, 132, 157, 190, 192, 226, 227
reification   26, 90
representation   16, 17, 32, 35, 36, 40, 43, 44, 46, 52, 55–7, 64, 69, 70, 85, 96, 113–15, 117, 130, 219, 225, 229, 231–3
reproduction   16, 26, 175, 219
reversibility   116, 131
rhizome   33, 34, 44, 100
Robinson, R.   37
romantic   22, 75, 76, 80, 81, 85, 103, 119, 120, 126
romanticism   75, 78, 102, 120
Rousseau, J-F.   76, 157

sacrifice   41, 88, 106, 111, 122, 187, 219, 222, 225
salvation   41, 207, 224, 233
Sapere aude   67
Sassen, S.   37
scape   10, 11, 26, 32, 83, 85, 88, 98, 115, 173–5, 222, 232, 233
Schelling von, F.   74, 77, 78, 85
Schiller, F.   76, 82
Schlegel, F.   76, 77
Schleiermacher, F.   76
Schopenhauer, A.   78, 86
scopic system   55, 56, 60
seduction   8, 15, 99–102, 105, 125, 223
self   2, 13–15, 17, 23, 28, 39, 42–3, 46–8, 54, 67–8, 72–5, 77–9, 81, 83, 85, 88–90, 105, 106, 108, 109, 117–21, 123, 125, 126, 132, 134, 136, 140, 155, 162, 166, 167, 170, 180–2, 191, 198, 219, 221–4, 230–3
silence   1, 22, 24, 33, 36–9, 109, 114, 118–20, 124, 128, 133, 140, 146–56, 160, 161, 175, 185, 194, 230, 232
Simmel, G.   127
simulation   8, 16, 41, 61, 63, 98, 101, 102, 125, 128, 132, 219, 221

sirens   20, 88, 89, 105
Sisyphus   14
situationalist   95–6, 127
Sloterdijk, P.   219
slow professor   4
solidarity   38, 89
soul   82, 83, 207, 221, 224
Southern perspective   39, 46
South Korea
    Obama debate   193
    obsession with grades   181–2
Socrates
    Socratic promise   14
space
    spatial turn   32, 51
spectacle   16, 24, 40, 95, 127, 221
Spinoza
    in Deleuze   43, 46, 55
    Monism   46
    Radical Enlightenment   242 n.103
spirit   12, 13, 16, 50, 71, 72, 74, 78, 79, 82, 83, 85, 96, 130, 143, 221, 230
structuralism
    structuralist   81
subjectivity   2, 26, 32, 55, 57, 67, 73, 74, 81, 85, 88, 91–4, 109, 118, 119, 224, 233
sublime   14, 23, 51, 119–21, 217
sugar daddies   203, 211

Taussig, M.   19, 130
Taylor, M. C.   237 n.30, 242 n.93, 248 n.211, 250 nn.18–19, 251 nn.27–9, 251 n.36, 251 n.47, 252 nn.52–7, 252 nn.62–6, 254 n.135, 255 n.136, 256 nn.1–2, 257 nn.5–8, 257 n.10, 260 nn.90–1, 264 n.3, 265 n.17, 265 n.27–8
teleology   28, 219
terrorism   63
Thatcherism   51
theory
    critical theory   86, 92
    fiction   17, 63, 115, 116, 232
time   6, 9–11, 16, 18–20, 23, 25, 26, 32, 33, 36, 38, 39, 43–5, 49, 50, 52–6, 62, 63, 67–70, 74, 76, 78, 79, 81, 85, 86, 93, 97, 103, 113, 114, 116, 124, 127, 129, 140, 144, 145, 149–50, 152, 156, 159, 160, 162, 164, 167,

168, 171, 172, 174, 176, 177–82, 185–7, 192, 194, 195, 200, 201, 206, 207, 217, 219, 222, 224, 225–30, 232, 233
Tobin, J. (Pre-school in three cultures), 51
Togo-shock   11
tragedy   12, 14, 18, 84, 85, 129, 228
transcendence   44, 78
transgression   6, 126
transparency   41, 99, 100, 113, 132
trickster   24, 116
truth   45
Tsing, A.
Tyler, S.   258 n.36, 265 nn.32–6

Ulysses   88
uncertainty   2, 6, 30, 34, 35, 63, 83, 89, 103, 105, 106, 120, 124, 130, 134, 217–34
unfinished   22, 91, 127, 128
unintelligible   102, 122
unity   12, 37, 52, 54, 56, 84, 95, 109, 124, 139, 143, 231
unruly   8, 12, 21, 131, 187
utopia   16, 19–21, 76, 79, 95, 97, 217–18, 221, 228, 229

validity   62, 93, 105
Van Gogh, V.   218
vignettes   7–8
Virilio, P.   219
virtual   36, 45, 76, 96, 116, 132, 133
virtue   25, 82, 171, 224
visible   31, 38, 74, 99–100, 115, 187, 222

wabi-sabi   65
Wagner, R.   84
Warhol, A.   3, 218
Washington consensus   28
Western
   science   2, 15, 38, 47, 61, 71, 102, 217
   thought   15, 39, 44, 47, 68, 71, 86, 125, 219, 231, 232
Westphalian (post), 10
Whitehead, A. N.   139
white rabbit (in Lewis Carroll), 50
Wittgenstein, L.   37
World
   disappearing   8
   messy   8
   post-Westphalian   10
   winner-take-all   9
writer   7, 9, 15, 24, 37, 101, 105, 113, 119, 121, 123, 125, 129, 130, 134, 139, 141, 176, 232
writing   1–4, 11, 18–20, 22, 23, 35, 37, 43, 67, 68, 78, 79, 81, 83, 87, 91, 99, 102, 105–37, 215, 219, 225–7, 232, 233

Yeats, W. B.   46

Zambia
   learner-centered pedagogy   190, 215
   sexual abuse   200
   vocational training policy   263 n.33
   witch doctor   191, 193
zeitgeist   10, 34, 62, 100, 127
Zen   139, 231, 232
Žižek, S.   219

www.ingramcontent.com/pod-product-compliance
Lightning Source LLC
Chambersburg PA
CBHW052154300426
44115CB00011B/1665